Susan Fenimore Cooper

Susan Fenimore Cooper

New Essays on *Rural Hours* and Other Works

Edited by Rochelle Johnson
and Daniel Patterson

THE UNIVERSITY OF GEORGIA PRESS
Athens and London

© 2001 by the University of Georgia Press
Athens, Georgia 30602
All rights reserved
Designed by Sandra Strother Hudson
Set in 10 on 13 Sabon by G & S Typesetters
Printed and bound by Thomson-Shore
The paper in this book meets the guidelines for
permanence and durability of the Committee on
Production Guidelines for Book Longevity of the
Council on Library Resources.

Printed in the United States of America
05 04 03 02 01 C 5 4 3 2 1

Library of Congress Cataloging-in-Publication Data

Susan Fenimore Cooper: new essays on Rural Hours
and other works / edited by Rochelle Johnson and
Daniel Patterson.
        p. cm.
Includes bibliographical references and index.
ISBN 0-8203-2326-8 (alk. paper)
    1. Cooper, Susan Fenimore, 1813–1894.   2. Natu-
ral history literature—United States.   I. Johnson,
Rochelle.   II. Patterson, J. Daniel.

QH13.45 .S87 2001
508—dc21   2001027078

British Library Cataloging-in-Publication Data
available

CONTENTS

Foreword

For a century after her death, Susan Fenimore Cooper was considered little more than a custodian of and ancilla to the career of her famous father, James Fenimore Cooper, who was the first American novelist to win enduring international fame. Only during the last decade has Susan Fenimore Cooper become recognized as a significant literary figure in her own right. A major turning point was the 1998 republication by Rochelle Johnson and Daniel Patterson of the original, unabridged edition of Cooper's most substantial book, *Rural Hours* (1850), the first major work of environmental literary nonfiction by an American woman writer, both a source and a rival of Thoreau's *Walden* (1854) in its meticulously probing and sensitive observation of the cycle of the year in a northeastern community set in the context of wide-ranging comparative reflections— ruminative, wry, sometimes trenchant—about emerging national and natural history, all illuminated by inventive linkages across continents and epochs.

Now Johnson and Patterson have assembled the first book-length critical work on Susan Fenimore Cooper, a compendium of essays that further strengthens the case for the importance of *Rural Hours* and begins to suggest her greater versatility of achievement and its full historical significance. A number of these critical essays probe further than any previous criticism into the interpretative strategies that *Rural Hours* requires, particularly into its adaptations of such modes and genres as picturesque, literary sketch, natural history essay, and treatise on domestic economy. The studies included here also consider Cooper's achievement in other venues: domestic fiction, the literary essay, anthology compilation, editorial and biographical commentary on her father's work. Still other essays situate her in relation to nineteenth-century conservationist thought about the relative claims of unmodified nature versus responsible domestication; debates about women's rights and women's sphere; religious controversies and the state of biblical interpretation; the critical reception of European ideas in the nineteenth-century United States; and the natural and social history of Cooperstown from its founding to the present day.

Any attentive reader of this collection, particularly one coming to Susan Fenimore Cooper for the first time, will never again believe that the literary history of Cooperstown effectively ended after James Fenimore's death; that his daughter played only a minor role in the shaping of his reputation; that Victorian American women who held conservative views about women's place and about the Christian faith were incapable of subtle, forceful, challenging thought and writing; that first-rate midcentury American nature writing stops with Henry David Thoreau; that "nature writing" can be thought of as a category sealed off from other genres; and that the culture of nature in the nineteenth century (or at any other time!) was necessarily thought to be in opposition to (critically self-aware visions of) "progress." These are only some of the insights that this collection of essays provides. It seems certain that these essays will further the Cooper revival now in progress within the academy and that they will encourage more readers—and not, I hope, professors of literature and their graduate students alone—to look more closely at her work.

Acknowledgments

Editing a collection of essays written by scholars, we've heard it said, can be something like herding butterflies. While the analogy preserves our most beloved myth of the professoriate, it does not reflect our experience as editors of this volume. Rather than guidance, the contributors to this volume needed little more than the suggestion that it was high time for a collection of essays on the literary career of Susan Fenimore Cooper. And once we were under way, an inspiring spirit of scholarly cooperation prevailed, pockets of information were opened generously from Cooperstown to the far reaches, and the book seemed to grow almost organically from its seed. As editors of this volume, we wish to thank the contributors for their participation in this project and for their expertise, professionalism, and generosity.

We wish also to thank Barbara Ras and Karen Orchard at the University of Georgia Press. Barbara consistently provided encouragement and wise suggestions, and Karen supported the project (as she did the earlier *Rural Hours* edition) practically from the moment of its inception.

We also acknowledge the work of several scholars who have helped give life to this volume. Larry Buell first presented Susan Fenimore Cooper's work as a significant and not fully understood alternative to the Thoreauvian tradition of American environmental writing and has since generously assisted others as they investigate this deeply textured area of literary and cultural history. Jessie Ravage of Cooperstown, New York, has shared her deep expertise and maintained, in the Cooperstown *Freeman's Journal,* what might be described as a journalistic vigil to the literary achievement of Susan Fenimore Cooper. Terrell Dixon was an early source of encouragement for developing this collection. Laura Dassow Walls provided insightful commentary on the introduction to the volume. We thank these individuals for their visible and invisible contributions to furthering Cooper studies generally and to this project in particular.

Albertson College of Idaho graciously provided various forms of needed institutional and material support.

For permission to quote from unpublished letters and manuscripts, we gratefully acknowledge the following: Allan Axelrad; Alderman Library, University of Virginia, Charlottesville; Archives and Manuscripts, Chicago Historical Society; Boston Public Library; Department of Rare Books and Special Collections, Rush Rhees Library, University of Rochester; Department of Special Collections, Memorial Library, University of Wisconsin—Madison; The Houghton Library, Harvard University; Mount Vernon Ladies' Association Library, Mount Vernon, Virginia; Manuscripts and Archives Division, New York Public Library; The New York State Historical Association Library, Cooperstown, New York; Rare Book and Special Collections Library, University Library, University of Illinois at Urbana-Champaign; Special Collections, Baker Library, Dartmouth College, Hanover, New Hampshire; and Special Collections, Haverford College Library, Haverford, Pennsylvania.

Nearly everyone pursuing Cooper studies is indebted to Hugh C. MacDougall, to whom we wish to dedicate this volume. We have benefited in many ways from Hugh's extravagant knowledge of the Coopers, as well as from his congeniality and persistence, the most recent examples of which are his discoveries of Susan Cooper's "Otsego Leaves" essays and her "Mission to the Oneidas," both of which were published during her lifetime but have since been forgotten. It is our hope that this volume expresses, in some way, our gratitude and respect.

Introduction

I t was the tremendous swell of interest in environmental writing that provided the conditions needed for a new edition of Susan Fenimore Cooper's *Rural Hours* in 1998.[1] However, Cooper herself would not have missed the irony that our late-twentieth-century ability to appreciate her accomplishment as a nature writer was completely dependent upon our continued degradation of the planet. Nevertheless, that edition has brought *Rural Hours* more readers and Susan Cooper's career closer scrutiny by scholars. The breadth, complexity, and quality of her literary production have rewarded the investigations of numerous scholars, and this volume was conceived in order to make public the fruits of much of that effort. Indeed, the Susan Cooper who emerges from this collective work is one of the premier nature writers of the United States, but for fifty years she was also an accomplished writer and editor in several other genres.

Susan Fenimore Cooper (April 17, 1813–December 31, 1894) had begun writing with publication in mind by the mid-1840s. By the time of her death she had published a romance; a book of bioregional nature writing; an anthology of nature poetry; an edition of the journal of a British naturalist; a number of short stories for adults and children; a theoretical essay on American landscapes; a tract to solicit donations for the restoration of Mount Vernon; several selections from her father's unpublished manuscripts; one book-length biography and several biographical essays; a lengthy philosophical essay against female suffrage; at least seven magazine articles treating aspects of the natural environment; fifteen substantial introductions to the "Household Edition" of her father's novels; an almanac, which she edited; numerous historical essays; and an array of other magazine and newspaper articles (see the list of Cooper's known publications in appendix 1). In addition, Cooper prepared at least two other book-length manuscripts for publication.

Susan Cooper was also the daughter of James Fenimore Cooper, a fact that often helped her publishing career while she was alive. Nearly every time her contemporaries mention her in reviews, they note her relation to "the American Scott" or "the famous novelist." But since her death, her father's shadow has more often obscured her own literary achievement. One purpose of the present volume is to consider that achievement in direct light.

Susan Fenimore Cooper's Literary Career: First Fiction

Following Susan Cooper's first thirteen years in Cooperstown, Westchester County, and New York City and following her European residence with her family from the summer of 1826 until the autumn of 1833, she began her literary career, not surprisingly, by writing fiction.[2] The earliest evidence we have showing that she was writing for publication is a letter from her father dated September 22, 1843, in which he promises to sell an undisclosed number of unidentified "tales": "I make no doubt of getting one or two hundred dollars for the whole." The successful author seems to imagine easily his daughter's future as a professional author herself: "A name will sell the remainder, and a little habit will set you up."[3] It is not clear, however, whether any of these tales was ever published.

It does seem clear, however, that these short fictions became pilots for the full-blown novel she then produced. By August 1844, Cooper had completed the manuscript of her 575-page *Elinor Wyllys,* which her father carried to New York City, had stereotyped, and sold to both Richard Bentley in London and Carey and Hart in Philadelphia (*Letters and Journals,* 4:470–71, 5:15, 25, 79, 82, 98, 101). From her late teens through her twenties, the author's father seems to have ushered her past several discussions and proposals of marriage, and at the end of that decade, she produced a novel in which the plain or even ugly young heroine is rewarded for her intelligence and goodness by the plot structure of the romance with a happy and financially secure marriage.

If the nonfictional dutiful daughter was unhappy to be unwed, no direct evidence survives. Certainly, Fenimore Cooper was a protective parent, and he may have had selfish motives, but his expressions of love for "dear little Suzy, meek little Suzy" strike one as genuine (*Letters and Journals,* 6:95). In the following words written in December 1849, just after he negotiated the terms of publication for *Rural Hours,* he even casts himself as a potential lover who settles for friendship: "How I love that child! Her countenance is like that of a sister I lost . . . by a fall from a horse, half a century since, and her character is very much the same. They were, and are, as perfect as it falls to the lot of humanity to be. I am in love with Sue, and have told her so, fifty times. She refuses me, but promises to live on in gentle friendship, and, my passion not being at all turbulent, I do not see but this may do" (*Letters and Journals*, 6:99). Three months later, we hear her expressing devotion to her father: "To satisfy yourself, and my dear Mother, has always been a chief object of my authorship, and hitherto I have met with little enough of encouragement from other quarters."[4] Their high regard for one another motivated them both and seems extremely important to the daughter's impetus to write.

Cooper's "The Lumley Autograph" was completed no later than November 1848 (*Letters and Journals*, 5:390). This is a playful but poignant variation on a device used by her father in his *Autobiography of a Pocket Handkerchief* (1841). Cooper was, however, already making studied observations of the plant and animal species native to her Otsego Lake region and planning a writing project in a genre her father would struggle to comprehend.

Rural Hours and Early Environmental Projects

In her preface to *Rural Hours,* Cooper tells us that she began recording her field observations "in the spring of 1848," but in a memoir dated January 25, 1883, she suggests that the quality of mind that would conceive a nature-writing project had much earlier origins. Recalling childhood days in Westchester County with her maternal grandfather, she writes:

> Our Grandfather De Lancey must have been a charming companion—he was very amusing with his grandchildren, and told us many pleasant things, as he drove us about in his gig and farm-waggon. . . . And my dear Grandfather soon commenced my botanical education—being the eldest of the little troop, I often drove with him, in the gig, about his farms and into his woods, and it was my duty to jump out and open all the gates. In these drives he taught me to distinguish the different trees by their growth, and bark, and foliage—this was a beech, that an oak, here was an ash, yonder a tulip-tree. He would point out a tree and ask me to name it, going through a regular lesson in a very pleasant way. Such was the beginning of my *Rural Hours* ideas.[5]

The author also, however, attributes shaping influences to the knowledge and experiences of three women in her family. Cooper recalls from her childhood, for instance, a walk during which her mother, Susan Augusta De Lancey Cooper (whose namesake she was), "picked up a broken branch of raspberry and set it in the ground, telling me that it would take root and grow." Cooper evaluates this early bit of botanical knowledge as "a fact which greatly surprised my infant mind" ("Small Family Memories," 10). Thus, more than seventy years after the event, the daughter paid homage in her 1883 memoir to the mother's presence at the birth of her affinity for plant life. She also fondly associates her grandmother De Lancey with her early awareness of plants: "She took great delight in flowers, and the south end of the long hall was like a greenhouse in her time. . . . Her flower garden was at the South of the house, and was considered something wonderful for the variety of flowers. There is a delicate little vine, called the Alleghany vine, Adlumia, growing in our hills; this was a favorite of hers" ("Small Family Memories," 12–13). From her aunt Pomeroy, Cooper recalls hearing accounts of the abundance of large mammal species living near Otsego Lake: "the Lake was almost entirely surrounded with forest. Game was still abundant, and on that occasion [that is, of the first lake party] the gentlemen of the party pursued and killed a deer in the Lake. Bears and wolves were common then, and panthers also. The bears would lie dormant in the caves on the hillsides. And my Aunt said she had often heard the wolves howl on the ice in the Lake, in winter" ("Small Family Memories," 18). In Cooper's record of these memories, written for her family members, it is clear that not only the patriarchs in her life but also the matriarchs contributed to her early conception of the flora, fauna, and environmental history of her native region.

Inspired and enabled by these early experiences, she found herself maturing as a writer amid dramatic alterations to her beloved landscape, and she composed *Rural Hours* to sway the human inhabitants of her place toward a wise restraint in their treatment of the physical environment: "No perfection of tillage, no luxuriance of produce can make up to a country for the loss of its forests; you may turn the soil into a very garden crowded with the richest crops, if shorn of wood, like Sampson shorn of his locks, it may wear a florid aspect, but the noblest fruit of the earth, that which is the greatest proof of her strength, will be wanting" (*Rural Hours*, 139). What we now call "nature writing" became, for this new author, a tool of suasion, a genre by which she could present her vivid plea for a human presence in her landscape that would be sustainable indefinitely into the future.

Her father wisely observed that the success of *Rural Hours* would be "eventual, for, at first, the world will not know what to make of it" (*Letters and Journals*, 6:151). Nevertheless, it was reviewed widely and favorably and appeared in nine editions and one abridgment over the next thirty-seven years. It became the work for which she was best known.

Two works from the beginning of the 1850s have disappeared and probably never were printed. In a letter to her father some four months before the July 1850 publication of *Rural Hours,* Cooper asks him to retrieve from a publisher "the M.S. of *Devotions for the Sick.*" She had no other copy of it and speculated, "Perhaps our Sunday School Publisher may take it one of these days."[6] This may be the work Fenimore Cooper refers to in May 1850: "I have not offered Susy's religious book to any one. I have thought it better to wait for R[ural] Hours, which will give value to all she does" (*Letters and Journals,* 6:187). No other reference to this manuscript is known.

The other lost work appears to have been at least partially in press at Putnam's. In George Putnam's letter to Susan Cooper dated December 2, 1851, he states that he has just received from Cooper "proofs of . . . 'The Shield.'" He closes by assuring her that he "shall proceed with . . . The Shield as rapidly as possible—presuming you can furnish the copy as rapidly as it is wanted."[7] In an August letter to Richard Bentley, the London publisher of *Rural Hours,* Cooper had provided the following description of "The Shield":

> The good success I have had in America has led me to prepare another work for the press, which will shortly be printed. It is called *The Shield, a Narrative;* and relates to the habits, and life of the red man, before his intercourse with the whites, or rather to his condition at the period of the discovery. Many historical essays, giving information on the antiquities and customs of the race, when first seen by the Europeans, have appeared here lately, and it is to embody these in a characteristic tale that the narrative has been written. It seems to me likely that in this case the tables may be turned, and *The Shield* from the nature of the subject may proove more intersting [*sic*] in the old world than a record of our simple rural life. Should such proove ti [*sic*] to be the fact it will also help the sale of Rural Hours. I have taken much pains to give the book accuracy in all its details. In your June letter you proposed to take the work on the same terms as Rural Hours, and I now wish to know if such are still your views. The first chapters will probably be printed within a month.[8]

Prior to this, in May of the same year, Fenimore Cooper had already characterized "The Shield" for Bentley as follows: "My daughter is preparing for Mr Putnam another book which will contain some of the surplus matter of Rural Hours, with large additions, in the same style; but the whole rendered more imaginative by a connection with a simple Indian story. It will be of about the size of Rural Hours. I should like to have an offer for it and that as soon as convenient as the work will shortly go to press" (*Letters and Journals*, 6:273–74). Although "The Shield" was advertised by both Putnam and Bentley, no copy of the book has been found, and no subsequent references to it appear.[9]

This large work's disappearance and the ensuing silence create an intriguing mystery, but we can draw several tenable conclusions from its author's characterization of it: she was interested in the history of Native Americans before European contact; she devoted a significant amount of time and creative energy following the publication of *Rural Hours* to a narrative based on historical essays she took to be factual; she hoped to become better known in Europe; and, to some extent, she conceived and designed the project so that it would enhance her reputation as an author and bring her some royalties.

Cooper's publications throughout the three years that follow her father's death on September 14, 1851, seem to spring from the concern with the human relationship to the natural environment that informs her *Rural Hours* work. In "A Dissolving View," an essay published in an expensive gift-book by Putnam in which she shares prominence with her father, William Cullen Bryant, and Washington Irving, Cooper meditates on a New England autumn landscape and provides a succinct statement of a premise that informs much of her environmental writing: "The hand of man generally improves a landscape. The earth has been given to him, and his presence in Eden is natural; he gives life and spirit to the garden. It is only when he endeavors to rise above his true part of laborer and husbandman, when he assumes the character of creator, and piles you up hills, pumps you up a river, scatters stones, or sprinkles cascades, that he is apt to fail."[10] As in *Rural Hours,* here she assumes a providential universe in which human restraint in the landscape is rewarded with success and in which the hubris of modern engineering is aligned with the sinful and ungodly.

Amid the early success of *Rural Hours,* Cooper continued to focus on the natural by writing an introduction and extensive natural history notes for an American edition of John Leonard Knapp's *Country Rambles in England* (1829).[11] She opens the introduction by placing Knapp's volume alongside Gilbert White's *The Natural History of Selborne* (1788) as among "the standards of English literature" (*Country Rambles*, 11). It seems clear that Cooper hopes her readers will place her own *Rural Hours* on this same shelf, since she associates her book with the nature writing of White and Knapp, whose books belong to that "choice class . . . written neither for fame nor for profit, but which have opened spontaneously, one might almost say unconsciously, from the author's mind" (*Country*

Rambles, 11). The ornamented title page also encourages this association by presenting the title "Rural Hours" in the same style and size of rustic, bold lettering used for "Country Rambles." And Cooper's introduction itself, while paying sincere homage to a fellow nature writer, finally implies that Americans ought to read books about American nature: "As a people, we are still, in some sense, half aliens to the country Providence has given us; there is much ignorance among us regarding the creatures which held the land as their own long before our forefathers trod the soil; and many of which are still moving about us, living accessories of our existence, at the present hour" (*Country Rambles,* 16). Because of "English reading," Americans habitually assume that plant and animal species are identical on both sides of the Atlantic simply because they have the same names: "And in this dream-like phantasmagoria, where fancy and reality are often so widely at variance . . . most of us are content to pass through life" (*Country Rambles,* 18). The bulk of her numerous natural history notes to Knapp's text are designed to remedy this particular ignorance. She wants her American readers to realize how lucky they are: "the nature of both hemispheres lies open before them, that of the old world having all the charm of traditional association to attract their attention, that of their native soil being endued with the still deeper interest of home affections" (*Country Rambles,* 18). Humbly and subtly, she works in this volume to prepare a readership and a market for American nature writing, works like *Rural Hours.*

In 1854 the Philadelphia publisher Willis P. Hazard brought out an illustrated edition of *Rural Hours,* keeping the attribution "By a Lady," which Cooper preferred. In the same year, Hazard also published *Rural Rambles; or, Some Chapters on Flowers, Birds, and Insects* with the same attribution, "By a Lady." There is, however, no clear proof that Cooper is the "Lady" who wrote, compiled, and edited this now-rare volume. Nonetheless, since the work is "generally credited to Susan Fenimore Cooper," it is worthwhile to consider *Rural Rambles* here.[12]

Nothing in the volume suggests that Cooper could not have been the compiler; on the contrary, all the qualities and features of the book seem completely consistent with those that inform her other work. *Rural Rambles* assembles a mix of natural history, personal observation, and poetry throughout its six main sections, each of which bears the name of a flower. Within each main section, the compiler focuses on various insects, birds, and flowers, bringing together poems, natural history findings, anecdotes, and her own observations on, as examples, "The Butterfly," "The Ant Lion," and "The Owl." The overall purpose of *Rural Rambles* is to bring readers closer to the pleasures and insights the compiler valued in native flora and fauna. The prose in its phrasing, tone, and meaning is also consistent with Cooper's other published prose:

> Next to the resolving of flowers into their component parts, and determining their species, genera, &c., the most delightful of all botanical pursuits is that of Floral Geography. The inquiring mind beholds in every nook where a flower can find room to open its delicate leaves, some new tribute to the unerring providence of God. Every leaf and bud suggest new thoughts, and in viewing the wonderful structure of the vegetable kingdom, the mind begins to form an adequate idea of that Being who not only supplies man with all the necessaries of life, but scatters beauty along his path, and speaks to him of hope and mercy, through the fragrant cups and emerald leaves of the flowers that blossom everywhere.[13]

Various aspects of this passage—the fluid clarity and measured pace of the prose, the avoidance of hyperbole and excess of sentiment, the advocacy of botany, the goal of training readers to perceive Providence in common flora—cause one to wonder whether this and other passages in the work might have their originals in the lost manuscript, "Devotions for the Sick." Nevertheless, despite the circumstantial evidence, *Rural Rambles* remains an open question in Cooper's career.

The Rhyme and Reason of Country Life, 1855

Certainly one of the earliest collections of poems about nature and rural life published in the United States, *The Rhyme and Reason of Country Life* reflects Cooper's desire to continue the cultural work she had begun in *Rural Hours*.[14] This anthology reflects her faith in the power of literature to influence—even change—minds; and it complements her earlier and later offerings of environmental prose by bringing poetry to the work of shaping the thoughts of Americans about nature and how human society—which she grants is also natural—ought to relate to it. Her introduction to this volume—more so possibly than any other single document—teems with insights into her thought and suggests how she understood her place in her culture and her work as a writer. For example, she theorizes about the motive behind nature writing. The ancient Greeks, she writes, did not write directly about their beautiful environment because they did not see themselves as independent of or distinguishable from nature. Americans in her day, by contrast, are motivated to write about nature by a "fear that she should fail them" (*Rhyme and Reason,* 14). Cooper also suggests that rural nature writers have one of the highest places in her culture. Whereas in past ages, the most important writers worked from within cities because only there were people educated (with the result that the "tastes and habits" of the culture were "necessarily . . . more or less artificial"), in Cooper's young nation, the much wider dissemination of education and the other advantages of civilization free the "rustic population" from the urban perception that they are "only fit for ridicule and burlesque" (*Rhyme and Reason,* 26). Instead, the American intellectual or artist can work effectively from rural settings: "He may read and he may write there with pleasure and with impunity. A wide horizon for observation opens about him to-day in the fields, as elsewhere." With general education "daily enlarging the public audience . . . [n]o single literary class is likely . . . to usurp undue authority over others—to impose academical fetters on even the humblest of its cotemporaries [*sic*]. Whatever is really natural and really worthy, may therefore hope in the end for a share of success" (*Rhyme and Reason,* 26–27).

The humbling influence of Christianity, however, is essential to the rustic writer whom Cooper would consider worthy of his or her place in the culture. We quote at length because of the importance of the following passage and because so few have a copy of the text at hand:

No system connects man by more close and endearing ties, with the earth and all its holds, than Christianity, which leaves nothing to chance, nothing to that most gloomy and most impossible of chimeras, fate, but refers all to Providence, to the omniscient wisdom of a God who is love; but at the same time she warns him that he is himself but the steward and priest of the Almighty Father, responsible for the use of every gift; she plainly proclaims the fact, that even here on earth, within his own domains, his position is subordinate. . . . Look at the simple flower of the field; behold it blooming at the gracious call of the Almighty, beaming with the light of heavenly mercy, fragrant with the holy blessing, and say if it be not thus more noble to the eye of reason, dearer to the heart, than when fancy dyed its petals with the blood of a fabled Adonis or Hyacinthus? Go out and climb the highest of all the Alps, or stand beside the trackless, ever-moving sea or look over the broad, unpeopled prairie, and tell us whence it is that the human spirit is so deeply moved by the spectacle which is there unfolded to its view. Go out at night—stand uncovered beneath the star-lit heavens, and acknowledge the meaning of the silence which has closed your lips. Is it not an overpowering, heartfelt, individual humility, blended with an instinctive adoration or acknowledgment in every faculty of the holy majesty of the One Living God, in whom we live, and move, and have our being? (*Rhyme and Reason,* 28–29)

In Cooper's subsequent cultural analysis, America becomes the site of literature's full maturity, and the rural poet of nature becomes the culture's most important artist. The main distinguishing characteristic of American poetry, Cooper claims, is "a deeply-felt appreciation of the beauty of the natural world" (*Rhyme and Reason,* 31). This national affinity for the natural becomes for Americans a moral guide past the "follies of idle ostentation and extravagant expenditure" encouraged and cultivated by the cities, the centers of commerce and manufacture (*Rhyme and Reason,* 32). By contrast, in America "[t]he influences which surround the countryman are essentially ennobling, elevating, civilizing, in fact" (*Rhyme and Reason,* 33). She concludes: "It can scarcely, therefore, be an error of judgment to believe that while in past generations the country has received all its wisdom from the town, the moment has come when in American society many of the higher influences of civilization may rather be sought in the fields, when we may learn there many valuable lessons of life, and particularly all the happy lessons of simplicity" (*Rhyme and Reason,* 33–34). Cooper's discussion in *Rural Hours* of the recent move to greater realism and accuracy in "descriptive writing, on natural objects" implies that literary representations of the natural can contribute to the "moral and intellectual progress" of the culture (*Rural Hours,* 208). Cooper's introduction to *The Rhyme and Reason of Country Life* provides a scholarly and philosophical analysis of her reasons for saying so.

The *Rhyme and Reason* introduction concludes a period of approximately six years during which Cooper devoted her literary labors exclusively to the cultural work of nature writing. Nearly five years pass before her next publication. The only other comparable gap—that between 1861 and 1868—includes the years of the Civil War. The fact that her first publications after the five-year silence were written in the service of other people—that is, a brief tract intended to encourage schoolchildren to donate funds for the restoration of Mount Vernon and a large memorial to her father's work—suggests that despite her earlier success, Cooper did not yet conceive of herself as—or commit herself to being—an independent, self-expressive author. She seems not to have any other nature-writing projects in mind; instead, she turns to the keeping—and shaping—of her father's literary reputation and to the establishment of a hospital and an orphanage in her town.

New Directions: Writing for Father and Society

Susan Cooper's commentaries in *Pages and Pictures, from the Writings of James Fenimore Cooper* (1861) begin her active public efforts to maintain her father's place in American letters. With the approach of the Civil War, however, her community would have other concerns, and she turned her intelligence and influence to the philanthropy that would eventually result in the Thanksgiving Hospital (dedicated on Thanksgiving Day, 1867) and in the Orphan House of the Holy Saviour (incorporated in March 1870).[15] Even as she announced the publication of *Pages and Pictures* to Rear Adm. William Branford Shubrick, the longtime family friend to whom she dedicated the volume, Cooper's focus was divided between her devotion to her father's memory and the imminence of war. She wrote to Shubrick on December 7, 1860:

> May the volume serve, my dear Commodore, to remind you of the heart-felt and life-long affection, borne you by my dear Father and may it remind you also occasionally of those who have so fully inherited that feeling!
>
> These are solemn days for us all, dearest Commodore. Charlotte and I from our quiet womanly home have been watching sadly, the dark clouds gathering over the country, and which all who have the good of the country truly at heart must so deeply deplore. Loyalty to the Union[,] fidelity to the interests of the country in every high, and generous sense of the word[,] we could never forget without treachery to the name we bear. Were he whom we mourn still with us his clear tones might now be heard, the influence of his powerful pen might be widely felt in this crisis. But there is scarcely any symptom of the present condition of public affairs so discouraging as the want of a sound healthful moral tone, of clear, and vigorous, and generous reasoning in behalf of great Truths, of disinterested devotion to the service of the nation, in the full meaning which that word should ever convey. The prominent public men, whether politicians, or writers, are to-day widely different in character . . . from those who have gone before them.

Cooper's high regard for her father here seems called up by her sadness and by her perception of the decline of effective national leadership. In the sympathetic company of her Commodore, she can comfortably lament, from her "quiet womanly home," the diminished character of the day's "prominent public men." This must have been a powerful letter for Shubrick. He was a native South Carolinian from Charleston and at the time of this letter was resisting great pressure to abandon his "Loyalty to the Union." South Carolina seceded on December 20, thirteen days after Cooper wrote these words describing qualities of leadership now absent from her nation. It is possible that Cooper intended her words to encourage Shubrick, forced now to be seen as disloyal to his native South. In her biographical sketch of Shubrick after his death in 1874, the traits of leadership she describes here are precisely echoed.

With the close of the war and with the establishment of the hospital and orphanage, Cooper's publishing career resumed. In the very first year of *Putnam's Magazine* (1868), she published excerpts from her father's diary in two separate issues. Having established this relationship with the magazine, she became a fairly active magazine writer and published at least thirty-five article-length pieces over the next twenty-five years in several of the nation's most reputable magazines.

The most clearly polemical of her writings from this period is her "Female Suffrage: A Letter to the Christian Women of America," published in *Harper's New Monthly Magazine* in August and September 1870. This is a carefully reasoned and logically developed argument against female suffrage, and it reflects the benevolence with which men treated Cooper throughout her life. Cooper argues that by divine creation, woman (with some rare exceptions) is physically and intellectually inferior to man and so must accept a subordinate position; woman, however, must always "connect self-respect and dignity with true humility, and never, under any circumstances . . . sink into the mere tool and toy of man."[16] While her argument rests mostly on Christian doctrine and the authority of centuries of past practice, she does mix in an element of essentialism:

> [T]he great mass of women can never be made to take a deep, a sincere, a discriminating, a lasting interest in the thousand political questions ever arising to be settled by the vote. They very soon weary of such questions. On great occasions they can work themselves up to a state of frenzied excitement over some one political question. At such times they can parade a degree of unreasoning prejudice, of passionate hatred, of blind fury, even beyond what man can boast of. But, in their natural condition, in everyday life, they do not take instinctively to politics as men do. ("Female Suffrage," 445)

This is an unusual moment in Cooper's oeuvre; here in her late fifties, she expresses a personal indignation that drives her nearly to the brink of satire. She did not, however, return to this subject for publication.

Outside of magazine writing, a major project she undertook beginning in the mid-1870s was a series of largely biographical introductions to Houghton Mifflin's "Household Edition" of her father's novels. Since her death, she has probably been best known as the rather silent author of these introductions. In 1876 the editions of the five Leatherstocking Tales appeared, and in 1881–84 editions of the ten other novels included in the series were published. Much research and labor went into preparing these introductions, and they consistently illuminate the history of the novels' compositions, settings, and characterizations. Cooper's commitment to this large and time-consuming project reveals her continuing devotion to her father's memory. When the last of these volumes was published, she was seventy-one years old, and her father had been dead thirty-one years. Some three years later, in February and October 1887, Cooper published two essays in the *Atlantic Monthly* that provide some biographical context for the composition and publication of three novels not included in the "Household Edition": *The Spy, The Wept of Wish-ton-Wish,* and *The Bravo.*[17] She was then seventy-four years old and did not again write about her father or his work for publication.

At nearly the same time that she completed the first five "Household" introductions in 1876, Cooper published two interesting biographical sketches, one of the national hero and her father's friend William Branford Shubrick and one of a Revolutionary War hero's wife, Mrs. Philip Schuyler. The Shubrick piece provides the readers of *Harper's* with a detailed chronology of this naval hero's life, emphasizing through vivid narrative his accomplishments during the War of 1812, during the war against Mexico, and at the beginning of the Civil War. Cooper's depiction of Shubrick's final visit to her dying father eulogizes a family friend but serves also to reflect some of Shubrick's light on her father's memory. Cooper's sketch of the life of Catharine Schuyler, "Mrs. Philip Schuyler," frames a memorial to womanly dutifulness and courage within a memorial to a local (that is, from Albany) male hero of the American Revolution.

"Otsego Leaves," 1878

Cooper produced a remarkable series of four essays published in *Appletons' Journal* under the collective title "Otsego Leaves." Since 1854 she had practically abandoned nature writing as a genre, but in 1878 she produced this rather nonchalant tour de force that is likely to be regarded, when it is more widely known, as her most mature and most fully realized contribution to American environmental writing. The four essays comprising "Otsego Leaves" are entitled "Birds Then and Now," "The Bird Mediæval," "The Bird Primeval," and "A Road-side Post-office." The last of these consists of a sketch of a coach ride that focuses exclusively on the behavior and qualities of the human inhabitants of her region and is a compelling sketch of rural life. The first three essays, however, compose a work of literary ornithology and will establish for Cooper a place in the history of that popular science in the United States, ornithology, which was second only to botany in Cooper's century.

She begins the series, in "Birds Then and Now," by documenting the decline of several of the most common bird species over the preceding two decades. She describes the bird populations of her region as they existed "Then," twenty years before, and then characterizes their reduction in numbers "Now." In her discussion of the causes of the decline, however, she becomes one of the earliest American voices trying to discern the reasons for a diminished biodiversity. The most tangible evidence of the decline in bird populations is Cooper's continuous counts over twenty and more years of bird nests: "When the leaves fall in November, the nests are revealed, and after snow has fallen, and each nest takes a tiny white dome, they become still more conspicuous." Because she has surveyed the same areas and been familiar with the same trees over many years, Cooper's conclusion seems sound: in the past, "you were never out of sight of some one nest, and frequently half a dozen could be counted in near neighborhood. To-day it may be doubted if we have more than one-third of the number of these street-nests which could be counted twenty years ago." [18] By modeling this method of monitoring bird populations in one area over many years, Cooper anticipates Aldo Leopold's encouragement of amateur ornithology in the 1930s. She moves beyond mere lament when she delineates the causes of the declining populations (that is, boys kill them, girls wear them on their hats, and travelers dine upon them in southern resorts). She writes now as an amateur ornithologist and engages readers in the possibility of restoring the reduced bird populations by understanding the causes and by ceasing the destructive practices.

In the second essay, "The Bird Mediæval," she models for her readers her method of culling environmental history from earlier Colonial texts. The opening dream-vision of bird life "about the homes of the early colonists" gives way to an unforgettable account of a visit to a Dutch farm on the "Upper Hudson," where she observed the many alliances the "Dutch negroes" kept with the birds. Central to her description of items set out in the spring as nesting places for the returning birds (old hats, gourds, some built bird houses, even the adorned skulls of domesticated mammals) is the image of the great barn and of the human and bird lives led there:

Seventy of those brown nests, many old, others new, and still unfinished,
might have been counted clinging to the vast, sloping roof, or clustering on the

beams. In and out through the great doors, in and out through smaller openings, high over the roof without, low over the broad river beyond, in shadow and sunshine, now grazing the heads of the noisy negroes, now gliding over the quiet cattle in the stalls, now whirling among the doves and martins, which also haunted that vast, hospitable barn-roof, were the sprite-like swallow-people. Yes, the great barn was full of merry, cheery life, in which the negroes, old and young, filled the largest space, no doubt, but in which the birds far outnumbered them.[19]

This vivid narrative of a human lifestyle that completely accommodates the needs of bird species becomes an antidote to the avian "holocaust" she exposes in the first essay.

She opens the third essay, "The Bird Primeval," with her regret that so much environmental history is irrecoverable; she then offers a narrative reconstruction of the life history of a three-hundred-year-old elm that occupied a slope overlooking Otsego Lake before Europeans first came to North America. The narrative center of this "history" is the image of the great hollow trunk of the storm-blasted elm and the scores of chimney swifts who build their nests in its shelter:

About the old elm there was more of winged life and movement than elsewhere on the mountain-side, but it was a noiseless life. One by one small, dark birds of a dull-brown color came wheeling above the old crow, their long wings and short bodies darting through the air with wonderful rapidity, and with scarcely a vibration of the wings, whirling, diving, darting to and fro, and vanishing, as it were, one by one, each diving with a singular rapidity and precision into the heart of the old elm. That aged trunk was hollow for some fifty feet downward from the open rift above. At the height of a man from the root it would have required three stalwart savage hunters to embrace the trunk in its outward girth. Within, the hollow space, at its widest point, measured twice the length of a man's arm in diameter. The entire hollow column was crowded with those singular birds, and had been their summer-house for half a century.[20]

These "primeval" swifts flourished in and experienced a state of nature now largely lost, as Cooper subtly explains to her readers. Her final maneuver in this essay is to lead readers from her image of the ancient elm's teeming trunk to their own chimneys, where the swifts of unrecorded history now nest and carry on their ancient survival.

Just as James Fenimore Cooper worked to give his country people a sense of *human* history, Susan Fenimore Cooper worked in "Otsego

Leaves" to give her country people a sense of *environmental* history. She worked to deepen Americans' knowledge of and thereby their affinity with the other-than-human environment. The style of her nature writing had matured beyond that of the late 1840s and early 1850s. She had developed a slower pace and a more thorough attention to detail, as well as a more authoritative voice, reflecting perhaps a greater confidence that these essays might have the desired effect on her culture.

Episcopal History and a Closing "Lament"

Nevertheless, Cooper did not return to nature writing for some fifteen years, during which time she produced one of the most thoroughly researched works of her career, "Missions to the Oneidas," a series of magazine articles relating the efforts of Episcopalian missionaries among the Oneida people in the region of Oneida Lake (near present-day Syracuse, New York). She was a devout Episcopalian her entire life, and her interest in the history of her church apparently increased in her final decade. Her adulatory biography of William West Skiles (1890) narrates the first establishment of her church in the most remote region of western North Carolina at midcentury. Although the title page presents Cooper as the book's editor, the narrative is so fluid and engaging that it seems clear that the "materials" she gathered from five ministers and one layman passed through much more than mere editorial changes. Her representations of the wild Appalachian settings show her affinity for nature description and provide further evidence that she authored—rather than merely edited—this book.

A short piece published in *Harper's* just over a year before her death, "A Lament for the Birds," while not the last of her published writings, evokes for us Cooper's lifelong interest in environmental history. This essay makes rather emphatically the point that from the time when she conceived of her *Rural Hours* project in the late 1840s until her death half a century later, the mind of Susan Cooper was focused radically on the natural environment and on the human impact upon it. This closing lament literally echoes concerns expressed in "Otsego Leaves" and in *Rural Hours,* and in paraphrasing observations first published in the 1850 book, she transforms that book into a source of the environmental history she argues is needed if humans are to stop or even slow their destruction of plant and animal species. By associating the disappearance of white pelicans with the disappearance of the original human inhabitants of her region, she makes her "Lament for the Birds" into a lament for all her region's vanished inhabitants. It is a beautiful, lyrical essay, but it sings no song of hope: "Alas for the vanished birds!"

If the phrase "EDITED BY" preceding Cooper's name on the title page of her last published book, the Skiles biography, is an understatement, so too is the epithet "author of 'RURAL HOURS,' ETC., ETC." Cooper has been remembered affectionately but neither fully nor accurately. The work is now under way to gather the pieces of and understand her considerable literary accomplishments.

The Present Volume

This brief overview of her publishing career provides, of course, only an introductory orientation to Cooper's life pursuits; the essays that follow take on the necessary work of exploring her achievements, explaining the various cultural contexts of her work, and analyzing her contributions to American literature. Fourteen scholars have contributed the results of their studies to this project.

The first four essays bring out important, subtle implications of various works by Cooper by considering them in the light of her relationship to her father and other family members.

Susan Cooper's tending of her father's literary career and reputation constitutes a key story of her life and work. Wayne Franklin surveys all the relevant biographical and textual material in order to demonstrate just where and how the daughter worked to influence subsequent generations' valuation of Fenimore Cooper. Franklin's close analysis also suggests that Susan Cooper once went so far as to merge "her own voice with his."

Allan Axelrad's study of Cooper's early tale "The Lumley Autograph" (1851) fully contextualizes its concern with the value of autograph collections in the social history of collecting autographs and in Cooper's personal history of maintaining her father's reputation. The tale satirizes the commodification of autographs by the rising commercial spirit of the mid-century. Axelrad demonstrates that while Cooper criticizes this superficial motive to collecting, "The Lumley Autograph" reveals Cooper's affinity for collecting that had its motive in a Romantic belief that an author's handwriting reflected qualities of the artist's mind.

Lisa West Norwood shows that Cooper's representation of George Washington's life at Mount Vernon after the Revolution in her *Mount Vernon: A Letter to the Children of America* both domesticates Revolutionary history in order to elevate domestic practice to the level of patriotism and reflects her conception of her own family and home, especially her grandfather and father. This study contextualizes *Mount Vernon* amid Cooper's introductions to *The Spy, The Pioneers,* and *The Prairie;* "A Dissolving View" in *The Home Book of the Picturesque;* and the references to George Washington in *Rural Hours.* Viewing *Mount Vernon* in this context shows that Cooper's domestication of the national monument complicates our understanding of antebellum private and public work as well as the connections between familial, regional, and national histories. Far more than a fundraising instrument, *Mount Vernon: A Letter* is a literary text that deepens one's understanding of its author and her other works.

Just as ecologists study changes in a place over long periods of time to discern large patterns of change, Michael P. Branch studies the literary representations of the Cooperstown region written by five generations of Susan Cooper's family to learn more about the relationship between language and landscape. How humans represent a landscape often determines how it is imagined, which in turn influences how humans treat it. *Rural Hours* bears close textual analysis, but it also has meaning in a diachronic study of how Cooper's native region has been imagined through two centuries of literary Coopers.

The second gathering of essays offers three studies of Cooper's lifelong concerns with landscape and the rural.

Although Cooper consistently maintained a humble rhetorical posture, especially in the introductions and prefaces to her books, she fully intended to influence her culture. Lucy Maddox discusses *Rural Hours* as a "rustic primer," bearing the customary humble sheen but also intended to instruct readers in how to shape America's future according to her rural ideology. Furthermore, as Maddox makes clear, since this rural ideology is advocated more often by women than by men, Cooper's primer suggests opportunities for women to be active in this rural strengthening of their culture.

Richard M. Magee's cultural analysis and close reading of Cooper's only novel, *Elinor Wyllys* (1845), cast light on the author's belief that a landscape reflects the moral character of its human inhabitants. We learn, furthermore, that this belief is fundamental to Cooper's landscape aesthetic. Magee demonstrates this through his argument that the moral center of the novel is not the nominal heroine, Elinor Wyllys, but the landscape artist, Charlie Hubbard. Although *Elinor Wyllys* has been neglected by critics in the past, Magee shows that it offers unlooked-for insight into Cooper's environmental philosophy.

Duncan Faherty considers *Rural Hours* and "A Dissolving View" in the context of the Jacksonian era and helps us see Cooper's opposition to the rampant commodification of nature that marked that period. In *Rural Hours* Cooper represents her town and region, subtly, as a model of respectful, balanced relations with the natural environment; in "A Dissolving View" she completes her argument that Americans have a chance that Europeans have missed to create a national architecture (and, by implication, other cultural forms) that is shaped by its democratic values. This remained possible for Americans because they had not yet irrevocably diminished the physical environment that gave rise to their values.

Division three of the essays presents new readings of Cooper's best-known work, *Rural Hours*.

How Susan Cooper read the Book of Ruth tells us much about how she expected to be read herself. Michael Davey provides a valuable discussion of the nineteenth-century Protestant hermeneutics that Cooper aligned herself with and shows that Cooper's treatment of Ruth in *Rural Hours* indicates that she wanted her readers to avoid interpreting *Rural Hours* too freely. Davey further demonstrates how Cooper's hermeneutic contributes to nineteenth-century discussions of language and meaning.

Two conceptions of time inform *Rural Hours,* as Jennifer Dawes explains. One is the linear model of progress, and it is essentially human-centered; the other is cyclical, following the annual round of seasons and emphasizing the human dependence upon natural processes and events. Cooper develops a tension between these two and offers a resolution in a model of time that redefines real "progress" as human development that occurs in ways that are sustainable indefinitely into the future. Dawes thus clarifies an understated but defining rhythm of *Rural Hours*.

Tina Gianquitto illuminates the discourse of *Rural Hours* by analyzing it in the context of several crucial contemporary concerns. Conceptions of the age of the earth and of humankind's place on it were changing rapidly at midcentury. Gianquitto discusses this climate of change and clarifies a dilemma that Cooper faced in the written representation of her experience of nature. She valued rural knowledge but found rural language inadequate to express the full meaning of the natural world. Similarly, she valued scientific knowledge but found in scientific discourse a tendency to obscure or devalue rural knowledge and the divinity of nature. Gianquitto shows that Cooper found a solution to her dilemma in a principle of the picturesque aesthetic.

The final four essays develop readings of works by Cooper by viewing them in the light of several contemporary authors and social issues.

By viewing *Rural Hours* in the context of the village sketch tradition, Erika M. Kreger exposes the debt Cooper owed to female writers of this popular genre, explaining that the village sketch rejected the required oppositions of traditional plot-driven narratives, instead emphasizing character and local knowledge in a vision of communal, interdependent rural living. Cooper expresses a similar aesthetic in *Rural Hours* but develops her vision beyond the strictly social concern of the village sketch to include the nonhuman environment in the web of rural life.

By studying Cooper's treatment of the domestic in *Rural Hours* alongside that of the chief theorist of the domestic in her day, Catharine Beecher, Robert Hardy is able to shed light on an important aspect of the conservationist ethic of Cooper's book. Whereas Beecher argues that women are to be self-sacrificing and tend to the needs of others, Cooper's use of the domestic suggests that women should tend to others by becoming stewards of the natural environment. By means of this innovation, Cooper moves toward an environmental theology developed more fully in the twentieth century by Rosemary Radford Ruether.

Cooper had a female nature-writing contemporary in Canada, Catharine Parr Traill. By studying the two writers together, Lisa Stefaniak is able to illuminate the respective influences of gender and class in their representations of nature. A close analysis of their different uses of the motif of gleaning leads Stefaniak to insights into the aestheticization of Cooper's nature and the utilitization of Traill's. Stefaniak also explains how both writers reflect boundaries set by their different cultures.

Susan Cooper's opposition to the woman's suffrage movement progressed from the indirect, in *Rural Hours,* to the polemic, in her "Female Suffrage: A Letter to the Christian Women of America." Jessie Ravage analyzes Cooper's thought on women's role in society by illuminating the relevant subtleties of *Rural Hours* and contextualizing the argument presented in an unpublished manuscript and the published essay. We see finally that the increasing energy and the ever more refined argumentation Cooper devoted to her opposition to the women's movement paralleled developments in the movement itself.

These fourteen studies present Susan Fenimore Cooper and her literary career as accomplished, complex, compelling, and significant. Of course, much research, analysis, and interpretation of Cooper's life and work remain to be done, and one purpose of this volume is to facilitate and inspire that further work.

1. Susan Fenimore Cooper, *Rural Hours,* ed. Rochelle Johnson and Daniel Patterson (Athens: University of Georgia Press, 1998). Hereafter cited in text.

2. Rosaly Torna Kurth weaves a convenient narrative from the primary biographical data. See her "Susan Fenimore Cooper: A Study of Her Life and Works" (Ph.D. diss., Fordham University, 1974), esp. 1–103.

3. James Franklin Beard, ed., *The Letters and Journals of James Fenimore Cooper,* 6 vols. (Cambridge, Mass.: Harvard University Press, 1960–68), 4:411. Hereafter cited in text as *Letters and Journals.*

4. Letter to James Fenimore Cooper, Cooperstown, March 3, 1850, Yale Collection of American Literature, Beinecke Rare Book and Manuscript Library, Yale University, New Haven, Connecticut. Hereafter cited as Beinecke Library.

5. Susan Fenimore Cooper, "Small Family Memories," in *Correspondence of James Fenimore Cooper,* ed. James Fenimore Cooper, 2 vols. (New Haven, Conn.: Yale University Press, 1922), 1:32–33. Hereafter cited in text.

6. Letter to James Fenimore Cooper, Cooperstown, March 3, 1850, Beinecke Library.

7. G. P. Putnam, letter to Susan Fenimore Cooper, New York City, December 2, 1851, Beinecke Library.

8. Letter to Richard Bentley, Cooperstown, August 6, 1851, Beinecke Library.

9. See Jacob Blanck, *Bibliography of American Literature,* 9 vols. (New Haven, Conn.: Yale University Press, 1955–91), 2:312. Two letters to George Putnam among the Putnam papers at the New York Public Library refer to "The Shield." On August 27, 1851, Susan Cooper tells Putnam that she does not think the "new book" can be ready for publication by October 1. In a rather wordy excuse, she attributes her delay to the irregularity of "our mails" and to her inability to visit New York City that autumn because of her father's illness. A few weeks later, on October 11, Cooper again explains her delay: "As regards my own book, *The Shield* I have not been very well, and scarcely fit for composition; the delay in sending the first chapters, however, has proceeded from another cause, they contain various allusions to items of natural history, and fearful of making some mistake I was anxious to confirm what had been written by examining one or two other books. My cousin M. De Lancey promises that I shall have the information desired very shortly, and as soon as these points are settled you shall have the first Chapters."

10. Susan Fenimore Cooper, "A Dissolving View," in *The Home Book of the Picturesque; or, American Scenery, Art, and Literature* (New York: Putnam, 1852; reprint, Gainesville, Fla.: Scholars' Facsimiles & Reprints, 1967), 82.

11. [John Leonard Knapp], *Country Rambles in England; or, Journal of a*

Naturalist with Notes and Additions, by the Author of "Rural Hours," Etc., Etc., ed. Susan Fenimore Cooper (Buffalo: Phinney & Co., 1853). Hereafter cited in text.

12. Blanck, *Bibliography of American Literature,* 2:312.

13. [By a Lady], *Rural Rambles; or, Some Chapters on Flowers, Birds, and Insects* (Philadelphia: Willis P. Hazard, 1854), 10–11.

14. *The Rhyme and Reason of Country Life; or, Selections from Fields Old and New,* ed. Susan Fenimore Cooper (New York: Putnam, 1855). Hereafter cited in text.

15. "The Thanksgiving Hospital" and "Orphan House of the Holy Saviour," in *A Centennial Offering. Being a Brief History of Cooperstown, with a Biographical Sketch of James Fenimore Cooper,* ed. S. M. Shaw (Cooperstown, N.Y.: Freeman's Journal Office, 1886), 180–82, 182–84.

16. "Female Suffrage: A Letter to the Christian Women of America," *Harper's New Monthly Magazine* 41 (August 1870): 440.

17. "A Glance Backward," *Atlantic Monthly* 59 (February 1887): 199–206; and "A Second Glance Backward," *Atlantic Monthly* 60 (October 1887): 474–86.

18. "Otsego Leaves I: Birds Then and Now," *Appletons' Journal* 4 (June 1878): 530.

19. "Otsego Leaves II: The Bird Mediæval," *Appletons' Journal* 5 (August 1878): 165.

20. "Otsego Leaves III: The Bird Primeval," *Appletons' Journal* 5 (September 1878): 274.

PART ONE

The Familial Context

Under the Table: Susan Fenimore Cooper and the Construction of Her Father's Reputation

One day in the spring of 1820, a man rose from his writing table and suddenly exited the drawing room of his rural Scarsdale, New York, home. In his absence, a seven-year-old girl, doll in hand, ventured into the room. She went to the table, lifted the hem of the cloth covering it, and soon was absorbed in silent play within the gloom below. Not long afterward the man came back, accompanied by his wife. As they settled into their seats, the girl did nothing to betray her own presence or acknowledge theirs. The man began reading his wife the latest chapter from a book he had been dared to write some weeks earlier. As his voice—remembered by his daughter decades later as "very fine[,] deep, clear, and expressive"—filled the air, the girl listened quietly but closely. To the amazement of her parents, her loud cries suddenly burst from beneath the table. They snatched the girl out of her "tent," puzzled by her presence and alarmed by her distress, and only gradually learned that her pain had been caused by the tale of woe her father had been reading aloud.[1]

Even at this tender age, Susan Fenimore Cooper thus proved an attentive witness to the creation of her father's art. Later she would be his amanuensis and the beneficiary of his keen interest in her own budding literary career, and ultimately she would serve as the guardian of his reputation. But it all started, so to speak, with her covert dalliance under that table in 1820. So keen was the child's interest in what he was about that James Cooper (who added the Fenimore to his name in 1826) feared she might divulge the secret of his turn toward authorship. When he took his wife, Susan Augusta, and the girl on a visit to the family of statesman John Jay that summer, carrying the not-yet-published *Precaution* with him, he intended to read it aloud to the Jays, passing it off as the work of someone else. Young Susan, put in the nursery with the Jay granddaughters during the reading, threatened to expose his secret as she kept wandering into the parlor while her father held forth. Later, as he began work on another novel, *The Spy,* she quickly learned its subject and working title and again started to blab: her father thus wrote his printer, Andrew Thompson Goodrich, that Susan had "long ears and longer tongue" and had "been *talking.*"

Privy to family occasions and private tales, Susan was to remain intimately involved in her father's career. Later, astute if not always accurate, she peddled James Fenimore Cooper's legacy even as she guarded it, tending his papers and passing on tales that, even at their more dubious points, continue to shape our apprehension of his work to this day. That she is rumored to have gone to her grave with the manuscripts of some of his journals in her grasp will suggest how complicated her self-appointed role was.[2]

Accuracy

Susan Fenimore Cooper often has been the object of doubt among scholars of her father's work. James Franklin Beard, whom the family appointed as the first official biographer in the 1940s, rarely had kind words to say about her stories. I recall that when Beard first read the proofs of my study of Cooper's settlement novels, the main comment he made in a letter was that she was not to be trusted. He thought I had given too much credence to her celebrated account of how her father had dictated a rough outline of the twelfth chapter of *The Last of the Mohicans* (containing the famous fight-in-a-dust-cloud between Chingachgook and Magua) while in a febrile delirium. Beard's own regard for accuracy was legendary, and he was indeed a very meticulous scholar, so much so that I have found very few errors in his transcriptions from Cooper manuscripts—so much so, too, alas, that he never managed to begin his biography of Fenimore Cooper, let alone complete it.

Beard's suspicions about Susan's reliability were healthy but exaggerated. For instance, in the case of her story about the dictation of that chapter outline for *Mohicans,* Beard supported his assertion that Susan was not reliable by noting that she had misdated the trip up the Hudson during which Cooper had conceived of that novel, placing it in the summer of 1825 rather than 1824. To be sure, anyone relying on Susan's account of that trip ought to double check her dating of it against other sources. More generally, one should be suspicious of any details culled from her many recollections if no confirmation is available. But the misdating of one anecdote does not in itself render the substance of that anecdote, let alone any others, false. Indeed, misdating is one of the most common failures of memory. And checking *any* recollection against other available sources is, of course, standard procedure. Susan's many recollections regarding her father do remain slippery, and, lacking corroboration from other sources, one must use them carefully in writing her father's biography.

Fair enough. Yet we should not miss a larger point here. What Susan believed about her father, whether narrowly confirmable or not, had an accuracy of its own. Once laid in the grave in 1851, the novelist became a kind of character in an ongoing family plot and as such underwent a variety of fascinating transformations that, if we attend to them imaginatively, may reveal the trace of larger truths. If, as I shall argue in other contexts, he himself recast the legacy of the Coopers and the Fenimores so as to shape a family background suitable to his sense of identity (our family stories are usually about the family we *wished* we belonged to), his own descendants did the same to his life. What they wished he had been will tell us, in other words, much about what they knew he actually was.

Historian Alan Taylor has demonstrated that Cooper's father, long thought by the family to have been sent to his death by a political assailant in the streets of Albany, actually died of more mundane bodily complaints in the bed of a tavern in that city. Yet the family anecdote about Judge Cooper's demise had a poetic truthfulness as well, reflecting his heirs' sense of the judge's public exposure, the volatility of his political milieu, and his heroic energy. It reflected as well, I think, their own desired entanglement in the Republic's bloody birth, something to which the Quaker pacifists who populated the family's past could not in themselves speak.[3] In the case of Judge Cooper's youngest son, I would suggest that Susan Fenimore Cooper's tales formed part of a larger poetic history of his life and the place which that life marked in his family's sense of itself.

Coverage

Susan Augusta Fenimore Cooper took up the question of her father's life on several occasions and for varying purposes, attending to different issues at different times and often revising some earlier tale (and her own texts) in later retellings. Despite the surprising bulk of material she eventually published regarding him, she felt some conflict about divulging any details of his biography from the outset. In this reluctance, she was acting on an injunction against authorizing a biography that the novelist had laid on the family shortly before his death. No last-minute whim, his opposition to such a biographical treatment grew from long-standing concerns about his mistreatment at the hands of the American press.

In the 1830s and 1840s Whig editors and papers had targeted Cooper because of his support for radical leftist interests in Europe, although their nominal charge was that he was contemptuous of American society and culture, a lie that enraged him all the more. The weary public disputes that ensued led to Cooper's ultimate victory in his libel suits against the editors (many of which he argued superbly himself), but the victories themselves gave him reason to fear that savage revenge would be exacted after he no longer could defend himself. He no doubt feared authorized biographers themselves to some extent, since he had suffered enough at the hands of so-called friends in the past. But his greatest fear probably was that even the most accurate biography would produce a flood of renewed attacks in unsympathetic papers and journals.

The family struggled with the resulting prohibition. Almost immediately after Cooper's death in September 1851, Mrs. Cooper was approached by their son-in-law publisher, Henry F. Phinney, who wished to issue an expanded edition of Cooper's 1838 political treatise, *The American Democrat*. She suggested including in it various public letters from the novelist (those addressed to literary societies or printers associations, for instance) but rejected Phinney's call for adding a biographical sketch of Cooper, citing his own "earnest charge, against any authorized biography" (*Letters and Journals*, 1:xxxvi). For Mrs. Cooper, the issue was clear.

However, following Mrs. Cooper's death early in 1852, the five surviving Cooper children showed a less certain attitude, in part because the family estate was impoverished, and peddling the family archive might generate badly needed funds. In May 1854, all the daughters thus were willing to strike a deal with the physician and author Dr. James Wynne, who proposed writing a five-hundred-page biography based on Cooper's journals and correspondence. The discussion went so far that Appletons' agreed to publish the book, and a contract was drawn up offering the Cooper daughters, whose approval was secured, a third of the profits from selling the copyright. In return, they were to give Wynne full access to the family papers and then check his manuscript for accuracy. The youngest child, lawyer Paul Fenimore Cooper, apparently took a stricter view of his father's prohibition, however, and the deal soon was quashed (*Letters and Journals*, 1:xxxvi).

Paul apparently won the war as well as this particular battle. When the first extensive biography of the novelist was published by Thomas R.

Lounsbury in the "American Men of Letters" series in 1882, almost thirty years after Wynne's proposal, its author noted at the outset that the old prohibition, still very much in force, had prevented his use of the novelist's papers.[4] Although some later biographers prior to James F. Beard's time did enjoy limited cooperation from family members, he was the first scholar to have complete access to the archive. Since his death late in 1989, it has been made available to others.

Rural Hours

Susan Fenimore Cooper gave her personal consent to the contract for that short-lived 1854 biography scheme. Even prior to her father's death, though, her exploration of the family's home ground, daily experience, and lore in her 1850 book, *Rural Hours,* had anticipated his rules. We know from his own records that James was in Cooperstown for much of the time in 1848 and 1849 when Susan kept the journals on which *Rural Hours* was based, but he casts only the dimmest of shadows across her pages. When Susan writes of her excursions in the landscape around Cooperstown in the first-person-plural voice, she in fact never indicates whether either of her parents accompanied her, although in many cases they almost assuredly did.

Take a single instance, the account of a coach ride to Burlington Green, a village west of Cooperstown, recorded in Susan's 1849 journal. Susan's parents, perhaps especially her mother, hardly would have missed that trip, since its object was the home of "Nanny" Disbrow, the much-loved nurse of the Cooper children who had married a Methodist farmer named Bloss and moved away from the old family home at Fenimore, on the shores of the lake, some thirty-five years before. The Coopers were both in Cooperstown in July 1849, but Susan, although she notes that a large group accompanied her, offers no clear indication that her parents did make the trip.[5] This one episode, too, is quite typical of many other similar ones in *Rural Hours.* If *Rural Hours* seems intimate, a further probing of its actual prose suggests that it deftly hides family business behind a veil.

The indirection in such instances may have been owing in part to her father's active intervention in Susan's literary career. For her first book, the novel *Elinor Wyllys,* he served as editor. Its title page declares this fact directly, while the copyright notice, like the copyright deposit form preserved in his papers, records his claims to be considered the book's *author,* probably a Victorian dodge aimed at protecting the supposedly delicate female writer from undue (or perhaps adverse) publicity. James also negotiated with the publisher of *Elinor Wyllys,* Carey and Hart, for the terms under which the book was to be published, arranging for payment of its proceeds to himself, probably again to "protect" his daughter.

The Victorian dodge, though, may have been more apparent than real. In the case of *Rural Hours,* published five years later, similar arrangements were made by James, but the survival of a fuller record allows us to read his control over Susan's works and career with more subtlety. Her dedication of the new book to him (more precisely, to "the author of *The Deerslayer*") might be taken to indicate that he once again served her as editor, and though there is no overt evidence that he did so, I have little doubt that he did. James also negotiated with the publisher, G. P. Putnam, for the 1850 book's first edition, but in this case he represented himself strictly as the author's agent. The payments due on the book's proceeds again were to be forwarded to him, not his daughter, but the executed copy of the agreement between Susan's father and Putnam, dated in New York on December 14, 1849, carries an endorsement in James's hand on its back: "This contract has been made by me as the agent of my daughter, Susan Augusta Fenimore Cooper, who is entitled to all its benefits." Perhaps Susan was emerging from her father's shadow a bit more here, or perhaps the fuller record states what we can only infer with regard to *Elinor Wyllys.* In any case, these details of the business arrangements for Susan's first two books will suggest, rightly I think, that her father also had a strong hand in helping shape the *contents* of both works.

We probably may conclude that the guarded references to family experience in *Rural Hours* reflected his precaution as much as hers, or that hers derived from his. Even if his only influence on such matters came from her knowledge that he would be reading her prose, that knowledge alone would have been sufficient to cause her suppression of more direct references. Ultimately, by the way, James swapped frontier lands he owned in Kalamazoo for some of Susan's proceeds from *Rural Hours,* a detail that sheds interesting light on her own commitment to preserving the landscape from rampant development. But the lands in question, acquired by James from a niece's husband as payoff for bad debts, were not something that James had eagerly sought to own. Susan in turn might be said to have applied her talent to redress wrongs against her father rather than to make a killing in Michigan real estate. From an ecocritical perspective, it nonetheless is intriguing that her book wasn't just made *from* trees—its proceeds helped level them.[6]

But let us return to the details of family life. Whereas little concerning the specific experiences of Susan's father can be culled from *Rural Hours,* the book does provide incidental insight into the patterns of life in the Cooper household. This point holds true in two ways. First, at several junctures Susan inserts small recollections from earlier days, especially from the years of the family's European residence (1826–33). She thus recalls seeing a German woman at work pulling a plow in the fields, harnessed together with a cow driven by the woman's husband, a scene that her father surely taught her to read as a mark of Old World oppressions happily escaped by American women (*Rural Hours*, 105). But such political vignettes are uncommon among Susan's family memories in *Rural Hours*. More typical is her recollection of her first glimpse of wild poppies, spotted in a field near Netley Abbey outside Southampton on the family's brief passage through England in 1826 (*Rural Hours*, 122); or, from the period following the Coopers' arrival in France and their establishment in Paris, her memory of how the nightingale's song would rise from the chestnut trees in the heart of the city just as the "market people and chimneysweeps" began to move about there each morning (*Rural Hours*, 136).

Aside from such precious glimpses of the family's long sojourn abroad, during which Susan reached adulthood, *Rural Hours* is rich in comments on the family's habits, material culture, and day-to-day life during the later 1840s back in Cooperstown. Although these items tend to be quite mundane and in few cases relate directly to her father's activities, by their sheer bulk they help flesh out one's sense of his ordinary surroundings, something essential for a well-rounded biographical treatment of most authors. To take a wholly representative example, in her entry dated September 7, 1848, Susan notes: "This evening we kindled our autumn fires" (*Rural Hours*, 176). Or, to cite a more dramatic case, during the following month Susan recalls how, when five bats invaded the Cooper family home the previous August, two of them yielded after a long fight, but the other three "kept possession of the ground all night" (*Rural Hours*, 213). Who precisely fought the invaders she doesn't reveal. Perhaps we may imagine her father, broom in hand, chasing the trespassers from Otsego Hall, the sacred ground of his ancestors, as he had flushed similar interlopers from the family grove at Three Mile Point, only to suffer the retaliation of having his works removed from the Cooperstown library and burned, as that story goes.

Otsego Hall is a special focus for Susan's comments in *Rural Hours*, as it happens. In fact, in this sense one might read her book as a fantasia on the theme of the Hall as the unofficial manor house of the larger region, an attitude she owed to her father, whose 1838 novel *Home as Found* has often been read as a celebration of the return of the Coopers to their proper social and spatial position. Since the Hall was in ruinous condition when Susan's father repurchased it in the 1830s, a great deal of work was done on it over the following decade, as well as on the grounds, which had been used in part as a storage area for lumber and other building materials. By the time of *Rural Hours,* the house had been properly Gothicized, a fact perhaps not evident from the book, and the three-acre grounds displayed the genteel landscape effects preached by the family's acquaintance Andrew Jackson Downing, as a careful reader, noting what Susan has to say about the plantings near the house, might not find surprising. Since the house was sold a few months after Mrs. Cooper's death in 1852 and then soon burned down, Susan's comments on life in and around it are all the more useful. While we are right to focus our attention on the natural themes in *Rural Hours,* as Lawrence Buell urges us to, we also might attend to the manner in which it reflects the domestic economy of its author's household.[7]

Not So Small Family Memories

Taken together, however, all such bits of family information in *Rural Hours* yield little insight into the creative habits (let alone the deeper energies) of Susan's father, which is for me the really interesting issue here. One way to begin to address that issue is to note the effect of his death on her own creativity. Her career as it had developed to that point fell into comparative silence soon afterward, so much so that it is common to observe that she never realized her considerable potential. We know that Susan was preparing a second novel, a frontier tale to be called "The Shield," by the end of 1850, when James signed a contract for it (specifically as *her* work) with Putnam.[8] This new book, although announced as "in press" at the end of the 1852 memorial volume published for her father and mentioned in other venues as late as 1854, was never actually issued, and we do not know why.[9] Following the collapse of that project, Susan did publish several other books, but with the exception of the short *Mount Vernon* of 1859, these involved her more as editor than author. She also published some dozen or so brief periodical essays.

Susan's muse hardly was dead; it merely had shifted focus. Nothing activated it in the years after 1851 more than the ever recurrent recollections of her father. His deathbed prohibition notwithstanding, Susan poured her own creative energies into recovering and indeed publicizing him, though in her own peculiar manner. Improvising various forms at different times, she never produced an orthodox biography and in fact seems rarely to have used the family papers that were at her disposal, as she would have needed to do in order to write one. Her sources clearly were not the scholar's; they were instead the memories welling up in her own mind, memories that stretched from that first sally of her father onto literary territory in the Scarsdale drawing room, through the European years from 1826 to 1833, the return to the United States (and to Cooperstown), and the final, most productive decade of his life, when he published fully half of his thirty-two novels. Of all his children, only Susan had lived through the whole sweep of his career. She had been under the table through it all, so to speak, and as noted above served him in later years as his amanuensis. The latter service helped discipline her own emerging talent while allowing her intimate insight into her father's.

Of the many items Susan published on her father, the most substantial was *Pages and Pictures, from the Writings of James Fenimore Cooper, with Notes by Susan Fenimore Cooper,* issued at Christmas 1860 but dated 1861. Lavishly illustrated with engravings and woodcuts derived from the Darley edition of her father's works and from other sources, the book was produced in large format and in several styles of binding, including a sacral version sporting deeply incised leather and gilt-edged pages. Susan's role in this work was more demanding than the title page's language ("Notes by Susan Fenimore Cooper") would indicate or the term "editor" (used in her dedication of the volume to her father's navy chum, Rear Adm. William Branford Shubrick) would suggest. The book runs to almost four hundred pages, not counting the unpaged engravings. Its bulk is composed of relatively self-contained excerpts from twenty-five of her father's thirty-two novels, usually whole chapters, but her own essays preceding each of those excerpts total about one hundred pages, some fifty thousand words. (This estimate does not include the substantial space taken up in Susan's essays by other excerpts from her father's prose, usually from the novel in hand or from the European travel books.)

Susan's contributions to the volume are significant as well as bulky. As the anecdote about the feverish composition of the twelfth chapter of *Mohicans* suggests, here she indeed tried to portray the inscape of her father's imagination. Her emphasis fell not on the embattled social thinker whom she knew well and whom the twentieth century, following the lead of Robert E. Spiller, rediscovered but rather on the mythopoeic figure, the man whose best inventions came from the inward dreaming that the *Mohicans* story stresses. This was the intensely private man who, as Susan also relates, decided to write *The Deerslayer* because of the visionary glimpse of the beautiful lake that he caught while the two of them rode home together from his hobby farm, the Chalet, up on the hills above Otsego's east side. (The Chalet was one of the sites that Susan repeatedly visited during the period covered by *Rural Hours,* presumably in the company of her father or both her parents, though the uninformed reader of that book would not explicitly learn of these regular visits.)

James's imaginative return to the Glimmerglass in this last Leather-stocking novel also had a profound social context, however, something Susan may have unconsciously admitted when she recalled that at the moment he received his inspiration he had been singing no Romantic lied but rather an old campaign song—one promoting, by the way, the party he had opposed! The novel pointedly wiped the landscape clean of its smudgy social signs, recovering the clean natural world underneath. And it did so not just because its author had that seemingly innocent vision of nature from the Vision, as he had named the hill in his first novel about Natty Bumppo, *The Pioneers.* It did so, too, because the author had been so deeply disappointed in American society in the intervening years: the new novel, in other words, erased the nation from the continent, even as it had to admit, in the figures of Hurry Harry and Floating Tom, that in the plot's imaginable future the evils Cooper already had seen would come to pass.

While Susan did not ignore her father's social thought or the squabbles that entangled him in the later 1830s and the 1840s, she favored an image of him as a solitary Romantic whose most significant social ties were bounded by the family's own tightly closed circle. What her essays in *Pages and Pictures* most typically focus on are the circumstances under which the work in hand originated—its "germ," as Henry James would later call it—or the relation of the story to the author's personal experience. Hers is a mostly private portrait, and in painting it she both obeyed and disobeyed her father's prohibition. Isolating him from society within her own pages, she played down the old entanglements that had made his last years so conflicted and in fact had led to the prohibition in the first place. But by foregrounding the private man in her own public text, she of course exposed him to wider scrutiny in her own era. If James managed Susan's talent in the later 1840s, she started managing his reputation in the early 1860s. In the materials she began to publish then, Susan thus became his agent, even at times his voice beyond the grave. As such, she extended the relationship that had obtained during the inception of her own career, when he had served as the mediator, instigator, or inspiration—or just the business manager—of her books and she as the copyist of his words.

Pages and Pictures remains the best known of her publications on her father. It is the one book in which she had her say about (and for) him, and it is the source most frequently cited by critics interested in Susan's views of her father. But it merely initiated, and at times timidly, a process carried on in a spate of later adumbrations and amendments that are more difficult of access but that are in many ways more revealing of the man and artist. Later on, for one thing, Susan could be more inclusive. In the 1861 book, apparently because of constraints imposed by the publisher (so her preface explains), she had to ignore seven of her father's novels, all but one of them from his last decade and fully five of them sea tales, so that the late nautical fiction suffered unduly. How she or the publisher selected the volumes to be bypassed then is unknown (two that had special auto-biographical significance, the Wallingford novels of 1843, were among those left out), but Susan was able to make up for most of the omissions when she later wrote a series of introductions for fifteen of the novels to be included in Houghton Mifflin's "Household Edition" starting in the mid-1870s. Of the seven novels omitted from *Pages and Pictures,* four (including the Wallingford books) were tapped for introductions in the new edition, and a fifth was given cursory treatment in the introduction to one of the others. As a result of these intersections, only two of her father's novels (*The Heidenmauer* and *The Ways of the Hour*) lack recollective commentary by Susan. We have a great deal of information from her about virtually the whole of her father's career.

I want to say something about the kinds of issues Susan raised in both *Pages and Pictures* and the "Household" introductions. First, though, I need to correct the false but widely shared perception that the "Household" introductions for the ten books also covered in *Pages and Pictures* largely just reprinted the essays prepared for the earlier venture. Susan clearly was approached by Houghton Mifflin not just because she was one of the Cooper children and something of an author in her own right but because *Pages and Pictures* existed. It would appear that the publisher actually wanted Susan to write "some authoritative account of her father's writings" and that Susan, mentioning her father's prohibition, offered instead to write "a series of papers which took the form of introductions to several volumes of the Leather-stocking and Sea Tales." [10] Whose idea it was to disbind the *Pages and Pictures* text, as it were, and refit the individual essays for this new purpose is not clear, though both publisher and author may have contributed to the notion.

Under its previous firm name of Hurd and Houghton, the publisher already had reissued the Darley edition in the early 1870s. Evidently, Hurd and Houghton had acquired the rights, or at least the reprinting rights, to the Darley edition from W. A. Townsend. At the same time, Hurd and Houghton may have acquired the rights to *Pages and Pictures*, which had first been published (and, we should note, copyrighted) by Townsend. Given these connections, Susan could easily have mined the older essays for the new venture. But she thoroughly revised and greatly expanded those essays, and in four (or four and a half) cases—for the books mentioned earlier that were not covered in *Pages and Pictures*—she provided wholly new introductions. For both *The Pathfinder* and *The Deerslayer*, perhaps the most striking examples of revision, she replaced very brief but important sketches in *Pages and Pictures* with texts about thirty pages long, texts that (as we shall see later) were among her most inventive forays onto the territory of her father's art and at the same time were at least tangentially related to her own lost novel, "The Shield." In every instance, however, Susan produced texts new enough—and she bargained shrewdly enough with Houghton Mifflin—that the copyright for the fifteen "Household" volumes she introduced was filed in *her* name, not the publisher's.

Despite such extensive changes, the misperception noted earlier probably continues due to two facts. First, the general suspicion that Susan was often wrong (or at least not quite right) in what she asserted about her father's works or life has led Cooper scholars to ignore *Pages and Pictures* and the "Household" introductions or at least not view them seriously enough to subject them to careful comparison. The differences, in other words, have been noticed but rarely studied. Second, the "Household Edition," even though it was intended to be a cheap, popular version of Cooper's works and was often reissued under other imprints, actually is elusive. Few research libraries have complete holdings: neither Harvard nor the American Antiquarian Society, for instance, reports more than a few scattered volumes. Anyone wishing to consult the "Household Edition" may find doing so surprisingly hard. It took me several months to assemble a complete set of copies of the fifteen volumes contributed to by Susan, and half of those are in photostatic form.[11]

Furthermore, some key facts about the history of the "Household" venture themselves remain elusive. Susan's first contributions to it focused on the Leatherstocking Tales, issued as a group by Houghton Mifflin in 1876, perhaps to coincide with the celebration of the centennial, which witnessed a resurgence of interest in the Colonial and early national frontier. To prepare her contributions to these and later volumes, Susan obviously had a copy of *Pages and Pictures* open before her. While the new introductions generally followed the sequence of topics in the older essays, however, Susan freely cut, condensed, and revised the latter, and she added considerable new material even when the original essays were sizable. For instance, in the case of *The Pioneers,* the *Pages and Pictures* essay ran to about fourteen pages, a total of some seven thousand words. From this total, Susan reproduced less than a third for the "Household" introduction. She omitted, for one thing, a long series of borrowings from her father's history of Cooperstown that *Pages and Pictures* had used as a means of intersecting the novelist's inventions with his own 1838 recollections of the village's past. These borrowings from *The Chronicles of Cooperstown* largely concern the diversity of early migrants into the Cooperstown region rather than family history per se; they also contain a brief account of the celebrated cannon, the "Cricket," to which reference is made in the pigeon-shoot chapter of the novel. Placed at the end of the 1861 essay, these borrowed passages were followed by a page-and-a-half excerpt from the novelist's 1851 revision of an earlier introduction to the book. (In 1876 the latter excerpt was left out because the whole of that 1851 introduction was separately printed in the volume.)

In addition to omitting all this matter derived from her father, the "Household" introduction to *The Pioneers* also altered Susan's own 1861 commentary on the novel. Some small passages were cut, others were skipped, and one long stretch was radically condensed. But Susan also made significant additions. The more interesting of the latter, I think, concern the divulging of personal information held back in 1861. For instance, in 1876 Susan for the first time named the "three or four boys" (*Pages and Pictures,* 51) who, as she reported in 1861, had been her father's schoolmates under the tutelage of the Rev. Thomas Ellison in Albany early in the nineteenth century. She also now informed her reader that these "boys"—"Judge William Jay, Judge Sutherland of Geneva, Dr. Van Rensselaer, [and] Mr. James Stevenson of Albany"—all "remained warm personal friends of Mr. Cooper through life." [12] Susan certainly had known these names in 1861. Perhaps she concealed them then because one of the boys, Dr. Jeremiah Van Rensselaer, still survived, and mentioning any of the names might have been a violation of his privacy. Van Rensselaer's death in 1871 removed such concerns, but it is likely that the inclusion of all the names in the "Household Edition" of *The Pioneers* also was owing to an enhanced openness on Susan's part about her father and the family in general.

In another case, she similarly expanded with more personal detail a story about her father's first teacher, the venerable Oliver Cory of Cooperstown. The 1861 essay had drawn on her father's history of the village in speaking extensively of Cory's service as the village schoolmaster. But it had little of consequence to say of James's personal relation to Cory, except for a story about how the teacher had commended the eight-year-old boy when, dressed in a faded cloak and leaning on a staff, he delivered a well-known declamation piece, the "Beggar's Petition" (*Pages and Pictures,* 50). In 1876 Susan considerably deepened the personal dimension of this part of her recollection. A new anecdote was added concerning a chance meeting of the two men in the summer of 1851, when, about to pass each other on the route leading up the east shore of Otsego Lake, they paused to reminisce. As Susan pointed out, her father already was afflicted with the illness that soon would claim his life, but he nonetheless jumped down from the seat of his wagon and went over to reach up and shake the now ancient Cory's hand. With "old-fashioned courtesy," however, Cory insisted on coming down from his own wagon, and the two men traded greetings and memories.

Had Susan ended her anecdote with this exchange on the public highway, it would be touching enough—focused on an image of her father tying together, as it were, the two ends of his life. But she made the story more personal still by relating how the two men went off together to "the Hall" (her term), where they "passed a pleasant morning together, talking over old times." Again, Susan extended and deepened a story whose outline had appeared in the 1861 essay. It is clear from her comments in the 1876 text, in fact, that among the topics of conversation between the two men at Otsego Hall that morning was the declamation delivered so many years before by the eight-year-old boy who later was to please a much wider audience with his representational powers (*Pioneers,* vii–viii). Susan knew this anecdote well in 1861, probably because she had personally witnessed Cory's 1851 visit to the Cooper home, but she chose to withhold it then, thus positioning her prose on public rather than private ground.

I want to bring in now two further points about the extended range of the introductions Susan Fenimore Cooper wrote for Houghton Mifflin in the 1870s and 1880s. As I noted earlier, she dropped from the introduction for *The Pioneers* sizable excerpts from her father's prose. In their place, she added a longer borrowing from that of her grandfather William Cooper. The latter, founder of Cooperstown, was not primarily a writer but had published a variety of items in the newspapers and had prepared a slim book for the press just prior to his death in 1809. The book was based on letters about his experiences in settling Cooperstown that he had written to Irish-American lawyer William Sampson, who saw the book

from the Writings of James Fenimore Cooper, with Notes by Susan Fenimore Cooper (New York: W. A. Townsend, 1861), 17. Hereafter cited in text.

2. James Franklin Beard, ed., *The Letters and Journals of James Fenimore Cooper,* 6 vols. (Cambridge, Mass.: Harvard University Press, 1960–68), 1:44, 63–64. Hereafter cited in text. For the rumor that some of her father's journals were buried with Susan, see *Correspondence of James Fenimore Cooper,* 1:3. Beard points out that there is no confirmation of the rumor (*Letters and Journals,* 1:xxxv).

3. Alan Taylor, "Who Murdered William Cooper?" *New York History* 72 (1991): 260–83.

4. Thomas R. Lounsbury, *James Fenimore Cooper* (Boston: Houghton Mifflin, 1882), "Prefatory Note."

5. *Rural Hours,* ed. Rochelle Johnson and Daniel Patterson (Athens: University of Georgia Press, 1998), 95–102. Hereafter cited in text.

6. Business papers, box 5, folders 21, 22, James Fenimore Cooper Papers, American Antiquarian Society.

7. Lawrence Buell, *The Environmental Imagination: Thoreau, Nature Writing, and the Formation of American Culture* (Cambridge, Mass.: Harvard University Press, 1995), 405–10.

8. Business papers, box 5, folder 21, James Fenimore Cooper Papers, American Antiquarian Society.

9. *Memorial of James Fenimore Cooper* (New York: G. P. Putnam, 1852), [107]; Susan's own copy of the volume, in my collection, is inscribed April 30, 1852, setting a terminus ad quem for the volume's publication. Rochelle Johnson informs me that "The Shield" was to deal with Native American life prior to the arrival of European settlers. It thus may have surfaced in part in Susan's later, lengthy introductions to *The Pathfinder* and *The Deerslayer,* on which more later.

10. Jacob Blanck, *Bibliography of American Literature,* 9 vols. (New Haven, Conn.: Yale University Press, 1955–91), 2:314.

11. I want to thank Allan Axelrad for sharing copies of several of the elusive introductions with me.

12. *The Pioneers* (Boston: Houghton Mifflin, 1876), x. Hereafter cited in text.

13. *The Chronicles of Cooperstown* (Cooperstown: H. & E. Phinney, 1838); S. T. Livermore, *A Condensed History of Cooperstown* (Albany: J. Munsell, 1862).

14. *The Pathfinder* (Boston: Houghton Mifflin, 1876), xxiii–xxv.

15. Blanck, *Bibliography of American Literature,* 2:314.

16. *The Deerslayer* (Boston: Houghton Mifflin, 1876), xxiv–xxv.

"The Lumley Autograph" and the Great Literary Lion: Authenticity and Commodification in Nineteenth-Century Autograph Collecting

Susan Fenimore Cooper's "The Lumley Autograph," a short story about autograph collecting, provides a light-hearted satire of the practices of the day. The story appeared in two parts in *Graham's Magazine* in January and February 1851.[1] It is narrated by Col. Jonathan Howard of Trenton, New Jersey, and details the eventful history of an autograph letter over several centuries. The story concludes by emphasizing an episode in London society in 1845. The narrative is mirthful and at times mischievous, but good humor is often a cover for other issues.[2] This story asks us to think about the value of a writer's autograph and the value of authorship. It also invites us to think about the author as the daughter of a famous author, James Fenimore Cooper, and their relationship.

The story begins on a "cheerless and dark" November day in late-seventeenth-century London. An "opaque canopy of fog" hung over the city. The "spirits of chill and damp" reached everywhere, but "in the wretched haunts of misery, they held undisputed sway." A "shabbily clad" figure is observed "dragging his steps wearily along, his pallid countenance bearing an expression" of uncommon "misery." We follow him home and learn that he is "a man of genius," but his "garret" contains "no food, no fuel, no light," and he is "suffering from cold, hunger, and wretchedness." In desperation he pens a letter to his patron:

"Nov. 20th 16——.

"My Lord—I have no light, and cannot see to write—no fire and my fingers are stiff with cold—I have not tasted food for eight and forty hours, and I am faint. Three times, my lord, I have been at your door to day, but could not obtain admittance. This note may yet reach you in time to save a fellow-creature from starvation. I have not a farthing left, nor credit for a ha'penny—

small debts press upon me, and the publishers refused my last poem. Unless relieved within a few hours I must perish.

"Your lordship's most humble,

"Most obedient, most grateful servant,

———— ————."

We then lose sight of the poet as he walks toward his patron's home. Whether he was admitted, we do not know. The poet's fate remains a mystery. But "the note written at that painful moment" has "a brilliant career" ("The Lumley Autograph," 31).

The letter first comes to light in 1745. It is discovered by the Rev. John Lumley, tutor to Lord G——. At this time the Reverend Lumley happened to be writing about the life of the seventeenth-century English poet and playwright Thomas Otway. He enthusiastically identifies his subject as the author of the letter, though it "was so illegible that it required some imagination to see in it, the name of Otway." Unfortunately, the Reverend Lumley takes sick and dies during a research trip to the Vatican. For twenty years the starving poet's letter is forgotten, until the reverend's nephew, "who inherited his uncle's antiquarian tastes," acquires his papers. His curiosity piqued by his uncle's manuscript copy of the dying Otway's letter, the nephew unsuccessfully tries to track down "the original letter," but he does manage to confirm the story during a chance meeting with Lord G—— ("The Lumley Autograph," 33).

News of the existence of such a letter is now out and about. Shortly thereafter, "the agent of a third person" attempts to purchase the original letter, if possible; if not, the manuscript copy. His employer is "believed" to be "that arch-gatherer, Horace Walpole, who gave such an impulse to the collecting mania." Walpole was a well-known novelist and essayist, but he was also a major autograph collector. In this instance, the letter that he seeks to add to his collection still has not surfaced, and the nephew refuses to sell his uncle's manuscript copy. The outcome of their negotiation is that "the manuscript gained notoriety, while the original letter became a greater desideratum than ever" ("The Lumley Autograph," 33).

A decade later, Doctor H——, while visiting a patient who worked as a trunk maker, spots "a soiled, yellow sheet of paper" in a "heap of rubbish." He does not know that this is the original Lumley autograph but he thinks the letter contains a worthy "sermon on charity." Dr. H—— has the trunk maker paste the letter onto the inside lid of a trunk he is having repaired for his son, a soldier about to depart for service overseas. As a result, the trunk with the letter joins the "soldier's wandering life." It is "besieged in Boston" and "made part of the besieging baggage at Charleston." It travels to the East Indies and spends twenty-five years in Bengal before returning home to England with its owner, now a highly decorated colonel. By this time a "corner" of the letter "had been carried away by an unlucky thrust from a razor—not a sword; while the date and signature had also been half eaten out by the white ants of Bengal." Yet the "time had now come," we learn, "when the Lumley autograph was about to emerge forever from obscurity, and receive the full homage of collectors" ("The Lumley Autograph," 34).

The colonel gives the battered letter, now something of a curiosity, to his future father-in-law, Sir John Blank, "a noted follower in the steps of Horace Walpole" ("The Lumley Autograph," 34). Although the signature is now completely indecipherable, "Sir John ingeniously pursuaded [sic] himself that what remained had clearly belonged to the signature of the great satirist" Samuel Butler, whose poverty was well known ("The Lumley Autograph," 34–35). A few years later, a gentleman who had just read Lumley's manuscript on the life of Otway chances to glance through Sir John's autograph album, and "the first sparks of controversy between the Otwaysians and the Butlerites were struck in Sir John's library." The controversy now rages throughout the collecting world, and the value of the letter increases astronomically. When Sir John dies, the letter passes to his daughter, the colonel's widow. However, financial distress prompts her to transfer the letter to Lady Holberton; in return, the widow's son obtains "a cornetcy in the regiment once commanded by his father" ("The Lumley Autograph," 35).

From this time forth the story takes place in contemporary London. Colonel Howard, the storyteller, observes and often participates in the events he relates. He chances to be a dinner guest of Lady Holberton the very day she obtains the letter. She is beside herself with excitement, having "at last triumphed in a negotiation of two years standing." She tells Colonel Howard that she now owns the "letter of poor Otway, actually written in the first stages of starvation," and then exclaims, "[O]nly conceive its value!" ("The Lumley Autograph," 36). Starving poets had special appeal, and Lady Holberton's reference to Otway's death by starvation echoed one popular but unsubstantiated view on the cause of his death.[3] Colonel Howard adds to the play upon values in the story by noting "the fine contrast" between the letter's "poverty-stricken air, torn, worn, and soiled, and the rich, embossed, unsullied leaf on which it reposed, like some dark Rembrant within its gilded frame," adding that one "could not have wished it a more elegant shrine than the precious pages of the Holberton Album," a "volume encased in velvet, secured with jeweled clasps, reposing on a tasteful *étagère*" ("The Lumley Autograph," 32).

That evening autograph collecting is the primary topic of conversation. One of the dinner guests, Theodosia Rowley, "also a collecting celebrity" ("The Lumley Autograph," 36), asks Colonel Howard if he could help her fill in some holes in her collection. She then hands him a list of "a hundred or two" names, "headed by Black Hawk." He points out that Black Hawk cannot write but volunteers a letter from a Cherokee friend. She also asks him if he knows "some *rowdies*" and if he would "oblige" her "with a *rowdy* letter" ("The Lumley Autograph," 97). He indignantly replies that his acquaintances are respectable. But the most "distinguished man" whose autograph she seeks, she says, "is called Uncle Sam, I believe." Her final request is that he "put her on track of a Confucius," if he has "any Chinese connections" ("The Lumley Autograph," 98).

The next day Colonel Howard hears that Lady Holberton has taken ill; the cause, it turns out, is the theft of the Lumley autograph. Lady Holberton suspects Miss Rowley, who, she says, "has all the principle of a Magpie" when "an autograph is concerned," and besides, "she is a Butlerite!" ("The Lumley Autograph," 99). Three months later, Colonel Howard happens to be in an autograph shop when a young girl comes in, hoping to sell an old letter she found lying on the road. It is the Lumley autograph. He purchases it from her. Knowing that a reward has been offered, he gives her Lady Holberton's address so that she can collect the money. Her reward is "a handful of guineas"—a stroke of great fortune for the girl and her needy family and "a sum by the bye just double in amount what the poor poet had received for his best poem." Colonel Howard presents the autograph to Lady Holberton, and "her health and spirits" recover ("The Lumley Autograph," 99). The colonel additionally contributes to an era of good feeling and harmony by distributing the contents of a just-arrived "cargo of American autographs" among the competing collectors, including "the letter of the Cherokee editor, the sign-manual of governors and colonels without number," and some "epistles from several noted *rowdies*" ("The Lumley Autograph," 100).

Lady Holberton seems to have learned her lesson, appointing "a new office in her household the very day after the loss of the Lumley autograph; this was no other than a pretty little page, dressed in the old costume of a student of Padua, whose sole duty it was to watch over the Album whenever it was removed from the rich and heavy case in which it usually lay enshrined." She gives a grand party to celebrate the autograph's return. When one of the guests casts suspicion upon Colonel Howard over "the extraordinary manner in which the precious Autograph had been lost and then found again," Miss Rowley rises to his defense. "I am proud to declare," she says, "the deed was mine." Lady Holberton's fiancé, Mr. T——, who was then examining the album, looks up and responds to Miss Rowley's audacious announcement with "a glance of intense admiration." Forgetting all else, he accidentally "touched the flame of a wax-light on the table." The album catches fire, and the Lumley autograph burns to ashes ("The Lumley Autograph," 100). The loss of the autograph ends the engagement of Lady Holberton and Mr. T——. He instead weds the thief, Miss Rowley, whose daring deed he so admires, thus uniting them "in the bonds of matrimony and collectorship." Lady Holberton is "inconsolable" ("The Lumley Autograph," 101), we suspect because of the loss of the autograph, not the loss of her fiancé.

Susan Fenimore Cooper's story about the Lumley autograph playfully pokes fun at overzealous autograph collecting in the Old World and the New World, for we are told that there are autograph collectors in America as well, even if their albums are mostly imported "from Paris and London" ("The Lumley Autograph," 36). Her identification of the eighteenth-century English Romantic writer Horace Walpole as a pivotal figure in the emerging popularity of autograph collecting is historically accurate, suggesting a link between autograph collecting and Romanticism.[4] The expansion of the practice in the nineteenth century provided substance for her satire.

In England at the time Susan's fictive characters fought over the Lumley autograph, autograph collecting had become, in the words of the British librarian A. N. L. Munby, "a cult of staggering dimensions" (*Cult*, 1). The cult strongly appealed to women. In a letter written in 1814, Emily Eden commented on the developing "fashion" of autograph collecting, stating that "it was quite ridiculous to see Lady Jersey and Lady Cowper and Lady E. Feilding and two or three others coming down of an evening at Middleton with their great books in satchells, like so many little school-boys, and showing each other their 'little treasures.'" Afterward, she explained, "the books are all locked up again," and each woman "wore the key of her manuscript book at her side, in case the others should get it by fair means or foul."[5]

The early decades of the nineteenth century saw an explosion in the demand for autographs in England. Authors frequently were beleaguered by collectors (Munby, *Cult*, 8, 81). Thomas Frognall Dibdin dubbed these "fiddle-faddling, indefatigable collectors" the "*Albumites*" (Munby, *Cult*, 8). Alexander Chalmers responded to one request with an apology, explaining that his "autographs had been woefully pillaged by seducing ladies" (Munby, *Cult,* 9). One woman reportedly accosted poets regularly with autograph book in hand, crying out, "Write, Sir write!"[6] Autograph poetry was highly prized by collectors. An author had to be willing to write an original poem in the collector's album. In 1831 in *Album Verses,* Charles Lamb published a collection of poems written for autograph albums, providing a small sample, according to Munby, of "the thousands" his contemporaries "were cajoled or blackmailed into providing" (*Cult,* 9).

In England autograph collecting had become fashionable. Its most zealous practitioners came from upwardly mobile mercantile families. By the 1830s their albums had become objects of conspicuous consumption, bound in sumptuous morocco, the letters inlaid in decorated mounts along with engraved portraits of the authors. Overzealousness led to misattributions, such as the wishful thinking that colored the identification of the fictive Lumley autograph. Less innocent were the forgeries and thefts.[7]

By the second quarter of the nineteenth century, autograph collecting had become a widely popular middle-class pursuit in America as well.[8] American authors were not necessarily flattered by this form of interest in their work. Washington Irving labeled collectors "musquitoes of literature" (Thornton, *Handwriting,* 86). Ik Marvel called the hobby "that dreadful fever."[9] James Russell Lowell thought that autograph albums were "an instrument of torture unknown even to the Inquisition."[10] Collectors who besieged American writers were sometimes known as "autograph harpies" (Thornton, *Handwriting,* 87), the epithet suggesting that they were predatory females like the Englishwomen Lady Holberton and Theodosia Rowley in Susan's story.

At the time Susan wrote "The Lumley Autograph," collecting was a popular hobby, and, no doubt, anecdotes abounded, especially in literary circles. In her epigraph, Susan provides an anecdote about "a German correspondent" who asked "an American author" for "'*a few Autographs*'— the number of names applied for amounting to more than a hundred, and covering several sheets of foolscap" ("The Lumley Autograph," 31). The anecdote may be fictitious, but the "American author" she had in mind most likely was her father, James Fenimore Cooper.

As the daughter of a famous author, Susan had a privileged view of what she referred to in the epigraph as "this mania of the day" ("The Lumley Autograph," 31). She grew to womanhood living with her family in Europe in the years 1826–33 at the height of "the cult of the autograph letter." She continued to live with her father until he died in 1851, enjoying a close personal and literary relationship. After they returned from

Europe, the Coopers lived in relative seclusion in the upstate New York village of Cooperstown; however, James continually received letters requesting autographs. While his daughter would have had numerous opportunities to hear humorous autograph tales told by her father and other writers, at home and abroad, some of these letters provided further fodder for her wit. One collector, for instance, politely asked James for his autograph, then added: "Could you favor me with an Autograph of your Father, the late Judge Cooper." [11] Another asked for a replacement for a "*stolen*" Cooper autograph, adding that he hoped that others "were more *honest* than some of my *friends* have proved" to be. [12] Some collectors wanted multiple autographs for themselves or others. [13] One collector asked James for his autograph *and* "such others as you may have in your collection." Then in a postscript he added: "Will you also include that of your daughter's?" [14] Another requested his autograph for a collection of "eminent and distinguished American Authors, Statesmen, & Military Commanders" plus letters from "foreign Authors" with whom he corresponded. [15] Still another asked James for his autograph and those of "other eminent literary men that you can spare." [16] One even asked his "permission" to retrieve from "the files of the Assembly of the year 1826 your petition for the authorized insertion of Fenimore as a middle name." [17]

Susan's close relationship with her father gave her an insider's view of a little-considered but routine aspect of literary fame. Requests for his autograph were part of their everyday life. [18] In this respect, their shared household was constantly subjected to uninvited intrusions. Victorian American gentlewomen were expected to behave politely, show restraint, and remain within the private sphere. The household was their domain. Susan was what Mary Kelley has called a literary domestic. [19] Working at home and armed with a pen, she protected her home and her father, striking back at these intrusions, her unfeminine aggression cloaked in "The Lumley Autograph" under the acceptable guise of humor.

Her father's experiences with autograph collectors provided Susan with the background and motivation for writing "The Lumley Autograph." He was connected with the story in other ways. During the course of the story, we are told that Thomas Otway, the starving poet who may have authored the Lumley autograph, wrote the play *Venice Preserved* ("The Lumley Autograph," 32). Otway's play opened in London in 1682. A century and a half later, *Venice Preserved* served as a source for her father's 1831 novel, *The Bravo*. From 1832 on, Susan assisted her father as his secretary. [20] In truth, the father's and the daughter's careers interconnected in a variety of ways. The famous author strongly encouraged his daughter's literary efforts, and he served as her literary agent. In the fall of 1845 he wrote his wife that their daughter's novel *Elinor Wyllys* would soon be published. He was optimistic about how well it would do since it had "sold in advance 1000 copies in New York."[21] As with Susan's second book, *Rural Hours* (1850), James handled the business arrangements and obtained the copyright in his name. For many years *Elinor Wyllys* would be attributed to the father, not the daughter.[22]

One story written by James, however, was attributed to Susan. After discussing Susan's novel, James went on to tell his wife that he had "given the quietus" to the "story" that their daughter, not he, had authored: *The Autobiography of a Pocket Handkerchief*, published serially in *Graham's Magazine* in 1843.[23] *The Autobiography of a Pocket Handkerchief* bears some resemblance to "The Lumley Autograph." Both tales satirize the hollowness of Victorian materialism by tracing the history of an object of consumption that is highly prized for its extrinsic value as a status symbol. The seamstress who embroidered the handkerchief and the poet who authored the autograph letter are not rewarded for their creativity. Value results from consumption, not production. The author of the handkerchief story and the author of the autograph story have similar values and share mutual concerns. But Susan did not write *The Autobiography of a Pocket Handkerchief*. Ironically, at the same time James reported that the rumor was false that their daughter authored the handkerchief story in *Graham's Magazine*, he revealed that he was trying to place a story that Susan actually had written in that very magazine.

James told his wife that he had "spoken to [George R.] Graham" about publishing "The Lumley Autograph." Graham "asked for the manuscript to look it over," he reported.[24] There is no record of what happened. Thus it is not clear that Graham saw the manuscript at this time. Nonetheless, James was obviously delighted with the story, for he spent some time and effort in the following years seeing the story to publication. In 1848 he shipped the manuscript to his English publisher, Richard Bentley, hoping to have it published in *Bentley's Miscellany*. "Depend on it it is clever," he told Bentley, "and will do your magazine credit."[25] After repeated inquiries in 1849 and 1850, the rejected manuscript was finally returned from London, and James placed it in *Graham's Magazine* after all.[26] "I shall put Sue up a few notches," he wrote. "As I go down, she will go up," the proud father told his wife, gloating over the fifty dollars Susan received for the story plus the exceedingly positive responses to her new book, *Rural Hours*.[27]

"The Lumley Autograph" was published in early 1851. James Fenimore

Cooper died later that same year at home in Cooperstown, his daughter close at hand. Susan became his literary executor. She was very devoted to her father in life and also in death, unswervingly striving to protect his accomplishments and values.[28] As the caretaker of his literary legacy, she had real decisions to make. Susan wanted to be faithful to his values without compromising her own. She succeeded admirably.

Over the years Susan received numerous requests involving her father's literary estate. Sometimes she responded favorably and sometimes not. She oversaw the posthumous publication of some remaining manuscripts, such as naval pieces, diary fragments, his account of an eclipse, and "New York," part of a larger unfinished study. She edited *Pages and Pictures, from the Writings of James Fenimore Cooper, with Notes by Susan Fenimore Cooper,* a beautifully illustrated book containing excerpts from his writings along with her very warm and personal commentary. Similarly, she provided affectionate and informative introductions to fifteen of the volumes included in the "Household Edition" of his works.[29] She also fielded many requests for her father's autograph.

It does not seem surprising that the author of "The Lumley Autograph" turned down requests from autograph collectors for her father's signature or handwriting. In a letter to a collector in January 1857, for example, she wrote: "We have received so many applications for my Father's autograph during the last few years, that we have been compelled to make it a general rule to decline them all, as otherwise we should deprive ourselves of the few remaining letters and papers of that nature still in our hands."[30] She was not being forthright, however. She denied requests not out of necessity but out of choice. She did not choose to give certain people samples of her father's handwriting.

Susan was very generous with others, however, so much so that in 1864 she told one collector that she had "long since parted with all the signatures" in her "Father's handwriting" that she could "yield." Instead she sent a manuscript page "taken from the *Water-Witch*" for this collector's "Album."[31] In the 1880s she was still honoring some requests for her father's handwriting. But in lieu of complete manuscript pages, she would now "enclose a scrap" or "a fragment" of a page from the manuscripts of novels such as *The Bravo, The Headsman,* or *The Water-Witch.*[32]

On the face of it, this behavior on the part of the author of "The Lumley Autograph" is quite surprising. Most of the secondary literature on autograph collecting is by collectors or dealers. They justify collecting by arguing that it has played an important role in the preservation of manuscripts that otherwise might have been lost to posterity. But they are not blind to destructive practices such as dispersing individual letters and in-dividual manuscript pages, and, worst of all, in Munby's words, "mutila-tion" in the form of the "horrifying dismemberment" of "the autograph manuscript" into "separate fragments for distribution to collectors" (*Cult*, 11). Such practices have had unfortunate consequences for James Feni-more Cooper's literary legacy. With individual manuscript pages dispersed and cut into fragments, it is now impossible to reassemble the manu-scripts in order to establish definitive texts for these novels. We might fault Susan Fenimore Cooper for her behavior. However, the author of "The Lumley Autograph" did not behave hypocritically; she was true to her own deeper values, and she did not violate her father's trust in her as his literary executor.

During his lifetime James had been very obliging to those who sought his autograph. "An autograph is so small a matter that I give them away almost daily to perfect strangers," he had written a woman friend, "and surely I cannot hesitate about giving you a dozen."[33] He also wrote poetry in autograph albums. The final two stanzas of one such poem, "To the Key to this Album," written in Paris in 1832, are flirtatious and flattering:

> The book reflects a lady's polished mind,
> The lock's an emblem of her modesty,
> And nearer viewed, repentant now I find
> A gentle coyness in the tiny key.
>
> These qualities may best adorn the fair
> This sweet reserve becomes the loveliest face,
> As hidden coquetry improves the air,
> And female mystery imparts a grace.[34]

Years later, "in complying with" Laura Jewett's "request for an auto-graph," James may have identified the woman for whom he had written the poem. "I formerly knew at Paris a Princess of Salm-Dy[c]k," he wrote. "She claimed to be the inventor of albums, and I had the honour of writing half a page in that father,—or mother—of all albums. Since that time I have done a good deal of work in that way, my female correspondents, in particular, being as numerous as, I dare say, they are handsome and agree-able."[35] James clearly was agreeable to autograph collectors and particu-larly responsive to female collectors, the primary target of "The Lumley Autograph." Moreover, he had never shown any desire to preserve his manuscripts intact. One autograph he furnished in this regard is especially noteworthy. Two years before Princess Victoria became queen of England,

James provided her intermediary with an autographed manuscript page from *The Bravo*.[36] Though a request for an autograph for Princess Victoria was quite special, overall the famous author seemed to be genial and obliging, his responses ranging from being flattered by requests to accepting them as part of the world associated with literary fame. He even authorized the insertion of original manuscript pages from *The Oak Openings* in copies of the Author's Revised Edition of his books published by Putnam in the years 1849–51 to increase sales.[37] The lessons Susan Fenimore Cooper would have learned from her father support her generosity and actual practices in accommodating collectors; they do not explain why she sometimes refused requests.

Actually, many of the autographs Susan provided did not go directly to private collectors. Instead, she found a very special and particularly meaningful use for them: she donated them to Civil War sanitary fairs. Civil War sanitary fairs resulted from a vast outpouring of energy and commitment by Northern women who wished to serve the Union cause. By spring 1864 Susan had sent "about two hundred" manuscript "pages" from her father's novels "to the different Fairs throughout the country."[38] In addition, that spring she published her father's unfinished manuscript "New York" in *Spirit of the Fair,* the magazine of the New York City sanitary fair. This was the most successful fair of all, raising a phenomenal sum estimated at $2 million to assist soldiers in the Union army.[39] The New York fair had a large number of autographs for sale, some of them quite extraordinary. From the Old World were numerous "kings, queens, dukes, nobles," "a splendid collection of the Bonaparte family," "a love letter of Lafayette," and an abundance of famous European authors (*Spirit of the Fair,* April 14, 1864, 99). Among the New World offerings were " 'the Star Spangled Banner,' in the handwriting and with the signature of Key," "the manuscript of the address of the President at Gettysburg," and "selections from ninety distinguished American authors" (*Spirit of the Fair,* April 12, 1864, 76). The ninety authors are not named, but we can be certain that manuscript pages from James Fenimore Cooper's novels were included among the offerings. Susan undoubtedly felt satisfaction because her father's unfinished work "New York" and the autographs she donated were used for a great cause.

Running through three issues of *Spirit of the Fair* (April 19–21, 1864) was an article by Joseph Green Cogswell on "Autographs and Autograph Collections," giving historical background and providing a rationale for— and giving us insight into—Susan's personal convictions about autograph collecting. His appraisal of the significance of the individual autograph is steeped in the Romantic origination of the widely popular practice of collecting. Autographs, he wrote, are the author's "living self, the spiritual essence of his mind." Compared to a painted "portrait," which "at best is a delineation of" the individual "only," he added, the "autograph is more or less a transcript of" the "mind"—in some "instances" also containing the "moral force" of someone's "character" (*Spirit of the Fair,* April 19, 1864, 150). Romantics celebrated human uniqueness, which could be divulged in the handwriting of especially talented individuals. Even more than an expression of admiration, collecting provided a spiritual engagement with genius and originality (Thornton, *Handwriting,* 78–85, 87).

In August 1851, not long after the appearance of "The Lumley Autograph," Susan expressed delight in "the compliment" paid to her by Samuel Francis in "wishing for a line of" her "hand-writing."[40] Susan did not write "The Lumley Autograph" out of any blanket disrespect for autograph collecting. She wrote it because the popular passion for collecting had commodified autographs, devaluing the creativity of the author and ignoring the real value of the autograph, violating her Romantic respect for the mystical potential of the autograph to transport the collector to a higher relationship with the individual genius of the author. In truth, autographs meant more to the daughter than to her father. He showed some pleasure when he received requests from charming ladies. In general, autographs had little meaning to him; supplying them on request was a duty that went with fame. For Susan, autographs meant much more. She responded favorably to collectors who seemed to share her belief in their Romantic meaning. She sent autographs to collectors who appreciated her father and valued his work, refusing others whose interest was insincere.[41]

Susan deeply believed in the intrinsic value of sincerity, which was a central tenet of the sentimental culture of her day. New money was producing rising classes, resulting in social flux that threatened the rock of sincerity upon which the good—the moral—republican society was founded. As a result, sincerity was giving way to hypocrisy and genuineness to artificiality.[42] "The Lumley Autograph" is a satire of the appropriation of autographs by a class of collectors who do not sincerely appreciate their real meaning and worth. The Lady Holbertons, Theodosia Rowleys, and Mr. T——s of the world are uninterested in the author or the work and indifferent to the Romantic value of handwriting. For example, when Miss Rowley asks Mr. Howard if he could get her an autograph from Uncle Sam, he starts to explain who Uncle Sam is, but she cuts him off: "'Only procure me one line from him, Mr. Howard, and I shall be indebted to you for life. It will be time enough to find out all about him when I once have his name—that is the essential thing'" ("The Lumley Autograph," 98). She is no more interested in Uncle Sam than she is in Black Hawk or Confucius. Such collectors do not sincerely value the personal accomplishments and qualities of the individuals that made their autographs desirable.

As Susan's story illustrates, the value of the Lumley autograph is artificial. It is, in fact, inversely related to the value of Thomas Otway's work. The autograph is valuable *because* no one would buy his work. Lack of remuneration and ensuing poverty resulted in starvation for the poet and, ironically, in the inflated value of his desperate letter. Even the poor girl who found the stolen autograph received more in the way of a reward than the poet had received for any poem. In this system, Susan Fenimore Cooper is telling us, the producer of the product is denied the true value of the work. For these collectors, the value of the autograph is artificially determined by the marketplace and the status it bestows. The quest for ownership was an exhilarating form of competition, mirroring the economic system that had produced the rising fortunes of the new collecting class. It is an amoral system that rewards indifference to human suffering, cutthroat aggression, and theft.

Although the tale takes place in England, Susan makes it clear that the moral points to both sides of the Atlantic. When the Lumley autograph was stolen, Mr. Howard had announced, "with a glow of national pride," that "in America we are much above pilfering autographs; when we do steal, it is by the volume—we seize all an author's stock in trade at one swoop" ("The Lumley Autograph," 98). The "author's stock in trade" that Susan was most concerned about was her father's. It included his extraordinary literary production and creative genius as well as the vision of the good society that his written words contained—in other words, the larger value of his work.

"The Lumley Autograph" is a study of values. Written during a time of change, the story juxtaposes sentimental sincerity and genuineness to the hypocrisy and artificial values of the ascendant economic class. It is noteworthy that the monetary value of her father's work was on a precipitous decline at the time she wrote "The Lumley Autograph." While in the 1820s he received as much as 45 percent of a novel's retail price, by the mid-1840s he was down to 20 percent; moreover, individual novels now sold for much less.[43] In this topsy-turvy world, the artificial value of the author's autograph might exceed the genuine value of the literary work itself. In *Rural Hours* Susan looked at threats to species due to environmental change around Cooperstown. In "The Lumley Autograph" at one point she wonders tongue in cheek "if the number of autograph-hunters were to increase beyond what it is at present," might it be possible "that the great lion literary, like the mastodon, will become extinct?" (35). "The Lumley Autograph" is a playful satire, but Susan was quite serious about protecting the value of her great literary lion's "stock in trade."

Susan was committed to producers of literature, not "producers of autographs," and her story pointedly targets autograph "consumers" ("The Lumley Autograph," 35). Broadly construed, "The Lumley Autograph" bears witness to the effacement of authenticity and the arrival of a new commercial culture. The story satirizes the nineteenth-century fashion in collecting that reduced autographs to commodities and status symbols. Yet Susan had great respect for the Romantic belief that handwriting afforded a special relationship with an author's mind and work. Later, as her father's literary executor, she acted on these principles by refusing some requests for autographs while honoring others. She honored requests from deeply meaningful charitable causes and from collectors who genuinely valued what the great literary lion had written. To the author of "The Lumley Autograph," the practice of autograph collecting embodied larger changes in nineteenth-century culture, pitting the older sentimental values that she esteemed against the rising spirit of commercialism.

NOTES

The author would like to thank Rochelle Johnson, Hugh MacDougall, Daniel Patterson, and Leila Zenderland for their advice and assistance.

1. Susan Fenimore Cooper, "The Lumley Autograph," *Graham's Magazine* 38 (January 1851): 31–36, (February 1851): 97–101. Hereafter cited in text.

2. In the only study to date of "The Lumley Autograph," Rosaly Torna Kurth dismisses the story as "simple entertainment" with no additional merit. See "Susan Fenimore Cooper: A Study of Her Life and Works" (Ph.D. diss., Fordham University, 1974), 199.

3. There were several popular versions of how Otway actually died. One story, that he was desperately hungry and choked to death on a mouthful of bread given to him out of compassion, supported the starving-poet story. The better documented story was that he died from a fever that resulted from his pursuit of the murderer of a friend. See Roswell Gray Ham, *Otway and Lee: Biography from a Baroque Age* (1931; New York: Greenwood Press, 1969), 212–15.

4. A. N. L. Munby, *The Cult of the Autograph Letter in England* (London: Athlone Press, 1962), 6. Hereafter cited in text.

5. Quoted in Christopher Fletcher, "Lord Byron's Unrecorded Autograph Poems," *Notes and Queries* 43 (December 1996): 426.

6. Quoted in ibid.

7. Charles Hamilton, *Scribblers & Scoundrels* (New York: Paul S. Eriksson, 1968), 94–104, 164–73; Adrian Hoffman Joline, *The Book Collector and Other Papers* (Greenwich, Conn.: Literary Collector Press, 1904), 49, 50, 62, 63; see also Munby, *Cult,* 10, 83.

8. Tamara Plakins Thornton, *Handwriting in America: A Cultural History* (New Haven, Conn.: Yale University Press, 1996), 86. Hereafter cited in text.

9. Quoted in Adrian H. Joline, *Meditations of an Autograph Collector* (New York: Harper & Brothers, 1902), v.

10. Quoted in Mary A. Benjamin, *Autographs: Key to Collecting* (1944; New York: Walter R. Benjamin Autographs, 1963), 17.

11. Lewis J. Cist to James Fenimore Cooper, January 15, 1843, Yale Collection of American Literature, Beinecke Rare Book and Manuscript Library, Yale University, New Haven, Connecticut. Hereafter cited as Beinecke Library.

12. The Rev. William Ware 3rd to James Fenimore Cooper, February 1, 1842, Beinecke Library.

13. See, for example, Robert B. Hariland to James Fenimore Cooper, December 17, 1842, and A. M. Harrison to James Fenimore Cooper, January 20, 1848, Beinecke Library.

14. George J. Gardner to James Fenimore Cooper, July [?], 1851, Beinecke Library.

15. Joseph B. Boyd to James Fenimore Cooper, December 20, 1850, Beinecke Library.

16. H. B. Whipple to James Fenimore Cooper, September 4, 1846, Beinecke Library.

17. D. B. Prindle to James Fenimore Cooper, March 29, 1847, Beinecke Library.

18. James Fenimore Cooper to Mrs. Hamilton Fish, August 1, 1850, in James Franklin Beard, ed., *The Letters and Journals of James Fenimore Cooper,* 6 vols. (Cambridge, Mass.: Harvard University Press, 1960–68), 6:210. Hereafter cited as *Letters and Journals.*

19. See Mary Kelley, *Private Woman, Public Stage: Literary Domesticity in Nineteenth-Century America* (New York: Oxford University Press, 1984); Karen Lystra, *Searching the Heart: Women, Men, and Romantic Love in Nineteenth-Century America* (New York: Oxford University Press, 1989), 37–38, 107–8, 125–27.

20. Kurth, "Susan Fenimore Cooper," xii.

21. James Fenimore Cooper to Mrs. Susan Augustus De Lancey Cooper, November 30, 1845, in *Letters and Journals*, 5:101–2.

22. In *A Descriptive Bibliography of the Writings of James Fenimore Cooper* (New York: R. R. Bowker, 1934), 209, Robert E. Spiller and Philip C. Blackburn place *Elinor Wyllys* in a list of writings incorrectly attributed to James Fenimore Cooper.

23. James Fenimore Cooper to Mrs. Cooper, November 30, 1845, and James Fenimore Cooper to Mrs. Cooper, November 26, 1845, in *Letters and Journals*, 5:102, 99.

24. James Fenimore Cooper to Mrs. Cooper, November 30, 1845, in ibid., 5:102.

25. James Fenimore Cooper to Richard Bentley, November 15, 1848, in ibid., 5:390.

26. See James Fenimore Cooper to Bentley, July 7, 1849, James Fenimore Cooper to Bentley, May 18, 1850, and James Fenimore Cooper to George R. Graham, September 14, 1850, in ibid., 6:53, 177, 214–15.

27. James Fenimore Cooper to Mrs. Cooper, September 30, 1850, James Fenimore Cooper to Mrs. Cooper, September 22, 1850, James Fenimore Cooper to Mrs. Cooper, September 14, 1850, James Fenimore Cooper to Mrs. Cooper, September 19, 1850, in ibid., 6:224, 222, 213, 218–19.

28. Lucy B. Maddox, "Susan Fenimore Cooper and the Plain Daughters of America," *American Quarterly* 40 (June 1988): 131–49.

29. James Fenimore Cooper, "Old Ironsides," *Putnam's Magazine* (May 1853): 473–87, (June 1853): 593–607; idem, "The Battle of Plattsburg Bay," *Putnam's Magazine*, n.s. (January 1869): 49–59; idem, "Fragments from a Diary," *Putnam's Magazine*, n.s. (February 1868): 167–72, (June 1868): 730–37; idem, "The Eclipse," *Putnam's Magazine*, n.s. (September 1869): 351–59; idem, "New York," *Spirit of the Fair*, April 5–9, 1864, 13–15; Susan Fenimore Cooper, *Pages and Pictures, from the Writings of James Fenimore Cooper* (New York: W. A. Townsend, 1861); James Fenimore Cooper, "Household Edition" of the *Works of James Fenimore Cooper,* introductions by Susan Fenimore Cooper (Boston: Houghton Mifflin, 1876–84).

30. See Susan Fenimore Cooper to Sir, January 26, 1857; Susan Fenimore Cooper to Sir, June 2, 1869, both in James Fenimore Cooper Collection (#5245), Clifton Waller Barrett Library, Special Collections Department, University of Virginia Library. Hereafter cited as Barrett Library.

31. Susan Fenimore Cooper to Dear Madam, April 2, 1864, private collection.

32. Susan Fenimore Cooper to My young Friend, February 21, 1884, American Antiquarian Society; Susan Fenimore Cooper to My young friend, Febru-

ary 17, 1885, Barrett Library; Susan Fenimore Cooper to ?, November 29, 1886, private collection; manuscript fragment from *The Headsman,* identified in Susan Fenimore Cooper's handwriting, private collection.

33. James Fenimore Cooper to Mrs. Hamilton Fish, August 1, 1850, in *Letters and Journals,* 6:210.

34. James Fenimore Cooper, "To the Key to this Album," June 2, 1832, private collection.

35. James Fenimore Cooper to Laura Jewett, January 5, 1850, in *Letters and Journals,* 6:106–7. In a footnote James Franklin Beard provides the princess's full name: Constance Marie (de Théis), princess de Salm-Reifferscheid-Dyck (ibid., 6:107).

36. James Fenimore Cooper to Aaron Vail, April 12, 1835, in ibid., 3:144–45.

37. Lance Schachterle, "Cooper's Revisions for Key Women Characters in *The Spy* and *The Last of the Mohicans,*" paper presented at the James and Susan Fenimore Cooper Conference, Oneonta, New York, July 12, 1999.

38. Susan Fenimore Cooper to Dear Madam, April 2, 1864, private collection. See also Susan Fenimore Cooper to My dear Sarah, March 11, 1864, Barrett Library.

39. Beverly Gordon, *Bazaars and Fair Ladies: The History of the American Fundraising Fair* (Knoxville: University of Tennessee Press, 1998), 68.

40. Susan Fenimore Cooper to Master Samuel Francis, August 29, 1851, Special Collections, Memorial Library, University of Wisconsin.

41. For example, see Susan Fenimore Cooper to My young Friend, February 21, 1884, American Antiquarian Society; Susan Fenimore Cooper to My young friend, February 17, 1885, Barrett Library.

42. Karen Halttunen, *Confidence Men and Painted Women: A Study of Middle-Class Culture in America: 1830–1870* (New Haven, Conn.: Yale University Press, 1982).

43. William Charvat, "Cooper as Professional Author," in Mary E. Cunningham, ed., *James Fenimore Cooper: A Re-Appraisal* (Cooperstown: New York State Historical Association, 1954), 135.

Susan Fenimore Cooper's "Home Book" of the Revolution: *Mount Vernon: A Letter to the Children of America,* Patriotism, and Sentiment

On July 12, 1858, Susan Fenimore Cooper wrote from Geneva, New York, to one of her sisters in New York City, expressing her pleasure at becoming involved in the purchase and restoration of George Washington's home and grave: "Most of us have more patriotism than we are aware of, and it is pleasant to have the feeling aroused under a form more generous and dignified, than a fourth of July Oration, (of the common sort), a Buncombe speech in Congress, or a fireman's procession— the usual channels into which one's everyday love of country flows." [1]

By the end of the year, Susan Fenimore Cooper had written a small text, *Mount Vernon: A Letter to the Children of America,* seeking donations for the cause and contributing to the plethora of written and visual statements on Mount Vernon's importance to the nation. [2] The text chronologically appears after Cooper's 1850 success with *Rural Hours* and before her extended efforts on her father's life and works, the 1861 *Pages and Pictures, from the Writings of James Fenimore Cooper, with Notes by Susan Fenimore Cooper* and the 1876–84 introductions to the "Household Edition" of James Fenimore Cooper's works. The same time period can be understood as the transition between her 1850s efforts on naturalist issues—with *Country Rambles in England; or, Journal of a Naturalist* (1853), *Rural Rambles; or, Some Chapters on Flowers, Birds, and Insects* (1854), and *The Rhyme and Reason of Country Life; or, Selections from Fields Old and New* (1854) published in addition to *Rural Hours*—and her 1870s philanthropic work in Cooperstown, highlighted by her founding of the Thanksgiving Hospital and the local orphanage.

With *Mount Vernon: A Letter,* Susan Fenimore Cooper brings Revolutionary sentiment into the home, domesticating history along with other contemporary women's projects. [3] The Mount Vernon preservation effort relied on domestic rhetoric, repeatedly extolling the need for female stewards of the home,[4] and Cooper's text fits neatly into this tradition. Yet while Cooper does stress Mount Vernon's importance as the home of George Washington (and, therefore, by extension, as a kind of national home), she does not intend to domesticate male history. Instead, her sense of civic involvement defies simple gender typing and encourages us to ask new questions about homes and memorials.[5]

Let me return to Susan Fenimore Cooper's letter to her sister. Patriotism to her seems potentially ungrounded—an everyday sentiment that tends to go unnoticed: "Most of us have more patriotism than we are aware of." It needs to be linked to a form. Yet the form of Mount Vernon appears not as a purely feminized space but as a "form more generous and dignified" than everyday domestic forms; it is separate from the "usual channels into which one's everyday love of country flows," channels that she identifies not with domestic concerns but with Fourth of July orations, congressional speeches, and the like—the very occasional effervescence of patriotic spirit that most would probably consider the male political domain, both then and now. This essay examines some passages in *Mount Vernon: A Letter* to see how Cooper domesticates Revolutionary history and what she considers the proper "home" for Revolutionary sentiment and memory. Her "home book" of the Revolution creates a new kind of Revolutionary monument, a monument that links everyday observances and patriotism.[6]

Although Cooper's *Mount Vernon: A Letter* domesticates Revolutionary cultural memory, its argument relies less on a sense of female subjectivity than on a sense of family and local history. Her conception of Washington at Mount Vernon draws heavily on her family legacy, with Washington doubling at times with her grandfather, at times with her father, and at times even with herself; it is this personalized touch that grants her the authority to assume that Mount Vernon could be central to others' lives as well as her own. Indeed, *Mount Vernon: A Letter* can be read as the first text she writes about her own family, several years before *Pages and Pictures*. The visual presentation of the texts supports such an argument, for *Pages and Pictures* includes similar frontispieces to those in *Mount Vernon: A Letter*: in each, there is a portrait of Washington and James Fenimore Cooper, respectively, followed by a picture of their respective ancestral homes, Mount Vernon and Otsego Hall. Yet *Mount Vernon: A Letter* also draws heavily from Cooper's earlier efforts, especially from the sense of place she explores in *Rural Hours*. Indeed, it seems that Cooper strives to link place and biography in *Mount Vernon: A Letter* as she did natural and cultural history in *Rural Hours.*

Before I continue with a discussion of Revolutionary sentiment and *Mount Vernon: A Letter,* I will outline the fascinating history of the preservation of Mount Vernon. Afterward, I will refer to *Rural Hours* to show how Cooper draws on her own sense of family history in her interpretation of Mount Vernon and Revolutionary sentiment.

The Preservation of Mount Vernon and *Mount Vernon: A Letter to the Children of America*

According to the Mount Vernon legend, a British naval officer passing the stately home on the Potomac during the War of 1812 tolled his ship's bell in reverence to the national site. The British display of deference became a tradition of respect followed by other ships as well, yet the respectful peal took on tones of lament as Washington's ancestral home fell into disrepair, since the heirs were unable to maintain it. Ann Pamela Cunningham's mother heard the peal while traveling past Mount Vernon in 1853 and described the sad state of the home to her daughter. Oddly recalling the death of James Fenimore Cooper's beloved sister Hannah, Ann had suffered a severe horseback riding accident in her teens and was an invalid, her physical impairment ending her reign as a Southern belle. Inspired by her mother's description of the disgraceful sight, Ann proceeded to organize women in the South to unite to save Mount Vernon. Her first appeal to the region occurred on December 2, 1853, in the *Charleston Mercury,* with subsequent calls for funding in other Southern papers in the same year. Soon the appeals took on a national note.[7]

Ann Pamela Cunningham's drive was not the only form of revived interest in George Washington. The 1850s saw a resurgence in the George Washington myth, with many writers using his image as an appeal to the Union, an attempt to find a figure that could supersede the sectional divisions of the nation. Many of these stressed Washington's long history of service, of which his leadership in the Revolution was only a chapter. In particular, his 1796 Farewell Address was cited again and again as a plea for Union, the Federalist concern with factions being reinterpreted as sectional interest, especially threats of secession.[8]

Many of these texts refer to Mount Vernon as Washington's much-loved place of quiet between public duties, but none took an interest in its actual preservation. Lack of interest was also rampant among private organizations and governmental bodies. In fact, both the state of Virginia and Congress turned down opportunities to purchase the home as a national site. Mount Vernon and the drive to purchase and preserve it did develop gendered associations that were apparent at the time.[9] Cunningham appealed to the women of the nation as the rightful inheritors of the site, the only ones who could protect it from the threats of the male political and economic world, "the grasp of the speculator and worldling."[10] She designed a counterpart to the American government as the best way to facilitate such national involvement of women: a union of American women, the Mount Vernon Ladies' Association of the Union, with a national regent and vice-regent per state. The vice-regent then could select local representatives for counties and towns. The Mount Vernon Ladies' Association preferred women who did not have to work and were not saddled with heavy family responsibilities. Widows and spinsters were the ideal candidates; their "families" truly could be aligned with the national interest.[11] That familial impartiality was a quality long associated with Washington himself, since he married a widow and accepted her children as his own but did not have any direct offspring. The legacy of his family relies on nephew bonds, brotherly affection, and surrogate roles.

The Mount Vernon Ladies' Association was not purely a Southern effort, although Cunningham's early appeals were intended for a Southern audience. It set the model for the midcentury preservation of other homes, with women claiming responsibility for cultural memory and perpetuating the belief that ancestral homes could impact the people of the nation. This pattern differs from the neglect earlier in the nineteenth century, with, for example, the destruction of John Hancock's house in Boston, and from twentieth-century examples, when professional men and national bodies became involved again in preservation matters. The Mount Vernon Ladies' Association can be seen as a predecessor to the Daughters of the American Revolution and other organizations that function on "genealogical" connections, which were not relevant in Mount Vernon's case— perhaps because of Washington's lack of direct descendants and the consequent sense that all Americans were heir to his cultural legacy.[12]

Although women spearheaded the movement to purchase and restore Mount Vernon, their fundraising efforts did not categorically exclude male contributions, nor did women raise all of the $200,000 necessary for the purchase. Edward Everett, the famous orator now mostly remembered as the "other" speaker at Gettysburg, traveled with his speech "The Character of Washington," soliciting funds and raising about a third of the total amount. He maintained a frequent and voluminous correspondence with Ann Pamela Cunningham and spoke warmly of the Mount Vernon Ladies' Association. He also wrote fifty-three weekly historical essays for the *New York Ledger* for the advance sum of $10,000, which he donated to the fund. These columns were later published by D. Appleton and Company as Everett's *Mount Vernon Papers*.[13] Other newspapers and magazines, including *Godey's Lady's Book* and *Harper's,* published appeals to the public. Currier and Ives lithographs of Mount Vernon were among the many different projects that contributed to the effort.[14]

After an initial period of resistance, John Augustine Washington Jr. signed a purchase agreement with the Mount Vernon Ladies' Association for $200,000. The contract specified February 1862 as the final payment date, but the fundraising proceeded more quickly than expected. By the end of 1859 the Mount Vernon Ladies' Association was within $10,000 of its original goal, although additional money was needed for restoration as well as purchase of the site.[15] The need for management plans and the increasing sectional tension delayed final possession until February 22, 1861.

While the preservation of Mount Vernon did not unite the North and South, it did provide a neutral ground near the locale of many of the early battles in the Civil War. Sarah Tracy, a Mount Vernon Ladies' Association representative, lived in the house with the groundskeeper (and a chaperone), and she upheld the integrity of the site as an apolitical realm. She received permission to cross enemy lines to obtain supplies and was promised protection by generals of both armies. In addition, soldiers from both armies toured the newly purchased Mount Vernon, with Tracy distributing souvenirs that could awaken interest in their homes when they returned from the war. They were not allowed to bring arms onto the grounds. Ironically, the lack of Civil War looting contrasts with the frequent pre-1858 seizure of items from the Mount Vernon house and lands by souvenir seekers and vandals.[16]

What was Susan Fenimore Cooper's involvement in the Mount Vernon Ladies' Association and in the purchase and restoration of Mount Vernon? In May 1858 Mary Morris Hamilton, granddaughter of Alexander Hamilton, was named vice-regent for the state of New York. In July 1858 Susan Fenimore Cooper wrote at least two letters, one to a sister and one to Mary Morris Hamilton, acknowledging her acceptance of a local role in the Mount Vernon project.[17] A copy of the *Mount Vernon Record* also records her name as a member of the New York Ladies' Standing Committee as well as a donor.[18] New York State was hugely successful in its efforts, contributing over $35,000 to the Mount Vernon Ladies' Association raised at balls and other events. Washington Irving even contributed $500. Susan Fenimore Cooper's *Mount Vernon: A Letter* was part of the fundraising effort, both soliciting funds with its message and also contributing the proceeds from its sales.[19]

Cooper's letter to Mary Morris Hamilton expresses willingness to help as well as deference to the vice-regent's talents and connections. It does not mention the text Cooper would publish within a few months. It also expresses a fear that she will not be very helpful due to the nature of her own home: "We live in a very quiet wood of the country; the population of our own county and that of half a dozen others adjoining it, is quite rustic, and matter of fact in character—very good Americans at heart no doubt—but not in the least prone to extraordinary demonstrations of patriotism."[20] Again, as in her letter to her sister, Cooper sees a split between everyday and extraordinary demonstrations of sentiment, associating Mount Vernon with the latter, not with the former. She specifically asks Hamilton about the minimal level of contribution, whether someone could give less than the one-dollar amount that entitled the giver to have his or her name listed in the *Mount Vernon Record,* a short-lived periodical designed for the cause. Although I have not found the specific totals attributed to the text, the trope of an appeal to children (and the associated plea for even pennies, not just dollars) did seem to have an effect. In fact, the *Mount Vernon Record* mentions a few New York school districts as contributors in 1859, so the appeal to "the children of America" was not an empty sentimental appeal.[21]

Mount Vernon: A Letter expresses many sentiments common to the cause, particularly the importance of Mount Vernon in establishing the moral character of Washington and the importance of women in preserving the home as a national shrine. The rhetoric at the end of the text demonstrates such domestic sentiment clearly:

> Children of America! We come to you to-day, affectionately inviting you to take part in a great act of national homage to the memory, to the principles, to the character of George Washington. The solemn guardianship of the home, and of the grave, of General Washington is now offered to us, the women of the country. . . . Let it become, for each of us, a public pledge of respect for the Christian home, with all its happy blessings, its sacred restraints—of reverence for the Christian grave, the solemn mysteries, the glorious hopes, shrouded within it. Let it become a pledge of our undying gratitude to him who lies sleeping so calmly yonder, on the banks of the Potomac.[22]

Cooper's address to the reader reveals the persuasive nature of the text, but it also recalls the novelistic convention of appeals to the reader found in midcentury sentimental novels, including *Uncle Tom's Cabin* (1851–52) and *The Wide Wide World* (1850). Yet despite the predictable language of Victorian domesticity, religion, and death, the text does not merely parrot Ann Pamela Cunningham's platform. I want to mention briefly two distinctions.

First, Cooper rhetorically appeals to the *children*, not the women, of America, positioning herself as a parental authority rather than as an equal member of a female American community. I find this approach significant to an understanding of Cooper's later works. Critics often have emphasized Cooper's role as a daughter, a position she seemed to fulfill even after the death of her father.[23] Yet here she takes on the opposite role, that of a parent appealing to the public as a younger audience. She specifically omits the role of daughter in her list of women's roles: "Happy are we, women of America, that a duty so noble is confided to us. And we, your countrywomen—your mothers, your sisters, your friends—would fain have you share with us this honorable, national service of love" (*Mount Vernon*, 68–69).[24] The narrative itself has the rhythms and language of a tale told to children, not a fundraising appeal to adults:

> Pause awhile, dear children; turn eye and heart towards that quiet country
> home on the Potomac. Remember all you have read, all that has been told
> to you, of the great man whose noble head was so long sheltered beneath that
> roof. Remember his honorable youth; see him first crossing the threshold of
> Mount Vernon, with his surveying instruments, when a growing lad of sixteen;
> see him bravely making his way on foot, through forests, over mountain and
> marsh, exposed to all winds and weathers, ever diligent, ever trustworthy, ever
> faithful to the task of the hour. (*Mount Vernon*, 10–11)

Washington appears not only as a great statesman and military leader but also as an exemplar of virtuous behavior for children: "Already, at that early day, he was fitting himself with care for the great work of life—by study, by forming good thought and worthy action" (*Mount Vernon*, 10). Such sentiments belong more firmly in the tradition of Washington lore popularized by Mason Weems in his 1800 *The Life of Washington*—the tradition of Washington as an adventurous, outdoor-oriented model for youths—than in the tradition of Mount Vernon appeals, which emphasize the home and grave over the woods.

Second, Cooper does not appear to have been connected with the

Mount Vernon Ladies' Association on the national level; her participation, as befitting her philosophy as expressed in *Rural Hours,* was more local and regional. None of the basic histories of the preservation movement mention her text or her involvement at all, although several mention the roles of other women prominent in literary and cultural circles, such as Horatio Greenough's widow, who was the vice-regent for Massachusetts.[25] In fact, Cooper's personal life and literary connections link her more with many of the men who participated in the wider Washington cult—such as Washington Irving, who wrote the magisterial *Life of George Washington,* and Horatio Greenough, who sculpted a statue of Washington—than with the national leaders of the Mount Vernon Ladies' Association. Her interest in the Mount Vernon project therefore does not align itself entirely along the lines of the domestic arguments of Cunningham and the vice-regents. Instead, like Irving and other writers not primarily concerned with the preservation of Mount Vernon, her interest in Washington foregrounds the question of cultural memory, including memory of the Revolutionary generation. The first quarter of *Mount Vernon: A Letter* uses language that not only stresses the rhetorical appeal to children but also appeals to a sense of a collective memory of Washington's life. She starts sentence after sentence with imperatives such as "Remember" or with the assertion "You remember," evoking a sense of a tale already familiar to her audience:

> Call to mind all his toil, all his perils, when . . . he travelled through the wilderness at mid-winter, bearing letters from the governor of Virginia to the French commander, on the shores of Lake Erie. You remember that long and perilous journey, with all its hourly dangers from the deep snows, the angry rivers, the cunning wiles of the enemy. . . . You know already how faithfully the papers intrusted to his care were guarded amid a thousand dangers, and, after more than two months of wintry peril in the wilderness, were safely delivered into the hands to which they were addressed. (*Mount Vernon,* 12–13)

While such language does fit the genre of writing for children, as I mention above, it also reveals how Washington's life had been internalized by successive generations. The phrases suggest that the events mentioned need only be called to mind or brought back into consciousness. Yet the specificity of her account suggests that certain items need to be highlighted—a perilous journey, the carrying of papers, as examples. Memory needs to be awakened or rehearsed, especially in its details. And, of course, the "children of America" in 1859 cannot remember Washington's feats; they can only remember the cultural expressions they encounter—the tales they hear and the monuments they see. Cooper's sentences therefore can be seen as performative; by asserting "you remember," she creates the necessary memories in her audience's mind, the details that narrate the internalized sense of Washington's greatness the way a single monument cannot. Thus, although *Mount Vernon: A Letter* expresses many sentiments common to the general Mount Vernon Ladies' Association project (the importance of Mount Vernon in establishing Washington's unbiased character and the necessary stewardship of women, not men, as custodians of Washington's home), Cooper used the opportunity to explore larger issues of the placement of Revolutionary sentiment and the meaning of monuments, as I will demonstrate in the next section.

Mount Vernon: A Letter to the Children of America and the Domestication of Revolutionary Sentiment

Amidst the predictable sentimental language in *Mount Vernon: A Letter,* Cooper presents a narrative of George Washington's life that domesticates the Revolution as well as the process of saving the ancestral home. She writes George Washington's life not as a series of departures for the national cause, as most eulogists did, but as a series of excursions away from home. She resists seeing Mount Vernon as the place of retirement, of an isolated private life, and instead sees it as a place of productive work, not unlike georgic visions of Cooperstown that abound in the three generations of Cooper writings. For example, she mentions Washington's role in trade as if he participated directly in the transactions, as trade occurs in rural villages: "The flour from the fields of Mount Vernon was sent in other ships to the West India Islands, and there, my children, the name of George Washington became known in the markets, not as that of a gallant soldier, not as that of a wise statesman, but as the name of an upright man, an honest farmer, faultless in good faith" (*Mount Vernon,* 17). This George Washington is not unlike the people in Cooperstown and other rural villages. Despite the scale of his enterprises, he is given a local presence "in the markets," presenting a model for rural trade as "an upright man, an honest farmer," not just the "father" of educated statesmen or landed gentlemen. Of course, the passage suggests to us today the issues of plantation economics and West Indian trade, issues that, along with land speculation, were admittedly part of Washington's life, although their role was minimized in the 1850s to maintain his status as a statesman. In this passage, for instance, these questionable practices were subsumed under the more benign epithet "farmer" for Susan Fenimore Cooper.

Cooper's image of Washington as "an honest farmer" recalls some of her views on the moral benefits of gardening in *Rural Hours*. She writes not only of the self-discipline that gardening inspires but also the generosity: "This head of cabbage shall be sent to a poor neighbor; that basket of refreshing fruit is reserved for the sick; he has pretty nosegays for his female friends; he has apples or peaches for little people; nay, perhaps in the course of years, he at length achieves the highest act of generosity—he bestows on some friendly rival a portion of his rarest seed, a shoot from his most precious root! Such deeds are done by gardeners." [26] Gardening results in surplus, which is not traded but is given away, bringing moral, not monetary, wealth to the worker. This moral development culminates in an act of sharing that transcends competition between gardeners even as it admits that such competition exists; until the end of the sentence, the reader has no clue that Cooper's image of the generosity of gardeners includes any kind of rivalry, not even a "friendly rival." Thus in this passage as in the passage on Washington as an "honest farmer," Cooper minimizes any sense of competition and emphasizes instead traits like generosity and shared enterprise, traits that fit ideals of a village economy more than contemporary models of plantation economics.

Not only does Cooper's narrative localize George Washington, but it also competes with the vision that Edward Everett proffers in his Mount Vernon speech, "The Character of Washington." [27] While Everett also emphasizes the importance of Mount Vernon in Washington's life, he envisions it as a rest between public offices rather than a settling for the civic lesson embodied in Mount Vernon itself. For Cooper, Mount Vernon the home was the central place of work, of moral work. Everett was known to appeal to his local audience, but in a way different from Cooper's in her text. He would arrange his talks around George Washington's visits to the place where he was giving the speech—such as his three visits to Boston, or his New York exploits in the war and afterward. [28] Everett chooses to show how Washington touched other places during these military and political departures from Mount Vernon; Susan Cooper chooses to conflate Mount Vernon itself with the place she loves—Mount Vernon and Cooperstown become doubles, not the opposites of country and city in the pastoral dichotomy.

If Mount Vernon and Cooperstown can be seen as doubles, then perhaps George Washington's excursions from the home are similar to Susan Fenimore Cooper's walks in *Rural Hours*. The observations that she provides the reader do not derive from within the house but from walks in the neighborhood. The pattern of leaving to gather knowledge and returning to compile it is similar to her expression of George Washington's leaving for adventures "on some worthy errand" and returning not as an escape but "as he returned to their [walls'] shelter, bearing with him, year after year, fresh claims upon the respect, the veneration, the gratitude of his country" (*Mount Vernon,* 54). The epistemology of learning is similar. One difference is that, for Susan Fenimore Cooper, all the county feels like "home"; since Cooper rarely ventures outside this broadened sense of home in *Rural Hours,* her text does not evoke the home-versus-world, private-versus-public tension found in most contemporary writings on George Washington.

Cooper not only focuses on the home as the central space of work in *Mount Vernon: A Letter,* but she even rewrites Revolutionary history into a calendar of natural history, repeating in miniature form the diary structure of *Rural Hours,* with George Washington as the author:

> Ere long, loving country life as of old, we find him keeping a diary of all the little events of interest. As the months went round, the days, marked so often in past years with the gloomy trial, the terrible battle, are now given to the peaceful work of the farm and the garden. Jan. the 10th—the period of the stormy winter campaign in the Jerseys, he now quietly notes that the thorn is still in full berry. Jan. the 20th—the anniversary of the bitter hardships of Valley Forge, the sufferings of his army, the plottings of his secret enemies in the Conway cabal—we now follow him into his pine groves, where he is happily busy clearing openings among the undergrowth. In April, the month of Lexington, he sets out willows and lilacs—he sows holly-berries for a hedge. . . . He sows acorns and buck-eye, brought by himself from the banks of the Monongahela. (*Mount Vernon,* 54–55)

This passage shows correspondence between national Revolutionary history and natural history, with nature taking over, the yearly occurrences both memorializing and replacing the "events" of the past, neutralizing them in an annual pattern of cultivation and observation. Here, nature helps make human events seem more like rituals, meaningful in their observation, not in their single occurrence.

Such a vision contrasts with the Emersonian tradition of transcendentalism most often associated with American antebellum nature writing. In transcendentalism, the viewer's mind—or Emersonian eye—passes from a natural object to a spiritual truth. The lilacs and willows lead not to universal currents but to specific connections, historical connections. The link is through the time of the year and through Washington's work in the garden or farm, not through any culturally relevant connection or natural symbolism. The lilac does not symbolize Lexington or the Revolution, does not itself evoke memory as it does in Whitman's elegy "When Lilacs Last in the Dooryard Bloom'd." While it seems that the connection may lack relevance, it links both the lilac and Lexington to a pattern of observation and ritual governed by the seasons, the rhythms of the natural world.

What kind of permanence does such a memorial provide? On the one hand, it links Revolutionary history not only to the "home" but also to the cultivated landscape, which, to Susan Cooper, contains the record of human history and American landscape changes. Consequently, Cooper domesticates Revolutionary sentiment not only by emphasizing the home but also by "domesticating" it as one does botanical species, transplanting it into the cultural memory as natural history. On the other hand, it raises the possibility that Revolutionary history could disappear under the repetitions of natural history. Will January 20 always recall the pine groves as it does Valley Forge? Or, to reverse the connection, will April always recall Lexington as it does willows and lilacs? The last example in Cooper's catalog, Washington's planting of buckeyes brought from the Monongahela River, perhaps shows the ultimate fate of such a link between national and natural history. The Monongahela was the site of a battle in the French and Indian War, not the Revolution. Thus in Cooper's catalog the French and Indian War, unlike the Revolution, no longer is tied to dates. The event itself has been erased, with its natural symbol overpowering it; bloody Monongahela has been transformed almost completely, translated in memory as acorns and buckeyes.

But what makes the Revolution able to fit a seasonal calendar and not the French and Indian War, whose "bloody Monongahela" has been nearly erased? The Revolution, unlike the French and Indian War, will not disappear as the botanical calendar incorporates it. It is the defining era of Cooperstown and of the Cooper family, their ideal moment of conception and creation. Judge Cooper first glanced over his lands shortly after the Revolution, and he associates Cooperstown with the immediate post-Revolutionary era: "In 1785 I visited the rough and hilly country of Otsego, where there existed not an inhabitant, nor any trace of a road. . . . In this way, I explored the country, formed my plans of future settlements, and meditated upon the spot where a place of trade, or a future village, should afterwards be established. . . . This was the first settlement I made, and the first attempted after the Revolution."[29] *The Pioneers* is set in Templeton, a double for Cooperstown, in the 1790s, and it deals with questions of inheritance introduced by the Revolution. Several of James Fenimore Cooper's other novels also rely on Revolutionary material, including *The Spy* and *The Chainbearers,* the middle book of the Littlepage trilogy.

Susan Fenimore Cooper continues the association of the end of the Revolution with the start of Cooperstown's history when she discusses a tree whose roots had been exposed by "a party of men from another valley" looking for buried treasure (*Rural Hours,* 232). "'But by whom did they suppose the money to have been buried? They must have known that this part of the country was not peopled until after the Revolution, and consequently no fear of Cow-boys or Skinners could have penetrated into this wilderness'" (*Rural Hours,* 232). She also mentions the era in her history of Cooperstown that centers on the pine-tree passage: "This village lies just on the borders of the tract of country which was opened and peopled immediately after the Revolution; it was among the earliest of those little colonies from the sea-board which struck into the wilderness at that favorable moment, and whose rapid growth and progress in civilization have become a by-word" (*Rural Hours,* 117–18). The Revolution will not disappear primarily because of these formative powers of the post-Revolutionary moment for three generations of the Cooper family. In *Rural Hours,* this era seems to absolve Judge Cooper and others from the criticism Cooper directs toward Colonial immigrants, those who bring Old World, nonnative species to the area. Focusing on the Revolution as the line between prehistory and history allows Cooper to avoid the repercussions of the contact narratives that she relates elsewhere in *Rural Hours.* As in *The Pioneers,* the changes in the landscape resulting from Colonial practices are minimized in comparison to those brought about by the end of the Revolution.

Furthermore, the fading of the French and Indian War will never be complete, even if it resonates less powerfully on the landscape than the Revolution. As Cooper explains in *Rural Hours,* plants can tell their own history as long as people remain familiar with reading the landscape. Native plants occur in isolated patches, pine trees stand as witness to the past, and the American landscape, as it is cultivated, can be read precisely for national as well as natural history (*Rural Hours,* 91, 116, 118). While it seems that the French and Indian War has been naturalized completely in Cooper's calendar, the connection between the Monongahela and the transplanted buckeyes renders it legible for anyone knowledgeable about the origin of different species in the landscape. The Revolution fits the seasonal calendar as living history, observed history. The French and Indian War must be read and interpreted; it belongs more to Cooper's sense of a prehistory than to history.

Let us return once more to Cooper's 1858 letter to her sister. Her sense of "everyday love of country" applies not only to her interest in the natural world, the calendar of changes and repetitions in the landscape, but also to a sense of patriotism that is grounded not in man-made monuments to the past, not in occasional speeches and celebratory events, but in the land itself, where it can be part of a national and domestic heritage. In her "observations," Cooper both notices and celebrates knowledge of the past as well as interest in the present.

George Washington, Revolutionary Sentiment, and the Cooper Legacy

What interests me about Susan Fenimore Cooper's reliance on the Revolutionary narrative in her account of George Washington is that most eulogists focus on the Revolution as one of several stages of public service in George Washington's life, neither more nor less important than the early western wars and exploration, the later presidency, and the delivery of the Farewell Address. Cooper, instead, relies more on the Revolution than on the other events of service even as she stresses the home more than public life. As I mention above, the Revolution, particularly the post-Revolutionary moment, is integral to the Cooper family legacy. Cooper seems to have brought that emphasis to her depiction of Washington in *Mount Vernon: A Letter,* making the connections between Mount Vernon and Cooperstown more apparent.

The connection between George Washington's wanderings on Mount Vernon and Susan Fenimore Cooper's excursions in Cooperstown become more salient when we realize how many potential connections there are between Cooper's sense of family heritage and the myth of George Washington. Otsego Hall, the Cooper family's counterpart to Mount Vernon, was constructed in 1799, the year of Washington's death. It too fell into disrepair, and James Fenimore Cooper repurchased it and restored it in the 1830s, after his family returned from Europe.[30] One of the "improvements" was the Gothic facade depicted in the frontispiece of *Pages and Pictures*. After James Fenimore Cooper's death, Otsego Hall was sold. It was destroyed by a fire in 1853, shortly after its renovation as a summer hotel.[31] Susan and her sister Anne Charlotte built their new home, Byberry Cottage, using bricks, oak doors, and other materials from the Otsego Hall remains.[32] Mount Vernon's preservation as a national home perhaps compensated Cooper for the loss of her own ancestral home; at least, her experience of the centrality of a home through several generations awakened her to the plight of Mount Vernon and the need to bring it under public protection.

Perhaps the strongest link between the Cooper family and the Washington myth lies in the local legend that Washington had viewed the land that would become Cooperstown prior to Judge Cooper's survey from Mount Vision in 1785. This account of Washington is retold in *Rural Hours:*

> A few months after the war was brought to an honorable close, Washington made a journey of observation among the inland waters of this part of the country; writing to a friend in France, he names this little lake, the source of a river, which, four degrees farther south, flows into the Chesapeake in near neighborhood with his own Potomac. As he passed along through a half-wild region, where the few marks of civilization then existing bore the blight of war, he conceived the outline of many of those improvements which have since been carried out by others, and have yielded so rich a revenue of prosperity. It is a pleasing reflection to those who live here, that while many important places in the country were never honored by his presence, Washington has trod the soil about our lake. But even at that late day, when the great and good man came, the mountains were still clothed in wood to the water's edge, and mingled with giant oaks and ashes, those tall pines waved above the valley. (117)

Cooper's description of Washington's thoughts parallels Judge Cooper's retelling of his own survey of the land in *A Guide in the Wilderness.* Washington not only "trod the soil about our lake" but also "conceived the outline of many of those improvements" carried out in particular by her father. Linking her grandfather and Washington not only potentially raises Cooperstown to national as well as regional prominence, but it also softens the criticisms that Judge Cooper's land speculation generated. The figure of the Judge reviewing the land is replaced with "the great and good man" whose image was, in the 1850s, beyond tarnish. The link between the two figures seems completed with the final paragraph in Cooper's introduction to *The Pioneers,* in which she quotes from her grandfather's *A Guide in the Wilderness:* "'After having been employed for twenty years in the same pursuit of improving lands, I am now, by habit, so attached to it that it is the principal source which remains to me of pleasure and recreation.'"[33] The Judge's adult life of purchasing, selling, and settling lands comes under the epithet "improving," rendering his activities benign in a way similar to Washington's Mount Vernon activities described by Susan in *Mount Vernon: A Letter.*

Cooper's constructions of her father and grandfather draw from her image of Washington in *Mount Vernon: A Letter*. In her introduction to *The Pioneers*, she details her father's childhood near Otsego Lake, emphasizing the importance of the place in a way that is similar to her discussion of Mount Vernon's early impact on Washington: "His first childish recollections were all closely connected with the forests and hills, the fresh clearings, new fields and homes on the banks of the Otsego." [34] Cooper continues to assert similarities in Washington's and James Fenimore Cooper's adult lives. She often describes her father as a gentleman farmer, most notably in her introduction to *The Crater:*

> In a garden the author felt almost as much at home as on shipboard. In his own garden he took very great pleasure, passing hours at a time there during the summer months, directing and superintending the work with his usual lively interest in whatever he undertook. It was his great delight to watch the growth of the different plants, day by day. His hot-beds were always among the earliest in the village, and great was his satisfaction when he could proclaim in early spring days to this or that friend, while strolling in the main street, the important fact that radishes or spinach were fit for the table, the tomatoes and melons growing rapidly. [35]

Furthermore, the lesson Cooper learned in constructing a home as a place of work carries into other introductions:

> "The Prairie" was chiefly written, as we have already observed, in the little study of the Rue St. Maur. . . . While writing "The Prairie," his little study crowded in the morning with the imaginary figures of mounted Indians and squatters, moving about Natty, the afternoons and evenings were passed in very different scenes. He was then making his first acquaintance with France and Parisian society, where he was received with all the graceful attention which never fails to be conceded to literary men of distinction in the Old World. [36]

Writing, although work, occurs in the home, and the excursions from the home, like her walks in *Rural Hours* and Washington's departures from Mount Vernon, appear in a calendar-like fashion, although on a daily, not yearly cycle. James Fenimore Cooper's excursions also provide a larger pattern that fits with Cooper's depiction of the rhythms of Washington's life; they tell a larger tale of journeys from Cooperstown and returns to the family home.

As the preservation of Mount Vernon perhaps compensates for the loss of Otsego Hall, the link with Washington absolves her father of the partisan criticism she battled upon returning from Europe. In her introduction to *The Crater,* she includes sentiments that seem directly drawn from the 1850s valorization of Washington: "The political characteristics of Mr. Cooper were strong and remarkable. He had no political idols. He did not worship the Goddess of Liberty, or the suffrage, or the caucus, or the primary meeting. He was purely generous and unselfish in his political views and aims; he was entirely frank, candid, and fearless in the expression of his convictions. In short, as a politician, he was thoroughly honest and thoroughly manly." [37] Cooper can create a Washington who resonates with features of her father's life, and, in turn, the image of the disinterested Washington purifies the reputation of her own father. Thus as the blood and turmoil of the Revolution become linked with natural occurrences, naturalized into the cultivated landscape for a benign memory, so does the legacy of Cooper's family, from the Judge as improver, to her father as landscape gardener and restorer of the ancestral home, and to herself as chronicler and observer.

We can end this discussion of the relevance of Washington and the Revolution to the Cooper legacy by returning to *Rural Hours.* Washington and the Revolution are closely linked with each other and with the process of inscribing the home book of the Revolution on the landscape. For example, Cooper's story of Washington's visit to the area occurs in the midst of her discussion of the group of pines near the village. The pines are associated with the pre-Revolutionary past, the memory of the time before Cooperstown was settled, before "the white man came to plant a home on this spot" (*Rural Hours,* 117). Notice the choice of the words "plant" and "home." Cooper contrasts the pines' association with prehistory and "with a state of things now passed away forever" with Washington's footsteps and the work of homemaking and planting (*Rural Hours,* 120). As in *Mount Vernon: A Letter,* Cooper domesticates the post-Revolutionary moment; history starts not just with the Revolution but with the establishment of homes—and with plantings. Yet unlike the Revolutionary calendar that Cooper creates on Mount Vernon's landscape, natural history still stands apart from national history in the pine-tree passage; the pines are juxtaposed with the post-Revolutionary moment, not linked within the same pattern of yearly observation.

Cooper's tale of the Revolutionary War veteran presents another attempt to create a home book of the Revolution, but one that is even more conflicted. The Revolutionary War veteran appears as a kind of muse or Wordsworthian figure. He, like Washington, had turned to working the land after the war:

[H]e loved the quiet solitude of the fields; and, unwilling to be idle, so long as he had strength to work, the good old man applied to the owner of the land in this direction for a spot to till; his request was complied with, and he chose a little patch within a short walk of the village. Early in the morning, before sunrise, he would go out into the woods, frequently remaining out the whole day, only bending his steps homeward toward evening. Often he might be seen at work with his spade or his hoe, about the little field which he was the first man to till. . . . It was like a blessing to meet so good a man in one's daily walks. (*Rural Hours,* 200–201)

Yet Cooper must complete the tale by telling her readers that old age and injury compelled him to abandon his plot and retreat into the home of his daughter:

The little patch of ground enclosed by logs, just within the edge of the wood, and the frequent turning-point in our walks, was the good man's clearing. It now lies waste and deserted. A solitary sweet-briar has sprung up lately by the road-side, before the rude fence. This delightful shrub is well known to be a stranger in the forest, never appearing until the soil has been broken by the plough; and it seems to have sprung up just here expressly to mark the good man's tillage. Tall mullein-stalks, thistles, and weeds fill the place where the old husbandman gathered his little crop of maize and potatoes; every season the traces of tillage become more and more faint in the little field; a portion of the log fence has fallen, and this summer the fern has gained rapidly upon the mulleins and thistles. The silent spirit of the woods seems creeping over the spot again. (*Rural Hours,* 201–2)

Cooper seems to want the sweetbriar, the sign of a domesticated landscape, to memorialize the efforts of the veteran, but she also admits that the fern, the species of the woods, is reclaiming the site from its markers of human disruption and cultivation. This image of plants erasing human history competes with the message of Mount Vernon's Revolutionary calendar, where the plants retain memory of the Revolution. Despite Cooper's interest in native species and the process of what we now call natural succession, her anxiety about the decay of the garden cannot be hidden from the reader.[38] *Mount Vernon: A Letter* provides the opportunity for Cooper to revisit these issues, to domesticate the Revolution and contain it in the cultural landscape of George Washington's home. The work of the Revolutionary War veteran may fade away, his marks on the land reduced to the sweetbriar and to Cooper's memorializing words, but Mount

Vernon's preservation can maintain similar marks longer in the cultural memory. Furthermore, the power of Mount Vernon's message is not limited to its physical location but can be applied to other places as well. The connection between plants and events allows numerous other sites to participate in the observation of Revolutionary history, with numerous other lilacs, willows, and pine groves tapping into the associations Cooper makes between natural and national history. Thus, unlike Cooperstown's irreplaceable ancient pine trees in *Rural Hours, Mount Vernon: A Letter* provides a home book of the Revolution that requires only observation for its persistence on the landscape; the connection between natural and national history will not fade as long as it is observed regularly.

NOTES

I would like to thank the staff at the Mount Vernon Ladies' Association Library, Mount Vernon, Virginia, for their assistance with this project.

1. Susan Fenimore Cooper, Geneva, New York, to My dear sister, July 12, 1858, Mount Vernon Ladies' Association Library, Mount Vernon, Virginia. Cited with permission from the Mount Vernon Ladies' Association Library.

2. Examples of writings, prints, and descriptions of other projects pertaining to the purchase of Mount Vernon can be found in the centennial exhibition catalog of the Mount Vernon Ladies' Association. See *Catalogue of the Centennial Exhibition Commemorating the Founding of the Mount Vernon Ladies' Association of the Union, 1853–1953* (Mount Vernon, Va.: Mount Vernon Ladies' Association, 1953).

3. For a nineteenth-century text that links women's issues and Revolutionary sentiment, see Elizabeth Fries Ellet, *The Women of the American Revolution* (New York: Baker and Scribner, 1848–50). For a recent secondary source, see Patricia West, *Domesticating History: The Political Origins of America's House Museums* (Washington, D.C.: Smithsonian Institution Press, 1999).

4. See Judith Anne Mitchell, "Ann Pamela Cunningham: A Southern Matron's Legacy" (master's thesis, Middle Tennessee State University, 1993); *Catalogue of the Centennial Exhibition*, 25.

5. For examples of other perceptions of Mount Vernon as a home and memorial, see *Catalogue of the Centennial Exhibition*, 25, 40, 56.

6. The term *home book* not only suggests the domestication of Revolutionary history but also refers to a publication that both Susan Fenimore Cooper and her father contributed to in 1852. *The Home Book of the Picturesque* was a compilation of essays about American scenery by well-known authors, accompanied by various engravings. The book not only brought images of outdoor America into

the home, but it also marked the home as a space that could participate in the discourse of the picturesque.

7. Several books tell the story of the purchase and preservation of Mount Vernon. The most complete narrative can be found in Elswyth Thane, *Mount Vernon Is Ours: The Story of Its Preservation* (New York: Duell, Sloan and Pearce, 1966). Other sources for general information on Ann Pamela Cunningham, the Mount Vernon Ladies' Association of the Union, and the purchase of Mount Vernon are Steven Conn, "Rescuing the Homestead of the Nation: The Mount Vernon Ladies' Association and the Preservation of Mount Vernon," *Nineteenth-Century Studies* 11 (1997): 71–93; Gerald W. Johnson, *Mount Vernon: The Story of a Shrine* (Mount Vernon, Va.: Mount Vernon Ladies' Association, 1991); Grace King, *Mount Vernon on the Potomac: History of the Mount Vernon Ladies' Association of the Union* (New York: Macmillan Company, 1929); Dorothy Troth Muir, *Presence of a Lady: The Story of Mount Vernon during the Civil War* (1946; Mount Vernon, Va.: Mount Vernon Ladies' Association, 1982); and West, *Domesticating History.*

8. For more information on the history of Washington's image, see Conn, "Rescuing the Homestead," 72–73, and Barry Schwartz, *George Washington: The Making of an American Symbol* (New York: Free Press, 1987). Writings on Washington in the 1850s include Washington Irving's five-volume *Life of George Washington,* published from 1855 to 1859, and Benson J. Lossing's *Mount Vernon and Its Associations, Historical, Biographical, and Pictorial,* published in 1859.

9. Conn, Mitchell, and West all agree that perceptions of gender and domesticity played important roles in the purchase of Mount Vernon.

10. "To the Ladies of the South," *Charleston Mercury,* December 2, 1853, reproduced in *Catalogue of the Centennial Exhibition,* 25.

11. Thane, *Mount Vernon Is Ours,* 78–79.

12. See Barbara J. Howe, "Women in Historic Preservation: The Legacy of Ann Pamela Cunningham," *Public Historian* 12 (1990): 31–61.

13. See Thane, *Mount Vernon Is Ours,* 29–76, for details of Everett's involvement with the Mount Vernon Ladies' Association. For discussion of Everett's traveling speech, see Ronald F. Reid, "Edward Everett's 'The Character of Washington,'" *Southern Speech Journal* 22 (1957): 144–56. The collected papers from the *New York Ledger* are published as Edward Everett, *The Mount Vernon Papers* (New York: D. Appleton and Company, 1860).

14. Muir, *Presence of a Lady,* 8. See, for example, "Mount Vernon as It Is," *Harper's New Monthly Magazine* (March 1859): 433–51.

15. Thane, *Mount Vernon Is Ours,* 131–61.

16. Johnson, *Mount Vernon: The Story of a Shrine,* 34–42; Muir, *Presence of a Lady,* 35–46, 53–58.

17. Susan Fenimore Cooper to My dear sister, July 12, 1858, and Susan Fenimore Cooper, Geneva, New York, to Mary Morris Hamilton, July 27, 1858, Mount Vernon Ladies' Association Library, Mount Vernon, Virginia. Cited with permission from the Mount Vernon Ladies' Association Library.

18. *Mount Vernon Record* 1 (1858–59): 17, 143. Cited with permission from the Mount Vernon Ladies' Association Library.

19. Minutes of the Council of the Mount Vernon Ladies' Association, Mount Vernon, Virginia, Mount Vernon Ladies' Association, 1929, pp. 79, 83. Cited with permission from the Mount Vernon Ladies' Association Library.

20. Susan Fenimore Cooper to Mary Morris Hamilton, July 27, 1858.

21. *Mount Vernon Record,* 168–74.

22. Susan Fenimore Cooper, *Mount Vernon: A Letter to the Children of America* (New York: D. Appleton and Co., 1859), 68–70. Hereafter cited in text.

23. See, for example, Lucy B. Maddox, "Susan Fenimore Cooper and the Plain Daughters of America," *American Quarterly* 40 (1988): 131–46.

24. The phrase "national service of love" neatly compresses the various forms of domestic sentiment that have received critical attention in recent years: the potentially political function of the home, the centrality of love or affection, and the dual sense of "service," encompassing both a discrete service rendered to the nation by women and a performed "service" or observation, like a church service. See, for example, Amy Kaplan, "Manifest Domesticity," *American Literature* 70 (1998): 581–606; Linda K. Kerber, *Women of the Republic: Intellect and Ideology in Revolutionary America* (Chapel Hill: University of North Carolina Press, 1980); and Lora Romero, *Home Fronts: Domesticity and Its Critics in the Antebellum United States* (Durham: Duke University Press, 1997).

25. See, for example, Thane, *Mount Vernon Is Ours,* 77–115. Elswyth Thane's history of the Mount Vernon purchase includes extensive information about the women involved as vice-regents.

26. Susan Fenimore Cooper, *Rural Hours,* ed. Rochelle Johnson and Daniel Patterson (Athens: University of Georgia Press, 1998), 81.

27. A version of Everett's speech "The Character of Washington" is published in Ronald F. Reid, *Edward Everett: Unionist Orator* (New York: Greenwood Press, 1990), 147–74.

28. Ibid., 153.

29. William Cooper, *A Guide in the Wilderness* (1810; Freeport, N.Y.: Books for Libraries Press, 1970), 9, 11.

30. Rosaly Torna Kurth, "Susan Fenimore Cooper: A Study of Her Life and Works" (Ph.D. diss., Fordham University, 1974), 70.

31. Samuel M. Shaw, "The History of Cooperstown, 1839–1885," in *A History of Cooperstown* (Cooperstown: New York State Historical Association,

1976), 51. For more information on the relationship between the Cooper family and their New York homes, see Kurth, "Susan Fenimore Cooper," 1–24, 68–92.

32. Kurth, "Susan Fenimore Cooper," 91.

33. Susan Fenimore Cooper, introduction to *The Pioneers; or, The Sources of the Susquehanna, a Descriptive Tale* by James Fenimore Cooper (Boston: Houghton Mifflin, 1901), xxxii; Cooper, *A Guide in the Wilderness*, 37.

34. Cooper, introduction to *The Pioneers*, v.

35. Susan Fenimore Cooper, introduction to *The Crater; or, Vulcan's Peak, a Tale of the Pacific* by James Fenimore Cooper (Boston: Houghton Mifflin, 1884), x–xi.

36. Susan Fenimore Cooper, introduction to *The Prairie; a Tale* by James Fenimore Cooper (Boston: Houghton Mifflin 1898), xxiii.

37. Cooper, introduction to *The Crater*, xvii.

38. Cooper's ensuing discussion of autumnal poetry and her criticism of the *feuille morte* tradition also reveal her desire to read something other than melancholy in a fading landscape. See Cooper, *Rural Hours*, 202–14.

MICHAEL P. BRANCH

Five Generations of Literary Coopers: Intergenerational Valuations of the American Frontier

Ecologists and conservation biologists devote considerable time and energy to longitudinal studies that attempt to measure ecosystemic changes across the generations of plants and animals that inhabit a particular place; through this sort of longitudinal study, we try to accurately imagine the landscape of the past, contextualize the landscape of the present, theorize the landscape of the future. The environmental literary historian is similarly employed; through study of generations of texts representing particular places or ideas, we try to imagine how people conceived of landscape, how they engaged with it, how they represented it in cultural forms such as art and literature. In this essay I attempt to more fully contextualize Susan Fenimore Cooper's literary accomplishments by looking both backward and forward from 1850, the year in which her book *Rural Hours* was published.

Given the historical circumstances under which Cooper wrote, *Rural Hours* is a remarkable accomplishment indeed. Working before the heyday of women's natural history writing that occurred in the later nineteenth century, Cooper manages a pioneering work that is rich and accurate in its natural historical detail. Living at a time when Victorian literary tastes strongly encouraged women authors to offer narrowly domestic, didactic, or sentimental parables, she takes to the fields and forests, where she allows her direct experiences of physical geography to inform and structure her book. Writing well in advance of organized efforts to protect American environments from excessive degradation, Cooper raises her voice with genuine conviction in support of forest conservation and preservation. And though her book was composed in the long shadow of her famous father, she demonstrates a strong, original style that reflects the family's literary gift while distinguishing her voice decisively from that of James Fenimore Cooper.

In order to fully appreciate *Rural Hours,* however, we need to inquire into the literary and environmental history of the region being described and celebrated in the book. How did writers working before and after Susan Cooper depict the Otsego landscape that is the setting and subject of *Rural Hours?* How did physical changes to the land inspire changes in the literary approaches by which it was understood and represented? How did developing ideas of the American frontier inform the way this particular place was perceived and depicted? Finally, how do changes in the literary representation of the Otsego landscape suggest larger changes in the American valuation of the natural world?

We have an unusual opportunity to pursue this inquiry without leaving the natural environs of Cooperstown and, indeed, without leaving the Cooper family. Susan Cooper's grandfather William Cooper (1754–1809), after whom Cooperstown is named, wrote a settlement tract called *A Guide in the Wilderness,* published in 1810, in which he describes the settlement of the Otsego wilderness and the foundation of Cooperstown while also offering practical instruction to readers who might wish to attempt a similar venture. In 1823 Susan's father, the novelist James Fenimore Cooper (1789–1851), published a fictional treatment of the Otsego landscape in his historical novel *The Pioneers,* which was also the first of his five famous Leatherstocking Tales. Then in 1850 the novelist's eldest daughter, Susan Fenimore Cooper (1813–94), published *Rural Hours,* a seasonally organized "country book" devoted primarily to the natural history of the Otsego region. In 1921 Susan's nephew, also named James Fenimore Cooper (1858–1938), published *The Legends and Traditions of a Northern County,* the first of his two historical and folkloristic studies of the Otsego country. Finally, in 1970, Susan's great-grandnephew Henry S. Fenimore Cooper Jr. (1933–) published his popular scientific book *Moon Rocks,* one of eight such books he has written since 1969.[1]

Taken as a single, discontinuous narrative, these five books cover the period from the initial settlement of the wilderness frontier of New York in the 1780s to the exploration of the new frontier of outer space in the 1960s. Examining these books in sequence, we find an intrafamilial, intergenerational trajectory of literary depictions of the frontier environment generally and the Otsego country particularly. I want to ask what this sequence of books reveals about the loss of wilderness that attended the settlement of the Otsego country and what it suggests about developments in the American imagination of the frontier. What might two centuries of literary Coopers teach us about changing perceptions and representations of one particular place?

William Cooper's *A Guide in the Wilderness* (1810)

I begin with William Cooper's *A Guide in the Wilderness*, a decidedly pragmatic book intended, as its subtitle advertises, to provide "useful instructions to future settlers." Structured as a series of letters from Cooper to his friend William Sampson, each letter is a response to an explicit query about the Otsego wilderness and how best to settle it. In this respect the *Guide* is structured very like Hector St. John de Crève-coeur's *Letters from an American Farmer* (1782) and Thomas Jefferson's *Notes on the State of Virginia* (1785), which use the letter and the query, respectively, to describe the American land and the patterns of use by which it is inhabited.

In his prefatory letter to the book, William Sampson attempts to glorify William Cooper's accomplishments in the wilderness even as he invites him to discuss those accomplishments in a series of letters: "And I should hope that the communication would be attended with some pleasure, and that the liberal and manly enterprise of reclaiming from its rude state the barren wilderness, and scattering the smiling habitations of civilized man in those dreary wastes . . . must be dear to the recollection of him whose courage and perseverance has triumphed over so many difficulties." Sampson then intensifies his paean to Cooper's "liberal and manly enter-prise" by comparing him to a great conqueror:

> Leave to Caesar the boast of having destroyed two millions of men; let yours
> be that of having cut down two millions of trees. He made men disappear from
> the fruitful soil where they were born; your labors made a new and happier
> race appear where none before you had been. To say that you have done all
> this for your own interest, does not take away the merit. . . . [Your readers]
> will be pleased to see by what means the face of nature can be altered, and
> how in half the span of one man's life, towns, roads, and cheerful seats, with
> all the comforts of civilized life, can be substituted for the gloomy monotony
> of the barren desert. (*Guide*, 2)

These passages help us appreciate the shared assumptions Cooper might have expected of his early-nineteenth-century readers. Heroism is associated with a successful war upon the forests, and the displacement of Native Americans is of so little concern that Sampson repeatedly indulges in an imperialist fantasy of erasure by which he simply pretends that no race preceded the white settlements. William's primary object in establish-ing Cooperstown—as he makes patently clear throughout his *Guide*—is to make a great deal of money; indeed, it is precisely his successful drive to amass wealth that Sampson believes qualifies Cooper as a truly expert "guide in the wilderness." Sampson's description of the forest as a "rude," "barren," "gloomy," and "monoton[ous] . . . desert"—an appraisal reminiscent of the antipathy toward wilderness typical of many seventeenth-century Puritan depictions of landscape—accurately reflects William Cooper's assumption that wilderness is a condition of degradation or waste that exists only to be redeemed by the improvements of human use. Cooper argues that the goal of every member of a settlement community should be to contribute "to the great primary object, to cause the Wilderness to bloom and fructify"; in reflecting upon his own accomplishments, he writes that he is "proud of having been an instrument in reclaiming such large and fruitful tracts from the waste of the creation." And a very effective instrument he was; in the *Guide* he makes the credible boast that "I have already settled more acres than any man in America" (6, 7).

As an account of the Otsego wilderness, William Cooper's *Guide* is deliberately selective. Having described the few animals he deems important, for example, Cooper explains that "[t]here are a number of other animals indigenous in the woods; but as they are unimportant to the farmer, neither yielding him advantage on the one hand by their flesh or their fur, nor on the other giving him any annoyance it would be wandering from our purpose to describe them." Cooper likewise provides detailed descriptions of the various species of trees he deems "useful" but almost wholly neglects mention of any nonagricultural trees or plants. Similarly, he devotes considerable attention to the abundance of edible or salable fish and game but omits the plethora of other species not considered to be in the pecuniary interests of the settler (*Guide,* 25).

Although he is a rich source of information about the practical uses of nature, Cooper makes no pretense to natural history, a subject he explicitly dismisses, leaving it "to be treated by the curious." "As to objects of natural history, or scientific research, whether vegetable or mineral" he writes, "they have never been my pursuit." Indeed, the *Guide* offers ample support for Cooper's claim that he is not interested in natural history. For example, the vast flocks of passenger pigeons that so inspired other writers of the period receive little more from Cooper than the comment that "[the pigeon's] squab is much preferred to the young of the tame species, being equally fat, and of a higher game flavor." Even Cooper's description of "noxious" animals such as the panther focuses on the profitability of exterminating such predators in order to collect the bounty placed upon them. In short, the *Guide* is a "how-to book" that provides instructions in profit seeking, and William Cooper's environmental ethic recognizes only the instrumental value of nonhuman nature. Despite the firmness of his anthropocentric environmental ethic, however, William does seem to predict his future granddaughter Susan Cooper when he writes that "[o]ne indeed who took delight in the study of nature, and was qualified to pursue her through her wonderful variety, might find this tract of country a rich and ample field, and abundant matter for beautiful and useful description" (*Guide*, 28, 26, 28).

James Fenimore Cooper's *The Pioneers* (1823)

While William Cooper's *Guide* is devoted explicitly to the subjugation and transformation of the Otsego wilderness, James Fenimore Cooper's novel *The Pioneers; or, The Sources of the Susquehanna* demonstrates an increased environmental sensitivity in its dramatization of the conflicts among several competing environmental ethics or approaches to the valuation of frontier wilderness.[2]

The first of these three approaches is exemplified by characters such as Richard Jones and Billy Kirby, who see wilderness not only as a larder but also as a kind of spoils. Immured in the myth of the inexhaustibility of natural resources, a myth that fueled the furnaces of westward expansion, they cannot believe in a significant depletion of trees, game, or soil fertility. In the justly famous chapter that describes the townspeople of Templeton—a fictional settlement that is based on the historical village of Cooperstown—slaughtering prodigious numbers of passenger pigeons (chapter 22), Richard Jones revels in his ability to achieve "victory" over the "enemy" pigeons, though he employs a swivel canon to do so. As in William Cooper's *Guide,* martial imagery dominates, and the human relationship to nonhuman nature is characterized by violence aimed at the subjugation of a presumably recalcitrant natural world. In the following chapter, which describes a comparable example of waste and exploitation, Jones prides himself on netting thousands of fish from Lake Otsego, though he intends to use but few. Speaking of the trees he fells for a living, Billy Kirby articulates an ethic very like Jones's: "to my eyes they are a sore sight at any time, unless I'm privileged to work my will on them; in which case I can't say but they are more to my liking. . . . I call no country improved, that is pretty well covered with trees." It is clear throughout the novel that Cooper's authorial voice condemns the actions of settlers such as Jones and Kirby, whose prodigality endangers the natural resources upon which the community depends (*The Pioneers,* 250, 229).

A more conservative approach to wilderness in *The Pioneers* is taken by Judge Temple, the patriarch of the settlement of Templeton whose character is based upon William Cooper. Temple's ethos of environmental concern, use, and restraint can most accurately be called "resource management." For example, Temple fears that reckless tapping of the sugar maple will prevent development of sugar production as a "branch of business." He likewise condemns the "expenditure" of overharvesting fish, which he values primarily because they would be "esteemed a luxury on the tables of princes." Unlike the historical William Cooper, who was so staunch an advocate of development, the Judge feels a genuine responsibility to conserve natural resources, to consider ethical obligations to future generations, and generally to hold development to a cautious, if not sustainable, standard of use. In one instance, Temple's paternalistic stewardship prompts him to remind Billy Kirby that the trees "are the growth of centuries, and when gone, none living will see their loss remedied." Nevertheless, the Judge's approach to conservation ultimately remains instrumentalist and utilitarian. He does not fear the destruction of wilderness as an aesthetic or spiritual loss but only as a loss of capital. Temple's vision is one of transformation, domestication, and control—a gospel of efficiency predicated upon the foundational imperative of utilization (*The Pioneers*, 222, 259, 228).

The most biocentric approach to frontier wilderness in *The Pioneers* is offered by Natty Bumppo, the "Leatherstocking" of Cooper's most celebrated novels. Despite his status as a vernacular and illiterate character, Natty's environmental ethic is informed by a highly developed aesthetic, spiritual, and moral valuation of nature. He is the only white character in the novel whose relationship to the Otsego wilderness can be described as one of membership rather than domination. Because he has a genuine sense of kinship with and sympathy for the "creators of the forest" and because he views the forest as God's work, Natty refuses to be in complicity with the pigeon slaughter. " 'Put an ind, Judge, to your clearings,' " he admonishes. " 'An't the woods his work as well as the pigeons? Use, but don't waste. Wasn't the woods made for the beasts and birds to harbor in? . . . I wouldn't touch one of the harmless things that kiver the ground here, looking up with their eyes on me, as if they only wanted tongues to say their thoughts.' " Natty's objection has been particularly poignant to readers of *The Pioneers* since 1914, the year the passenger pigeon was finally driven to extinction. It is a sad irony that the animal that best represented the myth of inexhaustible natural resources in which frontier settlers believed so devoutly—an animal that Cooper describes as migrating in seemingly interminable clouds—was extinguished by precisely the sort of wasteful behavior that Natty condemns (*The Pioneers*, 248).

Natty differs from Jones and Kirby in his genuine respect for nature and in his recognition that wilderness resources are not unlimited. He differs from Temple in that his valuation of wilderness is spiritual rather than simply economic. From his favorite peak in the Catskills Natty sees "all creation," but from the summit of nearby Mount Vision—which Temple has had partially logged in order to improve the view of Templeton—the Judge sees only the prosperous settlement that bears his name. While Temple's "vision" of America is Templeton (yet another version of John Winthrop's "city on the hill"), Natty's icon of American possibility is the hill itself, the nurturing wilderness, which he appreciatively calls "a second paradise" (*The Pioneers*, 292, 291).

Though fictional, *The Pioneers* offers a particularly insightful and accurate account of the tensions between wilderness and civilization that characterized the Otsego region and its settlement. Because it presents various environmental ethics in constellation and in conflict, the novel dramatizes the competing valuations of nature that were present on the American frontier. By implicitly condemning those who thoughtlessly waste nature and by attributing to Judge Temple some concern for the preservation of natural resources, Cooper demonstrates an environmental consideration that is absent from his father's *Guide*. By introducing and privileging Natty's spiritual valuation of wilderness, Cooper prefigures the yet more progressive ecological consciousness that animates his daughter's book, *Rural Hours*.

Susan Fenimore Cooper's *Rural Hours* (1850)

While James Fenimore Cooper's *The Pioneers* is broadly concerned with the frontier landscape and its transformation, his daughter Susan's work demonstrates a genuine knowledge of natural history and an explicit ethos of environmental concern. Although Susan published one novel, *Elinor Wyllys* (1845), much of her literary work was in the field we would now call nature writing. She edited English naturalist John Leonard Knapp's *Country Rambles in England; or, Journal of a Naturalist* (1853), and she assembled and edited *The Rhyme and Reason of Country Life* (1854), perhaps the earliest collection of American nature poetry. Her best-known work, *Rural Hours*, is, like her grandfather's settlement tract and her father's novel, set in the fields and forests surrounding Cooperstown. However, *Rural Hours* differs from the earlier Cooper books in the remarkable detail and accuracy of its natural historical observations and in its explicit call for preservation of the Otsego forests.

Like Henry Thoreau's *Walden* (1854), which it preceded by four years, *Rural Hours* is structured according to the seasonal cycle and provides an impressive record of the flora and fauna of the area it describes. And like Thoreau, Susan Cooper was particularly accomplished as a botanist. It was largely on the strength of her descriptions of plants, for example, that the 1855 London edition of *Rural Hours* was issued under the title *Journal of a Naturalist in the United States*. Although we are accustomed to celebrating *Walden* as a monolithic monument of mid-nineteenth-century nature writing, the accomplishment of *Rural Hours* makes clear that other important nature books were being produced in America during this period. Indeed, a reference in his *Journal* confirms that Thoreau read at least part of *Rural Hours*, and circumstantial evidence hints that some of the most memorable passages in *Walden* may have been suggested by several of Cooper's own passages on loons, wild berries, the perceived bottomlessness of the lake, and the seasonal breaking up of the ice.[3]

Despite a certain degree of false modesty that was inevitably required of her by Victorian social norms guiding the behavior of women, particularly women authors and scientists, Cooper shows herself to be a superb naturalist. Rather than being limited in her appreciation for plants to the sentimental symbology of culturally sanctioned Victorian ladies' "flower books," she is a close and patient observer who enjoys being in the field at all seasons and who brings genuine curiosity to her study of the natural world. She is unusually aware of the vital relationship between climate and flora and fauna, and she is sometimes brilliant in her speculation upon the interdependency of various species of plants and animals. And while her understanding of the natural world is experiential, visceral, and sensory, she also takes pains to study the published works of authorities in a number of fields of natural science. References in *Rural Hours* make clear that Cooper read not only regional natural histories such as those by James Ellsworth DeKay and John Torrey, but also that she studied the more ambitious works of such influential naturalists as Audubon, Bonaparte, de Condolle, Cuvier, Humboldt, Jefferson, Nuttall, and Wilson. Finally, Cooper's acumen as a naturalist is also visible in her willingness to admit ignorance and in the methodical, painstaking ways in which she seeks to answer her own good questions about the workings of nature. Her combination of patience and inquisitiveness is adequately suggested by notes such as this one: "Counted the flowers of a tall mullein spike, which measured thirty-three inches in length; it bore five hundred and seventy flowers, or rather seed-vessels, for it was out of blossom" (*Rural Hours*, 195–96). Finally, Cooper's sensibility gracefully combines an intellectual search for knowledge with an aesthetic appreciation for the beauty of the world; thus, the epistemology of *Rural Hours* distinguishes Cooper as a devoted amateur, a distinction that, as the etymology of the word suggests, identifies her as a lover of her subject of study.

Rural Hours is also a testimony to Susan Cooper's deep concern about the accelerating loss of wild places and wild creatures. Although the book has frequently received attention as a celebration of the Otsego countryside, it is rarely observed that the book also has a decidedly elegiac quality—that it measures environmental loss nearly as often as it rhapsodizes on natural beauty. In describing plants and animals, for example, Cooper frequently notes their increasing scarcity with alarm. Perhaps recalling the wasting of passenger pigeons and Otsego bass described in her father's novel, she laments that fewer and fewer wild pigeons visit the woods each year and that populations of fish in the lake have diminished despite attempts to protect them. She regrets that large mammals have been largely driven from the Otsego wilderness by trapping, hunting, and deforestation, and she repeatedly worries that "cupidity, and the haste to grow rich, shall destroy the forest entirely" (*Rural Hours*, 139). Indeed, a partial catalog of the plants and animals Cooper specifically notes as diminished or exterminated from the surrounding countryside is startling: quail, pine, passenger pigeon, martin, pitcher plant, moccasin flower, fragrant azalea, hemlock, rattlesnake, mountain lion, ladyslipper, whip-poor-will, old-growth trees (all species), killdeer, crested woodpecker, blue gentian, deer, oak, moose, beaver, red-headed woodpecker, ruffed grouse, ducks, bass, large fish (all species), herring, panther, bear, pinnated grouse, white pelican, wolf, bison, fox, otter, fisher, wolverine, rabbit, hare, and squirrel. If *Rural Hours* is a book inspired by an instinct of love and sympathy for nature, it is also one that recognizes the often exorbitant environmental costs of the sort of development promoted by William Cooper in his *Guide*. While Susan believes that "the earth is the common home of all," she also recognizes, sadly, that many species in the Otsego area "will entirely disappear from our woods and hills, in the course of the next century." "They have already become so rare in the cultivated parts of the country," she laments, "that most people forget their existence, and are more familiar with the history of the half-fabulous Unicorn, than with that of the American panther or moose" (*Rural Hours*, 56, 314).

As a response to this observed degradation of the Otsego environment,

Rural Hours is particularly impressive in its explicit call for the preservation of forests. After explaining that the current pace of deforestation exceeds the forest's ability to regenerate, Susan suggests selective thinning rather than clear-cutting, she proposes leaving untouched those trees growing on steep slopes, and she advocates the preservation of at least some of the old-growth forest. Commenting on the practice of setting out new trees, she notes that "[t]his is very desirable, but it is only the first step in the track; something more is needed; the preservation of fine trees, already standing, marks a farther progress, and this point we have not yet reached" (*Rural Hours*, 133). It is noteworthy that this prescient call for forest preservation was published four years prior to *Walden* and fourteen years prior to George Perkins Marsh's *Man and Nature; or, Physical Geography as Modified by Human Action* (1864), two books recognized as among the earliest to call for the preservation of American forests.

Equally important, Susan's valuation of the forest resembles Natty Bumppo's in its recognition of the aesthetic, moral, and spiritual importance of wilderness. Like Natty, who deplores the avaricious commercialism of his human neighbors, Susan Cooper directly questions the environmental ethic upon which her grandfather founded Cooperstown. "[I]ndependently of their market price in dollars and cents," writes Susan, "the trees have other values . . . they have their importance in an intellectual and in a moral sense" (*Rural Hours*, 133). Perhaps thinking of her grandfather, she further explains that even economic logic should prevent the mass destruction of forests:

> The first colonists looked upon a tree as an enemy, and to judge from appearances, one would think that something of the same spirit prevails among their descendants at the present hour. It is not surprising, perhaps, that a man whose chief object in life is to make money, should turn his timber into banknotes with all possible speed; but it is remarkable that any one at all aware of the value of wood, should act so wastefully as most men do in this part of the world. (*Rural Hours*, 132)

Throughout *Rural Hours*, Cooper forcefully admonishes that "[n]o perfection of tillage, no luxuriance of produce can make up to a country for the loss of its forests" (*Rural Hours*, 139).

As a third-generation Cooper representing the Otsego country in writing, Susan shares with her grandfather and father a deep connection to place. Like them, she thinks of the Cooperstown environment as home and as a place that is inspiring in its landscape and natural productions. But unlike William Cooper, whose *Guide* measured the wealth of the Otsego country only in dollars while leaving matters of natural history "to be treated by the curious," Susan Cooper measures natural wealth in terms of beauty, ecological value, and biological diversity. And unlike James Fenimore Cooper, whose *The Pioneers* worried about environmentally destructive behavior, Susan Cooper finds herself already obliged, by midcentury, to document the devastation such behavior has wrought.

Even in the face of the environmental losses she feels compelled to count, however, Susan Cooper, like Natty Bumppo, maintains a religious faith in the ennobling power of nature, as suggested by this lyrical description of the Otsego forest:

> [W]ithin the bosom of the woods the mind readily lays aside its daily littleness, and opens to higher thoughts, in silent consciousness that it stands alone with the works of God. The humble moss beneath our feet, the sweet flowers, the varied shrubs, the great trees, and the sky gleaming above in a sacred blue, are each the handiwork of God. They were all called into being by the will of the Creator, as we now behold them, full of wisdom and goodness. Every object here has a deeper merit than our wonder can fathom; each has a beauty beyond our full perception. . . . But it is the great trees, stretching their arms above us in a thousand forms of grace and strength, it is more especially the trees which fill the mind with wonder and praise. (*Rural Hours*, 125–26)

Although more eloquent than the vernacular hero of her father's novel *The Pioneers*, Susan Cooper shares with Natty Bumppo both a concern about the consequences of change in the local environment and a deep faith in the spiritual value of the Creation she finds manifest in the beauty of her home landscape.

James Fenimore ("Albany") Cooper's *The Legends and Traditions of a Northern County* (1921)

Although the literary Coopers who preceded Susan are better known than those who followed her, it is instructive to consider how the descendants of William, James Fenimore, and Susan Cooper encountered, represented, and refigured the changing landscape of the American frontier during the century that has passed since Susan's death in 1894. In examining the Cooper legacy since *Rural Hours,* we might begin with Susan's nephew James Fenimore ("Albany") Cooper, who was himself so concerned with the history of the Otsego region.[4] This James Fenimore Cooper was an attorney who practiced primarily in Albany, though he also lived in Cooperstown and founded the Otsego County Historical Society, which later became part of the New York State Historical Association. Albany Cooper also continued the family tradition of authorship by writing local history, two volumes of which were published as *The Legends and Traditions of a Northern County* (1921) and *Reminiscences of Mid-Victorian Cooperstown and a Sketch of William Cooper* (1936).[5]

While both of Albany Cooper's books take as their subject Cooperstown and its environs (the same place explored in William Cooper's *A Guide in the Wilderness,* James Fenimore Cooper's *The Pioneers,* and Susan Cooper's *Rural Hours*), *Legends and Traditions of a Northern County* is more useful to the present inquiry. In this book Cooper is deeply preoccupied with what he views as the region's romantic past. In particular, *Legends and Traditions* has in common with *Rural Hours* an attempt to document a loss—in this case, the loss of local cultural forms and institutions that were contingent upon the Otsego region's agricultural economy and landscape, which had, by the time of World War I, already undergone radical transformation.

Indeed, the prevailing mood of *Legends and Traditions* is unrelentingly nostalgic, even more so than normally required by the rhetorical conventions of local history. For the book not only contains the expected chapters on "Early Settlements and Settlers" and "Some Old Letters" but also broods on matters such as "Some Abandoned Houses" and "A Lost Atmosphere." Because *Legends and Traditions* is devoted so thoroughly to defining the Otsego region according to what it once was, will never be again, and yet cannot quite escape thinking of itself as, the chapter called "Ghosts—Ours and Others" might have provided an accurate title for the entire volume. Just as the literary historian chases the ghosts of ideas and the environmental historian stalks the ghosts of places, Albany Cooper wanders in the richly storied landscape of old Otsego, reviving, describing, celebrating, and lamenting the specters that rise in his path. As Cooper writes in the foreword to his book, he wrote *Legends and Traditions* "with the hope of preserving for future generations of my family the life and the thoughts of people living under conditions which are now gone forever" (vii).

Among the ghosts summoned forth by Albany Cooper are those of Great-grandfather William, Grandfather James Fenimore, and Aunt Susan, each of whom receives considerable attention in the book. Importantly, the mission of *Legends and Traditions* is not merely to remember, or to describe, or even to celebrate but rather to mythologize its subject. Thus William Cooper is heroically represented as an intrepid individualist who entered an uncharted wilderness and claimed it for his own, and his death is dramatically reported to have been caused by the vicious blow of a political opponent—a report now questioned by scholars.[6] Susan Cooper, described in the chapter entitled "Ghosts—Ours and Others," is not only "still remembered as a saint" for her service to the community but is credulously reported to have been empowered with an "animal magnetism" that allowed her to telepathically move heavy objects. And James Fenimore Cooper, Albany Cooper's namesake, is eulogized in an interpolated reminiscence by Susan—a reminiscence that includes the famous account of Cooper having spontaneously become a novelist when he vowed to his wife that he could personally improve upon the mediocre British novel they were then reading together. In short, the "lost atmosphere" that Albany Cooper seeks to revive is one that includes and mythologizes his own ancestors, those ghosts that haunt him so delightfully and so sadly. For this Cooper, the literary imagination of Cooperstown and its surroundings is inextricably braided with the various strands of his own rich family history (*Legends and Traditions*, 44).

The most haunting of the many ghosts in *Legends and Traditions,* however, is that of the environment itself—the much celebrated Otsego landscape that has, by Albany Cooper's day, been inexorably transformed by changes in the larger patterns of American economic production, transportation, and exchange. He is disturbed that lovely old millworks and stone buildings have been abandoned or ruined, and he laments that economic changes no longer make feasible the raising of hops in the Otsego region. He complains that use of the automobile, which was becoming more common by the time *Legends and Traditions* was published in 1921, was depriving people of a proper aesthetic appreciation for the landscape by denying them unmediated experiential contact with it, and he further regrets that the "serenity and beauty" of the Otsego lakefront has been "disfigured" by recently built boathouses and workshops. The historic charm of this agricultural region appears fully and finally transformed by the perhaps inevitable advent of recreational tourism, with its attendant commodification of both landscape and language. According to Albany Cooper, Cooperstown had become "a great summer resort. . . . The town was crowded with summer guests, and the lake with boats. All the desirable spots along the river bank were labeled: 'Lover's Retreat,' 'Calypso's Bower,' 'Shady Nook,' and similar signs attracted the idle pleasure seeker" (*Legends and Traditions*, 85, 111, 120, 130, 112).

In order to briefly measure differences in understandings of the Otsego landscape between the time of William Cooper and that of his great-grandson, we might consider an observation Albany Cooper made in his introduction to the 1897 edition of William Cooper's *A Guide in the Wilderness*—an introduction that is reprinted in *Legends and Traditions of a Northern County*. In his introduction, Cooper felt obliged to note that some of the rich agricultural lands named by his great-grandfather in the *Guide* had been doomed by watershed mismanagement. He explained that "[o]ne element in the speculative value of land, which investors apparently overlooked, was the effect which the clearing of the forests would have on the streams. Large tracts of land, then deemed valuable because they were located on the banks of some stream, navigable for scows and small boats, soon lost the advantage of such a location by the shrinking of the streams, due to the cutting away of the woods" (*Legends and Traditions*, 235–36). Seen in light of the ecological illiteracy that destroyed settlements by denuding forests and thereby depleting watersheds, William Cooper's accomplishments in the wilderness appear somewhat less heroic, even to his great-grandson. For while Albany Cooper is perhaps correct that the patriarch of Cooperstown was "a close observer of nature, a man who saw and understood the value of the natural phenomena among which he lived" (*Legends and Traditions*, 244), it is also the case that the instrumentalist environmental ethic so strongly advocated in the *Guide* had a number of unforeseen and sometimes disastrous ecological and economic consequences that had become apparent by Albany Cooper's day. If William Cooper advocated transformation of wilderness to commodity, and James Fenimore Cooper explored the possible consequences of such transformation, and Susan Cooper lamented the environmental losses caused by such transformation, then it might be said that Albany Cooper continued to resist the industrial and, ultimately, touristic results of that transformation. Perhaps it is his nostalgic sense of belatedness that drives him to write local history, for if the frontier represents the future, it may be the domestication of the frontier that drives us into the wilderness of the past.

Henry S. Fenimore Cooper Jr.'s *Moon Rocks* (1970)

We might conclude our intergenerational study of the Coopers and their home landscape by considering the work of Henry S. Fenimore Cooper Jr., the great-grandnephew of Susan Cooper and thus a sixth-generation descendant of William Cooper. Henry Cooper has enjoyed a long and successful career as a science journalist who has covered space exploration for the *New Yorker* and other magazines and who, though understandably less prolific than his novelist great-great-grandfather James Fenimore Cooper, has published eight impressive books of popular science on subjects relating to the exploration of space, Saturn, Mars, Venus, and the moons of Earth and other planets.

Moon Rocks, Henry Cooper's account of the famous 1969 *Apollo 11* voyage to the moon in which he describes the excitement and uncertainty surrounding the collection and subsequent study of the first moon rocks brought to Earth, was written largely while Cooper was living in the press area of the Manned Spacecraft Center outside Houston just before and after this flight. This engaging book bears a fascinating relationship to each of the previous Cooper books we've considered.

Like William Cooper's book, *Moon Rocks* is also a kind of *Guide in the Wilderness*—a book intended to educate its audience about the characteristics of the environment at the extreme edge of the culture's known territory. Indeed, Henry Cooper's book beautifully demonstrates the rhetorical conventions of a modern frontier narrative in which the frontier—now that of space and science rather than forest and field—has simply been expanded from Lake Otsego of New York to Mare Tranquillitatis of the moon. If such an expansion of focus seems jarring in scale, it may be helpful to remember that the frontier is never a fixed geographical location but rather a liminal place—a temporary meeting point of the far edge of human civilization and the near edge of the terra incognita beyond it. In 1969 Earth's moon was that edge, and Henry Cooper, like William before him, devoted his book to documenting the qualities of the new frontier that was capturing the imagination of his generation—just as the Otsego wilderness had captured the imagination of so many Americans of William's generation.

One of Henry Cooper's gifts as a writer is his essentially novelistic ability, like that of James Fenimore Cooper, to tell a good story in which dynamic characters embody and express conflicting opinions and values. In this case, the characters are lunar astrophysicists, geochemists, and exobiologists whose passionate attachment to various theories of lunar formation often only thinly veil their divergent environmental values. Whereas one scientist is devoted to the moon strictly as a noble subject for intellectual and scientific exploration, another has attached narrow, personal ambitions to its further exploration, while yet another wishes the surface of the moon could be bulldozed in order to simplify the mission of landing humans there. Several scientists express enthusiasm for the possibility of raising crops on the moon, while several others imagine ways in which the moon might be successfully colonized—an ambition that, however futuristic or implausible, is not substantially different from that held by the early settlers of Cooperstown. Henry Cooper's *Moon Rocks* is similar to James Fenimore Cooper's *The Pioneers* in that competing values cause conflicts between and among characters who have strong opinions about the environment—in this case the lunar environment—and the proper uses to which it should be put. In Henry Cooper's book the *Apollo 11* astronauts are the Leatherstockings of the twentieth century, heroic figures who embody the frontier virtues of resourcefulness, courage, and self-sufficiency. Indeed, Cooper variously compares the astronauts on the moon to John Wesley Powell in the Grand Canyon, the Wright Brothers above Kitty Hawk, and Admiral Peary at the North Pole.

Like Susan Cooper's *Rural Hours,* Henry Cooper's *Moon Rocks* is also an accomplished and successful work of popular science, or what in Susan's day would have been called natural history. Just as Susan Cooper complains that the artificiality and complexity of scientific nomenclature distance Americans from a salutary understanding of their land, Henry Cooper recognizes that the rarefied discourse of modern space science likewise prevented most twentieth-century Americans from understanding one of the most important and exciting exploratory endeavors of their historical moment. In the preface to his 1993 book *The Evening Star: Venus Observed,* Cooper explains that his writing was initially inspired by a concern "that science and the arts, which throughout most of history had been very close, had drifted apart in the last century and a half, largely because of the increased specialization of science, so that the scientists could scarcely be understood by their erstwhile colleagues. For me it became a challenge to help bridge the gap—to see whether I could explain to other non-scientists what scientists were doing." Cooper goes on to name Lewis Thomas, Carl Sagan, and Stephen Jay Gould—whom many today would call "nature writers"—as among the most brilliant practitioners of the sort of writing to which he has devoted his own career.[7] Henry Cooper also shares with Susan Cooper a sense that environmental concern can and should be the ultimate result of increased scientific understanding. In *Moon Rocks* he quotes British astrophysicist Fred Hoyle on the cultural impact of the first photographs of earth, a delicate blue sphere floating in the lifeless expanse of space: "'You have noticed how quite suddenly everybody has become seriously concerned to protect the natural environment. . . . Something new has happened to create a worldwide awareness of our planet as a unique and precious place.'" Just as Susan Cooper affirmed in *Rural Hours* that "the earth is the common home of all," Henry Cooper ended *Moon Rocks* with the observation that "[p]erhaps men had to go to the moon before they could clarify their picture of their own planet."[8]

Despite the otherworldliness of Henry Cooper's literary efforts on the frontiers of the solar system, he also shares with Albany Cooper a deep love for the earthly landscape of the Otsego region. Henry Cooper owns a farm outside Cooperstown and has maintained strong connections with the Cooperstown community. His most important efforts on behalf of his familial landscape have been carried forward by Otsego 2000, a regional environmental and historic preservation group of which he is founder and president. Established during the mid-1980s "to ensure that the natural beauty, wholesome environment, and varied economic landscape of [the Cooperstown] area is preserved for generations to come," Otsego 2000 is made up of "friends and neighbors in Otsego Lake Country, from many occupations and backgrounds, united by [a] love and concern for the environment in which [they] live." In the brochure for their organization, Henry Cooper and fellow members of Otsego 2000 write that "[w]e have seen what unplanned development has done to many other communities: Rivers and lakes polluted. Once valuable farmland converted into scrub brush and scattered building lots. Scenery scarred by bulldozers. Main streets deserted for ugly commercial strips. Everybody loses in the long run. Farmers, villagers, and summer residents. Families who have lived in a community for generations and new arrivals."[9]

In response to the erosion of the local agricultural base, the threat of poor land-use planning, and the pressures of industrial tourism, the members of Henry Cooper's Otsego 2000 believe, as did Susan Cooper, that environmental preservation is necessary; they also believe, as did Albany Cooper, that the protection of local cultural landmarks and customs is important to the vitality and health of the community. Cooper and his Otsego neighbors have asserted their hope for the environmental health of the region: "We can absorb new residents without destroying our farms, or the beauty of our mixed fields and forests. We can keep our lakes from dying from pollution or excessive nutrients. We can prevent strip development . . . while continuing to benefit from the visitors who seek out this area." The success of Henry Cooper and his fellow concerned citizens to protect the Otsego landscape is suggested by an important 1999 victory, in which the state of New York was persuaded to formally recognize the area around Lake Otsego as the Glimmerglass Historic District; the Glimmerglass District was consequently placed on the National Register of Historic Places, and will therefore receive special protection. It is apt that Henry S. Fenimore Cooper Jr.'s preservationist legacy will include the protection of Susan Cooper's beloved Otsego country under "Glimmerglass," the fictional name given by James Fenimore Cooper to Lake Otsego in his 1841 novel *The Deerslayer*—a novel set in the unbroken wilderness of a mythologized presettlement past before the arrival of men such as William Cooper changed the face of the landscape in ways that gave Albany Cooper such good cause for nostalgia.[10]

Conclusion: Reckoning the Legacy

We might conclude by briefly considering what can be learned from reading these five Cooper books in sequence. We learn, first, that the decimation of the frontier wilderness proceeded with remarkable swiftness. Where William speaks of shoals of herring entering Otsego Lake and saving the settlement during a grain famine, James Fenimore worries about overharvesting of the fish, Susan notes with regret that dams prevent the herring from entering the lake at all, Albany laments that the lake is choked with motorboats, and Henry documents a shift in American attention from the local Lake Otsego environment toward the frontier of outer space. Where William meditates on the gustatory value of passenger pigeons, James Fenimore implicitly condemns their merciless slaughter, Susan laments that so few remain to visit the Otsego woods, Albany writes at a time when the passenger pigeon is already extinct, and Henry describes the flights of humans to the moon while nevertheless working to protect healthy earthly environments that might save other species from the pigeon's fate. Where William explains the most effective means to eliminate trees, James Fenimore is concerned about the prodigal use of wood, Susan makes specific proposals for forest preservation, Albany notes the devastating ecological and economic consequences of deforestation, and Henry imagines the barrenness of lunar landscapes while also establishing a group devoted to environmental causes, including the protection of forests. Thus the intergenerational narrative established by these five Cooper books tells a powerful story of two hundred years of environmental degradation and biodiversity loss.

This sequence of books further suggests that the settlement and transformation of the Otsego frontier—and, by extension, the American frontier generally—resulted in a change from a purely instrumental valuation of wilderness toward a more aesthetic, moral, ecological, and even spiritual valuation of the land. While it is fruitless to portray early Coopers as environmental villains and later Coopers as ecological saints, since each writer is a product of his or her historical circumstances, it is valuable to recognize that such radically different understandings and valuations of a single place occurred not only within the same community but even within the same family. As the five Cooper books document, the settlement pattern of the Otsego wilderness describes a trajectory from wilderness, to exploitation of it, to concern for its disappearance, to nostalgia for its substantial loss, to efforts to preserve its remnants. The context established by this series of books suggests fascinating changes in the way the

Otsego country has been understood, used, and inhabited and how it has been represented in the literature of the past two centuries.

Finally, the discontinuous narrative of the five Cooper books strongly suggests the durability and plasticity of the American concept of the frontier. Where William took possession of a wilderness frontier in the name of economic prosperity, James Fenimore examined the ethical and environmental issues that plagued frontier settlement, Susan tested the frontier of environmental preservation, Albany lamented the technological frontier of motorboats, automobiles, and factories that threatened the Otsego landscape, and Henry allowed his literary imagination to follow and document American voyages to the frontier of space.

Of course, Susan Cooper's *Rural Hours* is itself a marker of several literary and historical frontiers, among the most important of which is the frontier of women's natural history writing. And while *Rural Hours* deserves and rewards close textual analysis, it is also important to place Susan Cooper's work in larger contexts, such as that established by the intergenerational literary environmental history of the Otsego country attempted in this essay. We need this larger context not only so that we can better understand Susan Cooper's accomplishment but also because the fate of the Otsego landscape will depend upon how it has been imagined in the past and how it will be imagined in the future. Perhaps we are on a new frontier—an ethical frontier in which we are challenged to transform our culture's valuations of nature in ways that may appear dauntingly dramatic and difficult. If so, it should be of some consolation that changes of comparable importance and magnitude have occurred before and that American writers such as the Coopers have attempted to document such changes for us.

NOTES

I wish to thank Dan Philippon, Rochelle Johnson, and Daniel Patterson for their useful comments on an earlier version of this essay. I especially wish to express gratitude to Hugh MacDougall, secretary of the James Fenimore Cooper Society, for his many helpful suggestions and for generously providing me with various materials that informed this article.

1. William Cooper, *A Guide in the Wilderness; or, The History of the First Settlements in the Western Counties of New York, with Useful Instructions to Future Settlers* (1810; Rochester, N.Y.: George P. Humphrey, 1897), hereafter cited in text as *Guide;* James Fenimore Cooper, *The Pioneers; or, The Sources of the Susquehanna* (1823; New York: Penguin Books, 1988), hereafter cited in text as

The Pioneers; Susan Fenimore Cooper, *Rural Hours,* ed. Rochelle Johnson and Daniel Patterson (Athens: University of Georgia Press, 1998), hereafter cited in text as *Rural Hours;* James Fenimore ("Albany") Cooper, *The Legends and Traditions of a Northern County* (New York: G. P. Putnam's Sons, 1921), hereafter cited in text as *Legends and Traditions;* Henry S. F. Cooper Jr., *Moon Rocks* (New York: Dial Press, 1970).

2. For other treatments of James Fenimore Cooper's environmental sensitivity, see Nelson Van Valen, "James Fenimore Cooper and the Conservation Schism," *New York History* 62, no. 3 (July 1981): 289–306; Donald R. Noble, "James Fenimore Cooper and the Environment," *Explorer* 14 (Winter 1972): 15–18; Alan Taylor, "'Wasty Ways': Stories of American Settlement," *Environmental History* 3, no. 3 (July 1998): 291–310; and Hugh C. MacDougall, "James Fenimore Cooper: Prophet of the Environmental Movement" (unpublished paper, 1990).

3. For commentary on Henry Thoreau's reading of *Rural Hours,* see David Jones's introduction to the 1968 edition of Susan Fenimore Cooper's *Rural Hours* (Syracuse, N.Y.: Syracuse University Press), xxxvii. For passages in *Rural Hours* that are suggestive of passages in Thoreau's *Walden,* see the following on loons (4), on wild berries (19, 101), on the depth of the pond (141), on the breaking up of ice (7, 18).

4. Alan Taylor refers to this James Fenimore Cooper as "James Fenimore Cooper the younger." See *William Cooper's Town: Power and Persuasion on the Frontier of the Early American Republic* (New York: Alfred A. Knopf, 1995), 365. However, I have followed Hugh C. MacDougall's practice of distinguishing this Cooper from his famous namesake by simply referring to him as Albany Cooper.

5. James Fenimore ("Albany") Cooper, *Reminiscences of Mid-Victorian Cooperstown and a Sketch of William Cooper* (Cooperstown, N.Y.: Freeman's Journal Company, 1936).

6. See Taylor, *William Cooper's Town,* 364–68.

7. Henry S. F. Cooper Jr., *The Evening Star: Venus Observed* (New York: Farrar, Straus and Giroux, 1993), x–xi.

8. Cooper Jr., *Moon Rocks,* 186.

9. "Otsego 2000," informational brochure (Cooperstown, N.Y., ca. 1988), n.p.

10. Ibid. Hugh C. MacDougall, secretary of the James Fenimore Cooper Society, reports that Otsego 2000 is also involved in a variety of other projects, including the successful Cooperstown Farmer's Market, which operates each Saturday during the summer.

PART TWO

Landscape and the Rural Ideal

LUCY MADDOX

Susan Fenimore Cooper's Rustic Primer

In a footnote to *Rural Hours* (1850), Susan Fenimore Cooper comments that her book is "offered to those whose interest in rural subjects has been awakened, a sort of rustic primer, which may lead them, if they choose, to something higher."[1] Four years later, in the introduction to her edited collection of poems on rural subjects, *The Rhyme and Reason of Country Life,* Cooper offers a more explicit commentary on her reasons for publishing books about rural life:

> Probably there never was a people needing more than ourselves all the refreshments, all the solace, to be derived from country life in its better forms. The period at which we have arrived is rife with high excitement; the fever of commercial speculations, the agitation of political passions, the mental exertion required by the rapid progress of science, by the ever-recurring controversies of philosophy, and, above all, that spirit of personal ambition and emulation so wearing upon the individual, and yet so very common in America, all unite to produce a combination of circumstances rendering it very desirable that we should turn, as frequently as possible, into paths of a more quiet and peaceful character.[2]

Cooper's comments suggest her awareness that the timing of her publications was significant, coming as they did at a moment when her American readers might have become more interested in "rural subjects" than they were in the past, more in need of the solace of rural life, and more aware that an interest in "something higher" is better stirred by country life than by city life. While Cooper protests that hers are modest works, intended only to serve the function of a "primer" or elementary text, she also suggests her consciousness of their contribution to the larger cultural project of bringing rural life—and what might be called a rural ideology—into contemporary discussions of the future direction of American political and social organization. Cooper's work can be seen, in retrospect, as a deliberate effort to forward the aims of the movement to locate the moral and ethical center of the United States in its rural populations.

83

More specifically, her work represents an effort to broaden the appeal and the effectiveness of the rural movement by opening up a space for women to participate in the work of civilizing the political culture of the country through an infusion of rural values.

Both the argument and the rhetoric of Cooper's advocacy of rural life are familiar in many ways. Midcentury rhetorical representations of the rural often cast the countryside as the source of both moral and social stability in American life. Andrew Jackson Downing's argument in *The Architecture of Country Houses,* published in the same year as *Rural Hours,* is typical: "Whatever new systems may be needed for the regeneration of an old and enfeebled nation, we are persuaded that, in America, not only is the distinct family the best social form, but those elementary forces which give rise to the highest genius and the finest character may, for the most part, be traced back to the farm-house and the rural cottage."[3] The effort to construct an idealized rural America and to celebrate the rural as the locus of peculiarly American values was fostered in a number of ways, including the proliferation of local horticultural and agricultural societies, the increased interest in landscape painting (and the popularized versions of it produced by Currier and Ives), and the dissemination of journals on horticulture and landscape gardening, such as Downing's well-known periodical, the *Horticulturist.* As Sarah Burns has noted, these activities produced carefully constructed images of rural life that "were identified with the best ideals of a society that celebrated both individualism and the breaching of fixed class barriers as the fruits of progress beyond the social order of the Old World."[4]

The definition of *rural* that underlay this public advocacy of country life was to some extent narrowly sectional; the celebration of rural values at midcentury was, in fact, almost entirely a celebration of life in the rural Northeast. As Angela Miller has observed, for example, the majority of the landscape painters practicing before the Civil War were located in the Northeast, and Northeastern subjects accounted for almost all of the illustrations in publications treating American scenery.[5] The very popular Currier and Ives prints used rural Northeastern settings almost exclusively for their "representative" American scenes. Agricultural and horticultural societies flourished in the Northeast, as did the fairs and shows they sponsored. The state horticultural society of Massachusetts, for example, enthusiastically advocated the practice of horticulture as a social and moral alternative to the materialism of the business world and encouraged the cultivation of local plants as an appropriate alternative to the importation of foreign varieties.

Cooper's home state of New York was one of the active Northeastern centers of rural advocacy. Downing, who spent his entire life in Newburgh, New York, began issuing the *Horticulturist* from there in 1846. Writing from Newburgh, Downing also published *A Treatise on the Theory and Practice of Landscape Gardening, Adapted to North America* (1841), *Cottage Residences* (1842), *The Fruits and Fruit Trees of America* (1845), and *The Architecture of Country Houses* (1850); George William Curtis published a collection of Downing's essays that appeared after his death as *Rural Essays* (1853). Closer to home, Cooper's father, James Fenimore Cooper, was instrumental in helping to establish the Agricultural Society of Otsego County as early as 1817, the first in New York. Fifty-one other New York counties quickly followed suit, establishing their own local agricultural societies. While the Otsego Society was disbanded in 1825, apparently because of dissension over control of the organization,[6] it was back in business at least by 1848, when Susan Fenimore Cooper reported enthusiastically (in *Rural Hours*) on the success of the annual county fair sponsored by the society. The Horticultural Society in nearby Albany sponsored its first public exhibition in 1847; the local newspaper, the *Albany Argus,* listed in detail the exhibitors and praised both the quality and the potential profitability of their fruit and vegetable products.[7]

The focus of artists, agriculturalists, local reformers, and writers alike was on the maintenance of what has been called the middle landscape, the settled and cultivated rural areas that provided a site of social, aesthetic, demographic, and moral balance between the extremes of wilderness and city on either side.[8] The conflation of these interests and energies produced what Sarah Burns has described as a "construct of ideology and values [that] is largely the product of the nineteenth century, when art and literature—popular and academic both—played a critical role in creating enduring and iconically powerful images of country life."[9] While there were surely many reasons for a surge in interest in rural advocacy at this particular historical moment, some part of the impetus behind the construction of an idealized rural North clearly reflects sectional interests and concerns; the independent Yankee farmer who succeeded by the work of his own hands stood in sharp contrast to both the slave-owning farmers and the sharecroppers of the South, and the picturesqueness of the sturdy Yankee's country life offered testimony to the superiority of his way of life.

Another part of the impetus seems to have been an effort to stem the tide of out-migration from the rural North, especially from New England. Hal Barron has documented the increase in public discussion of the problem of out-migration around the middle of the century, when the pull of speculative ventures in the West and Midwest raised concerns in rural towns and villages.[10] An additional source of concern was the lure of jobs in the factory towns of the Northeast that seduced young people, especially young women, away from their rural homes. In August 1847, the *Albany Argus* reprinted a notice from the *Plattsburgh Republican* that decried the flight of young women from New York towns and counties to the factories of Massachusetts: "One hundred girls passed through this village on the 30th inst., en route for Lowell, and some fifty for the same destination two weeks since. Agents are sent into this county, Franklin and St. Lawrence, and within the past year, more than four hundred have been 'picked up' and forwarded to the factories. . . . [E]verything is going to ruin—girls and all!"[11] Representations of the idealized rural life, therefore, were offered, at least in part, as a corrective to the disruptions of Southern sectionalism, the lure of fast money in the West, and the seductive promise of steady jobs in the industrializing towns of the Northeast.

Susan Fenimore Cooper's work is thoroughly consistent with this general interest in promoting the advantages of farm and village life as a national model that sets in relief the urban complications and excesses threatening the settled and orderly life of the republic. In *Rural Hours,* Cooper is careful to locate her town of Cooperstown securely in the middle landscape. She notes that, less than a hundred years before, the area was still "at the heart of a silent wilderness" and that, while it is near such "great cities" as Rochester and Buffalo, Cooperstown itself has grown slowly and methodically enough to preserve its village character and to stand as a model representation of American prosperity and moral health (*Rural Hours,* 117, 118). Because the land in the area is especially arable, Cooper explains, farms have proliferated and prospered. The settled nature of farming life has thus far protected Cooperstown and its county from the ills besetting those places where too much value has been placed on rapid growth and development and where the temptation to make money in a hurry has been unchecked by principle and foresight: "This general fertility, this blending of the fields of man and his tillage with the woods, the great husbandry of Providence, gives a fine character to the country, which it could not claim when the lonely savage roamed through wooded valleys, and which it must lose if ever cupidity, and the haste to grow rich, shall destroy the forest entirely, and leave these hills to posterity, bald and bare, as those of many older lands" (*Rural Hours,* 139).

As this passage begins to suggest, Cooper is especially concerned about what she calls, in the language of the day, "speculation," a matter that for her has moral and social implications as well as financial ones. (In her novel *Elinor Wyllys*, one of the characters observes ruefully that in America, "speculation and flirtation are too entirely the order of the day." [12]) Cooper notes with chagrin the contagion being spread in Otsego County by the 1848 news of gold in California and the haste of many men, young and old, to set off for the West. While this gold mania is troubling, Cooper still expresses her relief that the gold mines are in the West and not in her own rural Northeast: "Had the *placers* of California lain in the Highlands, in the White or the Blue Mountains, we should now, in all probability, have belonged to enfeebled, demoralized colonies, instead of occupying the high and hopeful ground where we now stand" (*Rural Hours*, 285–86). The county's only experience of anything like scarcity (a temporary shortage of wheat flour in the summer of 1838), she notes, was the result of a previous rash of speculative movement from East to West: "It was during the period of infatuation of Western speculation, when many farmers had left their fields untilled, while they followed the speculating horde westward" (*Rural Hours*, 245).

Throughout her work, but especially in *Rural Hours*, Cooper offers the constancy of country life as a moral alternative to the "fickle change" that has become a major temptation to her fellow citizens. Her implicit argument is that life on a farm or in a "rural and unambitious" town (*Rural Hours*, 69) like her own allows one not only to observe and participate in the gradual, natural round of the year and the orderly, purposeful unfolding of things but also to recognize the aptness—for personal and national life—of the lessons offered to humanity by the lives of plants, animals, and good country folk. Cooperstown and the county of Otsego are offered as "a good example of the state of the country generally" in its most imitable aspects. The growth of Otsego County "has always been steady and healthful; things have never been pushed forward with the unnatural and exhausting impetus of speculation, to be followed by reaction" (*Rural Hours*, 318).

In its general outlines, then, Cooper's work echoes that of many others of her contemporaries, including Downing, perhaps the most articulate and prolific midcentury promoter of things rural, including horticulture, landscape gardening, and an appropriate indigenous rural architecture. It also echoes the sentiment and the rhetoric of the numerous local agrarians in the Northeastern states who gave lectures and published poems and essays in the local newspapers, urging readers, as did one Vermonter in 1849, to "Fly from the city; nothing there can charm; / Seek wisdom, strength and virtue on a farm." [13] In his book on country-house architecture, Downing declared that "[i]t is the solitude and freedom of the family home in the country which constantly preserves the purity of the nation, and invigorates its intellectual powers. The battle of life, carried on in cities, gives a sharper edge to the weapon of character, but its temper is, for the most part, fixed amid those communings with nature and the family, where individuality takes its most natural and strongest development." [14]

Downing's affirmation of the moral superiority of rural life to city life is reflected everywhere in Cooper's work, sometimes by implication and sometimes very directly: "We conceive the spirit which pervades country life today, to be more truly civilizing in its nature than that which glitters in our towns." [15] Cooper also endorses the horticulturists' argument that the cultivation of plants is an activity with moral advantages for both the individual and the larger community: "Gardening is a civilizing and improving occupation in itself; its influences are all beneficial; it usually makes people more industrious, and more amiable. Persuade a careless, indolent man to take an interest in his garden, and his reformation has begun. Let an idle woman honestly watch over her own flower-beds, and she will naturally become more active" (*Rural Hours,* 81). While Cooper's dicta in this passage align her with contemporary rural reformers, the passage also indicates that Cooper was contributing at least one new element to the usual public discourse of rural reform. Her mention of the value of gardening for women as well as for men is a significant gesture, since one of the things that most distinguishes her work from that of her contemporary apologists for the rural life is her attention to the role of women in the project of identifying and confirming a set of values, rooted in the middle landscape of rural America, that are necessary for the preservation of the healthy life of the republic. Cooper is absolutely clear in her belief that home "will always be, as a rule, the best place for a woman; her labors, pleasures, and interests, should all centre there, whatever be her sphere of life" (*Rural Hours,* 100). At the same time, home, for Cooper, includes not only all of village life but all of the life and activity that is observable to her within the range of a day's walk or drive. Distinguishing herself from the "scientific gentlemen" (*Rural Hours,* 330, n. 33) from whose work she borrows or whose advice she seeks, Cooper places herself rather in the more modestly feminine role of teacher and commonsensical interpreter of the moral lessons inherent in the natural processes of the rural place. Her work is thus offered as a complement to the work of the men; the admonitions and lessons it contains are directed largely to the women in her audience, who have their own important role to play in the work of nation building.

By acknowledging the roles and obligations of rural women, Cooper may also have been lobbying, quietly, for an acknowledgment of the contributions that women were already making to the advancement of rural values and rural economies. At midcentury, many of the institutions that publicly supported agriculture, horticulture, and rural life in general were largely male preserves. The Massachusetts Horticultural Society, for example, did not admit women as members until 1864.[16] Provincial agricultural fairs, such as the one Cooper attended in 1848, typically made the productions of rural women, generally known as "domestic manufactures," a prominent part of the display; however, the exhibition of cattle and other farm animals remained the primary focus of the fairs, and it was the labor of men that received the most ceremonial attention. In describing New England agricultural fairs, Catherine Kelly has argued, "If the fairs recognized men and women, they did not honor them equally. The most popular events—speeches, races, and plowing contests—celebrated the rhetorical prowess of the republican gentleman and the physical strength of the New England yeoman."[17] In her account of the Otsego County agricultural fair in 1848, Cooper dismisses the livestock portion of the fair quickly, noting that "the stock of this county is not thought remarkable, I believe, either one way or the other." What Cooper found most remarkable and encouraging about the fair was the exhibition of women's work: "Our domestic manufactures, however, are really very interesting, and highly creditable to the housewives of the county" (*Rural Hours*, 193). Most of her account of the fair is taken up with lists and descriptions of the variety of these domestic manufactures: carpets, blankets, table linen, shoes and boots, embroidery, quilts, woolen stockings, bed quilts, and so on. From Cooper's point of view, the important work of the fair was not only its integration of women's labor and productions into the display of farm products—such as cattle and other livestock—that are most obviously associated with the labor of farming men but also the evidence it gave of the ability of the women to make a distinctive and valuable contribution to the rural economy.

In these comments on the industry of rural women who exhibit at the annual fair, Cooper's focus is on farm wives whose work contributes directly to the economic success of the farming family. Significantly, Cooper offers no evidence that she herself was an exhibitor at the fair; her perspective is that of the middle-class observer (and social theorist) who supports and applauds the useful work of the farm women. Reading *Rural Hours,* one is aware that Cooper was able to produce the book because she had not only the leisure to write it but also the leisure to spend a great many hours walking and driving in the vicinity of Cooperstown. Her general address is to other nonfarming women who also have the time for visiting, reading, observing life in the community, and both learning from the industry of farm women and perhaps offering advice to them. According to Cooper, one of the important roles that all rural women can play, whether they are farm wives or women in more elite positions, is to foster the strong attachment of their families to their rural homes. For those in rural communities, the threats to this attachment are many: they include the attractions of speculation elsewhere and the contentiousness of political disputes and divisions that might distract and divide a community—the "evil" that can be brought about by "small antagonist parties whose sympathies are not loyal to the nation at large" (*Rural Hours,* 266).

Cooper pays rather cursory attention to those larger distractions that are most likely to affect the men of the community—the ones who might be drawn away by the prospects of profit or drawn into divisive political arguments. She pays much more attention, throughout her work, to the sources of distraction that pose a danger primarily for women. Among these distractions is the wrong kind of reading, especially the reading of imported novels. Women comprised by far the largest proportion of novel readers at midcentury, and Cooper frequently offers to her women readers admonitions about their reading. More importantly, she offers her own books—those she wrote and those she edited—as examples of appropriate reading for women. In her novel *Elinor Wyllys,* she also provides a fictional instance of the far-ranging effects of misguided reading through her portrait of Mrs. Hilson, the silliest of the characters in the novel, who is prepared to emulate any fashion or posture she finds in her reading of foreign novels. The result is that Mrs. Hilson becomes a grotesque, both psychologically and physically: "Personally, she was thoroughly American, very pretty and delicate in form and features," but affecting Parisian manner and dress, reading English novels, and enamored of aristocracy in any of its forms. "Not a day passed but what cockney sentiments fell from her pretty little mouth, in drawling tones, from under a fanciful Parisian coiffure."[18] Predictably, Mrs. Hilson's behavior becomes more and more distressing to those around her and finally leads to her own moral ruin.

Continental books import a set of social models that are, in Cooper's view, completely inappropriate to American life, especially rural life. They also import a language and a set of names that are badly suited to the landscape and the republican ethos of the United States. Cooper issues frequent calls for a simpler and more localized approach to naming—of plants, animals, places, and even people. She is most vocal on the subject of place naming in *Rural Hours:* "Was there ever a region more deplorably afflicted with ill-judged names, than these United States? From the title of the Continent to that of the merest hamlet, we are unfortunate in this respect. . . . The Republic itself is the great unnamed; the States of which it is composed, counties, cities, boroughs, rivers, lakes, mountains, all partake in some degree of this novel form of evil" (*Rural Hours, 299*). Cooper calls for a simpler set of toponyms that reflect either the specific history of places or their natural features. She encourages especially the retention of Indian names, since they carry the traces of a very particular, indigenous history that Cooper sees as being retained in very few ways other than in the names of places. This same discomfort with ill-fitting names, especially imported ones, appears as well in her comments on the names of local plants:

> It is true, the common names of our wild flowers are, at best, in a very unsatisfactory state. Some are miscalled after European plants of very different characters. Very many have one name here, another a few miles off, and others again have actually, as yet, no English names whatever. They are all found in botanical works under long, clumsy, Latin appellations, very little fitted for every-day uses, just like the plants of our gardens, half of which are only known by long-winded Latin polysyllables, which timid people are afraid to pronounce. But, annoying as this is in the garden, it is still worse in the fields. What has a dead language to do on every-day occasions with the living blossoms of the hour? (*Rural Hours, 83*)

What concerns Cooper most is the use of non-English, imported names for local places and things. Her call for an indigenous, organic set of names is consistent with the similar argument offered by Downing (whom Cooper thanks in *Rural Hours* for his publications and his advice to her) for a rural architecture that is suited to the American place and appropriate to republican American values. In language similar to Cooper's, Downing celebrates the plain American farmhouse that does not try to imitate the pretensions of European houses: "Local truth in architecture is one which can never be neglected without greatly injuring the effect of country houses. And yet, such is the influence of fashion and false taste, and so little do the majority of citizens trouble themselves to think on this subject, that nothing is more common in some parts of the country than to see the cockneyism of three-story houses violating the beauty and simplicity of country Life." The American farmhouse, Downing asserts, "should rely on its own honest, straightforward simplicity, and should rather aim to be frank, and genuine, and open-hearted, like its owner, than to wear the borrowed ornaments of any class of different habits and tastes." [19] Downing's "borrowed ornaments" are reminiscent of Mrs. Hilson of *Elinor Wyllys,* with her foreign novels and Parisian gimcrackery; her "cockney" sentiments parallel the "cockneyism" of Downing's inappropriately grand American house; and the simple, frank, and genuine farmhouse of Downing's vision is reminiscent of the plain and honest eponymous heroine of *Elinor Wyllys,* a country girl who prefers all things American to all things foreign (including books) and whose most winning characteristic is her complete lack of affectation. Elinor provides a model for the young women of America, especially of rural America, and her eventual securing of a desirable and appropriate young husband holds out the promise of rewards for the life lived simply and unambitiously.

Mrs. Hilson and Elinor thus represent the poles of the rather predictable sentimental scheme of moral education for young women that is worked out in the novel. When *Elinor Wyllys* is set in the context of the rest of Cooper's work, however, the pedagogical aims of the novel begin to seem more complex, more specific to Cooper's own thinking about the values of rural life, and more distinctive from the efforts of her contemporaries— like Downing—who were offering their own arguments for locating the ideological center of America in the countryside.

In her appendix to John Leonard Knapp's *Country Rambles in England,* Cooper praises the English naturalist for his easy, unaffected comfort with his own surroundings and for his use of a language that has grown naturally from the experience of life in the English countryside. Knapp's familiarity with the local names of things Cooper takes as evidence of the settled gentility of rural culture in England: "It is one of the pleasing characteristics of an old and highly civilized country, that appropriate local names for the smaller hamlets, farms, and single rural dwellings, are in general and familiar use. Every thing which gives to the household home, whether of rich or poor, a pleasant distinctive character, and additional hold on the memory and the affections of its inmates, must always prove a merit." [20] At the same time, Cooper issues a quiet warning to the American reader of Knapp's book, pointing out the problem inherent in transferring Knapp's observations, and his language, to the American place. Americans are, Cooper notes in her introduction, still "half aliens to the country Providence has given us," since Americans know little about the natural history of their own country, while, at the same time, "English reading has made us familiar with the names, at least, of those races which people the old world." This combination of reading in foreign books and relative ignorance of their own natural surroundings means that "the forms of one continent and the names and characters of another are strangely blended in most American minds." The result is that most Americans spend their lives in a kind of "dreamlike phantasmagoria, where fancy and reality are often so widely at variance, in which the objects we see, and those we read of are wholly different"—a disorienting and ungrounded conceptual world in which language and experience are incompatible and in which language serves to distance one from home rather than attach one to it.[21] The borrowed names of things, that is, bury the possibility of an honest relationship with the American place beneath a layer of imported words that can only obfuscate and confuse.

The borrowed names of things are also antithetical to the production of an indigenous American literature that can help the newer country to enforce its independence from the Old World and to assert its distinctiveness. Cooper finds the most distinctive characteristic of American poetry to be its "deeply-felt appreciation of the beauty of the natural world,"[22] and she finds that American attention to the particularities of the natural landscape has even begun to have a salutary effect on British poetry, which has typically been prone to "vapid, conventional repetitions." American poets are teaching the Europeans to "look out the window more frequently"; when Americans look out their own windows, they need a language that allows them to name what they see, accurately and simply (*Rural Hours*, 208). Where the British have surpassed the Americans is in the writing of books of natural history, and as a result, in England, "many people . . . among the different classes of society, are familiar with these simple matters" (*Rural Hours*, 330, n. 30). Until the Americans begin to produce more books like *Rural Hours*, they will of necessity have to rely on British books, and the problem of an artificial naming system will continue.

Cooper specifically connects the project of developing an indigenous language to the project of developing an indigenous rural literature, and she sees an appropriate role for women in both of those projects, a role that she herself models. She distinguishes between the language of science, which is the province of the "scientific gentlemen," and the language of simple, local, natural history, which can and should be the province of the women of the country. Women can, appropriately, both write and teach. *Rural Hours* is one testimony to the ability of even the unambitious, homebound woman to produce books of local and natural history that will sit more comfortably on American shelves than will British and French novels. In addition, because they are the teachers of children and because they are—from Cooper's perspective—naturally attuned to local life in all its forms, women are the ones who are most suited to the task of reforming and domesticating the American language: "But if we wish those who come after us to take a natural, unaffected pleasure in flowers, we should have names for the blossoms that mothers and nurses can teach children before they are 'in Botany;' if we wish that American poets should sing our native flowers as sweetly and as simply as the daisy, and violets, and celandine have been sung from the time of Chaucer or Herrick, to that of Burns and Wordsworth, we must look to it that they have natural, pleasing names" (*Rural Hours*, 87). Women can teach children to speak an indigenous, local, American language before they learn the languages of science and before they begin to learn the language—and the morality— that foreign reading supplies.

In *Rural Hours* Cooper acknowledges the difficult work of pioneering that transformed the area of Cooperstown from a wilderness into an idyllic, rural, middle landscape. That work was done in the recent past (much of it by Cooper's grandfather) within the memory of some people still living in the town, and it was of necessity done by a "band of men" who prepared the ground for the women and children who would come to occupy the "cheerful dwellings of the village, the broad and fertile farms" (*Rural Hours*, 117). From their places in village and farm, the women can now do their own kind of pioneering and patriotic work, teaching children the simple and direct language that comes before the language of science or other technologies of knowledge and, in the process, giving them a means of articulating and reinforcing their attachment to their American rural homes.

NOTES

1. Susan Fenimore Cooper, *Rural Hours,* ed. Rochelle Johnson and Daniel Patterson (Athens: University of Georgia Press, 1998), 330, n. 33. Hereafter cited in text.

2. Susan Fenimore Cooper, ed., *The Rhyme and Reason of Country Life; or, Selections from Fields Old and New* (New York: Putnam, 1854), 30.

3. A. J. Downing, *The Architecture of Country Houses* (1850; New York: Dover Publications, 1969), xix.

4. Sarah Burns, *Pastoral Inventions: Rural Life in Nineteenth-Century American Art and Culture* (Philadelphia: Temple University Press, 1989), 3.

5. Angela Miller, *The Empire of the Eye: Landscape Representation and American Cultural Politics, 1825–1875* (Ithaca, N.Y.: Cornell University Press, 1993), 233.

6. Alan Taylor, *William Cooper's Town: Power and Persuasion on the Frontier of the Early American Republic* (New York: Knopf, 1995), 285.

7. *Albany Argus*, July 5, 1847, 1.

8. Miller, *Empire of the Eye*, 13.

9. Burns, *Pastoral Inventions*, 3.

10. Hal S. Barron, *Those Who Stayed Behind: Rural Society in Nineteenth-Century New England* (Cambridge: Cambridge University Press, 1984), 32.

11. *Albany Argus*, August 5, 1847, 2.

12. Susan Fenimore Cooper [Amabel Penfeather, pseud.], *Elinor Wyllys; or, The Young Folk of Longbridge. A Tale*, ed. J. Fenimore Cooper, 2 vols. (Philadelphia: Carey and Hart, 1846), 2:82.

13. Cited in Barron, *Those Who Stayed Behind*, 36.

14. Downing, *The Architecture of Country Houses*, xix.

15. Cooper, ed., *Rhyme and Reason*, 33.

16. Tamara Plakins Thornton, *Cultivating Gentlemen: The Meaning of Country Life among the Boston Elite, 1785–1860* (New Haven, Conn.: Yale University Press, 1989), 165.

17. Catherine E. Kelly, "'The Consummation of Rural Prosperity and Happiness': New England Agricultural Fairs and the Construction of Class and Gender, 1810–1860," *American Quarterly* 49 (September 1997): 582.

18. Cooper, *Elinor Wyllys*, 1:81.

19. Downing, *The Architecture of Country Houses*, 33, 138.

20. Susan Fenimore Cooper, appendix to [John Leonard Knapp], *Country Rambles in England; or, Journal of a Naturalist with Notes and Additions, by the Author of "Rural Hours," Etc., Etc.*, ed. Susan Fenimore Cooper (Buffalo: Phinney & Co., 1853), 281.

21. Cooper, introduction to [Knapp], *Country Rambles*, 16, 18.

22. Cooper, ed., *Rhyme and Reason*, 30.

An Artist, or a Merchant's Clerk:
Susan Fenimore Cooper's *Elinor Wyllys*
and Landscape

Before Susan Fenimore Cooper turned her observations of Cooperstown's seasonal natural environment into the popular *Rural Hours,* she tested her talents in the genre of domestic-sentimental fiction with *Elinor Wyllys; or, The Young Folk of Longbridge. A Tale.* The novel, which was published under the pseudonym Amabel Penfeather, was not successful, going through only one British and one American printing, a peculiar circumstance, perhaps, considering the general popularity of the genre in Cooper's day. Since its publication, *Elinor Wyllys* has been largely forgotten, ignored, or harshly criticized, especially by late-twentieth-century critics, who found that its convoluted plot, myriad subplots, and frequent moralizing tone display "little . . . artistic merit." [1] In spite of its dismissal by critics, however, *Elinor Wyllys* provides crucial insight into Cooper's environmentally informed works, that is, *Rural Hours* and "A Dissolving View." Specifically, *Elinor Wyllys* helps demonstrate that Cooper's understandings of environment and of landscape aesthetics are fundamentally imbued by her belief that a landscape reflects and embodies the morality of the human community that inhabits it.

Cooper believes, as she intimates in *Rural Hours,* that human communities shape their physical surroundings and that the landscape therefore reflects the community that resides in it. Through *Elinor Wyllys,* we find that Cooper also believes that an aesthetically pleasing landscape reflects the moral uprightness of its human inhabitants. Similarly, a community's well-being is dependent upon an environment that nurtures and sustains its morality. For Cooper, this notion of community as closely tied to the natural environment is crucial to the growth and development of American culture. Through *Elinor Wyllys,* Cooper seeks to present an integrated and complementary relationship between the natural environment and human endeavor and to suggest that the nation's decreasing concern for aesthetics—and its concurrent concern for profit—may lead to the nation's distance from the natural world, which would serve, according to Cooper's paradigm, as a direct indication of America's moral backsliding. A community that is closely tied to the local environment is therefore a crucial element in American culture. Thus Cooper's complex environmental philosophy is partially situated in the intersection of American culture, community, and aesthetics.

One particularly important subplot of *Elinor Wyllys* most clearly illustrates Cooper's belief. When Cooper focuses on the young artist Charlie Hubbard, she vividly outlines her aesthetic sense, which in turn allows us to understand more fully her environmental sense. Through the character of Charlie Hubbard, Cooper reveals that the moral foundation of a community is connected to the regional environment and may be apprehended most easily by a well-honed aesthetic sense or artistic appreciation of the landscape.[2] By looking at the vital role art plays in the novel and, by extension, in American culture, we can see how community—which includes both economic and moral aspects—and aesthetics both inform and are informed by environmental concerns. Furthermore, the moral dimensions of the sentimental literary tradition and picturesque artistic theory are reflected in Cooper's aesthetic and environmental concerns, which are always informed by an overarching moral structure.[3] It would not be going too far to say that the aesthetic and the environmental are the moral in *Elinor Wyllys,* and that Charlie Hubbard, as the representative of an important aesthetic ideology, serves as the moral center of this novel.

Before looking at how the novel makes important statements about Cooper's environmental vision, it will be helpful to provide a brief summary of the more important subplots in the novel, since the novel is today difficult to find.

The primary plot of the novel centers around the eponymous Elinor Wyllys, a young woman who has lived with her doting grandfather and aunt since the death of her parents. Elinor has the grace, the intelligence, and the moral uprightness found in the heroines of most novels of the genre, and she would fit the stereotype perfectly were it not for her plainness. The narrator notes over and over that Elinor is either very plain or even ugly. Nevertheless, Elinor is loved and respected by the community. The three Wyllyses live in an old-fashioned, comfortably large, though not ostentatious house in the country on the edge of the village of Longbridge. The village is situated on Lake Chewattan, and the entire setting is a slightly fictionalized version of Cooperstown.

One of Elinor's childhood friends, Harry Hazlehurst, proposes marriage early in the novel, and the young woman happily accepts. Hazlehurst, however, soon falls in love with another friend, the beautiful yet shallow Jane Graham, and breaks off the engagement. Jane, however, marries a man even more shallow than she. Hazlehurst, whose fortune was inherited from a kindly benefactor, finds his future threatened when the benefactor's alleged long-lost son shows up to claim his inheritance. During the long trial that follows, during which the son is represented by the sleazy lawyer Mr. Clapp, Hazlehurst renews his acquaintance with the Wyllys family and rediscovers his love for Elinor. When he loses the case and is penniless, he realizes that he cannot proclaim his love for Elinor because she is by now a wealthy heiress, and he would appear a grasping opportunist if he pledged his love anew. Things end happily, however, when the long-lost son is unmasked as an imposter, Hazlehurst regains his estate, and he and Elinor are married.

While these primary events unfold, Charlie Hubbard struggles to achieve his dream of becoming an artist. His father was a Presbyterian minister who died before the novel begins, and the large family survives with determination and the kindness of the community, especially the Wyllyses. Elinor and her grandfather get caught up in the drama at the Hubbard household, where Charlie is stubbornly resisting his older sister Patsey's pleas and his uncle's offer to become a clerk in New York City in favor of committing his life to art. Mr. Wyllys proposes a solution to the family turmoil: he will show some of Charlie's paintings to a friend, a prominent landscape artist. If the artist declares that Charlie has talent, he will be encouraged to train as an artist; if not, he will become the merchant's clerk.

Charlie passes the test and embarks upon his training and career, soon making a minor name as a landscape artist. His preferred subjects are the picturesque lakes, fields, and woods of rural New York, and his paintings show a remarkable facility for capturing the beauty and character of bodies of water. After Hazlehurst loses his court case and his fortune, he invites Charlie to go with him on a sailing trip around Long Island and Nantucket, knowing that the young artist will appreciate the beautiful scenery of the shore. While on the trip, Hazlehurst meets a sailor who tells him that the heir who usurped Hazlehurst's claim to the inheritance is an imposter. Just as the young man learns this good news, he looks up and notices that the boat Charlie is on has capsized, and the artist drowns. The happy ending of the novel is tempered by this tragedy.

The parallels between Cooper's domestic-sentimental novel and landscape-appreciation theory begin in the important historical changes taking place in the way artists chose to represent the natural landscape. The general trend in landscape theory from the mid–eighteenth to the mid–nineteenth century was away from the terror-inspiring grandeur of the sublime to the subtler charms of the picturesque. Angela Miller draws the following conclusions about the picturesque shift:

> The shift from the strenuous masculine associations of the romantic mountain sublime to an interest in space as a container of colored air marks a fundamental change in cultural preferences. The sublime as a category of experience did not disappear, but it was reformulated and extended. This redefinition emphasized subtle passages of feeling and mood associated with secondary attributes such as finely graded color rather than with the primary attributes of form. It coincided with, and was a part of, the appearance of a new language that couched social and moral formation in natural analogies, framing both in the language of gender. The new emphasis on feminine agency, signaled by the growing cultural potency of sentimental language, had important repercussions for imaging both nature and culture.[4]

The sentimental literature of Cooper's time also dealt with "subtle passages of feeling and mood" and emphasized a culturally transcribed morality that was expressed in a female-gendered discourse. Sentimental literature like *Elinor Wyllys* presented scenes constructed in the feminized language of human connection and interrelationships and valued the moral dimensions and didactic possibilities of the natural landscape, possibilities that Cooper fully exploits in her novel. As a sentimental novel, *Elinor Wyllys* appealed to the same sort of moral and aesthetic response that the picturesque tradition in landscape painting did.

Cooper's aesthetic sense, then, is grounded in the picturesque and is fully informed by nineteenth-century modes of landscape. Her appreciation of the natural environment is partially grounded in similar soil. Her aesthetics and her environmental awareness share a subject: rural nature partially mediated by human endeavor but not overwhelmed by buildings and agriculture. Cooper's exhibition of Charlie's aesthetics clearly demonstrates this shared origin. The first paintings Charlie shows to his family and friends are landscapes taken from the rural areas surrounding Longbridge. Charlie, the narrator tells us, "would sit for hours composing pictures, and attempting every possible variety in the views of the same little mill-pond, within a short distance of the house."[5] His subject choice is revealing: rather than paint a sublime scene of lake or mountains, Charlie focuses on a small, picturesque body of water that is man-made and created especially for rural industry.

By placing the human (the millpond) within the natural setting (and, indeed, inseparable from it), Cooper's landscape artist implicitly recognizes that humans can be a part of the natural environment; humans and the environment are not necessarily antagonistic or mutually exclusive. There is a very simple and practical side to this inclusive impetus. In order to appreciate the natural environment represented by landscapes, one must be able to see it. Cooper, writing as a genteel, mid-nineteenth-century woman, knows that she is neither willing nor able to trek across the wilds of America to view sublime, raw nature. The millpond—and Charlie's aesthetic appreciation of it—is required for those less hearty and rugged than her father's Natty Bumppo or for those born into a time when more sublime scenes have been altered or tamed by human hands.

Charlie's appreciation of a simple rural landscape and the concomitant environmental appreciation that the aesthetic signals helps us understand better Cooper's later and better-known works. In her 1852 essay, "A Dissolving View," Cooper writes of climbing a small mountain rising above Lake Otsego overlooking Cooperstown and describes the scene in aesthetic terms. "The hand of man," she notes, "greatly improves a landscape. The earth has been given to him, and his presence in Eden is natural; he gives life and spirit to the garden." [6] When this passage is read with Charlie Hubbard's landscapes in mind, its implications open up. Instead of thinking only of the "hand of man" operating on the landscape, we can also see the necessity that man's eye revere the landscape. Nature provides something to the landscape, the hand of man provides something, and the eye of the artist brings the two together in a symbiotic rather than parasitic relationship.

Charlie's choice of a man-made millpond as the subject of his very important test painting also links him to the American painters who were involved in creating the new nationalist aesthetic that became known as the Hudson River school of painting, and especially to Thomas Cole, the acknowledged founder of the movement. [7] For painters trained in the European style of landscape, the vastness and sparse population of the American countryside offered exciting new subjects while at the same time creating problems of what to do with all that space. The paintings that resulted often depict the wilderness held in tension against the encroachment of human endeavor, with the artist mediating. One of Cole's most famous works, *View from Mount Holyoke (The Oxbow)*, quite graphically illustrates this tension and the artist's position. [8] The left side of the massive canvas is dominated by the quintessentially sublime American wilderness: vast forest, rugged mountains, a broken tree, a wild thunderstorm. The right side balances this with the sun breaking through the clouds—cultivated fields and views of farms and cottages in the far distance. Standing in the middle foreground, almost exactly at the axis bisecting the two worlds, is the artist himself. The fictional landscape artist in Cooper's novel also places himself between the wild and the domesticated landscapes, though not so obviously as Cole does.

Other real-life artists and their works show intriguing parallels to Charlie Hubbard's aesthetic sense. Jasper Cropsey's 1851 painting, *American Harvesting*, represents, according to Sarah Burns, a "pictorial paean to the beauty of the harmonious, inhabited landscape. Its nucleus, the farm, is the center of a world of natural splendors that embellish but do not intrude upon man's domesticated acres."[9] In this painting, a farm clearing stands in the center, separated by a rough wooden fence from the huge trees in the left foreground and by a small lake from the rugged mountains in the background. The large expanse of sky behind the mountains glows and casts illumination upon the farmhands working at the harvest in the center. The figures are small, almost invisible, against the backdrop of domestic rural industry and wild nature.

Cooper's environmental aesthetic is situated in the same domestically rural landscape as Cropsey's painting, a fact that is made clear by another of Charlie's paintings. After Charlie proves his talent and takes the ubiquitous European tour, he returns to Longbridge, longing to paint the same kind of landscapes he had admired before his trip, the same kind of landscapes that artists like Jasper Cropsey were painting. Several of Charlie's patrons had commissioned him to paint scenes of Lake George, the picturesque lake in east-central New York that, by the mid–nineteenth century, had become an increasingly popular vacation destination. Charlie looks forward to painting this lake, which was still largely wild around its shores in spite of its growing popularity, and claims that he could never paint something sublime like Niagara, another important tourist destination.[10] The differences between the two waterscapes sum up Charlie's and thus Cooper's aesthetic, which values the environment that can be apprehended by the human spirit without the apprehension and terror inspired by the sublime.

Finding the correct balance in the landscape between human endeavor and the natural environment, however, is more complex than simply choosing between sublime and picturesque subjects, and Cooper's writing reflects this difficulty. One of the primary dangers in seeking this balance is that the wrong sort of human endeavor will succeed and undermine the moral order of the properly balanced landscape. When Charlie travels to

Lake George to sketch the studies for his commissioned paintings, he first stops at the nearby fashionable watering resort of Saratoga, where several of his Longbridge acquaintances are staying. One of these acquaintances is the flighty and snobbish daughter of Pompey Taylor, the richest businessman in Longbridge. The young woman is upset with her older, married sister, who has taken it "into her head to be romantic" and wants to spend part of the season at the less fashionable but more sublime Niagara (*Elinor Wyllys*, 2:19). The younger sister wishes to stay in Saratoga, where wealthy urban sophisticates engage in idle flirtations and morally suspect intrigues. The conflict between the two sisters indicates two important themes in the novel: the superior aesthetic sense of the older sister reflects a superior moral sense, and a proper appreciation for the natural environment is part of that moral sense.

That the wealthy urban sophisticates vacationing at Saratoga fail to understand the moral implications of the natural environment points to the economic aspects of Cooper's complex environmental dynamic. The dilemma that provides the title of this study—"an artist or a merchant's clerk"—illustrates the perils that face the community as desires for profit conflict with the desire to maintain an environmentally healthy landscape. Charlie's dilemma is common enough in the *Künstlerroman* tradition (that is, the "novel of the artist" in which the young artist must choose between art and commerce), but, like much of the action in the novel, Charlie's difficult decision has strong moral and environmental implications. These implications can best be seen by presenting the reactions of other characters to Charlie's ambition.

Charlie's first obstacle to artistic success takes the form of his older sister Patsey, who has had the charge of the family since their father died. Patsey worries constantly about money problems, and she fears that her baby brother will die destitute if he follows the foolish path of art. The persistent pressure of incipient economic disaster has hardened Patsey's aesthetic sense, and she is unable to understand the importance of art to her community. Simply put, the important things for Patsey are those that can put food on the table.

When Mr. Wyllys and his granddaughter lend their support to Charlie's artistic ideals, they indicate that they understand the position of artistry or aesthetics in the community. Mr. Wyllys's proposal that Charlie's early works be judged by a competent artist establishes the older man as the voice of equilibrium. Charlie must work to earn a living, but if he can work in a field that will allow him to celebrate the local landscape and the moral and aesthetic beauties of nature, then he should pursue that field.

Mr. Wyllys's opinions are most closely aligned with Cooper's own attitude toward the tensions that often arise between the aesthetic and the economic and toward the environmental concerns that underlie these tensions. In her book *Rural Hours,* Cooper often remarks on the sustainable rural economy that reveals itself to her on her rambles, and she reserves some of her harshest criticism for those who do not practice the same sort of economy. In a long entry dated July 28, Cooper describes in great detail the various types of trees found growing in the American forests as well as their various uses and virtues, finally listing the monetary value of the forest products to the New York economy. Money, however, is not the only or even most important thing taken out of the forest. "But independently of their market price in dollars and cents," she writes, "the trees have other values: they are connected in many ways with the civilization of a country; they have their importance in an intellectual and in a moral sense." She goes on to point out the process by which country dwellers eventually realize this more important value. At first, the "rude" pioneers managing a subsistence living need to "collect the conveniences and pleasures of a permanent home."[11] Eventually, once the basic needs are met, people realize that the forest is not just to be exploited, and an appreciation of the environment is a part of the intellectual and moral growth of the community. Charlie's sister Patsey has not yet reached the level of comfort necessary to grow enough to see the value of her brother's artistic ambitions, but the Wyllyses have.

If Patsey represents the "first rude stage of progress" and the Wyllys family the more enlightened and environmentally aware stage, then Pompey Taylor represents the most dangerous segment of society: the man who has reached a state of material comfort that allows him to appreciate the landscape but who chooses to be ever more rapacious in his quest for more wealth. Pompey Taylor is, as his name suggests, a pompous fool. He has not had the training to realize, as Thomas Cole puts it, that "Poetry and Painting sublime and purify thought";[12] his foolish thoughts of money and social standing are far from pure. Moreover, he is an urban pseudosophisticate who cannot appreciate the beauties of a rural existence or the conditions that make these beauties possible. His ostentatious and pretentious house is perhaps the best concrete example of Taylor's inability to connect with the others in Longbridge on the same terms of rural simplicity and economy. The house is huge and grand with three wings surrounded by a colonnade; when he makes an unexpected thirty thousand dollars "by one successful speculation," he orders the master builder to make a double row of columns instead of just a single row. The house is then named Colonnade Manor, causing the sometimes acerbic narrator to comment, "There is no accounting for taste in names, we suppose, any more than in other matters" (*Elinor Wyllys,* 1 : 111). Taylor also fails to understand, as Cooper puts it in *Rural Hours,* that "a fine tree near a house is a much greater embellishment than the thickest coat of paint that could be put on its walls, or a whole row of wooden columns to adorn its front" (*Rural Hours,* 133). Taylor's ostentation and lack of compassion for rural values is a threat to the community as well as an attack on the environment, because the builders had to cut down several lovely trees to add the unnecessary and vulgar ornament.

Taylor further demonstrates his lack of aesthetic understanding when several of the characters have gathered to admire Charlie's painting of the millpond. Charlie claims, "[T]here is nothing I like to paint so much as water," to which Taylor replies, "Do you intend to make use of watercolours altogether?" (*Elinor Wyllys,* 1 : 57). Shortly after this, when Taylor shows even more of his ignorance, Cooper's narrative voice somewhat testily intrudes with, "One is sometimes surprised by the excessive ignorance, on all matters concerning the fine arts, betrayed in this country, by men of some education" (*Elinor Wyllys,* 1 : 58). Readers are thus clearly informed about Cooper's opinion of the privileged place aesthetic education occupies. In order to appreciate and understand the natural landscape, one must be properly educated, something that mere wealth cannot provide.

The economic aspects of landscape appreciation in Cooper's novel have echoes in earlier English landscape traditions. Ann Bermingham suggests that the rise of English landscape painting after the enclosure movement "repeats a familiar pattern of actual loss and imaginative recovery,"[13] that the landscape artists were attempting to recapture or re-create the idyllic natural landscape that enclosure and institutionalized capital agriculture were destroying. Enclosure also had more insidious effects on the community, effects that Cooper implicitly recognizes and criticizes. When the people of the community were cut off from the land economically, they were cut off from it aesthetically, which meant that they had no stake in the environment either through their wallets or their senses. Consequently, the community's appreciation of the natural landscape is stunted, and further environmental damage is made easier. Charlie, and the Wyllyses through their support of Charlie, reject the easy economic fix (such as a relatively safe job as a clerk) in favor of a closer connection to the community and the local environment.

While the economic aspects of Cooper's environmental landscapes are important, a moral sense overarches and informs all other concerns in her presentation and critique of aesthetic ideology and environmental awareness. Charlie's desire to become an artist and his subsequent success have the force of a moral argument, and his actions in the second volume of the novel solidify his position as moral center.

The first indication that Charlie is the moral center of the novel occurs when he expresses his preference for the domestic landscape in his paintings. In the mid–nineteenth century, the most important part of a woman's duty was to serve as a moral teacher for her children, and the flowers, plants, and animals of the countryside were seen as lessons or living textbooks for such teaching. Numerous illustrated botanicals especially for women were published with the idea that a woman who could speak the language of flowers could use this language to impress children with moral sense.[14] In case actual landscapes were not available, the idealized landscapes of artists like Charlie were a useful and even desirable substitute. In a sense, then, Charlie's paintings can act as moral textbooks. Moreover, because the aesthetic and moral so often seem to overlap, a child who is imbued with the ability to appreciate a painting is seen as having moral qualities as well.

Finally, Charlie provides redemption for several other characters in the novel, which makes his position at the moral center firmer. In one of the last major conflicts of the novel, Hazlehurst stands to lose his inheritance if the man claiming to be the son of Hazlehurst's benefactor can prove his lineage. Charlie is particularly embarrassed by the claimant's representation since Clapp is married to one of Charlie's sisters. In spite of the familial tie that binds Charlie to the lawyer, he nevertheless remains loyal to his sense of right and supports Hazlehurst. When it becomes clear that Clapp has devised the entire inheritance plot with the help of a sailor who superficially resembles the lost heir, Charlie's allegiance to Hazlehurst is validated, and his moral courage is emphasized. Furthermore, by standing for what is right, Charlie redeems the family name, which had been sullied by connections to the devious Clapp.

Charlie's redemptive qualities culminate in the final dramatic events in the novel, and his tragic death indicates both his moral purpose and his connection to the natural landscape. Back in Longbridge, Elinor receives word that Hazlehurst, not Charlie, has drowned. Elinor's beloved has not drowned, of course, and, in a way, Charlie's death stands in for the other young man and redeems Hazlehurst to life. His death, moreover, occurs just as Hazlehurst's fortune—his economic and social life—is restored to him.

Charlie's death on the water has been subtly foreshadowed throughout the novel, most importantly by the artist himself. From his earliest paintings of the millpond, to his European studies of Alpine lakes, to his commissions to paint Lake George, Charlie's talent most obviously lies in his ability to capture the true spirit of water scenes. Thomas Cole's essay on American scenery also asserts the preeminence of water when he remarks that any scene without water is defective, since, "[l]ike the eye in the human countenance, water is a most expressive feature."[15] By connecting Charlie even more clearly with his nonfictional counterpart, Cooper illustrates the importance of Charlie's environmental landscape vision to American culture.

Not only does water lend expression and interest to the landscape, but it also has powerful mythic reverberations that reinforce Charlie's position as moral center of the novel. Since prehistoric times, water has been an important symbol of life, and water sources were often revered for their perceived supernatural qualities. Charlie's reverence for the water scenes he paints and his death in the water indicate his moral position as a redemptive figure. Because Charlie dies instead of Hazlehurst, as Elinor first feared, Hazlehurst and Elinor are able to marry in the end. Cooper points out throughout the novel that Elinor and Hazlehurst are not insensitive to the natural landscape, as opposed to Pompey Taylor, and their marriage, we are led to presume, will be a model for thoughtful, considerate living in the landscape.

Many of Cooper's works emphasize the local landscape and the need to respect, understand, and appreciate it. Charlie, as the mediator, preserver, and presenter of the local landscape, comes the closest in her novel to personifying the importance of the landscape and the spirit of environmental awareness. Because Charlie comes from a lower socioeconomic background than the other characters in the book, he represents those who are generally cut off from an aesthetic appreciation of the landscape and who, as a result, may pose a threat to that landscape's qualities in the eyes of the upper classes. Charlie, through his paintings, transcends class limitations and demonstrates that landscape appreciation need not rely on economic position. His paintings also stress the importance of living within the landscape, of balancing the requirements of civilization with those of the environment; that is, his paintings point out the responsibilities that civilization has toward the landscape. For Cooper, all of these responsibilities and motives are imbued with an undeniable moral force; protecting and caring for the environment by respecting the landscape is not just an aesthetic concern but a profoundly moral imperative.

1. Rosaly Torna Kurth, "Susan Fenimore Cooper: A Study of Her Life and Works" (Ph.D. diss., Fordham University, 1974), 124.

2. Cooper was well versed in the language of landscape, or the codified manner of observing and appreciating landscape developed by Edmund Burke, William Gilpin, Uvedale Price, Joshua Reynolds, and others in the eighteenth century. Such language permeates Cooper's descriptions and serves to emphasize the link between aesthetics and environment. The notion of the sublime that was most familiar to nineteenth-century Americans came from Burke's *A Philosophical Enquiry into the Origin of Our Ideas of the Sublime and Beautiful* (1756), which defined sublime as "[w]hatever is fitted in any sort to excite the ideas of pain, and danger, that is to say, whatever is in any sort terrible, or is conversant about terrible objects, or operates in a manner analogous to terror" (ed. Adam Phillips [Oxford: Oxford University Press, 1990], 36). In its simplest form, the picturesque is anything that makes an appropriate subject for a picture. In practice, the picturesque, as described by Gilpin or Price, is essentially a modification of Burke's sublime in which the terrible and dangerous aspect is less important than other elements of aesthetic appreciation. An important early work that articulates the picturesque aesthetic and its history is Christopher Hussey's *The Picturesque: Studies in a Point of View* (London: Putnam, 1927). For more on the picturesque or sublime in aesthetic theory, see Marjorie Hope Nicolson, *Mountain Gloom and Mountain Glory: The Development of the Aesthetics of the Infinite* (Ithaca, N.Y.: Cornell University Press, 1959; reprint, Seattle: University of Washington Press, 1997); Frances Ferguson, *Solitude and the Sublime: Romanticism and the Aesthetics of Individuation* (New York: Routledge, 1992); Elizabeth McKinsey, *Niagara Falls: Icon of the American Sublime* (Cambridge: Cambridge University Press, 1985); and Rob Wilson, *American Sublime: The Genealogy of a Poetic Genre* (Madison: University of Wisconsin Press, 1991).

3. For a definition of the sentimental genre, I rely upon Joanne Dobson, "Reclaiming Sentimental Literature," *American Literature* 69, no. 2 (June 1997): 263–88. Sentimental literature, the popular literature written largely by and for women in the mid–nineteenth century, is informed by a concern for the interconnections of human life and the domestic realm of hearth and home.

4. Angela Miller, *The Empire of the Eye: Landscape Representation and American Cultural Politics, 1825–1875* (Ithaca, N.Y.: Cornell University Press, 1993), 248. For more on the pastoral tradition and the links between landscape art and the domestic, see Sarah Burns, *Pastoral Inventions: Rural Life in Nineteenth-Century American Art and Culture* (Philadelphia: Temple University Press, 1989).

5. Susan Fenimore Cooper [Amabel Penfeather, pseud.], *Elinor Wyllys; or,*

The Young Folk of Longbridge. A Tale, ed. J. Fenimore Cooper, 2 vols. (Philadelphia: Carey and Hart, 1846), 1 : 51. Hereafter cited in text.

6. Susan Fenimore Cooper, "A Dissolving View," in *The Home Book of the Picturesque; or, American Scenery, Art, and Literature* (New York: Putnam, 1852; reprint, Gainesville, Fla.: Scholars' Facsimiles & Reprints, 1967), 82.

7. Louise Minks discusses Thomas Cole's position as the founder of the Hudson River school and traces his influence in *The Hudson River School* (New York: Crescent, 1989).

8. Cole's painting can be viewed in the Metropolitan Museum of Art in New York, gift of Mrs. Russell Sage, 1908.

9. Sarah Burns, *Pastoral Inventions: Rural Life in Nineteenth-Century American Art and Culture* (Philadelphia: Temple University Press, 1989), 11.

10. McKinsey points out that by the nineteenth century "the predominant feature of Niagara was its sublimity" (*Niagara Falls,* 38). Because it had a reputation as one of the most sublime landscape features in America, it soon became a popular vacation spot.

11. Susan Fenimore Cooper, *Rural Hours,* ed. Rochelle Johnson and Daniel Patterson (Athens: University of Georgia Press, 1998), 133.

12. Thomas Cole, "An Essay on American Scenery," in *American Art 1700–1960: Sources and Documents,* ed. John W. McCoubrey (Englewood Cliffs, N.J.: Prentice-Hall, 1965), 98.

13. Ann Bermingham, *Landscape and Ideology: The English Rustic Tradition, 1740–1860* (Berkeley: University of California Press, 1986), 9.

14. See Vera Norwood, *Made from This Earth: American Women and Nature* (Chapel Hill: University of North Carolina Press, 1993), for further discussion of the links between women's literature and nature. The sentimental botanical tradition and its aim to introduce nature to women as a moral didactic presence is particularly important to this discussion. Norwood provides illustrations of the women's "botanicals" that were printed from the eighteenth through the nineteenth centuries with an aim toward increasing interest in a properly "feminine" study of botany. Even more telling, the language used to describe the flowers is almost precisely that used to describe the ideal of womanhood.

15. Cole, "An Essay on American Scenery," 103.

The Borderers of Civilization:
Susan Fenimore Cooper's View of American Development

Within her best-known work, *Rural Hours* (1850), and in an important but long-neglected essay "A Dissolving View" (1852), Susan Cooper calls for the development of uniquely American cultural forms reflective of the nation's democratic doctrines. Intimately linked to this appeal was her description of nature as essential nourishment for the national imagination. Implicit in her argument was a second call: for the necessity of preserving this resource. By becoming familiar with their native environment, Americans would locate foundations for institutions in harmony with the landscape around them. As part of a broad-based cultural movement away from the commodification of nature that was a hallmark of the Jacksonian era, Susan Cooper charged Americans to stop imitating European cultural models, urging her generation to form a new national identity grounded in American nature.[1] Within these two texts, which need to be considered in tandem to appreciate fully her conception of American development, she argued that the absence of inherited architectural forms liberated Americans from the obstacles that faced their contemporaries in the Old World. European social development was subject to the constraints imposed by previous architectural productions. While Americans had not yet devised cultural forms to embody their democratic values, they had also not irrevocably altered their environment in ways that would prohibit them from so doing.

Susan Cooper firmly believed that cultural values were products of the combination of material culture (the entire shaped human environment) and the landscapes in and upon which it was fashioned. Petitioning Americans to pause before making further mistakes, she contemplates the delusory effects on American social development if the nation fails to rectify its current architectural practices.[2] She proposes the scrutiny of new building plans prior to construction, for "[t]here is a certain fitness in some styles of architecture which adapts them to different climates" (*Rural*

Hours, 297). By obscuring the natural negotiation between man and his specific environment, architectural failures threaten the stability of the culture. She teases out meaning on a local level, confining her examination to Cooperstown to illustrate her vision of national amelioration. Susan Cooper transforms Cooperstown into a "city upon a hill" to construct a jeremiad that decries current cultural practice, arguing that it mirrors much of the nation in economic and social progress at midcentury: "The growth of the inland region, to which our valley belongs, will prove, in most respects, a good example of the state of the country generally. The advance of this county has always been steady and healthful; things have never been pushed forward with the unnatural and exhausting impetus of speculation." Being spared the "unnatural" consequences of rampant speculation because of its geographical position, the environment of Cooperstown was shaped by the "industry of [its] population" and thus had grown "steadily and gradually" (*Rural Hours*, 318).[3]

As a post–Revolutionary War settlement largely unaltered by the rampant upheaval of Jacksonian commodification, Cooperstown reflected the social conditions of many rural American settlements. By recording its natural history, Susan Cooper hoped to teach others to respect the demands of the environment so that they might optimally arrange the human presence. Fashioned as a seasonal journal of observations of nature, *Rural Hours* catalogs the attempts of individuals in Cooperstown to shape and utilize their environment. The wealth of data collected in *Rural Hours* functions as source material for her more pointed arguments in "A Dissolving View."

In the "Autumn" section of *Rural Hours*, Susan Cooper considers the impact of the American wilderness on the writing of natural history. She describes a process of cross-pollination through which Europeans reconceived their environment in light of a new respect for American scenery, asserting that "all descriptive writing, on natural objects, is now much less vague and general than it was formerly; it has become very much more definite and accurate within the last half-century." Cooper notes the popularity of landscape painting and the propensity for a "natural style in gardening" as possible causes of this transition. But, she contends, social patterns are rarely altered by discrete factors: "It is seldom, however, that a great change in public taste or opinion is produced by a single direct cause only; there are generally many lesser collateral causes working together, aiding and strengthening each other meanwhile, ere decided results are produced" (*Rural Hours*, 208). Cooper's caveat forestalls reading cultural trends reductively, revealing her deep concern with tracing the complexity of alterations in social attitudes. Furthermore, it underscores her concern with how "causes" combine to produce change.

Susan Cooper employed the languages of both natural history and social refinement to interrogate the current state of her society. The question of American social maturation was intrinsically tied to natural history for Susan Cooper: she perceived that the Republic's social structures had grown out of the management of its natural resources. Cooper's nuanced understanding of the "collateral causes" that collectively shape "public taste" exhibits her attempt to refine various disparate narratives in circulation. In *Rural Hours* and "A Dissolving View," she promulgated the notion that American cultural behavior, both in practice and planning, ought to take into account and somehow represent America's environmental uniqueness. Familiar as she was with nineteenth-century natural histories, her own work deploys these source texts, and ideas derived from them, to deliberate about America's social, architectural, and cultural practices.

Susan Cooper's refusal to admit a "single direct cause" as responsible for cultural transformations reminds us that for most of her contemporaries the embrace of nature as model for culture was not intended to transcend their material lives but to complement them. Cooper's conception of nature and the patterns nature offered represents a paradigm shift in the way natural history writing was understood in the early nineteenth century. This shift emancipated treatments of American nature from the confines of eighteenth-century European descriptions of New World nature. Liberated from the restraints of such residual practice, Susan Cooper demanded that Americans, in order to define themselves, turn toward nature rather than continue to reject its primacy.

Susan Cooper's connections with her locale were deeply rooted; she understood that the natural environment and social development of Cooperstown were tied directly to her familial history. Susan Cooper was the third Cooper to describe the natural environment of central New York State, following both her grandfather Judge William Cooper and her father, the novelist James Fenimore Cooper.[4] The views expressed by these three authors, writing of the same region over a forty-year period (1810–50), document significant shifts in the history of American attitudes toward nature. William Cooper held a primarily utilitarian vision of wilderness: writing to attract Europeans contemplating immigration, he described the economic possibilities of New York State. James modified his father's vision by questioning his predecessor's interaction with nature, while simultaneously claiming the American wilderness as a setting for the historical romance. Susan Cooper infused her writing with a scientific consciousness absent in her forefathers' writings. Thus the movement from William to Susan Cooper mirrors developments in American natural history writing while also suggesting the great depth of her intellectual rootedness in her region.

By the mid–nineteenth century, when Susan launched her career as a writer, Americans—at least those who lived in New York—were no longer burdened either with fashioning a civilization out of wilderness or with validating their enterprise to a skeptical European audience. For the first post-Revolutionary generation of American writers, including Charles Brockden Brown, James Fenimore Cooper, and Washington Irving, the wilderness offered a fictive realm where they might rehearse the tensions that the formation of a national identity evoked. Empowered by developments in natural history and by the successful literary foundations of their predecessors, midcentury American authors employed nature toward very different ends. For this later generation of writers, nature was not an uncultured realm but an arena unfettered by the constraints of dogma. Freed from the need to defend American art, Susan Cooper figured nature not as a symbolic trope but as an element that evinced social life.

Born in 1813, Susan Cooper came of age in an America very different from that of her father. A mythic reinterpretation of the War of 1812 created a heretofore unknown sense of national cohesion that rapidly supplanted, in the popular imagination, the fact that the conflict had come perilously close to dissolving the union.[5] After weathering several challenging collapses and panics, the American economy had, by the 1840s, largely stabilized, transforming the nation from an economically stratified society to one with capital held predominantly by an emergent middle class.[6] Popular iconography figured America as the nation of the future, and youth and possibility became central themes of the new American narrative. Moving beyond an earlier tendency to measure American achievement against European models, Susan Cooper grounds her consideration of national identity in the determining role of the natural environment.

Throughout the 1830s and 1840s efforts to locate the sources of national identity were manifested in a broad-based interrogation of the institutions of the Republic and their effects in forming post-Revolutionary subjectivities.[7] Beginning in the 1830s, America witnessed a massive increase in the publication of advice manuals and conduct guides.[8] Coupled with this trend was an increased attention to domestic economy, registered in the novels of Susan Warner, Harriet Beecher Stowe, and Maria Susanna Cummins, in handbooks by Lydia Maria Child and Catharine Beecher, and in popular journals such as *Godey's Lady's Book* (1836) and the *Home Journal* (1846).[9] The abundance and success of these publications speak retrospectively to a cultural desire for instruction on matters of identity formation. These texts responded to a Jacksonian cultural anxiety concerning the effects social migration and the commodification of nature—caused by the shift away from an agriculturally based economy—might have on the construction of a national culture. If Americans secured their identity through a primary connection to nature, what would be the cost of urban expansion and industrialization? Linked to this attention to the domestic was an increasing interest in forming scientific and educational associations dedicated to the study of natural history. The creation of these institutions responded to the emerging belief in a correlation between the natural environment and character development.

The advent of gentility in America during the mid–nineteenth century was, as Richard Bushman notes, yoked to a "beautification campaign," which insisted that "everything from houses to barns to village streets was to be made beautiful; every scene was to be turned into a picture."[10] In *Rural Hours* Susan Cooper argues for the congruence of interiors and exteriors by unearthing "how large a portion of our ideas of grace and beauty are derived from the plants, how constantly we turn to them for models" (316). Look at "all the trifling knick-knacks in the room," Cooper directs, "and on all these you may see, in bolder or fainter lines, a thousand proofs of the debt we owe to the vegetable world" (*Rural Hours,* 316). Cooper urges the incorporation of interior decorations that match America's exterior environments, rather than relying on foreign models. While Cooper's remarks recall the tenets of European *Naturphilosophie,* they are more properly read as a careful adaptation of that doctrine. Susan Cooper shuns the idealization of nature, insisting instead that Americans adopt realistic forms from their immediate environment.[11]

As Rochelle Johnson and Daniel Patterson note in their introduction to *Rural Hours,* Susan Fenimore Cooper avidly read natural history. Cataloging the volumes she is believed to have consulted, they document Cooper's repeated requests that her father purchase for her specific scientific and protoscientific texts. Familiar with the works of Louis Agassiz, Andrew Jackson Downing, and Charles Lyell, Susan Cooper also immersed herself in the writings of John James Audubon, François Chateaubriand, Georges Cuvier, Alexander von Humboldt, DeWitt Clinton, Thomas Jefferson, Alexander Wilson, and other natural historians.

Chief among these new natural historians was Charles Lyell, whose scientific discoveries had considerable impact on natural history writing in the United States after the publication of his *Principles of Geology* (1830–33). Lyell toured the Republic in 1841, lecturing to overcrowded halls in most of the nation's major cities.[12] In his speeches and writings, Lyell observed that the age of the earth far exceeded previous understandings, implying that European pride in its "ancient" civilization was misplaced. If the heritage of the West was dwarfed by the reality of the earth's age, then the relative youth of the Republic was inconsequential. By lengthening the frame of history, introducing what Foucault calls "the irruptive violence of time," Lyell indirectly helped assuage American anxiety about national identity.[13]

Lyell contended that the entirety of the past could be successfully interpreted by examining forces still operant in nature.[14] Such a reconceptualization reversed the prevalent Whig notion of progress, liberating the present from a deterministic past by inverting the figures in the equation. If, to understand the past, one must scrutinize the present, then America's failure to attain some prescribed plateau was irrelevant. These developments in natural history, spearheaded by the work of Lyell, enabled midcentury American writers to imagine nature not simply in a unidirectional relationship with cultivated European landscapes but as a fragment of a much older, more intricate picture. As a result of this recalibration of the earth's age, Susan Cooper could investigate the correlation between the society of the Republic and New World nature without privileging European social structures as the primal scene.

Lyell's American tour sparked a turn during the 1840s toward science as a vehicle for explaining the state of American culture. The first publication of *Scientific American* (1845) was followed in short order by the establishment of the Smithsonian Institution (1846). Harvard sought to rival European centers of learning by hiring Louis Agassiz and promoting his work through the foundation of the Lawrence Scientific School (1847). While such highbrow activities might seem divorced from the popular success of texts concerned with domestic economy, these trends were intrinsically connected with the creation of a uniquely American style of interior design, with landscape composition, and with stylistic developments in architecture. Intriguingly, Susan Cooper registers this phenomenon by speculating on the linkages between terra-forming strategies and social structures.

A major influence on Susan Cooper's conception of landscape aesthetics was Andrew Jackson Downing, whose widely celebrated *Treatise on the Theory and Practice of Landscape Gardening, Adapted to North Amer-*

ica (1841) was the first American work devoted to landscape design.[15] In Downing's work Susan Cooper found a voice that counseled patience and the cultivation of nature as the optimal means of advancing American cultural development. In a nation searching for domestic instruction, Downing quickly rose to prominence. Promulgating the cultivation of gentility, Downing argued that as nature could be shaped and husbanded, so too could social practices, and that alterations in the landscape would provoke shifts in cultural habit.

In an editorial in the *Horticulturist,* a journal Downing edited from 1846 until his death in 1852, he cautioned that "to live in the new world" meant leaving foreign preconceptions behind.[16] Downing called for moderation in the cultivation of the landscape rather than the typical American "goaheadism," urging his readers to have reasonable expectations and to appreciate the impossibility of forming a picturesque garden overnight. If America was to develop a refined native culture (autonomous, yet comparable to European society), then its citizens must proceed with caution. For Downing, landscape and social structure were directly linked. The cultural institutions Americans created must be grounded in an interior and exterior architecture that represented the democratic tenets of the Republic, for as Downing advanced in *The Architecture of Country Houses,* "different styles of Domestic Architecture" were "nothing more than expressions of national character."[17]

Immediately after the Revolution and well into the first quarter of the nineteenth century, American artists were largely ignored when they mourned the landscape's destruction. In an earlier appeal for preserving the American forest, Thomas Cole enumerated the glories of the New York wilderness, pointing out that it had yet to be "destroyed or modified" to "accommodate the tastes and necessities of a dense population."[18] In the 1830s, the United States was only beginning to confront the consequences of development, and Cole enjoined his audience to moderate the rate of progress, for "the ravages of the axe are daily increasing" and "the most noble scenes are made destitute." Writing during the height of large-scale terra-forming projects in New York, Cole realized that "such is the road society has to travel," yet he hoped this would "lead to refinement in the end."[19] Jacksonian America was not preoccupied with maintaining picturesque views but with improving market access and building a workable infrastructure. Over a decade later, after the American economy had stabilized and capital was more equally distributed, Downing's popular pleas for patience and preservation—which Susan Cooper echoed—

found a more receptive audience. Cooper's arguments about American development were more pointed than Downing's, for the consequences she envisioned were not abstract but extremely personal.

In *Rural Hours* Susan Cooper investigated American social mores as an extension of the Republic's relationship to its natural environment. In a pivotal essay that appeared two years later, she advanced her argument more specifically, mapping the historical terrain of American architecture and its connection to the landscape. In "A Dissolving View," which appeared in the handsome 1852 gift-book *The Home Book of the Picturesque*, Cooper entreated readers to emancipate themselves from received practice, to imagine their own location in nature as the central experience of their worldview. In "A Dissolving View," she recapitulates residual conceptions of American social evolution and considers how emerging interests in natural history and landscape aesthetics departed from that inherited tradition.

Dedicated to Asher Durand, president of the National Academy of Fine Arts, *The Home Book of the Picturesque* sought to capitalize on cultural preoccupations with natural history and interior design, while also contributing to the cultivation of an American aesthetic.[20] The dedication underscores this intention by stating that the volume was "an initiatory suggestion for popularizing some of the characteristics of American Landscape and American Art."[21] Aspiring to fulfill consumer demand, Putnam undertook the volume "as an experiment," asserting that it would provide an American alternative to popular European gift books by illustrating "the picturesque beauties of American landscape."[22] Both nationalist and market-conscious, Putnam's editors canonized the productions of American artists while advancing an argument about the picturesque aesthetic.

On the title page of *The Home Book of the Picturesque*, the editors at G. P. Putnam list their contributors in ranking order. Susan Cooper's is the fourth name on that page, preceded only by Washington Irving, William Cullen Bryant, and her father, James Fenimore Cooper. Susan Cooper's prominent listing is not surprising, since Putnam's published *Rural Hours* as its 1850 presentation volume and profited from its considerable success. Susan Cooper's relation to the writers whose names precede hers on Putnam's title page is not, however, simply a matter of contemporary literary reputation. Her essay, "A Dissolving View," conveys its readers from the landscape aesthetic of Irving, Bryant, and her father to a more localized and less romantic conception of American scenery.

America's foremost popularizer of "the Picturesque," Andrew Jackson Downing, defined that aesthetic mode as "an idea of beauty or power strongly and irregularly expressed," as opposed to "the Beautiful," which is "calmly and harmoniously expressed." [23] In creating a picturesque scene, Downing observes, "everything depends on *intricacy* and *irregularity*." He began from an assumption that nature was not inherently picturesque but required arrangement and embellishment to be formed, and that this shaping "springs naturally from a love" for the terrain. To express a wild yet cultivated nature, landscape gardening must be tailored to its region. In America the progress of landscape gardening was not impeded by a lack of resources but by a failure to adapt European ideals to the demands of America's geographical and historical particularities: "Even those who are familiar with foreign works on the subject in question labor under many obstacles in practice, which grow out of the difference in our soil and climate, or our social and political position." [24] Downing's equation of regional differences with sociopolitical factors demonstrates how closely linked are these seemingly divergent agendas. A landscape aesthetic must reflect the demands of a given environment while representing a nation's heritage. It is precisely this new vision of a landscape aesthetic that informs the creation of *The Home Book of the Picturesque* and, in particular, Susan Cooper's "A Dissolving View."

Susan Cooper situates "A Dissolving View" during autumn in Cooperstown. Her choice of season grounds her essay within (as she conceives it) the paradigmatic American season. Beginning in *Rural Hours*, Cooper argues that America's autumnal palate offers unrivaled vistas. "Our native writers, as soon as we had writers of our own, pointed out very early both the sweetness of the Indian summer, and the magnificence of the autumnal changes," which uncovered, Cooper continues, "the precise extent of the difference between the relative beauty of autumn in Europe and in America: with us it is quite impossible to overlook these peculiar charms of the autumnal months," whereas in Europe "they remained unnoticed, unobserved, for ages" (*Rural Hours*, 209). While it is customary to associate nature with vernal scenes, the explosion of color during an American autumn affords a spectacle unfamiliar to Europeans. These diverse tints are the most difficult to reproduce, for "there is no precedent for such coloring as nature requires here among the works of old masters, and the American artist must necessarily become an innovator" (*Rural Hours*, 215). Autumn is, Cooper argues, an unworked genre, delivering American artists from the constraints of unfavorable comparisons with the artistic conventions of Europe. Representing American autumn required painstaking attention to fleeting scenery. The best vantage point a seeker of picturesque scenes could have is in "the hanging woods of a mountainous country" where the "trees throwing out their branches, one above another, in bright variety of coloring and outline" sufficiently frame the intricacy of the scene (*Rural Hours*, 211). Susan Cooper's narrator occupies such a position at the opening of her meditation on the development of Cooperstown.

Cooper opens "A Dissolving View" with a familiar account of the beauty of the autumnal American landscape. That rendering is complicated when she describes autumn as protean. During fall an observer is unbalanced, never knowing "beforehand exactly what to expect," for "there is always some variation, occasionally a strange contrast." Yet Cooper quickly reveals that the human transformation of the multihued landscape generates the picturesque: "I should not care to pass the season in the wilderness," for while "a broad extent of forest is no doubt necessary to the magnificent spectacle," there "should also be broken woods, scattered groves, and isolated trees." She continues, "it strikes me that the quiet fields of man, and his cheerful dwellings, should also have a place in the gay picture." Fall contains "a social spirit," for its "brilliancy" draws attention to the human presence in the landscape ("A Dissolving View," 80, 82, 81).

Cooper locates her narrator on the trunk of a fallen pine tree that "overlooked the country for some fifteen miles or more," framing her field of vision and enabling her perception of the picturesque. A nearby "projecting cliff" and "the oaks whose branches overshadowed" the narrator's seat, creating a natural Claude glass, guide her vision, imparting a graduated scale to the objects in the background.[25] Situated within the forest, Cooper's narrator overlooks a cultivated landscape that figures the progressive development of American settlement: "the lake, the rural town, and the farms in the valley beyond, lying at our feet like a beautiful map." From this topological position, the favorite perch of the Hudson River school, Cooper's narrator witnesses—and records—the history of American social evolution while ruminating on the consequences of all human development.[26] She concludes that although "the hand of man generally improves a landscape," there is a danger that terra-forming projects partake of the hubristic. In such work, man "endeavors to rise above his true part of laborer and husbandman," assuming "the character of creator" ("A Dissolving View," 81, 82).

For Cooper, this hubristic inclination has contaminated architecture since its advent. Europe is replete with architectural projects that compete with nature rather than harmonize with it: "Indeed it would seem as if man had no sooner mastered the art of architecture, than he aimed at rivalling the dignity and durability of the works of nature which served as his models; he resolved that his walls of vast stones should stand in place as long as the rocks from which they were hewn; that his columns and his arches should live with the trees and branches from which they were copied; he determined to scale the heavens with his proud towers of Babel" ("A Dissolving View," 84). While such "imposing" ancient piles stir up wonder in viewers, they also recall the combative cultures out of which they arose.[27] The "very violence" of the past and its "superstitious nature" created monuments to dissolute empires and forged structures to withstand the continual danger of eradication ("A Dissolving View," 86).

Should Americans mourn the absence of ancient edifices redolent of antagonistic cultural values? If a cultivated landscape should epitomize the specific social and cultural values of its population, as Cooper believes, then is it tragic that the United States lacks monuments to monarchies and feudalism? European cities are burdened by buildings that were formed by the "prevalence" of a "warlike spirit." These medieval buildings "are likely" to "outlast modern works of the same nature," for those who built them imagined a future dedicated to the same principles that governed them: "They not only built for the future, in those days, but they expected posterity to work with them; as one generation lay down in their graves, they called another generation to their pious labor." While Americans are "in some measure influenced by those days of chivalry and superstitious truth," they are not bound by them ("A Dissolving View," 86–87).

Susan Cooper recognized just how much materiality matters in shaping a coherent social philosophy. By affirming agency, Cooper extends her contention that European architecture is ill suited for America; like the effect of a canopy formed by towering trees, the shadows of the past prohibit new growth from taking root. "Thus it is that there is not in those old countries," she observes, "a single natural feature of the earth upon which man has not set his seal." Cooper finds a triumphant strength in "how different from all this" the "fresh civilization of America" is. Within the United States, "there is no blending of the old and the new," for "there is nothing old among us" ("A Dissolving View," 88–89). Much of the Republic's nature remains wild, and thus for Cooper, Americans fashioning a modern nation are not burdened by the detrimental decisions of their ancestors.

Critical of the current state of national life, Cooper complains that Americans are "the reverse of conservators," failing to preserve markers of their own history. Here Cooper's position reproduces contemporary, class-based arguments against the depredations of laissez-faire capitalism. Yet for Cooper there is freedom in Americans being "the borderers of civilization," for that position enables them to "act as pioneers." She extends her examination of American society by freighting the landscape with predictive power; Cooper observes that "the peculiar tendencies of the age are seen more clearly among us than in Europe" ("A Dissolving View," 89). The unfolding of the American scene—measured by its architecture, its landscape design, and its consequent social refinements—is a matter of more than local interest. It is a barometer of the age, a register of the future.

Inheritors of Western social tradition, yet free from the constraints of modern Europe's determining environment (for "many parts" of the Old World "have an old, worn-out, exhausted appearance"), the United States should fashion an architecture suited to the more "subtle" nineteenth century. America's historic monuments are not to be found in man-made ruins but within nature itself. Paraphrasing Louis Agassiz, Cooper notes that "as the surface of the planet now exists, North America is, in reality, the oldest part of the earth," simultaneously more ancient and more vigorous than the natural environment of Europe ("A Dissolving View," 89, 90). While Americans failed as historic conservationists, they have not yet irrevocably denuded their landscape and so can still alter their interaction with it.

Cooper continues by returning to Agassiz, who "tells us that in many particulars our vegetation, and our animal life, belong to an older period than those" of Europe ("A Dissolving View," 90). Agassiz believed that vegetation that existed only in a fossil state in Europe continued to flourish in North America. By the 1850s, Agassiz was the most prominent natural historian in the United States, and Cooper's citation of his work testifies to her familiarity with contemporary natural history.[28] Agassiz wanted to understand nature through, as Edward Lurie suggests, "the perceptions provided by direct experience." While Agassiz straddled "the two worlds of empiricism and idealism," he also knew "that nature, if it meant anything at all, was to be understood as a whole, a historical and contemporary unit of experience."[29] Agassiz's conception of nature, which dominated natural history prior to Darwin's 1859 publication of his *Origin of Species,* rested on the assumption that local environments were shaped by divine power for particular ends. Advancing this notion of separate creations, he argued in *Lake Superior* (1850) that "the geographical distribution of organized beings displays more fully the direct intervention of a Supreme Intelligence in the plan of Creation, than any other adaption in the physical world."[30] Agassiz's sense of the uniqueness of each territory's natural history undergirds Cooper's promotion of a specific American architecture or interaction with the landscape. If, as Agassiz maintains, nature is separately created for a particular, divine purpose, then Americans, who have not completely disrupted their environment, are positioned to interpret properly their physical world. And by accurately reading their landscape, they can build dwellings in harmony with their surroundings.

Cooper ends her essay with an enigmatic turn. Seizing a "sprig of wych-hazel," Cooper's narrator plays a "game of architectural consequences" in which she imagines the landscape as it might have appeared if the culture that had formed it had been driven by different forces. The inroads of civilization disappear, and with a wave of the wand the landscape is restored to wilderness. But "merely razing a village" and restoring the valley to its virginal state "did not satisfy the whim of the moment," and so the spell is cast again until she "beheld a spectacle which wholly engrossed" her attention ("A Dissolving View," 91–92).

The conjuring wand produces the valley as it would have appeared "had it lain in the track of European civilization during past ages; how, in such a case, would it have been fashioned by the hand of man?" In the midst of this reverie, in which everything is "so strangely altered," the narrator requires "a second close scrutiny to convince [herself] that this was indeed the site of the village which had disappeared a moment earlier." Only through an intense examination of "all the natural features of the landscape" is she assured that it is the valley, and not herself, that has been recast. Noting the geographically appropriate vegetation and recognizing the familiar contours of the lake shore, she understands that it is the history of cultural production that has mutated the landscape. Quickly, "all resemblance ceased," for the "hills had been wholly shorn of wood," and the "position of the different farms and that of the buildings was entirely changed." The little town "dwindled to a mere hamlet" ("A Dissolving View," 92–93).

The valley is now dominated by two structures, the church and an "old country house" that give the surrounding habitations their meaning, or at least arrange them in "various grades of importance." The church and manor house define the social structure of this European village: all its citizens share one religion, and just as clearly, they are cast into a delineated social hierarchy based upon architectural style. Cooperstown's bustling industry becomes, in the "European" hamlet, "two or three small, quiet-looking shops"; its wooden bridge is replaced by a "massive stone" one guarded by "the ruins of a tower" ("A Dissolving View," 93).

By recomposing the scene in the form of a European village, Cooper underscores the difference between American and European society. While the denuded European landscape contains buried "ancient coins" and the ruins of "feudal castles," the relationship of its current occupants to their environment is entirely predetermined ("A Dissolving View," 93). Unlike the less-ordered American scene, the social roles of Europeans are always already fixed. In sharp contrast, the current state of architecture and civic planning in the United States permits the natural proliferation and change of the social relations of Americans.

The narrator's reverie is disrupted by "a roving bee, bent apparently on improving these last warm days, and harvesting the last drops of honey" ("A Dissolving View," 94). As Washington Irving reminds us, bees were widely perceived as "the heralds of civilization, steadfastly preceding it as it advanced from the Atlantic borders."[31] The bee, cast here as a symbol of an intrusive market economy, quite literally stings the narrator out of her Hudson River fancy and reminds her that the rural location from which she views the American scene might soon fall victim to the energies of regnant capitalism. Or, perhaps, having imagined the appearance of the valley as if it had been shaped by European cultural advancement, readers of her essay would have understood the danger of choosing foreign models as social guides.

Prior to her wych-hazel fancy, Cooper contemplates the current state of American architecture, suggesting that "it is yet too unformed, too undecided to claim a character of its own, but the general air of comfort and thrift which shows itself in most of our dwellings, whether on a large or a small scale, gives satisfaction in its own way" ("A Dissolving View," 91). This critique is not melancholic; rather, it is framed as a recognition that America is a nation whose identity will be decided in the present, a borderland between a determining past and an unknown future. While American architecture may lack a character of its own, that absence will not obstruct the progress of future generations. She encourages a movement toward preservation that would enable the development of an American aesthetic cognizant of the particular character of the nation's environment. By registering the vulnerability of older aesthetic perspectives that proceed from a reliance on European cultural models, she argues for their rejection. Anything built on such foreign foundations was doomed to collapse; alien to New World soil, they could never take root without damaging the natural environment. At the same time, she maintains that Americans need not pursue heedlessly forms of architectural and landscape design capable of reflecting a democratic cultural order.

Only by considering her two texts in tandem can a reader fully appreciate Susan Cooper's conception of the linkage between cultural forms and nature as dependent upon the imagination. Instead of further damaging their environment by constructing badly designed buildings, Americans, she argues, should imagine the consequences of their choices before plunging ahead, working with—rather than in opposition to—their natural environments. Since assembled aesthetic failures encumber the formation of a national culture by articulating inappropriate social codes, she promotes the imagination (and not the landscape) as the arena for testing the consequences of any new construction. Moving beyond residual aesthetics, requiems for an America that failed to import European cultural models, Susan Cooper makes a case for preserving the wild as the locus of the imagination.

NOTES

I thank Joan Richardson and Kimberly Engber for reading versions of this essay. I am deeply indebted to Bill Kelly; without him this essay would not have been possible.

1. Susan Cooper's distaste for the importation of European cultural forms registers in her critique of the unfortunate practice of naming American settlements after European cities. See Susan Fenimore Cooper, *Rural Hours,* ed. Rochelle Johnson and Daniel Patterson (Athens: University of Georgia Press, 1998), 298–309. Hereafter cited in the text. References to "A Dissolving View" are to *The Home Book of the Picturesque; or, American Scenery, Art, and Literature* (New York: Putnam, 1852; reprint, Gainesville, Fla.: Scholars' Facsimiles & Reprints, 1967), 79–94. Hereafter cited in text.

2. Cooper's interest in architecture as a record of American social practice reflects its status during the first half of the nineteenth century. Prior to its professionalization in the last quarter of the century, considering architecture one of the fine arts was a common practice, as even the Library of Congress (following Jefferson's cataloging schema) shelved architectural treatises along with works of poetry, fiction, and other artistic texts. Susan Cooper was also most likely familiar with Andrew Jackson Downing's *The Architecture of Country Houses* (1850), in which he argued that the aim of architecture, like that of "every fine art is the art of so treating objects as to give them a moral significance" ([New York: Dover, 1969], 38). Additionally, Cooper would have been familiar with her father's own speculations on this question, figured most prominently in *Home as Found* (1838) and *The American Democrat* (1838).

3. Cooperstown's distance from both the Erie Canal and existing railroads in the 1850s meant that it was relatively unaffected by the boom-and-bust economy of the Jacksonian period.

4. William Cooper published his study of Cooperstown, *A Guide in the Wilderness; or, The History of the First Settlements in the Western Counties of New York with Useful Instructions to Future Settlers* (Dublin: Gilbert and Hodges, 1810), at the close of the century's first decade, while James Fenimore Cooper repeatedly explored the terrain of New York State in his fiction starting in the 1820s.

5. The best critical accounts of the nationalist myths born from Jackson's victory at New Orleans remain Marvin Meyers, *The Jacksonian Persuasion: Politics and Belief* (Stanford, Calif.: Stanford University Press, 1957) and John William Ward, *Andrew Jackson: Symbol for an Age* (New York: Oxford University Press, 1955).

6. For a discussion of this economic phenomenon nationally, see Charles Sellers, *The Market Revolution: Jacksonian America, 1815–1846* (New York: Oxford University Press, 1991). For more specifically regional examinations, see Paul E. Johnson, *A Shopkeeper's Millennium: Society and Revivals in Rochester, New York 1815–1837* (New York: Hill and Wang, 1978) and Mary Ryan, *Cradle of the Middle Class: The Family in Oneida County, New York, 1790–1865* (New York: Cambridge University Press, 1981).

7. For an extended discussion of the shifting representation of America's Revolutionary heritage, see Michael Kammen, *A Season of Youth: The American Revolution and the Historical Imagination* (New York: Knopf, 1978).

8. For examinations of the effects of this increase in the publication of manuals and guides, see Karen Halttunen, *Confidence Men and Painted Women: A Study of Middle Class Culture in America, 1830–1870* (New Haven, Conn.: Yale University Press, 1982).

9. Among the key critical studies of the emergence of the cult of domesticity are Gillian Brown, *Domestic Individualism: Imagining Self in Nineteenth-Century America* (Berkeley: University of California Press, 1990); Ann Douglas, *The Feminization of American Culture* (New York: Doubleday, 1977); and Jane Tompkins, *Sensational Designs: The Cultural Work of American Fiction, 1790–1860* (New York: Oxford University Press, 1985).

10. Richard L. Bushman, *The Refinement of America: Persons, Houses, Cities* (New York: Vintage, 1993), xiv.

11. Consistently in *Rural Hours,* Cooper suggests that Americans manufacture interior decorations based upon the superior variety of colors and shades found in nature around them rather than continue to follow foreign trends.

12. For a detailed discussion of Lyell's importance in the United States, see Leonard G. Wilson, *Lyell in America: Transatlantic Geology, 1841–1853* (Baltimore, Md.: Johns Hopkins University Press, 1998).

13. Michel Foucault, *The Order of Things: An Archaeology of the Human Sciences* (New York: Vintage, 1994), 132.

14. See Stephen Jay Gould, *Time's Arrow, Time's Cycle: Myth and Metaphor in the Discovery of Geological Time* (Cambridge, Mass.: Harvard University Press, 1987).

15. Downing's influence reached into other aspects of rural life: see, as examples, his *Fruits and Fruit Trees of America* (1845), *Cottage Residences* (1842), and *The Architecture of Country Houses* (1850). For in-depth treatments of Downing's influence, see Judith K. Major, *To Live in the New World: A. J. Downing and American Landscape Gardening* (Cambridge, Mass.: MIT Press, 1997); David Schuyler, *Apostle of Taste: Andrew Jackson Downing 1815–1852* (Baltimore, Md.: Johns Hopkins University Press, 1996); and Adam Sweeting, *Reading Houses and Building Books: Andrew Jackson Downing and the Architecture of Popular Antebellum Literature, 1835–1855* (Hanover: University Press of New England, 1996).

16. As quoted by Major, *To Live in the New World*, 2.

17. Downing, *The Architecture of Country Houses*, 26.

18. Thomas Cole, "Essay on American Scenery," in *Thomas Cole: The Collected Essays and Prose Sketches,* ed. Marshall Tym (St. Paul: John Colet Press, 1980), 8.

19. Ibid., 17.

20. The dedication to Durand is testimony to his prominence, but possibly the editors were also trying to invoke the spirit of one of his most famous paintings, *Kindred Spirits* (1849). Commissioned to paint a portrait of Thomas Cole and William Cullen Bryant, Durand depicted them in *Kindred Spirits* in complete harmony with the American wilderness. For a sense of the reception of Durand's painting, see Barbara Novak, *Nature and Culture: American Landscape Painting 1825–1875* (New York: Oxford University Press, 1980) and James T. Callow, *Kindred Spirits: Knickerbocker Writers and American Artists, 1807–1855* (Chapel Hill: University of North Carolina Press, 1967).

21. From the title page of *The Home Book of the Picturesque.*

22. Ibid., 7.

23. Andrew Jackson Downing, *Landscape Gardening and Rural Architecture* (1852; New York: Dover, 1991), 54. This volume is a reprint of the seventh edition of *A Treatise on the Theory and Practice of Landscape Gardening* (1852).

24. Ibid., 82, 19, 7.

25. A familiar tool for those searching for the picturesque, the Claude glass (named for the French landscape artist Claude Lorraine) was a convex mirror used to concentrate the features of a landscape. Here Cooper suggests that the cliff and trees create a natural frame for her vision.

26. Employing a tactic familiar to Hudson River school painters, Cooper locates her narrator within wild nature but casts her field of vision into a settled

landscape. See Angela Miller's reading of Cole's *The Oxbow* (1836) in *The Empire of the Eye: Landscape Representation and American Cultural Politics, 1825–1875* (Ithaca, N.Y.: Cornell University Press, 1993), 39–48.

27. Cooper in particular singles out the architectural styles of Babylon, Greece, and Rome for their fortitude in surviving numerous attacks at the hands of "savages" and "barbarians."

28. The best account of Agassiz's importance is Edward Lurie, *Louis Agassiz: A Life in Science* (Baltimore, Md.: Johns Hopkins University Press, 1988), see esp. chaps. 4 and 5.

29. Ibid., 82, 52, 50.

30. Louis Agassiz, *Lake Superior: Its Physical Character, Vegetation, and Animals, Compared with Those of Other and Similar Regions* (1850; New York: Arno Press, 1970), 144.

31. Washington Irving, *A Tour of the Prairies* (1832; Norman: University of Oklahoma Press, 1956), 50. Cooper would have also been familiar with her father's treatment of this myth in his novel *The Oak Openings; or, The Bee-Hunter* (1848).

PART THREE

Theorizing *Rural Hours:* Audience, Time, and Aesthetics

Reading Susan Reading Ruth: Audience, Response, and the Historical Hermeneutics of *Rural Hours*

Writing to his wife in 1850, a few weeks prior to the American publication of his daughter Susan's *Rural Hours,* James Fenimore Cooper expressed some hesitant but cogent reservations about the book's impending reception: "I have written to Sue to say how much I am pleased with her book—It is not strong perhaps, but . . . I do not doubt, now, of its eventual success—I say eventual, for, at first, the world will not know what to make of it." [1] In confiding these thoughts to his wife, James was not simply expressing the anxiety a father would naturally feel for the work of a beloved daughter. Rather, his comments need also to be considered in light of both antebellum views on genre and antebellum reading practices specifically.

Nineteenth-century audiences and critics were especially sensitive to an author's combining of familiar narrative modes. Although debates raged for much of the period about the extent to which writers were allowed to use mixed forms, most readers at least expected an author's use of genre to be consistent and not disorienting. [2] "[W]hat to make" of Susan Cooper's book should thus also be understood as an expression of her father's specific concern about how readers would react to the fact that the book's genre was not self-evident. Writing to Richard Bentley to negotiate the book's British publication, James called *Rural Hours* a "diary" that included observations of local flora and fauna but also "a great deal of information in it, besides." [3] In the preface to the first edition (1850), the author describes her book as a "journal" of "notes" revealing "rural life" as well as observations about nature specifically. In short, both Susan Cooper and her father were unsure how to categorize her book, a fact entirely consistent with the historical conditions of the text's production and reception. As Rochelle Johnson and Daniel Patterson note, "Even though the genre of nature writing had fully emerged by the late eighteenth century, it was new enough in 1850 to find readers still expecting that natural history and travel writing would keep to their respective genres and publishers' lists."[4] Clearly, at the time of the book's publication, writers, publishers, and critics were still constructing ways of describing and classifying what we now consider to be a mixed but relatively stable narrative mode.[5]

This aspect of the book's production and reception history is worth bringing into relief because, as rhetorical critics have demonstrated, genre plays an immensely important role in audience response.[6] Although antebellum anxiety about genre was a product of a variety of issues related to nineteenth-century debates about poetics, aesthetics, and the ethics of reading and writing,[7] from a late-twentieth-century perspective it is also possible to see that questions about genre are always also questions about reading practices—about hermeneutics. Conventions establish expectations in the reader, and every text either conforms to or violates its generic expectations, usually doing both to some degree or another, depending on the author's purposes. Conventions thus exist simultaneously both in the text—as established modes of literary representation and figural expression—and outside it—as socially prescribed rules for making what Wolfgang Iser calls the latent "virtual dimension" of the text actual.[8] As Peter Rabinowitz puts it, "Literary conventions are not in the text waiting to be uncovered, but in fact precede the text and make discovery possible in the first place."[9] Identifying a book's genre is thus a crucial component of determining how to respond appropriately to its use of convention—in effect, in determining how to read the text.[10]

A natural question that arises along these lines in regard to *Rural Hours* is whether the text itself provides any clues as to how Cooper expected her readers to respond to her use of convention. In other words, does *Rural Hours* contain any evidence of the particular hermeneutics its author assumed would inform the response(s) of her audience? In their study of antebellum reader response among Boston's upper class, Ronald Zboray and Mary Zboray note that the record of the responses of real readers from the antebellum period is scant, especially in regard to the "page-by-page experience" of texts.[11] Such evidence that does exist takes the form of letters and diaries as well as published literary criticism.[12] Accordingly, I argue that *Rural Hours* is important precisely because it provides a rare glimpse at an antebellum reader reading and responding to a text—specifically, Cooper reading and explicating the Book of Ruth.

Coming very near the end of the section "Summer," Cooper's reading of Ruth is the longest "digression" in the book, which may explain why it was not included in the abridged 1887 edition published by Houghton Mifflin, the same edition reprinted by Syracuse University in 1968. As I will show, however, how Cooper reads the Book of Ruth has much to tell us about how she expected her readers to read *her,* allowing a rare opportunity to examine the hermeneutics that informed the author's own writing process and thus to recover what Cathy Davidson calls the "interpretive grid" that Cooper expected would shape her audience's response.[13] Specifically, I will argue that Cooper's reading of the Book of Ruth functions rhetorically as a sophisticated hermeneutic model for reading *Rural Hours,* in effect asking her audience to read her own work according to a rather narrow conception of the limits of reader response—asking her reader, in effect, to limit the exercise of his or her textual power.[14]

For Cooper, reading for convention meant adhering closely to the hermeneutic rules that an author's historical moment and choice of genre dictated. Deeply concerned with her public image as a woman writer and with how her book would be interpreted and thus received, Cooper in effect asked her reader to read *Rural Hours* straight—to resist engaging in the sort of overreading (what we might call more simply *interpretation*) she accuses Voltaire and others of doing in their discussion of Ruth's moral character. By thus limiting what readers could infer from her use of available narrative modes, Cooper tried to insure that her audience would be as kind to the author of *Rural Hours* as she had been to the author of the Book of Ruth.

Although at first glance such a conception of the author-text-reader economy might appear naive, I hope to show that the means by which Cooper goes about influencing her readers to limit the exercise of their textual power is in actuality one of the book's greatest strengths. The hermeneutic model the author enacts in her reading of the Book of Ruth, although conventional for the period, is at the same time extremely powerful in terms of the experiences it makes available to its readers. That is, she reads the Book of Ruth as any midcentury, educated, pious, Episcopalian woman would have done. In doing so, however, she positions her reader to entertain a variety of complex, subtle, and provocative ideas about language, hermeneutics, and interpretation, concerns she shared with other prominent antebellum writers and language theorists. As such, her inclusion of these concerns in a book of nature writing begs us to reconsider her place among other nineteenth-century theorists of the relation between language and meaning.

As the work of the editors of the two most recent editions of *Rural Hours* attests, determining the genre to which the book belongs and thus the hermeneutic that should best inform our reading and response is an issue that has remained as relevant for twentieth-century readers as it had been for Cooper's father. David Jones, in his preface to the 1968 reissue of the abridged 1887 edition, argued that there were essentially two reasons for reading *Rural Hours*. First, it provided a detailed glimpse at mid-nineteenth-century life in "a small, rural, upstate New York community," [15] and its value was thus as an historical record primarily. Second, the view of life that emerged from Cooper's "gentle reflections" was "refreshingly bright," sophisticated, and moral. Finally, in no way did Jones suggest that the book had very much aesthetic value, especially compared to other major works from the period. According to Jones, *Rural Hours* was not like *Walden*. In framing the book in this way, Jones was in effect telling his readers how *not* to read Cooper's book. Do not come to *Rural Hours* with the expectation of finding another masterpiece of the antebellum period—you will only come away disappointed.

Responding to Jones, the editors of the most recent edition have taken a very different and much more compelling tack in establishing the book's hermeneutic framework. In preparing us to read Cooper's book, Johnson and Patterson have successfully resituated the book as an important moment in the history of American nature writing and thus as a prophetic precursor to more recent writing on the environment. In their words, "By means of the form of the natural history essay and through narratives and descriptions of Cooper's walks and excursions, *Rural Hours* presents what ultimately emerges as Cooper's argument for a sustainable balance between human culture and its natural surroundings." [16] Such a rendering of what is intelligible about Cooper's book is only possible, they argue, because one result of the worsening environmental crises that continue to unfold in the fin de siècle is that we have become "better readers of nature writing." [17] This reconceptualization of *Rural Hours* is extremely useful because it recovers a more historically accurate sense of the book's genre and purposes (as well as its cultural capital) than allowed for by Jones's late New Critical biases. Most importantly, Johnson and Patterson's approach correctly positions the starting point of our collective critical focus on both the book's genre and on the hermeneutics that follow from it.

My own work is thus meant as a contribution to what James L. Machor would call *Rural Hours*'s historical hermeneutics, a focus that combines reader-response theory with the contextual (and thus historical) emphasis of reception theory in an effort to "reconstruct the shared patterns of interpretation for a specific historical era [and] to define the reading strategies of particular interpretive communities."[18] In doing so, the critical focus is on how a reader's response to a text is a function of historically specific ideological and interpretive practices and thus of the assumptions about reading and about interpretation they adhered to as community members. Ideally, such an approach focuses on "the area where reading codes, ideological assumptions . . . and the textual construction of audience intersect."[19] Accordingly, in writing about Cooper's reading of the Book of Ruth, I will not be addressing its rich potential for thematic discussion.[20] Rather, I will be focusing on establishing both the historical-theoretical context for her own exegesis and on her specific rhetorical use of that exegesis at the end of "Summer."

Reconstructing the interpretive grid from within which Cooper would have worked as a member of an historically specific community of readers of biblical narrative (to be defined in more specific terms shortly) must precede close analysis of the function of the Ruth sections in Cooper's own rhetoric, especially analysis of the story's thematic implications. Accordingly, our concern is not with how the Book of Ruth can be interpreted ideationally but with the conventions for reading biblical narrative that dominated the mid–nineteenth century and especially with the role Cooper's brand of Protestantism would have played in her reading and rhetorical use of Ruth's story.

Cooper's reading of the Book of Ruth was influenced most by her membership in two communities of readers, primarily, nineteenth-century proponents of historical-critical methods of biblical exegesis and orthodox American Protestants. Historical-critical methods of biblical interpretation came to prominence in the nineteenth century and were a direct result of rationalist attacks on religion that had begun during the Reformation. Gerald Bray points out that in response to these attacks, theologians and church leaders early on developed a "rational orthodoxy" that "sought to harmonize basic Christian doctrine with the findings of natural science."[21] As the seventeenth century waned, however, the deep and often politically charged debates about the status of the Bible as a source for truth—in any rationalist, scientific sense of that term—deepened.[22] Textual criticism and eventually historical-critical analysis were seen, at least by moderates among the orthodoxy, as providing methods of scriptural analysis that could place the Bible firmly in its historical context but at the same time preserve it as a sacred document compatible with rationalist thought. Renaissance humanists had first recognized that a text is best understood in terms of its original context, but it was not until the nineteenth century that historical-critical methods of biblical interpretation gained widespread acceptance by scholars and lay people alike, although acceptance by the general public (especially in the United States) lagged far behind acceptance by scholars.

There were five principles that defined the historical-critical method in regard to Old Testament scholarship in particular. First, adherents of the new historical criticism believed interpretation must be based on solid knowledge of the original documents, including especially the language in which they were written and the material-historical context in which they were composed. Second, a reasonable explanation must be sought for every phenomenon. Third, evidence gleaned indirectly from a text was of more value than direct statements or claims because it was less likely to have been the result of propaganda. This meant reading was essentially inference making. Fourth, historicist scholars believed there was an evolutionary drift from the simpler to the more complex; therefore, more complex ideas and practices date from a later time. Finally, monotheism was seen as a higher form of religion than polytheism and therefore as having developed later (*Biblical Interpretation*, 301–3).

Turning from intellectual history and the world of ideas, we need to focus on the world of lived religion, especially as it was practiced by Protestants in the United States. By the year *Rural Hours* was first published, Protestants had lived through a degree of change to organized and popular religion not seen in this country since the Great Awakening and not to be seen again until the genteel, middle-class religious boom following World War II.[23]

The revivalism that swept through the United States from approximately the end of the War of 1812 until the 1840s—by which time the last vestiges of the revival movement were almost completely absorbed by more genteel reform movements (including abolition and temperance)— left no Protestant middle-class home untouched. The first Great Awakening had died out completely by the early national period. Deism specifically, as well as the general rationalism that was affecting English and Continental thought, effectively extinguished the last remnants of the country's first widespread spiritual movements. But by the Peace of Ghent, a new wave of spiritual revivalism was sweeping the country. As the immigration of New Englanders to upstate New York as well as the settlement of the frontier farther west created new challenges for established denominations, church leaders, as well as what we might describe as independent religious activists such as Charles Grandison Finney, responded to the spiritual malaise by calling for a literal revival of man's faith and experience of religious devotion. "Revival" thus meant a rekindling of the feverish spiritualism that had characterized the first spiritual awakenings in the United States and had contributed to the mushrooming of Protestant denominations throughout the country. Most importantly, the emotionalism of this new revivalism was its hallmark and included the sort of extreme displays of religious devotion that are still part of some rural and fundamentalist Protestant denominations in the United States today. In short, the religion of revivalism, especially on the frontier, was "uninhibited, emotional, and extremely personal, lacking all formality."[24]

Most interesting for our discussion of Susan Cooper is that nowhere was the advent of revivalism more profoundly felt than in the "burned-over" district of central and western New York State. Indeed, no area of the country saw a more diverse or more concentrated practice of revivalism than this region.[25] Many converts from the first Great Awakening had moved out of New England and into the mountains of Vermont and extreme western New England. The descendants of these rural peoples eventually immigrated across Lake Champlain and down the Hudson to Albany before moving up the Mohawk, taking their religious practices with them. As Whitney R. Cross in his seminal discussion of revivalism in this region notes, the newly arrived immigrant to the burned-over district "could scarcely evade a religious experience in New York. For ten years at most he might dwell in some isolated spot, but settlers inevitably arrived, churches formed, and revivals occurred."[26]

Cooperstown lay on the extreme eastern edge of the region defined by Cross, but it was by no means outside of the influence of the myriad spiritual and reform movements that passed through the region. Lying between the two most important routes for immigration into the region (the Mohawk Valley and the Susquehanna River), Cooperstown and greater Otsego County were regular stops for revivalists.[27] In sum, the Coopers of Cooperstown came to power and prominence during one of the most tumultuous periods in the history of religion in this country in a region that became synonymous with revivalism, crackpot spiritualism, and, only later, reform.

To its detractors, revivalism was inherently anti-intellectual, substituting emotion for theological debate and biblical exegesis.[28] Reactions against revivalism were strongest among Presbyterians, German Lutherans and German Reformed, Congregationalists, and Episcopalians. In the burned-over district, most Episcopalians were descended from the eighteenth-century aristocracy of New York, Pennsylvania, and Virginia and thus maintained a "cool dignity amidst the fiercest storms of fervent revivalism."[29] One general reaction among all the antirevivalists, especially among the orthodox Protestant denominations, was to establish clear, specific doctrines that reaffirmed their orthodox creeds, stressing the "purity of the 'true church,' with its proper liturgy, sacraments, and ministry."[30]

From what evidence there is in the family history, and as might be expected given their membership in the Episcopalian Church, the Coopers' orthodox and essentially conservative religious beliefs seem to have remained unaffected by the advent of revivalism. This does not mean, however, that they would have been unfamiliar with the perceived vagaries of the various spiritual movements or that they would not have had strong feelings regarding the movements' general validity or characters. William Cooper, Susan's grandfather, was not a pious man, but he supported through patronage the established conservative religions, especially the Presbyterians. Alan Taylor notes that he gave no support whatsoever to the denominations closely associated with revivalism in Otsego County—the Baptists, the Methodists, and the Christian Connections.[31] As an ardent but deposed Federalist in the very early 1800s, Judge Cooper saw orthodox religion as a means for curbing democratic tendencies in the general public. Revivalism and its emphasis on emotional outbursts and extreme, individualistic expressions of conversion and worship seemed to Federalists simply the latest among a whole slew of dangerous applications of democratic principles to American life. The Judge thus actively supported the establishment and growth of the orthodox denominations in Otsego County and believed as well that Episcopalianism in particular was a "genteel faith that would help polish the manners of his sons and enrich their cosmopolitan connections to the urban gentry," especially among the influential Episcopalians he associated with at the state capital, Albany.[32]

James was thus sent to an Anglican school in Albany, St. Peter's, before attending Yale, and he and his family's conservative (and later dogmatic) adherence to orthodox Episcopalianism had its roots in his early childhood. His daughter was thus raised in a climate that fostered as much reverence for the received teachings of the Episcopalian Church as it did hostility to anything that smacked of vulgar expressions of democracy or of unorthodox religious practice, especially practices that might violate established standards of social decorum. Her mother's people were from one of the most aristocratic regions in New York. As such they had inherited "Huguenot blood, the Dutch patroon system of land tenure, and American Tory political philosophy."[33] Educated in New York City and in Europe, Susan Fenimore Cooper was her father's daughter. Unlike William, who saw in religion merely a moral opiate for the vulgar masses, James was a devout and active member of his chosen church, especially in the last years of his life, including the period of *Rural Hours*'s publication. There are no indications Cooper broke with family doctrine at any point in her life.[34] Indeed, the frequent but gentle challenges to superstitious folk beliefs throughout *Rural Hours* should be seen as trace remainders of the spiritual upheavals of the period. Raised to consider herself part of the American elite, Cooper and her family would have had nothing but disdain for the revivalism of the period. The silence in the family record about the revivalism they could not have avoided encountering indicates not that they were unaware of what was going on regularly all over the county, the state, and the country but just how far beneath them they must have considered the religious fervor of the times.[35]

Most importantly, Cooper's adherence to orthodox Episcopalianism meant that in the face of revivalism the integrity of the Bible and so of proper biblical exegesis would have been crucial components of her personal beliefs. Adherence to received teachings about scripture as well as received principles for private exegesis—as opposed to mere individualistic, emotional expressions of conversion—set a good Episcopalian's religious practice off from the vulgar forms of worship going on elsewhere. Because it was anti-intellectual, revivalism and the sects closely associated with it during this period were completely unaffected if not unaware of the rise of historical-critical methods of biblical interpretation.[36] As my reading of the Book of Ruth sections will show, however, just the opposite was apparently the case with educated, orthodox Protestants like Susan Fenimore Cooper. Such persons would have been extremely receptive to "scientific" advances in hermeneutics and exegesis that could be used to combat the low-brow revivalist sects cavalcading across the country. As one historian of Protestantism has described it, "The foes of revivalism could do little to stop it. They could only stand as a corrective to it, reminding Christians that it was not the only nor the purest form that Christianity takes."[37]

At some point in her life, surely while living in Europe, Cooper was apparently exposed to Continental ideas about biblical exegesis, including historical-critical methodologies. One result of this was that she embraced a set of hermeneutic principles she enacted in her discussion of the Book of Ruth, providing both a model of rational piety for like-minded Protestants and a model of reading she expected her own audience to adopt in reading *Rural Hours*.

The discussion of the Book of Ruth comes in the entry for Monday, August 21. After quoting gleaning references from Leviticus and Deuteronomy, she immediately turns to a discussion of the biblical sources for gleaning—but not from a theological or thematic standpoint. Rather, her focus is on the Bible as an historical document. The following passage is worth quoting in full because it contains several important hallmarks of nineteenth-century biblical criticism and thus reads like a passage from a handbook for historical-critical exegesis:

> Whether a custom of this kind [gleaning] already prevailed in the ancient world before the days of Moses, we cannot determine. . . . Some of the precepts of the Mosaic code, however, are known to be merely a confirmation and repetition of those given still earlier, such as those which enjoin sacrifice and circumcision, &c., &c. Many others doubtless flowed first, at the period of the Exodus, from Almighty wisdom and mercy, like the raising of the tabernacle, the establishment of the Levitical Priesthood, &c., &c. The protection of the gleaner may have belonged to either class of precepts; but its minuteness partakes very much of the character of the Hebrew law, and it is quite possible that it may have been first inculcated from the lips of Moses in the wilderness.[38]

Here the issue is the origin of the tradition of gleaning. Cooper argues there is no earlier source than the Pentateuch (the first five books of the Old Testament, traditionally thought to have been written by Moses) and that there are thus two possibilities for the origin of this form of Judeo-Christian charity: either it was part of earlier Jewish law, and Moses merely included it when he put Jewish law into writing, or he included it after he was inspired by God to do so during the Exodus. From a secular, late-twentieth-century standpoint, such a debate may seem like counting angels on the head of a pin, but the issue for the present study is neither theological nor philosophical but hermeneutic, discovering thereby what Cooper's discussion of gleaning reveals about the type of reader she was of biblical narrative. What we discover is a reader (and writer) engaged in a discussion of the Pentateuch entirely along historical-critical lines.

Recall that two of the major hallmarks of this mode were that interpretation must be based on solid knowledge of the original documents—the language in which they were written, and the context in which they were composed—and that a reasonable explanation must be sought for every phenomenon. In this passage and throughout her discussion of the Book of Ruth, Cooper adheres closely to these tenets. The hermeneutic she thus adopts and enacts in her discussion can be defined as follows: reading is inference building, but it is a process that is always also informed by one's understanding of the historical context in which the text was constructed and thus by the related rules or conventions for interpreting the text in question. Accordingly, Cooper takes her reader through the story of Ruth, filling in the gaps in the narrative as her understanding of the text's historical context dictates. As a rational but pious antebellum reader of the source material, she believes that Moses was a mortal man inspired by God to write the first five books of the Bible. As a real, historical figure, he thus must have borrowed from older Jewish sources he would no doubt have been familiar with as a leader of his people. Her handling of this part of her discussion is thus classic in its commitment to both rationalism *and* to its underlying belief that all scripture is divinely inspired, a respected position among nineteenth-century historical-critical scholars.

As her reading continues, this hermeneutic manifests itself in primarily three ways: in her focus on the meaning of individual words, in her invocation of historical knowledge to construct inferences based on textual evidence, and in her refusal to project anachronistic ethical standards back onto the distant past. The first type of inference can be represented by her discussion of the differences between Ruth and Orpah and evidences Cooper's close attention to the language of her source material:

> Naomi again urges their leaving her: "Turn again, my daughters, why will ye go with me?" "And Orpah kissed her mother-in-law, but Ruth clave unto her." This is the first sentence that betrays the difference between the young women; both had been kind and dutiful to their husbands and mother-in-law, but now we see one turning back, and the other *cleaving* to the poor, and aged, and solitary widow. No positive blame is attached to Orpah, but from that instant we love Ruth. (*Rural Hours,* 161)

Here Cooper embellishes the description of Naomi by making several common-sense inferences ("poor, and aged, and solitary"), bringing into relief three facts about Naomi's condition entirely consistent with the textual record. Most noteworthy in this section is the focus on the word "clave" as evidence of Ruth's worthiness of the reader's admiration—a linguistic emphasis entirely in keeping with the historical criticism informing her reading. Cooper's handling of this aspect of the biblical text is thus from her viewpoint academic, revealing how committed she is to a reasoned understanding of her received religion.

The next type of historicized inference building in which Cooper engages involves invoking historical information about the period during which Ruth may have lived: "Doubtless, in those ancient times, the people all lived together in towns and villages for mutual protection, as they did in Europe during the middle ages—as they still do, indeed, to the present hour, in many countries where isolated cottages and farm-houses are rarely seen, the people going out every morning to the fields to work, and returning to the villages at night" (*Rural Hours,* 161). This seemingly obvious observation, as well as others like it—many of them quite detailed—are actually indications of the extent to which Cooper was steeped in the latest history and the latest methods of biblical exegesis. Archaeological digs in Palestine and other areas in the Middle East had a profound effect on biblical scholarship in the nineteenth century. Most serious scholars began the century doubting seriously whether an essentially nomadic tribe of primitive people could have reached a level of development by the time of Moses (then considered to be 1400–1200 B.C.E.) sophisticated enough to have supported complex writing and/or complex religio-mythic thought. But discoveries throughout the century about Babylon and Mesopotamian culture confirmed that just the opposite was true—so much so that eventually "a man like Abraham was no longer regarded as a primitive, half-civilized nomad, but as the inheritor of an ancient and highly developed Mesopotamian culture. A knowledge of writing and of law-making was [thus] seen as entirely compatible with an early dating of the patriarchal narratives" (*Biblical Interpretation,* 300). Cooper demonstrates early on in *Rural Hours* that she is familiar with these advances. Writing about whether the 137th Psalm is more accurately translated as depicting the Israelites hanging their harps on willows specifically or simply on trees, she writes:

> Another evidence that [a] kind of willow [gray osier] was formerly common on that ground [in Mesopotamia], is found in the ruins themselves. M. Beauchamp, in the account of his investigations of the remains of Babylon, during the last century, says: "The bricks are cemented with bitumen. Occasionally layers of oziers in bitumen are found." Other travellers speak of reeds also in the bitumen; so that the plant, and the tree, named by Sir R. Porter, as now found on the banks of the Euphrates . . . are thus proved, by the most clear and positive evidence, to have also existed there in ancient times. (*Rural Hours,* 32)

Here Cooper shows she is an astute and informed reader, deeply interested in language, in history, and in what other writers have to teach her and *her* readers about the complex relation between sacred and profane history as well as between truth and its representation in language.

Writing on the response to the influence of the scientific method on all facets of nineteenth-century religious life, historians have found that in this period there were essentially three responses by orthodox denominations to the challenges such influences posed for established religion: some groups embraced the findings of science and sought to modify traditional faith in drastic ways to compensate; a second class sought a middle ground, hoping that science and religion could eventually be reconciled; and a third class resisted the inroads of science strongly, insisting on the absolute validity of traditional orthodoxy.[39] Cooper's response places her in the second group, for in her view science clearly has much to contribute to religion and to orthodox belief. Given the then-ongoing debates about proper scriptural interpretation in the face of advances in science, her discussion of the Book of Ruth would have functioned rhetorically for other pious persons—especially those who considered themselves to be antirevivalist—as a model of rational piety. As a lay person, Cooper's familiarity with an historical-critical approach and with the archaeological and historical sources she quotes from throughout *Rural Hours* is unusual. Her adherence to historical-critical principles thus evidences an enlightened and undogmatic brand of orthodoxy. Although conservative, Cooper's discussion is at the same time a model for other persons interested in reconciling science with religion. And again, we are not interested in the viability of such an enterprise considered in the abstract but in how Cooper's membership in a specific community would have informed her reading practices and thus her understanding of the reading practices of *her* audience.

The final general type of historical inference building Cooper engages in is her refusal to read back into history an inappropriate standard of conduct. Discussing allegations by biblical commentators about Ruth's display of sexual modesty in presenting herself to Boaz, she writes:

> Upon this ground only, M. De Voltaire has not scrupled to apply to Ruth one
> of the most justly opprobrious words in human language. . . . As though in
> a state of society wholly simple and primitive, we were to judge of Ruth by the
> rules of propriety prevailing in the courts of Charles II. and Louis XV. Ruth
> and Boaz lived, indeed, among a race, and in an age, when not only the daily
> speech, but the daily life also, was highly figurative; when it was the great
> object of language and of action to give force and expression to the intention
> of the mind, instead of applying, as in a later, and a degenerate society, all

the powers of speech and action to concealing the real object in view. (*Rural Hours*, 163)

Appropriately (for an historical critic), Cooper claims here that Ruth's actions must be understood and judged according to the standards extant at the time of the story's narration and by no others. At first glance her concern for the integrity of Ruth's moral fiber might appear simply theological or perhaps merely the result of her pre-Victorian sense of decency. Regardless, it is at the same time a concern for the integrity of the textual source as an historical document and further evidences her consistent awareness of and commitment to her hermeneutic and thus to her rational orthodoxy.

It is important to emphasize, however, that Cooper's interest in providing a hermeneutic model for her readers was not driven by religious concerns alone. Indeed, at the end of her discussion of the Book of Ruth, two additional principles become manifest, revealing that her interests in history and in interpretation were not those of a mere pious dilettante but extended to a sophisticated concern with the authority of authors and with the textual power of readers.

From Voltaire's condemnation of Ruth, Cooper's focus turns to an almost polemic defense of a narrow conception of authorial intent and of its implications for the limits of audience response. Specifically, her handling of the Book of Ruth figures a hermeneutic model wherein readers are obliged to read no further into a text than allowed by both its historical context and its use of convention. Accordingly, there is no interpretation possible per se. Rather, the transaction among writer, reader, and text is strictly governed by the limits placed on the reader by convention. The inclusion of such a discussion in a supposed book of nature writing raises questions about its function in Cooper's rhetoric. As I am about to argue, the answers lie in seeing her concern with proper scriptural exegesis as a manifestation of her related concern for the proper exegesis of and thus proper response to *Rural Hours*. In effect, Cooper uses her discussion of Ruth to direct her reader not to read very far beyond anything implied directly by her book—an aspect of *Rural Hours* I will argue in my conclusion that has implications for our own twentieth-century work on Cooper's book.

Continuing to address Ruth's modesty in presenting herself to Boaz, Cooper writes: "the impartiality of the sacred biographers, from the first to the last books of the Holy Scriptures, is so very striking, so very peculiar to themselves . . . that reason alone requires us to receive each narrative simply as it is given. . . . The writer of the narrative has not, by one word, imputed sin to either. How dare the mind of the reader do so?" (*Rural Hours,* 164). The focus here is on the liberties readers like Voltaire might take in interpreting and responding to the text of the Book of Ruth and, as we have seen, is the result of both Cooper's religious background and her commitment to a specific method of exegesis. But her discussion reveals also a concern with how *her* audience might read and respond to *Rural Hours.* In effect, Cooper argues for a rather narrow conception of authorial intent and especially for a limited brand of audience textual power—"the writer of the narrative has not, by one word, imputed sin to either. How dare the mind of the reader do so?" Such a conception of the limits of audience response is an attempt to rein in the reader via a theory of language wherein the potential for language to signify—in effect, to oversignify and thus to become ambiguous—is controlled sharply by its context or by what speech theorists might call its illocutionary aspect.

Cooper continues this tack, concluding her discussion by noting:

> There are but three positions which the infidel can take upon the subject: he may, with the Christian, believe the Book of Ruth to be true, in which case he is bound to receive the facts as they are given; he may hold the narrative to be a compound of fiction and truth, and then plain justice requires that those points upon which the Scriptural writers have always shown such marked impartiality be charged to the side of truth . . . he may, lastly, declare the book to be, in his opinion, wholly fictitious; in this case he is bound, by common sense, to receive the narrative precisely as it is written, since it is a broad absurdity to judge fictitious characters otherwise than as they are represented. If he suppose one act or one view beyond what the writer presents or implies, he may as well sit down and compose an entire fabric of his own, and then the world will have one Book of Ruth in the Holy Bible, and another among the works of Mr. A., B., or C. (*Rural Hours,* 164)

In this passage Cooper lays out the three possible types of biblical audience in terms of the fact/fiction distinction, and although each audience's stance in regard to the truth content of the Bible is radically different, her claim is that in not one of them is the reader in a position to read beyond what is imputed by the text itself. How one determines what the text itself imputes is unclear, yet Cooper's point remains unambiguous: there are limits to proper reader response.

Although problematic in certain respects, especially given debates in literary studies over the last twenty years, Cooper's narrow conception of textual power and thus of the limits of audience response is not based on a simplistic understanding of the difference between literal and figurative discourse. Indeed, the hermeneutic she espouses based on her understanding of the difference between the two includes a rather modern version of the role of convention in reader response. Writing about Ruth's presentation of herself to Boaz, Cooper notes: "When Boaz found Ruth lying at his feet, he immediately understood the action as figurative. . . . Her whole answer is figurative, like the act. Spreading the skirt, or wing, was a common Hebrew phrase, implying protection, and it is said to be, to this day, a part of the Jewish marriage ceremony. Boaz well knew that the action and the words were intended to remind him of the law, that the 'near kinsman' should marry the widow" (*Rural Hours*, 164–65).

For Boaz, the key to reading and to interpreting Ruth's gesture appropriately rests in his recognition that her act is figurative as well as in his familiarity with the context in which that gesture is made. Because her audience is familiar with the conventions extant in Hebrew culture governing what are essentially figurative speech acts as well as with Hebrew laws pertaining to levirate marriage, Ruth's gesture, although figurative, clearly and unambiguously represents her intentions. Recognition and acceptance of the gesture's figural dimension thus unlocks its symbolic potential but along an established, almost preknown trajectory. There is thus no remainder in this transaction. As a result there is no ambiguity, very little room for interpretation, and thus no chance for miscommunication. The figurative is set off here from the literal by its indirectness but also by the conventions the audience—in this case Boaz—brings to the transaction. As such, the figurative does not result in indeterminability but in determinability within a specific frame of reference. As Rabinowitz has described it in more modern terms, reading for convention is "a matter of social convention rather than of individual psychology . . . [it is] the acceptance of the author's invitation to read in a particularly socially constituted way that is shared by the author and his or her expected readers."[40]

The implications of such an understanding of the limits of reader response for *Rural Hours* are primarily twofold. First, Cooper clearly hoped her reader would treat her book as she advocates treating the Book of Ruth, in effect asking her reader not to look too deeply into *Rural Hours*, because doing so will only lead to misinterpretation of either text or author or both. Second, this suggests that whatever larger ideational or rhetorical content the book includes is not hidden but on the surface. That is, Cooper's own hermeneutic, the interpretive grid she assumed readers would bring to her work, contradicts or at least complicates attempts to read beyond *Rural Hours*'s rather straight-forward use of available conventions. As Nina Baym has argued, the antebellum reader was not a "construer of meanings, interpreter of value systems, or supplier of bridges over gaps in signification. These concepts of reader behavior lay far in the future, and they imply a profoundly different kind of activity from that assumed" in the nineteenth century.[41] Accepting the tacit contract offered by *Rural Hours*'s use of available narrative modes thus meant accepting a limited active role in unlocking the work's virtual—borrowing Iser's term—dimension. And to be sure, Cooper's concerns in regard to just how far readers might go in reading and interpreting *Rural Hours* were entirely consistent with the conditions of authorship for the period.

Although stabilizing rapidly, professional authorship in 1850 was in a state of flux, and for women writers in particular becoming a professional writer meant assuming an especially complex relation to the reading public, sacrificing a certain degree of privacy, and thus exposing themselves to a degree of scrutiny that required women writers to protect themselves from possible attacks on their propriety and modesty (among other things).[42] Publishing *Rural Hours* with a frontispiece indicating that it was written by "A Lady" shrouded its author behind a discreet veil of anonymity but at the same time signaled unambiguously that the figure behind the veil was a genteel and respectable member of the middle class. The work of Zboray and Zboray indicates that Cooper's concern with how readers would perceive an author, especially in regard to the extent to which she would be held accountable for the content of her books, was well founded. Antebellum readers did not accept the twentieth-century distinction between implied authors and flesh-and-blood writers, except in the case of what critics called "fictional autobiography."[43] By this term they meant first-person narration narrated by a character in the fictional world, or what in more precise terms we might call a homodiegetic narrator. Any other type of book, and certainly all nonfiction, was considered by readers to reflect the ideas and values of its author. This meant that readers' response to a text was heavily influenced by the image of the author they constructed in light of what they read. Readability, length, verisimilitude, diction—all of these determined readers' evaluation (positive or negative) of a book and thus of its author: "In discussing the text, readers could pass judgment not only upon the author's ability to render an experience believable but upon the writer's integrity as well. By making themselves the arbiters of truth and falsehood, these readers empowered themselves."[44] Indeed, Zboray and Zboray found that readers would at times exert their textual power by emphasizing an author's personality over the text that author wrote and that curiosity over the private lives and personalities of writers could take precedence over discussion of the content of the works themselves. Finally, two important characteristics readers looked for were pedagogical value and practical application. For example, most readers "spoke in terms of moral benefits or religious uplift upon finishing a text."[45]

As a relatively new professional writer but an astute antebellum reader, Cooper was well aware that her own character would become an issue if her work did not provide the moral uplift or pedagogical value readers expected. The inclusion of the sections on the Book of Ruth as well as the other "digressions" in the book can thus be seen as having been included in order to complement the book's detailed observations of rural life and of nature, giving it the moral and pedagogical use-value readers sought in nonfiction. Accordingly, such discussions are not digressions so much as important moments when the author was able to move from discussions of nature and rural life to discussions of the sort of religious and pedagogical issues readers expected. Writing about the reading habits of women in England from 1837 to 1914, Kate Flint has shown that young women, especially during the first decades of the period in question, were expected to read the Bible "carefully and thoughtfully." Indeed, warnings abounded against "uncritical acceptance of no matter what form of Christian writing." As she puts it, "The lessons offered, particularly in the New Testament, set down the moral foundation by which all other forms of reading might be judged or interrogated."[46]

Biblical hermeneutics thus functioned as models of general audience interpretation and response, something Cooper could count on in making her reading of Ruth a model of both rational piety and respectful—for the author—exegesis. Like other antebellum readers, she believed that the truth content of a book—its moral, pedagogical, and thus practical value—were what separated great works from those that merely obscured "the real object in view." The concerns she addresses through her handling of the Book of Ruth are thus those of a nineteenth-century woman writer whose education, worldliness, and sophisticated understanding of hermeneutics and language combined to reveal to her that there was more at stake in what her readers decided to make of *Rural Hours* than mere profit. As such, she included an explicit discussion of the limits of proper reader response, in effect cajoling her reader not to read too far into her own gentle observations of life in and around Cooperstown. Although problematic (perhaps), Cooper's reading of the Book of Ruth also places her reader in an especially complex and illuminating position regarding the relations among authors, readers, conventions, and meaning.

Finally, Cooper's shift from an historical-critical discussion of the Book of Ruth to a discussion of authorship and of the limits of audience response forces us to examine her discussion of language and interpretation in relation to other midcentury discussions of authorship, of language, and of the distinction between literal and figurative discourse. Specifically, Cooper's ideas about convention and its role in reader response need to be considered in light of the then-ongoing effort by antebellum American writers and thinkers to respond to the general crisis in language engendered by European intellectuals, language theorists, and biblical critics.[47]

Debates about language and about biblical exegesis in the antebellum United States were so interdependent in this period that it is impossible as well as historically inaccurate to treat them as separate concerns. Schematically, European language theorists and biblical scholars in the first part of the century forced American intellectuals to recognize that the relation between words and things was not as stable as was once thought. This in turn influenced American theologians as well as American writers to confront established notions about writing, meaning, and interpretation in an effort to reconnect language to the world it was meant to describe. For example, Emerson's notion of a spiritual link between words and things, which he first described in the language section of *Nature,* is only one of many such efforts by American thinkers to arrive at a theory of language that could preserve the power of language to discover and to represent truth.

Further, as Philip Gura has shown, the work of such figures was "conducted almost solely with reference to [its] implications for Protestant theology."[48] That is, the dominant paradigm (at least in the United States) informing the work on language by such figures as Emerson, Thoreau, and Rowland Gibson Harder, whose *Language: Its Connexion with the Present Condition and Future Prospects of Man* was published in the same year as *Nature* (1836), was theological and Protestant and not strictly linguistic and philosophical. Gura argues that as a result it was figures like Horace Bushnell and Alexander Bryan Johnson and not Kant and Hegel who had the greatest impact on antebellum American theories of language, writing, and interpretation, forcing Americans and European Romantics alike to embrace "a new 'paradigm' for the organization of knowledge, one within which writers of the American Renaissance could express the multiplicity which had come to characterize their moral and intellectual universe."[49] Johnson and Bushnell thus represent the two poles between which midcentury writers formulated their responses to this crisis. Johnson believed that man must return to nature as the standard by which the meaning of words were to be judged, arguing for a strict correspondence between words and things. His intensely empirical theory of language stressed the empirical verification of the words men used and was a direct influence on the correspondence theories of language of both Emerson and Thoreau. Bushnell went in a completely different direction, arguing instead that language's very ambiguity gave it its power to represent truth. In Bushnell's words, "[W]e never come so near to a truly well-rounded view of any truth as when it is offered paradoxically; that is, under contradiction; that is, under two or more dictions, which taken as dictions, are contrary one to the other." [50]

Cooper's account of the relation between literal and figurative discourse should thus be seen as a compelling compromise between these two poles and one that prefigures more modern conceptions of the role of convention in shaping how readers construct meanings out of their experiences of the books they read. As someone who would have been very uncomfortable with the radical sort of ambiguity and thus threatened indeterminability Bushnell's position allowed for, Cooper argues implicitly for an awareness of the role of convention and thus of genre in both reading and interpretation. Just as Boaz, who, by virtue of his knowledge of the conventions of levirate marriage and of Hebrew culture, is able to accurately read Ruth's actions, so too are readers able to read the Book of Ruth appropriately once they arrive at an understanding of the text's historical context and of the conventions for reading that go along with it. Cooper's position in the antebellum debates about language and interpretation represented in her reading of the Book of Ruth thus presages the emphasis on convention espoused by late-twentieth-century rhetorical critics responding to poststructuralist claims about the inherent indeterminability of texts both figurative and literal. As a nineteenth-century woman steeped in the issues and discourse that prompted the sudden flowering of American literature in the period, Cooper was thus an individual both representative in many ways of her historical moment and at the same time unique—a model, enlightened member of an essentially conservative denomination who in her discussion of the Book of Ruth participated in two of the major theoretical debates of the period—the crisis in language as well as the resulting crisis in biblical hermeneutics and exegesis.

Reading practices and genre conventions are always also historically specific, yet as Machor has observed, many critics often bracket this fact and instead produce readings that merely "privilege the critic's own response by positing themselves as the ideal readers of the text(s) in question."[51] For example, the tendency among critics of recovered authors in particular is often to search for a subversive rhetorical or narrative strategy that demonstrates the author's importance based on his or her capacity for social, political, or ideological criticism. Yet in ignoring the work's historical hermeneutics, the critic often reveals merely his or her own late-twentieth-century critical interests rather than the equally significant ideological implications of the writer's own rhetoric, especially as seen from a properly historical perspective.

My contribution to our collective understanding of Cooper's work should be seen as a gentle corrective to any such work on *Rural Hours*. As critics and teachers we understand that readers will exercise their textual power in a variety of ways, often with quite compelling results. What I hope my discussion has shown, however, is that equally compelling are those readings that attempt simply to recover the readings available to readers and writers from the text's own period. William Charvat argued that "literary history has been much too busy trying to prove that past writers shouted loud enough to be heard by posterity. We should be more interested in knowing how far their voices carried in their own generation."[52] In Cooper's case, I have attempted to show just how far she hoped her own voice would carry—and then stop. This does not mean we should not continue to investigate either how far her voice might have continued to carry for antebellum readers, in spite of her best efforts to limit their responses, or how her voice continues to carry for ourselves; rather, the study of the historical hermeneutics of *Rural Hours* should be seen as an effort to establish compelling starting points for further building a vital community of readers of Susan Fenimore Cooper's work. In short, readings like mine are not meant as ends in themselves but as starting points for the further exercise of our individual and collective textual power. The results, I think, will be that we will continue to discover the different ways in which Susan Fenimore Cooper was an exceptional woman writer, but an exceptional woman writer very much of her time.

NOTES

1. James Franklin Beard, ed., *The Letters and Journals of James Fenimore Cooper,* 6 vols. (Cambridge, Mass.: Harvard University Press, 1960–68), 6:151.

2. See Nina Baym, *Novels, Readers and Reviewers: Responses to Fiction in Antebellum America* (Ithaca, N.Y.: Cornell University Press, 1984), esp. 13–25, 196–224.

3. Beard, ed., *Letters and Journals*, 6:156.

4. Rochelle Johnson and Daniel Patterson, introduction to Susan Fenimore Cooper, *Rural Hours*, ed. Rochelle Johnson and Daniel Patterson (Athens: University of Georgia Press, 1998), xi.

5. This is not at all to suggest that Cooper's purposes are not recoverable or that the book lacks cohesion as a result. It is merely to argue that recovering an historical understanding of the book's production and reception requires avoiding a hermeneutic framework that does not account for this fundamental component of the book and its horizon of expectations.

6. See, among others, Thomas Kent, *Interpretation and Genre: The Role of Generic Perception in the Study of Narrative Texts* (Lewisburg: Bucknell University Press, 1986); Peter J. Rabinowitz, *Narrative Conventions and the Politics of Interpretation* (Ithaca, N.Y.: Cornell University Press, 1987); and James Phelan, *Reading People, Reading Plots: Character, Progression, and the Interpretation of Narrative* (Chicago: University of Chicago Press, 1989).

7. See Baym, *Novels, Readers and Reviewers*, 196–223; Sheila Post-Lauria, *Correspondent Colorings: Melville in the Marketplace* (Amherst: University of Massachusetts Press, 1996); and James L. Machor, ed., *Readers in History: Nineteenth-Century American Literature and the Contexts of Response* (Baltimore, Md.: Johns Hopkins University Press, 1993), 54–84.

8. Wolfgang Iser, *The Implied Reader: Patterns of Communication in Prose Fiction from Bunyan to Beckett* (Baltimore, Md.: Johns Hopkins University Press, 1974), 279.

9. Rabinowitz, *Narrative Conventions*, 27.

10. By *appropriately*, I do not mean determining authorial intent. As critics from Booth to Rabinowitz have made clear, at least in regard to reading fiction, what we might loosely call "reading for convention" is in fact "a matter of social convention rather than of individual psychology. . . . [It is] the acceptance of the author's invitation to read in a particularly socially constituted way that is shared by the author and his or her expected readers" (ibid., 22).

11. Ronald J. Zboray and Mary Saracino Zboray, "'Have You Read . . . ?': Real Readers and Their Responses in Antebellum Boston and Its Region," *Nineteenth-Century Literature* 52 (1997): 143.

12. See ibid. as well as Baym, *Novels, Readers and Reviewers*.

13. Cathy Davidson, *Revolution and the Word: The Rise of the Novel in America* (New York: Oxford University Press, 1986), 4. For a strictly narratological

approach to reconstructing such grids, see Susan Stanford Friedman, "Spatialization: A Strategy for Reading Narrative," *Narrative* 1 (1993): 12–23.

14. See Robert Scholes, *Textual Power: Literary Theory and the Teaching of English* (New Haven, Conn.: Yale University Press, 1985).

15. David Jones, introduction to *Rural Hours* by Susan Fenimore Cooper (Syracuse, N.Y.: Syracuse University Press, 1968), xi.

16. Johnson and Patterson, introduction, ix.

17. Ibid., xvi.

18. Machor, "Historical Hermeneutics and Antebellum Fiction," in Machor, ed., *Readers in History*, 60.

19. Ibid., 61.

20. The opportunities for investigating Cooper's handling of Ruth from a thematic perspective, especially given recent work on gendered and feminist readings in particular, are great. The Book of Ruth is a story about women, told from a woman's point of view, and possibly written by a woman, at least in its earliest versions. As Nancy M. Tischler has remarked recently, women in the Bible "seldom serve as more than accessories to the men, who are the main event" ("Ruth," in *A Complete Literary Guide to the Bible,* ed. Leland Ryken and Tremper Longman [Grand Rapids: Zondervan Publishing House, 1993], 157). The Book of Ruth breaks with these conventions of both early Hebrew literature and scriptural narrative and is thus highly atypical. It is hardly surprising, then, that recent work by feminist readers, including biblical scholars and secular literary critics, has made much of the rich potential for thematic signification and thus thematic criticism that Ruth's story holds. See Athalya Brenner, ed., *A Feminist Companion to Ruth* (Sheffield: Sheffield Academic Press, 1993); Phyllis Trible, "A Human Comedy: The Book of Ruth," in *Literary Interpretations of Biblical Narratives,* ed. Kenneth R. R. Gros Louis et al., 2 vols. (Nashville: Abingdon, 1974), 2:161–90, and *God and the Rhetoric of Sexuality* (Philadelphia: Fortress Press, 1978); and Edward F. Campbell's introduction to Ruth in the Anchor Bible, 45 vols. (New York: Doubleday, 1975), 7:1–42. The issue of Ruth's authorship is highly contentious. See foremost Adrien J. Bledstein, "Female Companionships: If the Book of Ruth Were Written by a Woman," in Brenner, ed., *A Feminist Companion to Ruth,* 116–32; and Fokkelien van Dijk-Hemmes, "Ruth: A Product of Women's Culture?" in ibid., 134–39.

21. Gerald Bray, *Biblical Interpretation: Past and Present* (Downers Grove, Ill.: InterVarsity Press, 1996), 196. Hereafter cited in text. I rely heavily on Bray throughout my discussion for my account of the history of biblical exegesis.

22. In many ways, these debates were simply between literalist and figurativist interpretations of the Bible. But as we shall see, the roots of Cooper's biblical her-

meneutics extended beyond simple debates about whether, for example, Jonah was really swallowed by a whale. One result was that Cooper adopted a rather complex position in relation to available modes of reading and of interpreting both the Bible and secular writing.

23. See Jerald C. Brauer, *Protestantism in America: A Narrative History,* rev. ed. (Philadelphia: Westminster Press, 1965); Charles H. Lippy, *Being Religious, American Style: A History of Popular Religiosity in the United States* (Westport, Conn.: Praeger, 1994); William A. Clebsch, *American Religious Thought: A History* (Chicago: University of Chicago Press, 1973); George C. Bedell et al., *Religion in America* (New York: Macmillan, 1975).

24. Brauer, *Protestantism in America,* 111.

25. See ibid., but especially Whitney R. Cross, *The Burned-Over District: The Social and Intellectual History of Enthusiastic Religion in Western New York, 1800–1850* (Ithaca, N.Y.: Cornell University Press, 1950).

26. Cross, *The Burned-Over District,* 8.

27. See ibid., 287–321. Interestingly, Finney had extremely close ties with Otsego's Episcopalian minister, Daniel Nash—the same Nash who had presided over Hannah Cooper's funeral in 1800 and later convinced Cooper's grandfather William to finance the construction of Christ Church, which was built adjacent to Otsego Hall in Cooperstown. See Alan Taylor, *William Cooper's Town: Power and Persuasion on the Frontier of the Early American Republic* (New York: Vintage, 1995), esp. 309, 349–50.

28. See especially Brauer, *Protestantism in America.*

29. Cross, *The Burned-Over District,* 67.

30. Bedell et al., *Religion in America,* 221.

31. Taylor, *William Cooper's Town,* 348–51.

32. Ibid., 350. As James Fenimore Cooper's biographer, Robert E. Spiller, describes William, "Judge Cooper, in spite of his Quaker heritage, apparently early adopted the view of the New York aristocracy that there might be ways of getting into heaven other than that of the Church of England, but that no gentleman would choose any of them" (*Fenimore Cooper: Critic of His Times* [New York: Russell and Russell, 1963], 30).

33. Spiller, *Fenimore Cooper,* 61.

34. Her nephew James's comments that at a very late age she had acquired psychic powers but gave them up for religious reasons are the only evidence we have that she ever moved very far beyond received, orthodox, Episcopalian religious practice (Jones, introduction, xv). Yet in light of both her exposure to revivalism and her devout adherence to Episcopalian orthodoxy, this odd quirk of late old age is actually quite understandable. As Brauer notes, "Throughout the

'burned-over' revival districts where various revivals had come and gone, strange beliefs persisted. Some men believed they had special powers of prophecy. Others had sticks they called divining rods with which they supposedly located lost treasures or received divine revelations" (*Protestantism in America*, 160).

35. Interestingly, Cross indicates the period from 1825 to 1837 as the peak of revivalism in the burned-over district. This period includes, of course, the Coopers' residence in Europe, indicating not only that they may have missed out on some but not all of what went on but raising questions about the extent to which revivalism may have contributed to their desire to leave the country.

36. As Brauer notes, "There was little intellectual side to their [the revivalists'] faith because there was little intellectual life on the frontier. There was much theological disputation but little arbitration in terms of doctrinal consistency or proper biblical exegesis" (*Protestantism in America*, 113).

37. Ibid., 123.

38. Susan Fenimore Cooper, *Rural Hours,* ed. Rochelle Johnson and Daniel Patterson (Athens: University of Georgia Press, 1998), 159–60. Hereafter cited in text.

39. See especially Bedell et al., *Religion in America*, 207–10, 223–51.

40. Rabinowitz, *Narrative Conventions*, 22.

41. Baym, *Novels, Readers and Reviewers,* 63.

42. See Mary Kelley's *Private Woman, Public Stage: Literary Domesticity in Nineteenth-Century America* (New York: Oxford University Press, 1984), esp. 111–37.

43. See Baym, *Novels, Readers and Reviewers,* 146–48.

44. Zboray and Zboray, "Real Readers," 153.

45. Ibid., 162.

46. Kate Flint, *The Woman Reader: 1837–1914* (Oxford: Clarendon Press, 1993), 80.

47. See Bray, *Biblical Interpretation,* and especially Philip F. Gura, "Language and Meaning: An American Tradition," *American Literature* 53 (1981): 1–21.

48. Gura, "Language and Meaning," 2.

49. Ibid.

50. H. Shelton Smith, ed., *Horace Bushnell* (New York: Oxford University Press, 1965), 103.

51. Machor, "Introduction: Readers/Texts/Context," in Machor, ed., *Readers in History,* vii.

52. William Charvat, "Literary Economics and Literary History," in *The Profession of Authorship in America, 1800–1870,* ed. Matthew J. Bruccoli (New York: Columbia University Press, 1992), 283–84.

A Farther Progress:
Reconciling Visions of Time in
Susan Fenimore Cooper's *Rural Hours*

This fresh green hue of the country is very charming, and with us
it is very fugitive, soon passing away into the warmer coloring of
midsummer. . . .

But allowing even that hundreds of years hence other trees were at
length to succeed these with the same dignity of height and age, no
other younger wood can ever claim the same connection as this, with
a state of things now passed away forever.

SUSAN FENIMORE COOPER, *Rural Hours*

In *Rural Hours,* Susan Fenimore Cooper presents what she
calls in her preface "the simple record of those little events which make up
the course of the seasons in rural life."[1] She shapes her narrative around
the seasonal changes in Cooperstown, New York, and its natural environs
over the course of one year. As Cooper watches one season pass into the
next, she discusses the changes in the land that have occurred in her lifetime and that are harbingers of the end of a way of life that is passing away
before her eyes. These changes represent a shift in the human perception
of time and the actions that are shaped by that perception.

Cooper focuses her narrative around three ways of perceiving time that
profoundly impact the natural environment. The first—a cyclical, seasonal view of time—involves human interaction with nature on nature's
own terms. Cultivation, plowing, planting, and reaping all occur within a
cyclical, natural pattern that shapes the relationship between humans and
the land as in, for instance, farming. This is the world Cooper sees slowly
slipping away as development of the landscape diminishes the agrarian,
rural world.

In contrast to the perception of time as a seasonal cycle, the second way
of perceiving time promotes development and progress—it is a genera-

tional time that advances a linear approach to time framed in strictly human terms. This view allows for abuses of the land, since the human perspective is the only frame of reference. Cooper sees the depletion of natural resources as a result of the break with the cyclical patterns of nature—the circle is broken; that which is taken is not restored. Ultimately, as a reconciliation of these conflicting views of time, Cooper proposes yet a third view of time that she calls a "farther progress" by which humans can learn to prevent or mitigate harm to the environment. While she recognizes that development of the land is inevitable, Cooper argues that Americans must begin to see that their residence in the land comes hand in hand with responsibility toward the land in the form of preservation—a learned behavior acquired over the course of time: "But time is a very essential element, absolutely indispensable, indeed, in true civilization; and in the course of years we shall, it is to be hoped, learn farther lessons of this kind" (*Rural Hours*, 133). These visions of time are central to Cooper's narrative and critical to any understanding of Cooper's predicament of being caught between two worlds with opposing values. They illuminate this conflict and allow us to understand the impact of the changes she witnesses in her region.

An effective way to discuss Cooper's presentation of these different perceptions of time is through Mikhail Bakhtin's concept of "chronotopes." A chronotope is an individual's conception of time and space—or, in effect, how one perceives time and acts according to this perception. Bakhtin uses chronotopes to discuss fiction, as have most critics, where the characters' perceptions of time direct their actions and shape the plot of the novel.[2] Although chronotopes have been used primarily to discuss fiction, they provide a practical language through which to explore nonfiction and, in this case, nature writing. Cooper's chronotopes emplot her narrative as she perceives and portrays the changes in her natural landscape. In Cooper's narrative, we see three chronotopes: seasonal time, which is cyclical and based on natural patterns; human time, which views progress as development of the land; and Cooper's proposal for a farther progress, which identifies the need for preservation within the context of development.

Cooper's chronotopes of the seasons and of progress correlate to those in Bakhtin's "Forms of Time and Chronotopes in the Novel," although each writer gives importance to a different vision of time. Cooper's view of seasonal time is represented in Bakhtin by what he calls "folkloric time," in which human life and the natural world are inextricably bound together: "The agricultural life of men and the life of nature (of the earth) are measured by one and the same scale, by the same events."[3] This view of time, which is present in the idyll, is cyclical and similar to the seasonal cycle of Cooper's narrative. Whereas Bakhtin critiques the cyclical aspect of folkloric time as "one that limits the force and ideological productivity of this time,"[4] Cooper privileges the seasonal with its cyclical aspect. According to Bakhtin, cyclicity retards growth. What Bakhtin perceives as a trap, however, Cooper sees as positive.

Similar to Cooper's perception of progress in human terms, Bakhtin presents individual time as a break with the communal/cyclical view of life; instead of portraying death and rebirth, it presents a more linear approach to life, one in which death is seen as a finality. Simultaneously, historical time, which is separate from but parallel to individual time, concerns itself with the life of the state, government, humanity. Individual and historical time are both examples of the linear temporal thinking that Cooper represents as destructive.

Cooper implicitly critiques the idea that cyclical chronotopes are limiting in scope and less desirable than other perceptions of time as she presents the world she inhabits as tied to the seasons. In the sections that follow, I will examine Cooper's opposition of cyclical and linear chronotopes and trace her creation of a chronotope designed to accommodate a future in which humans preserve their natural surroundings and take responsibility for their actions toward the land.

Seasonal Time

From her family home in Cooperstown, New York, Cooper recorded for posterity the daily changes in her natural environment and her musings about these changes. As spring unfolds into summer and summer passes into autumn, which gives way to winter, Cooper narrates the transformation of the land from one season to the next, and, in doing so, she promotes a cyclical, seasonal view of time upon which her narrative is based. When the "green hue of the country" passes into the "warmer coloring of midsummer," and the return of one season signals the end of another, Cooper anticipates these changes and relishes them, always emphasizing that the death of the one means the rebirth of the other in a perpetually repeating pattern (*Rural Hours,* 59). Natural time is viewed as a cycle, and the change of the seasons occurs in a cyclical pattern in which all of nature participates. Nature, itself, provides a structure and a source for Cooper's narrative. She frequently points to cyclical/seasonal changes in the land and uses them as a contrast to the human changes that are acting, within her lifetime, to alter the landscape of her region.

By creating a narrative that follows the change of the seasons, spanning one year in the life of Cooperstown and its natural environs, Cooper is able to make powerful statements about place and change. In her place-based narrative, Cooper presents intimate details about her region. She gives her readers a thorough description of the landscape she encounters, including the folklore and the natural history of the region. This is no abstract discussion of what could happen "somewhere"; Cooper presents a concrete picture of one place that is slowly being altered through development. The fact that this development was mirrored in other places—as, for example, the railroad began its stretch across the continent—makes Cooper's narrative all the more powerful in its identification of specific changes in a distinct place that are representative of a larger shift.

It is important to point out that Cooper's contrasting views of time do not dichotomize development and wilderness. Instead, Cooper prizes the agrarian, "middle" landscape, what Leo Marx calls the pastoral ideal, which is located in "a middle ground somewhere 'between,' yet in a transcendent relation to, the opposing forces of civilization and nature."[5] Marx's middle landscape is an agrarian space—a land that has been cultivated. Similarly, Bakhtin's folkloric time emphasizes the collective cultivation of the land.

Just as Bakhtin's folkloric time is inextricably tied to the land, Cooper's seasonal view of time derives from and responds to her local natural environment.[6] It is a time that is *profoundly spatial and concrete* (emphasis in the original).[7] Cooper grounds her narrative on her passion for her local, natural environment, and she favors a sense of time—a chronotope—that harks back to the folkloric time Bakhtin describes. Cooper's narrative is driven by her ties to her local landscape as she proposes her ideal, both aesthetic and ecological, landscape. Her privileging of the rural, agrarian life that is being compromised stems in part from her place in time on the cusp of industrial activities and development that will forever alter the world she knows. The world Cooper inhabits shapes her view of nature and time, which is central to the narrative she produces.

Cooper possesses not only a sense of place developed through interaction with her local landscape but also a sense of time that is cyclical and tied to the seasons. The structure of Cooper's narrative reflects the chronotope of cyclical time. Although the entries for *Rural Hours* were gleaned from journal entries from two years, Cooper crafts them into a narrative that reflects one year in the life of Cooperstown and environs. The shaping of her narrative to fit into the pattern of four seasons points not only to the constructedness of her book but also to the importance seasonal continuity had to Cooper's argument as she emphasizes the cycle of death and rebirth and the constancy of nature. In her "Spring" section, Cooper writes about the dying of the winter: "The withered leaves of last autumn are whirling, and flying over the blighted grass of the lawns, and about the roots of the naked trees—a dance of death, as it were, in honor of winter as he passes away" (*Rural Hours*, 9). As Cooper describes the passing of one season into the next, she also emphasizes the idea of return—of the rebirth of one in the death of the other. As the seasons change, they also bring back former experiences with the natural world, underlining the constancy of nature. In a journal entry for Thursday, April 27, Cooper writes,

> How pleasant it is to meet the same flowers year after year! If the blossoms were liable to change—if they were to become capricious and irregular—they might excite more surprise, more curiosity, but we should love them less; they might be just as bright, and gay, and fragrant under other forms, but they would not be the violets, and squirrel-cups, and ground laurels we loved last year. Whatever your roving fancies may say, there is a virtue in constancy which has a reward above all that fickle change can bestow, giving strength and purity to every affection of life, and even throwing additional grace about the flowers which bloom in our native fields. (*Rural Hours*, 29)

Although the unusual in nature may delight or surprise, it is the constant elements that bring true joy to the observer. Later, in Cooper's section on autumn, she again finds the same patterns of seasonal change in her local environment: "Every year, as the foliage falls, and the trees reappear in their wintry form, the eye wonders a while at the change, just as we look twice ere we make sure of our acquaintance in the streets, when they vary their wardrobe with the season" (*Rural Hours*, 231). Seasonal changes in the landscape can be surprising at first and yet also familiar; trees clothe themselves in different attire as do their human neighbors in response to the seasons.

While she does portray her life as bound to a local sense of place and season, Cooper nostalgically responds to the chronotope of an agrarian, preindustrial past. Even as she favors the seasonal time within which she lives, she also reflects back on what she considers a more idyllic past when the ways in which people actually experienced nature were most important. Nature was understood through personal experience unmediated by scientific discourse. In her discussion of the scientific naming of plants, Cooper expresses disdain for what she perceives as a ridiculous practice of giving plants Latinate scientific names:

> They are all found in botanical works under long, clumsy, Latin appellations, very little fitted for every-day uses, just like the plants of our gardens, half of which are only known by long-winded Latin polysyllables, which timid people are afraid to pronounce. But, annoying as this is in the garden, it is still worse in the fields. What has a dead language to do on every-day occasions with the living blossoms of the hour? Why should a strange tongue sputter its un-couth, compound syllables upon the simple weeds by the way-side? (*Rural Hours*, 83)

Cooper admits that if these names were confined to the pages of scientific works, she would accept their use. However, she laments the common use of such names as "Batschia, Schoberia, Buchnera, Goodyera, Brugmannsia, Heuchera, Scheuzeria, Schizanthus" (*Rural Hours*, 85). Her indignation at what she feels are ridiculous naming practices causes her to recall a simpler time: "Before people were overflowing with science—at a time when there was some simplicity left in the world, the flowers received much better treatment in this way. Pretty, natural names were given them in olden times, as though they had been called over by some rural party—cherry-cheeked maidens, and merry-hearted lads—gone a-Maying, of a pleasant spring morning" (*Rural Hours*, 83–84). This older practice of naming was tied to the way people actually experienced the plant. For instance, according to Cooper, "spicy gilliflowers, a corruption of July-flowers, [were named] from the month in which they blossomed" (*Rural Hours*, 84). The old names echo an unmediated experience with the natural world that contrasts with an ordered scientific taxonomy—instead of being told what to call a plant, people derive the name of the plant from their own interactions with it. Cooper's valuing of the older forms of interaction with nature reflects her desire to preserve the simplicity of rural, agrarian life—a life lived close to nature—that is fading before her eyes.

In this as in other instances, Cooper also emphasizes that in order to truly know and understand the nature of a region, one must get outside and experience it for oneself. To know a region is to experience it first-hand—to inhabit the time and place or chronotope of a particular place. Cooper is concerned with promoting a landscape aesthetic that praises these older ways of interacting with the landscape, even as she understands that encroaching development will alter this landscape. Writing during the mid-1800s, Cooper is situated between this older, agrarian world with its focus on the seasonal and a new world that views progress as forward movement—as taking from the land and moving on when the land stops giving back.

The Progress of Human Time

As Cooper promotes a cyclical chronotope based on season changes, she laments the coming of "progress," which alters the land through depletion and extinction of local flora and fauna and drives the Native Americans out of their former home. In contrast to natural time, the human or generational conception of time results in abuse of the land because it does not account for continued inhabitancy of one place.[8] In one, there is always the promise of return; in the other, the finality of death or extinction thwarts naturally occurring cycles. Because Cooper is focused on her specific region and its ecological health, she sees the destructive tendencies of development on her local landscape. She recognizes changes in the landscape in her own lifetime, as she also speculates about the past and the future. Loss of types of flora, particularly trees, greatly concerns Cooper as she explores her landscape on daily walks. She also names and discusses the animals that have been driven from her region. Cooper contrasts the change of the seasons and the migration of animals, which are based on cyclical patterns, with abuse of the land such as the depletion of the forests—a type of use that takes away but does not replenish. Cooper conflates the plight of Native Americans with that of the land as she examines how they have disappeared from lands they once freely roamed. She imaginatively depicts the past as she "daydreams" about the role the Native American once played in the landscape.

In the mid–nineteenth century, as Americans moved into what was once a wilderness, they changed the landscape—sometimes irrevocably. Cooper records these changes as she examines the ways her local environment has been damaged. She views the older trees still standing as spectators to the changes in the land: "And throughout every act of the work, those old pines were there. Unchanged themselves, they stand surrounded by objects over all of which a great change has passed" (*Rural Hours*, 118). The old pine trees have watched the land being transformed as its inhabitants have changed. Cooper imaginatively portrays the possible ramifications of future destruction of the landscape. Cooper understands the magnitude of the changes around her as she describes what may be lost in the felling of old trees: "But allowing even that hundreds of years hence other trees were at length to succeed these with the same dignity of height and age, no other younger wood can ever claim the same connection as this, with a state of things now passed away forever; they cannot have that wild, stern character of the aged forest pines" (*Rural Hours,* 120). The old trees are connected with a time and landscape that is gone and cannot be regained. They are important to Cooper's argument against uncontained development, as their destruction represents the death of a chronotope that unites humans with the natural world. Cooper presents the felling of these trees as one of the gravest dangers of development because it indicates a mindset that does not take responsibility for the land. If the trees were destroyed, there would be no record of this earlier time, and it would take centuries to replace them. But more importantly, if the trees, which inspire awe in Cooper for having stood for hundreds of years in the region, are destroyed, then what is to stop development from encroaching on the entire region and altering it irreversibly? The felling of these trees represents not only an actual occurrence but a shift in mindset about time and the value of the natural world.

Just as Cooper sees the old trees as witnesses to the past, she portrays the Native American as a spectator to the changes in the land and a representative of the old world that is passing away. Cooper conflates Native Americans with the natural environment as she examines white attempts to "civilize" them and their movement out of the area and away from "civilization." On one of her many walks, Cooper comes upon a spring where she imagines the Native American in an earlier time: "When standing beside these unfettered springs in the shady wood, one seems naturally to remember the red man; recollections of his vanished race linger there in a more definite form than elsewhere; we feel assured that by every fountain among these hills, the Indian brave, on the hunt or the war-path, must have knelt ten thousand times, to slake his thirst" (*Rural Hours,* 57). Cooper must recall the "ghost" of the Native American, which is still felt among the springs in the "shady wood," because he no longer physically inhabits this place. Cooper portrays the Native American as an element of the scenic landscape much like the old trees she admires. She does not recognize the Native Americans' impact upon the land, nor does she see their habitation of the land as indicative of its age, because the native people are a part of the landscape: "In the first years of cultivation, they [pine stumps] are a very great blemish, but after a while, when most of them have been burnt or uprooted, a gray stump here and there, among the grass of a smooth field, does not look so very much amiss, reminding one, as it does, of the brief history of the country" (*Rural Hours,* 90). Throughout her narrative, Cooper frequently refers to "uncultivated land" or "recent cultivation" as well as to the "new country" and the "brief history of the country." Cooper ignores Native Americans' cultivation of the land and the ways they interact with the natural world as well as the history of these people in this land. Their chronotope is not her own, nor does she recognize its existence.

As new chronotopes emerge that sever the connections between the native peoples and the land they have inhabited for thousands of years, they are driven from this land. Cooper presents the decline in the Native American population in her region as implicitly tied to the white encroachment on the land: "It was but yesterday that such beings peopled the forest, beings with as much of life as runs within our own veins, who drank their daily draught from the springs we now call our own; yesterday they were here, today scarce a vestige of their existence can be pointed out among us" (*Rural Hours*, 58). Later in her narrative, she explains that in many parts of the country Native Americans are no longer present at all; it is rare to see them, and many of the white inhabitants of the region have never seen them. Although Cooper laments the disappearance of the Native Americans from the area, she portrays them as outside the scope of "civilization." Upon viewing a group of Iroquois in a white community, Cooper notes, "The first group we chanced to see strike us strangely, appearing as they do in the midst of a civilized community with the characteristics of their wild race still clinging to them; and when it is remembered that the land over which they now wander as strangers, in the midst of an alien race, was so lately their own—the heritage of their fathers—it is impossible to behold them without a feeling of peculiar interest" (*Rural Hours*, 108). This "peculiar interest" that Cooper feels for the Native Americans is but one example of her ambiguous reactions to them. As representatives of an older society existing in a "folkloric" variety of time, the Native Americans' passing is lamented. However, their status as heathens complicates Cooper's response. She explains her response to the Native Americans by blaming the negative influences of civilization and the weakness of the Native Americans to vice: "But such is only the common course of things; a savage race is almost invariably corrupted rather than improved by its earliest contact with a civilized people; they suffer from the vices of civilization before they learn justly to comprehend its merits. It is with nations as with individuals—amelioration is a slow process, corruption a rapid one" (*Rural Hours*, 112). By blaming the corrupt aspects of civilization, Cooper can both idealize the older generations of Native Americans now passed away while she simultaneously castigates the newer generations who, instead of benefiting from the good of civilization, suffer from its vices. Whether through dispossession and relocation or corruption, the disappearance of the "noble savage" is lamented in Cooper's narrative.

Likewise, Cooper documents and mourns the gradual demise and extinction of local animal populations. In a prescient passage, Cooper even predicts the extinction of the buffalo. Noting the victory of Long Islanders in preserving their deer population, Cooper laments that Otsego County has ignored issues of preservation, and she predicts the demise of many creatures in her area as well as ultimately devastating effects for the United States as a whole if people do not begin to focus their efforts on conservation and preservation: "In this county very little attention has been paid to this subject, and probably everything of the kind will soon disappear from our woods. The reckless extermination of the game in the United States would seem, indeed, without a precedent in the history of the world. Probably the buffaloes will be entirely swept from prairies, once covered with their herds, by this generation" (*Rural Hours*, 190). Cooper sees the extinction of native animals as a sign of the impending development of the land and with it the destruction of the natural world. Progress in the linear sense of development threatens the older cyclical patterns that focus around the rejuvenation of the land and its creatures.

Cooper does support economic uses of the land. However, she proposes that conservation of natural resources will enable people to reap a greater yield from the land. She links the cultivation of the landscape to both economic and aesthetic purposes, finding the cultivated "middle" landscape aesthetically pleasing:

This general fertility, this blending of the fields of man and his tillage with the woods, the great husbandry of Providence, gives a fine character to the country, which it could not claim when the lonely savage roamed through wooded valleys, and which it must lose if ever cupidity, and the haste to grow rich, shall destroy the forest entirely, and leave these hills to posterity, bald and bare, as those of many older lands. No perfection of tillage, no luxuriance of produce can make up to a country for the loss of its forests. (*Rural Hours*, 139)

Here Cooper valorizes the cultivation of the land while she also calls for moderation in felling the trees of the forests. She warns against greediness as she indicates the possible end result of the "haste to grow rich." Cooper emphasizes that the economic fate of a people is tied directly to the condition of the land they work. If the land is abused, it will no longer yield sustenance. Toward the end of her narrative, Cooper describes the slow and moderate development of Otsego County and explains how what she calls "improvement" benefits its citizens:

> The advance of this county has always been steady and healthful; things have never been pushed forward with the unnatural and exhausting impetus of speculation, to be followed by reaction. Neither do we possess a railroad or a canal within our limits. We have not even a navigable river within our bounds; steamboats and ships are as great strangers as the locomotive. It will be seen, therefore, that we claim no striking advantages of our own, and what prosperity we enjoy, must flow from the general condition of the country, and the industry of our population. (*Rural Hours,* 318)

The condition of the land indicates the fate of its people. According to Cooper, care must be taken to conserve natural resources for future use and to preserve the beauty of the natural landscape.

A Farther Progress

In an attempt to reconcile her yearning for the agrarian past with the reality of uncontained development, Cooper proposes the chronotope of a farther progress as one that takes into account human prosperity (in utilizing and developing the land) as well as the aesthetic and ecological condition of the land. In this chronotope, humans will begin to see that a linear approach to development that does not take into account the natural cycles of the land is detrimental to their own tenancy in the land. In Cooper's vision of a farther progress, there is no contradiction between human good and the state of the natural landscape. Cooper views the prosperity of humans as tied to the land—if the land is depleted, then it is of little use.

Cultivation of the land, practiced with a sensitivity to the land and recognizing the need to replenish natural resources, is favored in Cooper's narrative as aesthetically, economically, and ecologically desirable. She portrays conservation as simple common sense, even to the businessman:

> It is not surprising, perhaps, that a man whose chief object in life is to make money, should turn his timber into bank-notes with all possible speed; but it is remarkable that any one at all aware of the value of wood, should act so wastefully as most men do in this part of the world. Mature trees, young saplings, and last year's seedlings, are all destroyed at one blow by the axe or by fire; the spot where they have stood is left, perhaps, for a lifetime without any

attempt at cultivation, or any endeavor to foster new wood. One would think that by this time, when the forest has fallen in all the valleys—when the hills are becoming more bare every day—when timber and fuel are rising in prices, and new uses are found for even indifferent woods—some forethought and care in this respect would be natural in people laying claim to common sense. (*Rural Hours,* 132)

Cooper points out that the destruction of the trees is indiscriminate, and the forests have been recklessly denuded. At the same time, she calls for those making a profit from this destruction to become less concerned with immediate financial gain and more aware of the long-term effects of heedless logging and, as a result, their future profits. Cooper believes that these future profits must be tied to an awareness of the natural cycles of the land, and, as a result, she presents a way of looking at time and place that honors these natural cycles as beneficial to nature and to humans. The chronotope of a farther progress that she proposes accounts for both the health of the land and the profit to be made from it.

But even as she calls for conservation, she recognizes that this stage has not yet been reached by her society: "the preservation of fine trees, already standing, marks a farther progress, and this point we have not yet reached" (*Rural Hours,* 133). This kind of progress is antithetical to that of uncontained development, which does not heed the call for moderation. The farther progress promotes a view of time that honors the cycles of her regional environment. Cooper explains what reaching this stage would mean for humans' interaction with the land:

And when we have made this farther progress, then we shall take better care of our trees. We shall not be satisfied with setting out a dozen naked saplings before our door, because our neighbor on the left did so last year, nor cut down a whole wood, within a stone's throw of our dwelling, to pay for a Brussels carpet from the same piece as our neighbor's on the right; no, we shall not care a stiver for mere show and parade, in any shape whatever, but we shall look to the general proprieties and fitness of things, whether our neighbors to the right or the left do so or not. (*Rural Hours,* 134)

At this future time, humans would place more importance on the needs of the environment than on the short-sighted desires of society.

For Cooper, conservation does not concern only humans but is a behavior through which they demonstrate a larger respect for God's creation. She portrays reckless development as showing a lack of proper respect and thankfulness for the gift of God's creation: "A careless indifference to any good gift of our gracious Maker, shows a want of thankfulness, as any abuse or waste, betrays a reckless spirit of evil" (*Rural Hours*, 134). Those who willfully destroy the land transgress God's preordained patterns of life that sustain and nurture both the land and its human inhabitants. To Cooper, the cyclical workings of nature are divinely ordered: "Let us remember that it is the Supreme Being who is the Creator, and in how many ways do we see his gracious providence, his Almighty economy, deigning to work progressive renovation in the humblest objects when their old forms have become exhausted by Time!" (*Rural Hours*, 134). In this passage, Cooper refers to rejuvenation through natural processes and patterns—literally, the cycle of death and rebirth. For Cooper, then, her proposition of a farther progress is not simply a call for conservation but also a religious plea for respect for God's creation.

As an example of her farther progress, Cooper describes her own county. She discusses Otsego County's contained development, citing the circumspect approach to progress as crucial to perceptions of development:

> The advance of this county has always been steady and healthful; things have never been pushed forward with the unnatural and exhausting impetus of speculation, to be followed by reaction. Neither do we possess a railroad or a canal within our limits. We have not even a navigable river within our bounds; steamboats and ships are as great strangers as the locomotive. It will be seen, therefore, that we claim no striking advantages of our own, and what prosperity we enjoy, must flow from the general condition of the country, and the industry of our population. (*Rural Hours*, 318)

Cooper depicts the inhabitants of her county as living in a symbiotic relationship with the land. What they have must come from the land, and if they are to receive sustenance from it, then the land itself must be sustained.

As a chronotope, a farther progress works toward a reconciliation of ideas of progress with the cyclical functioning of the natural world. Cooper's view of time as a farther progress, which accounts for development, responds to the inevitability of what is to come—the movement toward industrialization and the slow move away from the older agrarian world. Cooper is realistic about what is happening around her, but she advocates a concern for the environment as essential to any future progress that will be beneficial to humans. If the fate of humans is inextricably tied to the land (a lesson learned from the cyclical folkloric view of time), then any development must not exceed that land's ability to remain healthy and to sustain life. As Cooper examines various ways of interacting with the

natural world, she presents linear and cyclical views of time that characterize vastly different human responses to the land, and the attendant tension between these two chronotopes provides the central tension of her
narrative. This tension is resolved in Cooper through her discussion of
real progress as a notion that accounts for and addresses environmental
concerns.

NOTES

1. Susan Fenimore Cooper, *Rural Hours,* ed. Rochelle Johnson and Daniel
Patterson (Athens: University of Georgia Press, 1998), 59, 120. Hereafter cited
in text.

2. In her essay "The Chronotope of the Asylum: Jane Eyre, Feminism, and
Bakhtinian Theory," Suzanne Rosenthal Shumway defines the chronotope as "the
time/space continuum that gives shape to a novel, directing and in some ways even
generating its existence. The chronotope functions, we might say, as a form of
setting for the novel. But more than merely a device to locate the plot within a
specific time and place, the chronotope actively works to shape and create the plot
itself, becoming, in the end, a formal, as well as a thematic, feature of the plot" (in
A Dialogue of Voices: Feminist Literary Theory and Bakhtin, ed. Karen Hohne
and Helen Wussow [Minneapolis: University of Minnesota Press, 1994], 157).

3. Mikhail Bakhtin, "Forms of Time and Chronotopes in the Novel," in *The
Dialogic Imagination,* ed. Michael Holquist (Austin: University of Texas Press,
1981), 208.

4. Ibid., 209–10.

5. Leo Marx, *The Machine in the Garden: Technology and the Pastoral Ideal
in America* (London: Oxford University Press, 1964), 23.

6. In folkloric time, as in Cooper's narrative, humans have deep ties to their
natural environment in the form of agricultural labor. The sustenance of human
life is incumbent upon the land. This stage of development precedes historical moments perceived as "progress" such as the Industrial Revolution. Folkloric time
ultimately declines and reappears nostalgically in the form of the idyll. According
to Bakhtin, all idylls share several common features based upon a relationship of
time to space in which individuals are tied to place—what Bakhtin calls "an organic fastening-down, a grafting of life and its events to a place, to a familiar
territory with all its nooks and crannies, its familiar mountains, valleys, fields,
rivers and forests, and one's own home" ("Forms of Time," 225). Life becomes
anchored to a real, tangible location. Human life is closely linked to nature in the
idyll as the events of human life are tied to the rhythms of the natural world.

7. Ibid., 208.

8. The chronotope of time as human progress that Cooper depicts corresponds to Bakhtin's ideas of linear time—both individual and historical. Bakhtin writes of a movement away from folkloric time that begins to focus on the individual rather than the communal. The individual becomes separate from the natural world of folkloric time. Parallel to but separate from this individualistic view of time is historical time, which emphasizes the big picture—the major events of history—rather than the smaller lives of individual people. Visions of time become compartmentalized, and the focus shifts away from the unity of time, humanity, and nature. As humans become separate from the natural world, nature becomes simply a backdrop to human experience. People no longer work the land together as a community; instead, lives are divided one from another and each from nature itself. From this perspective, nature becomes a stage for human action and does not figure in the action. As humans grow separate from the natural world, no longer collectively dependent on the land for daily sustenance, this disunion allows for the kind of abuses of the land that Cooper documents in her narrative.

TINA GIANQUITTO

The Noble Designs of Nature:
God, Science, and the Picturesque in
Susan Fenimore Cooper's *Rural Hours*

In the preface to *Rural Hours*, Susan Cooper gives her readers an easy way to fix the identities of both author and text through the metaphor of gleaning. "The Lady" of the preface is a mere collector who "naturally gleans many trifling observations of rustic matters" while "wandering about in the fields" and who then recollects these scraps for the pleasure of her friends.[1] Gleaning or gathering together the scraps left by regular gatherers is by nature a humble activity performed by humble figures, and Cooper here allies herself with the other gleaners that people her text: the "mothers, children, and the aged"; Ruth, the gleaner of the Old Testament; the newly arrived immigrant women; and the birds, squirrels, and other small animals (*Rural Hours*, 159). These unassuming figures perform their secondary activity only after the real work of reaping has been completed.

If we are to believe the rhetoric of the preface, then, Cooper is not an author; she is simply a domestic woman who shares her "trifling observations" with her friends by the fireside. Nor, as she vehemently protests, is she a scientist. Although the "simple events" she records in her journal include descriptions of migratory bird patterns and the gradual decimation of both species and habitat, she makes "no claim whatever to scientific knowledge" (*Rural Hours*, 3). As a writer of a "rustic primer" on the subject of America's native birds, trees, plants, butterflies, and insects, Cooper metaphorically gleans the fields of other, more proficient reapers of knowledge—theologians and philosophers, botanists and ornithologists, landscape artists and theorists. Yet these same gleanings also show her grappling with the interpretive shifts in nature's "meaning" that theology, philosophy, botany, and ornithology were bringing to nineteenth-century America.

If the preface pledges that *Rural Hours* will be a simple journal comprised of modest observations, then the text of *Rural Hours* far exceeds that humble promise. *Rural Hours* is not "the simple record of those little events which make up the course of the seasons" (3); it is instead an intricate, expansive investigation into the shifting portrait of the landscape surrounding the author's Cooperstown home. In fact, Susan Fenimore Cooper is anything but a "mere recorder" (to use Mary Austin's words) of the events around her home. She not only strives to apprehend the natural events of Cooperstown; she also struggles to interpret those events as part of a larger narrative of home, nation, history, and divinity. Even the terms of the preface are misleading. Cooper describes events as "trifling" and her locale as "rustic." In fact, the changing of the seasons, the passage of time, and the effects of human habitation on the landscape—in other words, the natural and national histories chronicled in *Rural Hours*—are not trifling occurrences. And just as Cooper transforms the meaning of "trifling" in her text, she performs a similar alchemy with the term "rustic." The reader of *Rural Hours* quickly discovers that Cooper is both familiar with and critical of scientific terminology. Rather than privileging the scientist's "strange tongue sputter[ing] its uncouth, compound syllables upon the simple weeds by the way-side," Cooper prefers the rustic's knowledge with its functional, descriptive, and utilitarian terms (*Rural Hours*, 83).

In *Rural Hours,* Susan Cooper attempts to make a comprehensible whole out of her gleanings and to reconcile the competing discourses that govern her representations of nature. For Cooper, God remains firmly entrenched in the details of the natural world; these details, in turn, reveal the particulars of a divine plan. Yet Cooper, despite her stance as a faithful Christian and traditional woman who extols the virtues of the domestic realm, is often not content to confine her descriptions within the limiting rhetoric and metaphors of a domesticated natural theology. As an active participant in the culture, politics, and science of her times, she wants to prove herself as a skilled naturalist well versed in the scientific advances of her day. She observes the minutiae of the plants, animals, and especially birds that inhabit her landscape. She knows her sources—Audubon, Lyell, Wilson, and Humboldt, for instance—and has honed her observational skills in the field. Like the scientific sources to which she turns to explain the objects of the natural world, Cooper guardedly participates in a discourse that is overtly critical of received definitions.

Rural Hours records Cooper's struggle to find a mode of representation that will allow her to produce an accurate, morally viable record of her observations and experiences of the natural world. Her problems with descriptive language reveal her as being caught in her historical moment.

She values the specificity that scientific observation and language offer but worries that the terms of science threaten to remove both the local and the divine from the picture produced. She privileges rustic knowledge and language but expresses concern that the local cannot accommodate the universal designs of the natural world. Cooper finds relief for her representational dilemmas in the picturesque aesthetic that governs her apprehension of the landscape. This painterly aesthetic, adopted by nineteenth-century America as a way to comprehend its vast and largely uncharted landscape, relies on relations of parts to a whole, on an attention to how minute details function in creating a panoramic vista. Cooper immediately recognizes the value of this aesthetic for her contemplative exercises. In particular, it allows her to use the tools of science (careful observation and precise description) to ground her conception of the web of moral relationships that govern the natural world. In doing so, she creates a holistic picture of a landscape already subject to the fragmenting tendencies of scientific investigation.

The seasonal journal form that Cooper employs to track the rhythms of the environment in *Rural Hours* reflects her desire to unite local detail to a universal design. As Lawrence Buell notes, the seasonal form mimics "the motions of the environment itself" and relies on "nature's motions to provide the central organizing device."[2] I would add that the seasonal form, which emphasizes environmental structure and process, also allows Cooper easy access to natural theology. Seasonal changes that do manifest themselves in such trifling details as melting ice and chirping birds are, according to the terms of natural theology, a general providence of God. The natural laws that govern the seasons, the obvious manifestations of such changes, and the relative ease with which those changes can be observed provide even the most casual observer a map to God. "Nature considered *rationally,* that is to say, submitted to the process of thought," as Cooper reads in Humboldt's *Cosmos,* reveals "a unity in diversity of phenomena; a harmony, blending together all created things, however dissimilar in form and attribute; one great whole animated by the breath of life."[3] As LeMahieu observes, this "theology of purposeful relationships" privileges reason and empirical proof over subjective emotions in its search for God; a reasoned excursion into the design of natural phenomena reveals not only the existence but the character and attributes of the deity.[4]

In his influential *Natural Theology* of 1802, William Paley argues by analogy that just as a watch found in a field must, of necessity, imply a watchmaker, so must the works of nature, which "surpass the contrivances of art in the complexity, subtlety, and curiosity of the mechanism," imply the "*existence* of an intelligent Creator."[5] Furthermore, because those "marks of design" in so vast and encompassing a system as nature surpass the abilities of any one person to create, the designer must be God.[6] Natural theology imbues the environment with a valuable morality; careful observation of the intricate structures and intimate connections of the natural world provides humans not only with a record of their accomplishments but with a model upon which to base their future actions. Although the specific and isolated details of nature may seem trifling, Susan Cooper knows that these details become, "through 'sheer accretion,' a unity in themselves," as Barbara Novak observes.[7] They produce a panorama that reveals God and consequently produces a "moral . . . energy that could be translated into action."[8] For Cooper, this moral energy extends outward from the environment, to the home, through the village, and into the nation.

Cooper's insistence upon the moral imperatives encoded in the landscape relies upon an understanding of the close connections between human and nonhuman families rooted in natural theology. This ontological system provides the underpinnings of the obviously (and relentlessly) domestic metaphors that Cooper uses to describe the natural world.[9] Cooper domesticates nature in order to reveal the close, morally infused relationships between human and nonhuman. Birds, insects, flowers, and trees play an important role in this domesticated nature; these objects, in their designed fitness for their natural environment, make it possible to read moral lessons in their existence. Cooper employs a flower, the may-wing, for one such lesson for her readers. She writes that although the may-wing exhibits in its habits of growth an "innate grace," "a unity, a fitness, in the individual character of each plant to be traced most closely, not only in form . . . but also in the position it chooses, and all the various accessories of its brief existence," it knows "nothing of vanity, its trivial toils and triumphs!" (*Rural Hours,* 53). This lesson of the woods would be well heeded by the "young girls about [the] villages," who are "often wildly extravagant in their dress, and just as restless in following the fashions" (*Rural Hours,* 99). Like Jonathan Edwards before her, Cooper also uses insect parallels to meditate on human character; a "cunning and designing man" is as reviled as the wily and suspicious spider, who "lives by snares and plots." Cooper justifies her extraction of these moral lessons by recalling that even despised "insects have their merits and their uses, since none of God's creatures are made in vain" (*Rural Hours,* 61).

It is in her discussions of bird families, though, that Cooper makes clear the importance of natural creatures as models for human behavior. That birds of all species are everywhere in Cooper's text is no surprise, given the particular appeal of ornithology for nineteenth-century women.[10] In part, the appeal for Cooper of these "honest creatures" lay in their mimetic function—vigilant, selfless mothers happily submit to "voluntary imprisonment" for their offspring, while their "remarkably good husbands" cheer and provide for their mates (*Rural Hours*, 23). By correlating the actions of bird "homes" to human homes, Cooper manipulates and extends the definition of "nature" to mean "home"; these domestic arrangements produce ideal (and natural) societies, making bird families exemplary neighbors for human communities.[11]

This interconnectedness of home and environment governs the *representations* of both home and environment in the text; nature offers a divine and fixed model for a human community that is continually in flux. Cooper's formulation recalls Emerson, who writes in "Nature" that the natural world is "the present expositor of the divine mind." "It is," he continues, "a fixed point whereby we may measure our departure. As we degenerate, the contrast between us and our house is more evident. We are as much strangers in nature, as we are aliens from God. We do not understand the notes of the birds. . . . We do not know the uses of more than a few plants, as corn and the apple, the potato and the vine."[12] Cooper, like Emerson, sees the order of the natural world beyond human control, but the objects in nature that *Rural Hours* depicts are continually subject to human whim and action. Her reading of nature as an extension of the human home reveals these relational models at the root of her understanding of the natural world. Specific instances in the text where, for example, Cooper exclaims that were it not for a principle of restraint, she and her companions might have struck animals that crossed their path with their parasols indicate that the environment Cooper accesses is always under human control (*Rural Hours*, 41, 178). That world remains invariably in Cooper's firm interpretative grasp as well; as a result, she is able to assign each individual object she encounters during her walks a functional definition or a specific role within a larger, well-ordered system.

Cooper makes clear early in *Rural Hours* that the model of nature as what Peter Bowler has called "a harmonious system animated by spiritual forces" governs her reading of the landscape surrounding her home.[13] As a result, the text abounds with examples of God's Providence as expressed in natural mechanics; for instance, a little, fallen sparrow in her path reminds her that both human and nonhuman creatures are ever "heeded and remembered before God" (*Rural Hours*, 259). The nonhuman occupants of Cooper's world also reveal through their "fitness" for their environment how humans should behave; they teach lessons of humility, fidelity, constancy, and comportment. She opens *Rural Hours* with an injunction for women to venture outside: "After facing the cold bravely," she writes in her journal's opening entry, "one brings home a sort of virtuous glow which is not to be picked up by cowering over the fireside." Interaction with the outside world invigorates the "inside" world, and Cooper assures her reader that "the effort brings its own reward" (*Rural Hours*, 4). In the case of the observant adventurer, the effort of interacting with the natural world brings the reward of a deeper understanding of that world and an individual's place in it. Moreover, the walker in Cooper's excursive model, like Thoreau's saunterer who "'rove[s] about the country . . . going *a la Sainte Terre*,' to the Holy Land," experiences firsthand the fact of God's goodness rather than relying simply on the speculation of that goodness.[14]

Cooper concludes as much during a walk on a warm, cloudy, "sweetly calm" spring day (*Rural Hours*, 45). Walking far from the village to a point where the meadows and woods "shut one out from the world," Cooper spends long hours contemplating "nothing but the river flowing gently past, and a few solitary birds flitting quietly to and fro." Such contemplation leads her directly to God as she writes: "At hours like these, the immeasurable goodness, the infinite wisdom of our heavenly Father, are displayed in so great a degree of condescending tenderness to unworthy, sinful man, as must appear quite incomprehensible—entirely incredible to reason alone—were it not for the recollection of the mercies of past years, the positive proofs of experience" (*Rural Hours*, 45). Cooper's discussion of the spiritual transformation effected by nature's redemptive work rests on tactile experience of the natural world—as air courses into the lungs and herbs are crushed underfoot, the observer/participant moves easily from "nature to nature's God," to borrow Elizabeth Keeney's phrase.[15] But, as Christopher Manes observes, biblical exegesis teaches that the objects in nature are "mere *littera*" or signs that serve as an occasion for discovering "a moral truth established by God."[16] Thus, Cooper's springtime penitent will necessarily turn for comfort from the "Word of God" to the "Work of God." One sentence effects the transformation from scripture to nature, from revealed theology to natural theology, as she writes: "And, from the Book of Life, let the mourner turn to the works of his God; there, the eye . . . will be soothed with beauty and excellence; the ear . . . will gladly open to sounds of gentle harmony from the gay birds, the patient cattle, the flowing waters, the rustling leaves" (*Rural Hours*,

46). In this passage, Cooper draws on what Perry Miller identifies as the "correspondence of idea and object, of word and thing" in establishing the necessary relationship between natural and revealed theology.[17] Since God both authors the design of the natural world and provides a record of that creation in the Bible, natural and revealed theology must exist in harmony.[18] As she writes, scriptural study or "reason alone," if divorced from the "proofs of experience" available in nature, renders the divine "incomprehensible" (*Rural Hours*, 45).

If this passage shows Cooper resting securely in her belief of the correlation between the narrative of the Bible and the corresponding proofs accessible in the natural world, other passages in *Rural Hours* show Cooper grappling with problems of representation and translation in the Bible itself.[19] For instance, willows spied during a spring walk inaugurate an inquiry into the willow of Psalm 137, and the result is one of the most rhetorically impressive passages of the text. Cooper opens her entry for May 1 with a small complaint against the weather—"showery; not so bright as becomes May-day" (*Rural Hours*, 30). Cooper's walking party was "obliged to be satisfied with following the highway," until, enticed "off the road into a low boggy spot" by a bright cluster of marsh marigolds, Cooper spies a golden willow coming into leaf (*Rural Hours*, 30). In Cooper's text, roads, sidewalks, and particularly fences often impede rather than promote her naturalist ramblings. In fact, Cooper frequently complains when conditions require her to "plod humbly along the highways" (*Rural Hours*, 288), as she prefers to roam the trackless expanses, experiencing nature free from prescribed definitions. In this case, the physical move off the well-worn track and into the boggy marsh mirrors the textual digression from describing the "native willows of America" to interrogating Psalm 137's "willow of Babylon, in whose shade the children of Israel sat down and wept" (*Rural Hours*, 31). The move from the "track" to the "trackless" in this passage initiates an interpretative move away from established interpretations and translations and charts a new definition composed of but still distinct from writings she surveys. The willow passage records Cooper's process of discovery, which, as Gilian Beer notes, "is a matter not only of reaching new conclusions but of redescribing what is known and taken for granted."[20]

Cooper's knowledge of the habitat required to sustain a willow tree inspires her to ask a simple question: What kind of tree inhabits Psalm 137? She writes: "When we read of those willows of Babylon . . . we naturally think of the weeping willow which we all know to be an Asiatic tree. But the other day, while reading an observation of a celebrated Eastern traveller, the idea suggested itself, that this common impression might possibly be erroneous" (*Rural Hours*, 31). Is it a weeping willow, the tree mentioned most often in translations of the Bible, or is it a variety of the species more suited to the desolate landscape of Babylon? After presenting her seemingly unassuming question, Cooper mines noted travel narratives of the region to get a picture of the habitat of the area and to look for clues to indicate the presence of the noble weeping willow. These recorded observations fail to satisfy her curiosity; instead, they lead her only to demand that she "would like to see the proofs clearly made out in behalf of the weeping willow" (*Rural Hours*, 32). Alas, she seeks to no avail—the only willow mentioned is the "*gray ozier*," a tree deemed "insignificant in size, and of an inferior variety." Cooper's tone in this passage is confident, and she states, "[T]he question may be very easily settled by those who have learning and books at command." Cooper wastes no time in assuring her readers that she has such "learning and books" at her disposal, and she fills the next paragraphs with observations from such diverse sources as Herodotus, Beauchamp, Porter, and two translations of the Hebrew Bible. While her search fails to provide the necessary evidence on behalf of the weeping willow, Cooper's careful survey does convince her that the lowly gray osier has been "thus proved, by the most clear and positive evidence, to have also existed there in ancient times" (*Rural Hours*, 32).

But why is this detail so important? The answer to this question becomes apparent in the concluding paragraph of the May 1 entry, where Cooper awards her patient reader with a meditation on the meaning and effect of the scriptural passage under scrutiny. Cooper boldly proposes a third option here, a new translation composed of the writings surveyed but independent of the male writers she cites as her authorities, and she treats her reader to an interpretation of the passage based on her new reading: "What sublime, prophetic power in those simple words—'who art to be destroyed'—when addressed by the weeping captive to the mighty city, then in the height of her power and her pride! That destruction has long since been complete; Babylon is wasted indeed; and we learn with interest from the traveller, that beside her shapeless ruins, stand the 'gray ozier willows, on which the captives of Israel hung up their harps;' mute and humble witnesses of the surrounding desolation" (*Rural Hours*, 33). The "common impression" of the noble weeping willow does not, in fact, fit into this new interpretation of the biblical passage—the import of the passage requires that the humble osier, the tree that both mimics the attitude of the captives and also fits naturally into the desolated landscape of Babylon, stand next to the banks of the river.

Why does the problem of the willow of Psalm 137 so occupy Cooper's attention? Cooper's insistence on solving the riddle of the willow's identity pinpoints a moment of cultural tension as it forces her to ask whether the Bible can be trusted despite empirical evidence that might disprove biblical narratives. Cooper must establish the primacy of the Bible as the ultimate source for the nature observer in order for the scheme governing the apprehension of natural objects in *Rural Hours* to work. Cooper argues here that the seemingly insignificant details of both species and translation are essential elements in an accurate interpretation of the Scripture. If the facts recorded in the Bible are wrong or misrepresented, then the "mourner" who looks from the "Word of God" to the "Work of God" will not find the two in harmony. Cooper, of course, neatly avoids the deep religious and philosophical dilemmas that would surely result from this train of thought by focusing specifically on the Bible as a translated text. As such, the fault lies not in the representation of the natural phenomena but rather in the translations of that representation. Cooper willingly offers the community her new translation of the biblical passage—a translation whose authority derives from individual observation, not communal consensus. In doing so, Cooper responds to what Michael Halloran astutely identifies as the cultural shift in the locus of moral authority from institutions to the individual.[21]

In order to establish the "truth" of the details related in the Bible, Cooper demands proofs of an almost scientific nature. She constructs her discussion on the identity of the willow as a kind of scientific inquiry: she posits a hypothesis, seeks her proofs in empirical observation, and presents a new conclusion based on those observations. Cooper must perform this investigation because if natural theology fails, if the details observed in the natural world do not conform to a larger design inspired and effected by God, then the natural world as a model for human actions similarly fails. The moral lessons encoded in the natural world become meaningless if the foundation upon which those lessons are based can be dismantled. A scientifically attuned eye, with its ability to unmask representational inaccuracies, could threaten Cooper's apprehension of her natural world. Yet as this passage shows, science, with its attention to empirical observation and classification, is, as Keeney calls it, "an ally, not an enemy, of religion."[22]

Cooper takes advantage of both natural theology and science (botany) to discern the significance of the biblical willow in this passage and in doing so reveals the tensions that run throughout the text. *Rural Hours* documents Cooper's efforts to unite increasingly competing ways of understanding the natural world: a religious view that regards the design of nature as a direct product of God made for the benefit of humankind and a scientific view that begins to present the world as a web of interrelated systems of which man is simply a part. Although natural theology, with its reliance on order and fixity, works well with the artificial, taxonomic nature of Linnaean classification that dominated botanical study well into the nineteenth century, Cooper, like most naturalists operating in the mid–nineteenth century, finds the rigidity of Linnaeus's closed systems incapable of accommodating the open-ended, organic metaphors that were coming to dominate the presentations and understandings of the natural world.[23]

Cooper senses that the traditional definitions offered by natural theology, which often overlook detail in presentations of the design, are inadequate. Scientific advances, particularly geological discoveries that challenged conventional notions of the age of the earth and universe, put an enormous stress on the causal links upon which natural theology depended.[24] Cooper finds herself pressured to address nature as an exclusively scientific construct—an object to be observed, identified, investigated, and interpreted outside of a moral frame. Although Cooper is dedicated to a view of nature that is threatened by scientific advances, she understands, as an amateur naturalist, the real value of scientific research and language and often feels compelled to demonstrate her knowledge of this alternative system. She has read current geological, botanical, and zoological texts and crafts descriptive passages that are as accurate as those of the naturalists whose works she both admires and seeks to emulate. In fact, during the coldest winter days, Cooper shares her passion for bibliographic references with her readers and turns to her library to deepen her knowledge of the species and habitat she might see, if she were outside.[25] Cooper's citations, which include texts by Lyell, Cuvier, Condolle, and Wilson, clearly indicate her familiarity with the debates raging around her, but she adheres to the older model of harmonious nature despite its flaws and contradictions.

Cooper's conflicted and often contradictory responses to science reveal the deep tensions caused by the intersections of the theological and scientific discourses that inform *Rural Hours*. Cooper longs for the simplicity of a localized perspective but acknowledges the global movement of natural organisms. She presents sharp criticisms of the inadequacies of contemporary naming systems yet provides the very Latin terms she condemns as footnotes to her descriptions (*Rural Hours*, 52, 53, 64). She accesses scientific texts of all varieties to inform her own representations of the landscape yet quarrels with professional naturalists in their reluctance to accept "simple truths" in their creation of unnecessarily elaborate theories (*Rural Hours*, 167). And while she laments the "little attention" that has been paid to subjects like entomology, she seems uncomfortable with the increasing specialization of the sciences, as this specialization distances the amateur observer, or "rustic fancier," to use Cooper's terminology, from the scene (*Rural Hours*, 174). Cooper's uncomfortable position is further indicated by the sources she chooses to access in her text, many of whom, like Humboldt and Cuvier, were associated by Cooper's time with an outmoded, static view of nature.[26]

As a result, Cooper, though versed in the language of scientific description, remains wedded to an interpretative schema that resembles the "floriography" of popular sentimental botanies and floral dictionaries, texts that revealed the moral "meanings" of flowers for the purpose of guiding women through nature to God. As Ann Shteir notes, this floral language privileges the moral imperatives expressed in the relationships between natural objects and provides participants in the flower culture a "constructed knowledge system with a universal code of meaning."[27] Though Cooper draws on the form of what Keeney terms "botanical natural theologies" for many of her meditations on nature,[28] she uses *Rural Hours* to add her voice to a chorus of complaints against these texts as they arise at midcentury.[29] Lucy Maddox notes that Cooper presents herself as a reader as well as a writer in *Rural Hours;* as a result, she assumes the right to discuss the "social and moral implications of what women read."[30] Floral botanies are insufficient as field guides because the numerous errors that pepper the texts make proper identification of flowers impossible. Nor can they function as devotionals; descriptive inaccuracies cause the individual observer of nature to doubt the veracity of her own observations and distract her from contemplating God. Cooper does not quarrel with the function of these texts as moral primers; after all, *Rural Hours* performs much the same tasks. She does, however, find fault with their form. Written by supposedly distinguished authorities, these texts carelessly overlook details in their hasty presentations of nature.

Cooper continually turns her honed analytical eye to the texts that she reads; in a sharply critical entry she takes "the distinguished" Martin Tupper to task for the observational inaccuracies present in his *Proverbial Philosophy*, a "great work" that "has been a source of so much pleasure and advantage to half the world" (*Rural Hours*, 72). In her entry for June 15, Cooper turns her attention to her "little friend" the humming-bird. In a language that implies a long intimacy with the habits of the creature, Cooper provides a brief description of the types of flowers most commonly frequented by the bird and notes specifically how the shape of certain flowers particularly suits it. She writes: "There is something in the form of . . . tube-shape blossoms, whether small or great, which suits their long, slender bills, and possibly, for the same reason, the bees cannot find such easy access to the honey, and leave more in these than in the open flowers" (*Rural Hours*, 71). She then turns to Tupper and the "pretty compliment" he pays to the hummingbird. "Personifying Beauty," Cooper writes, "[Tupper] says, she 'Fluttereth into the tulip with the humming-bird'" (*Rural Hours*, 72). Tupper's "compliment," however, does not imply any real understanding of the bird or its habits, as Cooper claims that after *she* watched "the humming-birds for several seasons," she has not only "never seen one in a tulip," she has in fact "often observed them pass these for other flowers" (*Rural Hours*, 72). Although Cooper modestly notes that the error "may have been accidental" or that Tupper may refer here to a variety of the bird with which she is not familiar, she defends her criticism by noting the fruits of her own thorough observation: "there is something in the upright position of that flower which, added to its size, lends one to believe that it must be an inconvenient blossom for the humming-bird, who generally seems to prefer nodding or drooping flowers, if they are at all large, always feeding on the wing as he does, and never alighting, like butterflies and bees, on the petals" (*Rural Hours*, 72). Cooper dismisses her complaints by calling them the "very trifling" points of "some rustic bird fancier." But the astute reader, recalling the rhetoric employed in the preface, will acknowledge the force behind Cooper's modest justification that "we are busying ourselves wholly with trifles just now" (*Rural Hours*, 72).

What troubles Cooper about Tupper's text is her impression that the mass of readers will trust this "distinguished" author and will become careless in their own reading of the natural environment. By extension, Cooper worries over the lingering effects of floral dictionaries, decrying the fact that although "every young girl can chatter largely about 'bouquets,' and the 'Language of Flowers,'" these same children, as well as the adults around them, can seldom remember the "common names of plants they must have seen all their lives" (*Rural Hours*, 83). But if the excesses of traditional flower languages obscure accurate observation and description of the local landscape, Cooper finds the proliferation of the Latinate terms of botanical texts equally problematic. Scientific terminology denies nature its poetry, and while Cooper appreciates the specificity scientific language allows, she finds the artificial distance it inserts between the object and the observer problematic. In her complaints against scientific naming, Cooper demands to know how an observer/participant in nature can feel an impulse to act morally if thus distanced from the natural object. In this, Cooper responds to the burgeoning "organic metaphors" of the new sciences, metaphors that present the environment as a complex web of open-ended relationships that replace the constant and the fixed with the unexpected and the unpredictable.[31]

Despite Cooper's insistence on the primacy of the individual observer, however, *Rural Hours* is the portrait of a communal space. Accordingly, Cooper privileges the rustic parlance that assigns flowers, trees, and animals names that reveal those objects' distinguishing communal characteristics; these expressive terms establish linguistic, historical, and cultural relations between the observer and the objects observed. Local language domesticates the wilderness, and since in Cooper's view moral energy emanates from the home, it makes the transition from the human home into nature's household an easy one.[32] Science, with its "big books" and "long-winded Latin polysyllables," on the other hand, removes the beauty and mystery from the natural world as it distances the local folk from the plants around them (*Rural Hours*, 83). In her views on science, Cooper mirrors Emerson, who is not opposed "to science *per se*," as Arnold Smithline writes, "but to science which had forgotten the poetry of ideas in the assurance that the sensible fact . . . was sufficient."[33] She acknowledges the benefits scientific texts can have on a deeper understanding of the natural environment but warns her readers of the "additional weight of moral responsibility" that comes with "every new science introduced into the school-room" (*Rural Hours*, 228). That Cooper feels compelled to address the mechanistic impulse of Linnaean terminology as an "evil [that] is spreading over all the woods and meadows" indicates the degree to which scientific perspectives were being absorbed by the culture at large—so much so, in fact, that Cooper warns "mothers and nurses" to teach the "natural, unaffected" names of flowers to their children "before they are in 'Botany'" (*Rural Hours*, 83, 87).[34]

Rustic terms and local language encode and display the history of an entire community and give natural objects an identifiable place in the workings of human culture; the local community therefore has an equal obligation to fidelity in crafting its descriptive terms. Simplicity is paramount for Cooper, and, accordingly, the best names for America's flora and fauna are honest ones, ones that truthfully identify that item's form or function. She rails against names like "chick wintergreen" for a plant that "has nothing in the world to do with chicks, or weeds, or winter" and celebrates those like "gay-wings" for a flower that is "in truth one of the gayest little blossoms we have" (*Rural Hours*, 52–53). Rustic terms that recall "cherry-cheeked maidens, and merry-hearted lads" tromping through the woods and fields also make poetry and literature possible (*Rural Hours*, 84). Although Cooper provides her reader with several exemplary passages from English authors such as Chaucer and Shakespeare, her demand for a local language expresses a determined nationalism and derives from her "wish that American poets should sing our native flowers as sweetly and simply as the daisy, and violets, and celandine have been sung from the time of Chaucer or Herrick" (*Rural Hours*, 87).

Cooper's complaints about both the excesses of floral languages and the mechanistic impulses of Latinate botanies as well as her demands for accuracy in writings about nature indicate a larger concern for the moral and intellectual health of the American nation. Her own descriptive passages, which synthesize observation and research, the individual and the communal, serve as examples of how natural and national histories should be performed. Her investigations into translations of Psalm 137, her censure of Tupper's hummingbird passage, and her criticism of Latinate terms reveal the desire to craft a terminology and an aesthetic that provides a "truthful description," a "correct picture of a landscape, a tree, a building" and, by extension, of a community (*Rural Hours*, 329, n. 29). And a truthful picture of the Cooperstown landscape is precisely what Cooper imagines *Rural Hours* to be. It is therefore fitting that the author employs the painterly aesthetic of the picturesque as a means of accommodating her desire for both descriptive fidelity and moral impact in representations of the landscape.

Cooper's use of the picturesque as an organizational device is not surprising given her close relationship with her father, James Fenimore Cooper, and his works. As Blake Nevius notes in *Cooper's Landscapes,* the picturesque, with its reliance on artistic, visual aesthetics and its "awareness of the pictorial values to be sought in the natural landscape," dominates James Fenimore Cooper's mode of representing the American landscape.[35] But Susan Cooper does not rely solely on her father's representations of the American wilderness when fashioning her own response to the rural scenes she inherits from him; she is writing during that moment when the picturesque reached its height of influence on American environmental writing and painting. The vastness of the American landscape, so threatening to colonial America, was, as Novak argues, in the process of becoming the locus of an American culture and "the repository of national pride." The suddenly tamer landscape was becoming for many something to experience rather than subdue. Thus American "nature"—cultivated, organized, controlled—supplanted American "wilderness"—wild, disordered, unrestrained—and metamorphosed into an "effective substitute for a missing national tradition." [36]

The revival of the picturesque aesthetic by American landscape artists, architects, and writers is in part responsible for the improvements that Cooper notes in the accuracy of descriptive writing on natural objects. She attributes this shift to an enlightened public's desire for something "more positive, more real" in descriptive writings on natural objects (*Rural Hours*, 208). [37] Halloran notes that the picturesque aesthetic demands the acute attention of the observer to visual detail in representations of the environment and depicts through "harmonious visual composition . . . an inviting natural landscape lightly touched by human civilization." [38] The picturesque likewise encourages the landscape viewer to consider the artistic qualities and potentials of a vista and to provide that vista with a frame that will organize its disparate elements into a comprehensible whole. Alison Byerly calls the picturesque a "specific mode of pictorialism" in which "the viewer stumbles upon a scene or a prospect in which the elements are arranged 'as if' in a picture"; the "apparently 'accidental' manifestation of the picturesque implies that the scene's properties are inherent, ready to be discovered." [39] Cooper's responses to the views she encounters on her walks often conform to the "conscious aesthetic framing of the landscape" that Byerly identifies as a key trope of the picturesque. [40] For instance, she entraps one prospect in an "archway of green branches, and between noble living columns of pine and hemlock" and gazes at the now-enclosed lake below her as "through the elaborate mouldings of a great Gothic window—a fine frame for any picture" (*Rural Hours*, 21). Cooper projects herself into an interior space here and in the process subdues and domesticates her landscape by enclosing it within man-made structures.

But the presence of the observer of the picturesque scene is not, in fact, accidental; like the observer in *Rural Hours*, the picturesque spectator actively participates in defining and controlling the scene and infuses that accidental landscape with both history and moral significance. [41] The active role that the viewer takes in constructing the landscape is most apparent in Susan Cooper's meditations on the aesthetic as expressed in "A Dissolving View," her contribution to Putnam's lavish *The Home Book of the Picturesque*. Cooper's entry in this popular volume of essays and illustrations opens with a celebration of the "brilliant novelty" and "strange beauty" of the American autumn. Yet Cooper, in observing her scene from a hilltop vantage point, notes that America has not produced an architecture or a conservation ethic that will encode the culture's history indelibly in the landscape. Since the nation has not accomplished this task, Susan Cooper, as the interpretive observer of the piece, will perform it for her readers, and she ends the essay with an imaginative act that literally transforms the valley below her into the picturesque "view of the valley in the condition it would have assumed, had it lain in the track of European civilization during past ages."[42] In this passage, the narrator participates in the production of what Ann Bermingham calls the "pure spectacle" of landscape aestheticization;[43] she gathers "a sprig of wych-hazel, and waving it over the valley," watches as the "comparatively slight and fugitive" dwellings below her "vanished like the smoke from their own chimneys" ("A Dissolving View," 91).

Not content with merely "razing the village," the narrator of "A Dissolving View" once more waves the witch hazel and watches as a forest and then a "mere hamlet" reappear below her. Cooper has no quarrel with the natural features of the American landscape and assures her reader that they "remained precisely as we had always known them; not a curve in the outline of the lake was changed, not a knoll was misplaced." Even the vegetation, she insists, "was such as we had been long familiar with, and the coloring of the autumnal woods precisely what it had been an hour earlier." "But here," she remarks, "all resemblance ceased." Below her appear almost immediately "low, picturesque, thatched cottages," "a monument of some past historical event," "a castle of gray stone," "beautiful lawns and broad masses of woods," and finally "the ruins of an ancient watchtower" rising from a far hill ("A Dissolving View," 92). The scene that she relates to her reader has all the necessary, conventional marks of William Gilpin's picturesque beauty, which includes "contrasts in light and shadow; rough textures, or 'ruggedness,'" "compositional unity within the varied elements of a scene," and "historical associations."[44] The picturesque eye organizes those varied elements into a unified panorama and allows Cooper to submit nature to Humboldt's "process of thought"; it reveals a cohesive narrative of nature and nation and shows the cultural, historical, and moral progress of a civilized community. Cooper's fanciful act of investing the American landscape with a decidedly European quality, however, serves as a stern reprimand to her own culture, which she sees as determined to "pull down" its historical markers in its quest for "novelty" ("A Dissolving View," 89).

The elements of the constructed landscape of "A Dissolving View" take on a more specifically American nationalist perspective when read in conjunction with Cooper's comments about history and landscape in *Rural Hours*. Cooper's celebration of the American autumn in this passage—and her calculated move to retain the distinctive American woodlands in her new landscape—stems from her delight with the effect the vivid colors of the season have had on the eyes of America's poets and painters. "[T]he march of Autumn through the land," she remarks in a lengthy discussion of the literary representations of the season, "is not a silent one. Scarce a poet of any fame among us who has not at least some graceful verse, some glowing image connected with the season; and year after year the song must become fuller, and sweeter, and clearer" (*Rural Hours,* 209–10). Cooper's examination of the pictorial qualities of the autumn scene leads her to turn her studied eye to its individual components. While her painterly appreciation enables her to take in the "magnificent picture [that] meets the eye," from the "woods that skirt the dimpled meadows" to the "trees which line the streets and road-sides," her training as an amateur naturalist allows her to distinguish the "brilliant scarlet" of the sumac's "long, pinnated leaf" from the "deep, rich red" of the flat-leafed oak and the orange linden from the "wrought gold" aspen (*Rural Hours,* 211). Yet Cooper, always the reverent observer who seeks to extract the moral significance from the scenes surrounding her, necessarily concludes her passage with a meditation on autumn's effect on the faithful observer as she writes: "In very truth, the glory of these last waning days of the season, proclaims a grandeur of beneficence which should rather make our poor hearts swell with gratitude at each return of the beautiful autumn accorded to us" (*Rural Hours,* 213). In this passage, Cooper produces a "fitting" blend of representational modes: her scientifically astute eye allows her to investigate the parts of the scene; her aesthetically informed glance enables her to create a unified whole from those parts; and her theologically rooted understanding of that whole empowers her to derive the moral significance from the scene.

As Lucy Maddox aptly notes, Susan Cooper's *Rural Hours* completes the chronicle of the domestication of the Cooperstown landscape that begins with William Cooper's confrontation of the wilderness, as recorded in his *A Guide in the Wilderness,* and continues with James Fenimore Cooper's records of the subjugation of that wilderness. *Rural Hours,* Maddox writes, provides "the final documentation of the moral and cultural significance of the great undertaking" that "ends with the daughter's inheritance of a place that is no longer wild but comfortably rural."[45] While it is true that Cooper inherits a place whose wildness has been subdued by the controlling hand of human culture, Cooper seeks to do more than just record the comfortable, "simple events" of life in that inherited rural space. Indeed, her complex and complicated text seeks to fix meanings to natural objects during a historical moment in which, as Paul Brooks describes, "the fundamental beliefs about the origin of the earth and man's place in it were shattered beyond repair."[46] Cooper, despite her humble rhetoric, responds directly to these interpretative shifts in religion, science, and philosophy, and *Rural Hours* records her successful struggle to find a mode of representation—that of the picturesque aesthetic—that can accommodate her competing desires. Her writings, moreover, gesture toward an organic (or proto-ecological) model of both the natural world and the representational modes that are employed to understand that world, and she uses the space of *Rural Hours* to compel her readers to interrogate their own understandings of the natural world—their place in it and their responsibilities toward it.

NOTES

1. Susan Cooper, *Rural Hours,* ed. Rochelle Johnson and Daniel Patterson (Athens: University of Georgia Press, 1998), 3. Hereafter cited in text.

2. Lawrence Buell, *The Environmental Imagination: Thoreau, Nature Writing, and the Formation of American Culture* (Cambridge, Mass.: Harvard University Press, 1995), 220.

3. Alexander von Humboldt, *Cosmos: A Sketch of a Physical Description of the Universe,* 5 vols. (London: Henry G. Bohn, 1848), 1:2–3.

4. D. L. LeMahieu, *The Mind of William Paley: A Philosopher and His Age* (Lincoln: University of Nebraska Press, 1976), 172.

5. William Paley, *Natural Theology; or, Evidence of the Existence and Attributes of the Deity Collected from the Appearances of Nature,* ed. Frederick Ferre (1802; New York: Bobbs-Merrill, 1963), 13, 20.

6. Ibid., 44.

7. Barbara Novak, *Nature and Culture: American Landscape Painting 1825–1875* (New York: Oxford University Press, 1980), 25.

8. Ibid., 6.

9. For an excellent discussion of morality and domesticity in *Rural Hours,* see Vera Norwood, *Made from This Earth: American Women and Nature* (Chapel Hill: University of North Carolina Press, 1993), 25–41.

10. For a discussion of ornithology and professional naturalism, see Charlotte

Porter, *The Eagle's Nest: Natural History and American Ideas, 1812–1842* (Tuscaloosa: University of Alabama Press, 1986), 26–51.

11. Cooper's bird families define what Nancy Cott identifies as the social ethic of domesticity, a space where "mother, father, and children grouped together in the private household ruled the transmission of culture, the maintenance of social stability, the pursuit of happiness; the family's influence reached outward, underlying success or failure in church and state, and inward, creating individual character" (*The Bonds of Womanhood: "Woman's Sphere" in New England, 1780–1835* [New Haven, Conn.: Yale University Press, 1977], 1). For a compelling discussion of the role of the home in *Rural Hours,* see Norwood, *Made from This Earth,* 27–42. For an examination of the "Cult of True Womanhood," see Barbara Welter, *Dimity Convictions: The American Woman in the Nineteenth Century* (Athens: Ohio University Press, 1976), 21–41; and Carroll Smith-Rosenberg, *Disorderly Conduct: Visions of Gender in Victorian America* (New York: Oxford University Press, 1985), 173–76. For a discussion of the competing ideal of the "Real Woman," see Frances B. Cogan, *All-American Girl: The Ideal of Real Womanhood in Mid-Nineteenth-Century America* (Athens: University of Georgia Press, 1989), 4–61.

12. Ralph Waldo Emerson, "Nature," in *The Selected Writings of Ralph Waldo Emerson,* ed. Brooks Atkinson (New York: Random House, 1950), 36.

13. Peter Bowler, *The Environmental Sciences* (New York: W. W. Norton, 1992), 204.

14. Henry David Thoreau, "Walking," in *The Writings of Henry David Thoreau,* 20 vols. (Boston: Houghton Mifflin, 1906), 5:205.

15. Elizabeth Keeney, *The Botanizers* (Chapel Hill: University of North Carolina Press, 1992), 100.

16. Christopher Manes, "Nature and Silence," in *The Ecocriticism Reader: Landmarks in Literary Ecology,* ed. Cheryll Glotfelty and Harold Fromm (Athens: University of Georgia Press, 1996), 19.

17. Perry Miller, *The Transcendentalists: An Anthology* (Cambridge, Mass.: Harvard University Press, 1950), 53. On the doctrine of correspondence, see Perry Miller, *Jonathan Edwards* (New York: Delta, 1949), 165–95; for an excellent discussion of language theories and theology in nineteenth-century America, see Philip F. Gura, *The Wisdom of Words: Language, Theology, and Literature in the New England Renaissance* (Middletown, Conn.: Wesleyan University Press, 1981), 75–105.

18. Keeney, *The Botanizers,* 103.

19. In questioning the reliability of biblical translations, Cooper gestures toward the larger debates of the biblical "higher critics" (i.e., Johann Herder and J. G. Eichorn), who suggest that the Scriptures, as a written record of a spoken

word, should be treated as a literary text in critical analysis. The inroads the higher critics made into the authority of translations of biblical texts make Cooper's investigations into alternative translations possible. For discussions of higher criticism and biblical authority in the American context, see Gura, *The Wisdom of Words*, 15–31, and Barbara Packer, "Origin and Authority: Emerson and the Higher Criticism," in *Reconstructing American Literary History*, ed. Sacvan Bercovitch (Cambridge, Mass.: Harvard University Press, 1986), 67–92.

20. Gilian Beer, *Open Fields: Science in Cultural Encounter* (New York: Oxford University Press, 1996), 149.

21. Michael S. Halloran, introduction to *Oratorical Culture in Nineteenth-Century America: Transformations in the Theory and Practice of Rhetoric*, ed. Gregory Clark and Michael S. Halloran (Carbondale: Southern Illinois University Press, 1993), 11.

22. Keeney, *The Botanizers*, 103.

23. Bowler, *The Environmental Sciences*, 163–64.

24. See ibid., 190–305. The burgeoning idea of the environment as an organic system—a web of interrelated parts—with a diverse past and adaptable future put serious strain on the picture of the natural world as a divinely constructed, static entity. As Bowler notes, discoveries in such areas as biogeography (the geographical distribution of organisms), botanical geography, and fossil-based geology, as well as prevalent theories of transmutation and other evolutionary notions that preceded Darwin's *On the Origin of Species* worked together to remove God from the workings of the natural world.

25. Buell, *The Environmental Imagination*, 406.

26. Bowler, *The Environmental Sciences*, 208. Bowler notes that despite the major contributions both Humboldt and Cuvier made to various fields of scientific inquiry, both were soundly criticized by succeeding generations of scientists who were trying to distance themselves from the conceptual limits of arguments from design. Cooper cites only Humboldt's South American travel narratives in *Rural Hours* (75, 302) and not his monumental *Cosmos*. She cites Cuvier twice. In the first instance, he firmly settles a question of the identity of the ibis (*Rural Hours*, 267); in the second, she dismisses his interpretation of the actions of bank swallows, noting that the ideas he supported are "quite abandoned for want of proof" (*Rural Hours*, 329, n. 24).

27. Ann B. Shteir, *Cultivating Women Cultivating Science* (Baltimore, Md.: Johns Hopkins University Press, 1996), 158. See also Beverly Seaton, "The Flower Language Books of the Nineteenth Century," *Morton Arboretum Quarterly* 16 (1980): 1–11.

28. Keeney, *The Botanizers*, 99.

29. For contemporary complaints against sentimental botanies and science

education for women, see Margaret Fuller, *Woman in the Nineteenth Century* (New York: W. W. Norton, 1971), 94–95; Elizabeth Wright, *Lichen Tufts from the Alleghanies* (New York: M. Doolady, 1860), 30–32. Wright concludes her blistering criticisms of sentimental botanies with the comment: "If these books, and the counterfeit 'language' they teach, had not usurped the place of the beautiful science on which they have grown like parasites, they would not be worth the trouble of chastising. But when sensible people come to the conclusion that botany amounts to little more than the language of flowers, and that language such idiotic gibberish as I have quoted from, surely it is time to enter a protest against such usurpation and desecration."

30. Lucy Maddox, "Susan Fenimore Cooper and the Plain Daughters of America," *American Quarterly* 40 (June 1988): 141.

31. Bowler, *The Environmental Sciences*, 166.

32. See Norwood, *Made from This Earth*, 38.

33. Arnold Smithline, *Natural Religion in American Literature* (New Haven, Conn.: College and University Press, 1966), 97.

34. For a good description of the popularization of the sciences in the 1820s and 1830s, see Margaret W. Rossiter, *Women Scientists in America: Struggles and Strategies to 1940* (Baltimore, Md.: Johns Hopkins University Press, 1982), 1–26.

35. Blake Nevius, *Cooper's Landscapes: An Essay on the Picturesque Vision* (Berkeley: University of California Press, 1976), 89.

36. Novak, *Nature and Culture*, 20.

37. For a discussion of Cooper's connections to Ruskin's realist aesthetics, see Buell, *The Environmental Imagination*, 90, 409.

38. Michael S. Halloran, "The Rhetoric of Picturesque Scenery: A Nineteenth Century Epideictic," in *Oratorical Culture*, ed. Clark and Halloran, 239. Many critics contest the reading of the picturesque as creating a clear, detailed picture of the landscape, claiming instead that the picturesque imposes a narrative of national destiny over local details and leads to a distinct blindness to the realities of the landscape (i.e., labor and poverty) and is a determining factor in environmental exploitation. For discussions of the problems of the picturesque, see Stephen Copley and Peter Garside, eds., *The Politics of the Picturesque* (New York: Cambridge University Press, 1994), and Kim Ian Michasiw, "Nine Revisionist Theses on the Picturesque," *Representations* 38 (1992): 76–100.

39. Alison Byerly, "The Uses of Landscape: The Picturesque Aesthetic and the National Park System," in Glotfelty and Fromm, eds., *The Ecocriticism Reader*, 54, 55.

40. Byerly, "The Uses of Landscape," 53.

41. Halloran, "The Rhetoric of Picturesque Scenery," 243.

42. Susan Cooper, "A Dissolving View," in *The Home Book of the Pictur-*

esque; or, American Scenery, Art, and Literature (New York: G. P. Putnam, 1852), 92. Hereafter cited in text.

43. Ann Bermingham, "The Picturesque and Ready-to-Wear Femininity," in *The Politics of the Picturesque*, ed. Copley and Garside, 85.

44. William Gilpin, "On Picturesque Travel," in *Three Essays: On Picturesque Beauty; On Picturesque Travel; and On Sketching Landscape: to which is added a poem, on Landscape Painting*, 2nd ed. (London: R. Blamire, 1794; Westmead, England: Gregg International, 1972), 42, quoted in Beth Lueck, *American Writers and the Picturesque Tour: The Search for National Identity 1790–1860* (New York: Garland, 1997), 6. For a good discussion of the compositional elements of the picturesque scene, see Stephen Copley and Peter Garside, introduction to *The Politics of the Picturesque*, ed. Copley and Garside, 3–25.

45. Maddox, "Susan Fenimore Cooper and the Plain Daughters of America," 141.

46. Paul Brooks, *Speaking for Nature* (Boston: Houghton Mifflin, 1980), xv.

PART FOUR

Susan Fenimore Cooper
among Her Contemporaries

ERIKA M. KREGER

Rustic Matters: Placing the Rural Community Narratives of Alice Cary, Susan Fenimore Cooper, and Caroline Kirkland in the Context of the Nineteenth-Century Women's Sketchwriting Tradition

Although early critics were quick to conclude that Susan Fenimore Cooper wrote *Rural Hours* (1850) "without benefit of any American precedent,"[1] more recent scholarship has correctly observed that her work derives from a "thriving local sketchbook tradition" that may have originated with Mary Russell Mitford in England but, by the mid–nineteenth century, was dominated by women writing in the United States.[2] Cooper had no need to look across the Atlantic for literary mentors who presented realistic observations about their surroundings in nonlinear, nonfictional prose. She had only to pick up one of the many popular magazines of her day to find numerous examples of such writing exhibited in journalistic sketches—short prose works emphasizing character and description rather than plot—that were also frequently collected in best-selling volumes.[3] A hybrid form, the sketch exhibits elements of autobiography, fiction, and essay. Its flexibility made it a favorite choice of the women editors and authors who were a vital part of American print culture during the antebellum era.

Considering *Rural Hours* in the context of the sketch tradition, we see that Cooper did not necessarily step out alone and "set the stage for women nature essayists."[4] Instead, she joined the established ranks of American female writers producing realistic accounts of rural communities.[5] By placing Cooper's nature diary alongside the community narratives of her successful contemporaries, Caroline Kirkland and Alice Cary, it becomes apparent that all three share the common concerns, subject matter, and viewpoint of the American woman sketchwriter. Although each presents a distinctive persona (Kirkland's more assertive, Cary's more somber, and Cooper's more subtle), they all clearly borrow and develop the techniques of their sketchwriting predecessors. Each approaches her work with the matter-of-factness of a journalist, explicitly arguing for both the value of simple prose and the significance of quotidian events. Each rejects the constraints imposed by plot-driven literary forms and culturally constructed oppositions, instead crafting a cyclical narrative that illustrates the possibility of intermingling the domestic, natural, and public worlds. Each claims both a female perspective and an authoritative voice, engaging in dialogue with other observers whose comments require correction. All three of these writers record local history, helping their readers to see the value of an interdependent rustic life driven by communal rather than capitalistic forces and challenging conventional assumptions of what matters in both life and literature.

Noting Cooper's debts to predecessors and similarities to contemporaries should not, however, obscure her unique contribution to American nature writing and environmental thought. While she employs a participant-observer narrator and emphasizes rural location in the manner of the female sketchwriters, she does not choose to foreground the narrator's individual consciousness as many of these other female authors do. This desubjectified perspective has been critiqued by those justifying the obscurity of *Rural Hours* in comparison to Henry David Thoreau's similarly constructed but more forcefully individualistic *Walden* (1854).[6] Cooper does indeed reject the self-involved romantic voice. Instead, as Lawrence Buell points out, she develops remarkably detailed "environmentally informed descriptions" that "show more . . . place consciousness than Thoreau attempted in print."[7] In fact, *Rural Hours* evokes a consciousness of more than one kind of "place." Cooper pairs her account of the physical environment with an argument regarding humanity's position in the continuum of ecocultural history. In her view, if humanity knows its place as inheritor, cultivator, guardian, and chronicler of the landscape, then both human communities and natural environments will thrive. In *Rural Hours,* Cooper demonstrates that people need to position themselves as parts of a social and ecological network. While taking much from the structure, style, and spirit of the village sketch, Cooper's adaptation pushes the form's communitarian ethic one step farther, incorporating nonhuman life into its cooperative social vision. To show readers her "place," both her geographic region and her communal role, Cooper must reveal not the inward-looking musings of one idiosyncratic person but rather the outward-directed observations of a representative figure participating in the interdependent ecocultural activities of her rural location.

Cooper appreciated landscapes depicted in the "natural style" that provides, as she defines it in *Rural Hours,* "something more positive, more real" to an audience "grown tired of mere vapid, conventional repetitions."[8] She admired those writers who "recently began to look out of the window more frequently; when writing a pastoral they turned away from the little porcelain shepherds and shepherdesses, standing in high-heeled shoes . . . and they fixed their eyes upon the real living Roger and Dolly in the hay-field" (*Rural Hours,* 208). It is this second kind of "real living" pastoral vision that Cooper, Kirkland, and Cary all adopt in their community narratives. Before moving on to an examination of their works, it will be helpful to review briefly both the basic elements of this type of American pastoral and its relationship to the women's sketchwriting tradition.

As critics such as Annette Kolodny have noted, American writings idealizing an intermediate space between wilderness and civilization—such as the women's western narratives that depict the frontier as a garden—contrast with the typical male frontier myths wherein heroes flee to the wilderness to escape a suffocating society characterized as feminine.[9] Such descriptions of a gardenlike frontier not only run counter to the masculine frontier vision but also perpetuate the age-old pastoral ideal of a human-created middle ground between raw nature and corrupt culture. Often depicting rural communities that possess the potential of becoming such ideal spaces, many nineteenth-century sketchwriters advocate eighteenth-century values associated with Thomas Jefferson. Jefferson, as Leo Marx reminds us, put forth "a pastoral, not an agrarian, vision," a vision based not on profit-oriented economics but "on the allegedly superior moral integrity of people who live closer to the soil."[10] Such people occupy the same intermediate realm associated from ancient times forward with the shepherd, who when viewed "against the background of the wilderness . . . appears to be a representative of a complex, hierarchical, urban society," yet "against the background of the settled community . . . appears to epitomize the virtues of a simple unworldly life" (Marx, "Pastoralism," 43).

This pastoral vision held particular appeal for American settlers, who during the nineteenth century saw no contradiction in embracing "simultaneously and as if perfectly compatible—both the progressive and pastoral ideals," believing that "[t]o establish a society of the 'middle landscape' it was first necessary to transform the wilderness into a garden" (Marx, "Pastoralism," 49). Kirkland, Cary, and Cooper all idealize this "middle landscape" in their community narratives and, as women of their time, occasionally fail to recognize any inconsistencies in pairing progressive and pastoral goals. Like the other writers drawn to the "new pastoralism" that Marx discusses, they do not wish for "a return to some imagined state of unmodified nature" ("Pastoralism," 58). Rather, "[w]hat matters most to them, as it had to Thomas Jefferson, is the proper subordination of material concerns to other, less tangible aspects of life—whether aesthetic, moral, political, or spiritual" (Marx, "Pastoralism," 59).

What distinguishes most women's community sketches from other nineteenth-century texts presenting the Jeffersonian ideal is that the sketch-writers typically offer a plan for perpetuating a pastoral environment, a plan they believe can work. Considering only male-authored narratives, Marx notes that most "classic American literary texts" are "pastoral[s] of failure" that convey "both the enormous appeal that this pastoral motive holds" and its "impotence in the face of . . . practical, material motives" ("Pastoralism," 59). In contrast to such stories of failure, women sketch-writers like Cary, Cooper, and Kirkland wrote pastorals of possibility that, even when depicting the flaws of a given settlement, argue for the attainability of the ideal middle ground.

This positive outlook is very much in evidence in the writings of Mary Russell Mitford, the British author whose best-selling series *Our Village* (1824–32) popularized the village sketch on both sides of the Atlantic. Mitford's active narrator, clear prose, sharp wit, and communitarian values provided a model for many American women searching for a way to present their vision of rural life.[11] Subtitled *Sketches of Rural Character, Our Village* models the clarity and concreteness Mitford argued for in both her public literary reviews and private correspondence.[12] Unlike the wide-ranging fancy sketches—also popular during this era—that imitated the aristocratic style and removed perspective of Washington Irving's *Sketchbook of Geoffrey Crayon* (1819–20), Mitford's life sketches offer an insider's view of quotidian events taking place in a single locale.[13] But though they focus on everyday objects and ordinary people, the sketches of *Our Village* paint what some considered an overly cheerful portrait of rural life.[14] Therefore, American writers who wished not only to describe but also to improve their local communities adapted Mitford's form to their purposes by pairing her vivid detail with pointed critique.

The most successful American adapter of the village sketch form, Caroline Kirkland, acknowledges in the preface to her first book, *A New Home, Who'll Follow?* (1839), "that Miss Mitford's charming sketches of village life . . . suggested the form of my rude attempt."[15] Yet the reader needs only to read a few pages of *A New Home* to recognize that though

Kirkland has borrowed the structure of *Our Village,* she has an assertive narrative style all her own. In her vivid and often satiric description of a nascent Michigan settlement, Kirkland presents authentic life sketches, using vivid characterizations, authentic local dialect, and unromanticized anecdotes to show the region as it really was and offers witty commentary to both inform and amuse her readership.

Kirkland purposely chose the nonlinear form and realistic style she felt would further her goal of debunking fashionable ideas about the frontier contained in other authors' "elegant sketches of western life" (*A New Home,* 49). Employing the interactive style characteristic of the era's periodicals, she fits her work into an ongoing national literary dialogue. Before heading west herself, she had read the works of Charles Fenno Hoffman and James Hall but soon discovered that "these pictures, touched by the glowing pencil of fancy," had given her all sorts of misconceptions about living in a new settlement (*A New Home,* 6). Early in her own narrative, she repeatedly advises her audience to expect neither linear development nor fanciful imaginings: her "meandering recital of common-place occurrences" will offer only an "unvarnished transcript of real characters" and an "impartial record of every-day forms of speech" (*A New Home,* 3). Those who might have expectations of finding aristocratic musings are put on notice by the author: "I make my confession at the outset, warning any fashionable reader who may have taken up my book, that I intend to be 'decidedly low'" (*A New Home,* 4).

The critical and popular success of *A New Home* attests to the fact that readers had no objections to such "low" subject matter and "every-day" speech but rather welcomed what was heralded as the first accurate account of life on the American frontier. One of the best-selling books in the United States up until that time, *A New Home* went into three editions in three years and soon replaced *Our Village* as the point of departure and comparison for any author or reviewer discussing rural communities or domestic existence.[16] Although she published both *A New Home* and its sequel, *Forest Life* (1842), under the pseudonym Mary Clavers, Kirkland's real identity was soon widely known, and from the mid-1840s onward her work appeared under her own name. Whether writing as Clavers or Kirkland, she spoke her mind, repeatedly defending her (and all women's) right to both possess and publish strong opinions. Even after enduring angry reactions from her neighbors in the village of Pinckney, the real-life model of *A New Home*'s Montacute, Kirkland still, in the preface to *Forest Life,* insists on her rights: "I shall not renounce my privilege of remarking freely on all subjects of general interest. In matters of opinion I claim the freedom which is my birthright as an American, and still further, the plainness of speech which is a striking characteristic of this Western country." [17]

Kirkland employs this authoritative, plain-speaking persona in all of her western sketches. Like Mitford before her and Cary and Cooper after her, she writes as a knowledgeable insider whose authority derives from living in the community and sharing the experiences of the people she describes. The reader follows along as the Clavers persona gets stuck in mud holes, smoked out of her cabin, and surprised by snakes. We accompany her as she circularly moves in and around—rather than linearly through—her environment. As she makes visits, manages housekeeping disasters, wrangles children and pets, struggles to plant a garden, and so on, she laughs at herself and her circumstances and then learns how to adapt. Witty and self-deprecating, she is no less an example of female agency for all of her flaws. Her character as well as her sketches model the processes of community formation. Kirkland learns from her neighbors, relinquishing some of the individualistic and elitist ideas that hinder communal prosperity, while her multivocal narrative incorporates opinions and perspectives other than her own, reflecting the negotiations involved in building a truly democratic community. Although directed at an urban middle-class audience that knows as little about frontier life as the narrator, *A New Home* repeatedly gives the last word to the dialect speakers, often showing at the conclusion of a sketch "that the common sense was all on their side" (42).

At the beginning of *A New Home,* the educated Mary Clavers persona is distressed by her unschooled Michigan neighbors, who refuse any "acknowledgment of inferior station" (39). She soon comes to understand, however, the interdependent nature of frontier life, realizing the absurdity of maintaining a "proud distinction" where any daily crisis "may throw you entirely upon the kindness of your humblest neighbor" (*A New Home,* 65). Even though the practical reasons for such interclass associations are readily apparent, it is only after "the barriers of pride and prejudice are broken" that she can see the less tangible benefits of these interactions and "discover a certain satisfaction in this homely fellowship" that well repays the "concessions" she had to make (*A New Home,* 185). Her "philosophy was of a slow growth," but in the end she has no "regret [about] having been obliged to relinquish what was, after all, rather a silly sort of pride" (*A New Home,* 40).

Of course, the sophisticated Kirkland never entirely reconciles herself to rustic manners, such as those exhibited by Mrs. Jennings, who agrees to come in and "chore around" but expects to share family meals, "drink tea from the spout of the tea-pot," and dip "her own spoon or knife into every dish on the table" (*A New Home,* 51). Rather, Kirkland maintains faith in her fellow settlers' potential for growth and improvement, optimistically hoping that "the silent influence of [her] example is daily effecting much towards reformation" of her neighbors' "most unpleasant . . . habits" (*A New Home,* 53). Until such reform takes place, however, she learns "many ways of *wearing round,*" blending Eastern and Western habits just as her text often blends erudite and dialect speech, and so is able to live "very much after my own fashion, without offending" her rustic companions (*A New Home,* 52).

Kirkland sees the development of a community, like the reformation of a person, as a gradual process. The West may be mismanaged, but she does not consider the situation there as any less correctable than the bad manners of her neighbors. So while *A New Home* offers readers sketches that critique, among other things, the waste of resources in the West (11, 77), the land sharks who inflict economic hardships on unwary investors (31, 55, 121, 126), and the misguided romantics unprepared for frontier realities (78, 99–107, 156, 160–67), it also provides numerous glimpses of the advantages—of both people and place—that could help the region fulfill its pastoral potential.

Though the practical Mrs. Clavers is hardly one to sit around "picturesquing" like a vacationing college student, once she has given "due weight to the many disadvantages and trials of a new-country life," she takes time to describe the natural beauty of her environment and the "compensating power of the wilderness" (*A New Home,* 162, 148). Like the ancient shepherd and his flocks, Montacute stands in that fortunate position distanced from both the city comforts "apt to make us proud, selfish, and ungrateful" and the "unwatched and unbridled license which we read of in regions nearer to the setting sun" (*A New Home,* 183, 147). In this intermediate realm, Kirkland witnesses "the placid contentment, which seems the heritage of rural life" and "the harmony which the Creator has instituted between the animate and inanimate works of His hand" (*A New Home,* 148).

Such harmony is threatened, however, by profit motives that disrupt the balanced resource allocation of the rural ideal and thwart the process of community development. Kirkland laments that many settlers sacrifice the palpable "*home*-feeling, which is so large an ingredient in happiness," to the pursuit of intangible wealth (*A New Home,* 22). This type of farmer neglects "domestic comfort[s]" because they "will not add to the moneyed value of his farm"; he concentrates instead on acquiring land because "the possession of a large number of acres is esteemed a great good, though it makes but little difference in the owner's mode of living" (*A New Home,* 22). By contrast, Kirkland herself sees no value in real estate or currency unless it impacts one's daily existence. Although well aware of the power of the "almighty dollar" in other regions, she tells the reader that "money has never seemed so valueless to me since I have experienced how little it will buy me in the woods" (*A New Home,* 52, 120). Appreciating only the use-value of things, Kirkland is a model of the occupant of the middle ground who is immune to the corrupting forces of capitalism. These forces are personified in *A New Home* by the land speculators of the neighboring settlement of Tinkerville, "cunning and stealthy blood-suckers" who care nothing about developing a livable community but only want to turn acres into cash (121). When Tinkerville fails, however, readers receive a clear indication of the negative repercussions of unchecked capitalistic impulses.

After witnessing "the distress among the poorer classes of farmers" who lost money in the Tinkerville scheme, Kirkland has a renewed apprehension of "the inequalities in the distribution of the gifts of fortune" in her nation (*A New Home,* 186). Although these disparities "are not greater in the country than in town, but the contrary," they still hinder Kirkland's plan for community development. Having gained insights into the situation, Kirkland wants her account of these problems to bring "wholesome and much-needed instruction home to those whom prosperity and indulgence may have rendered unsympathizing" (*A New Home,* 186). This indulged audience is, of course, the middle-class, city-dwelling readership to whom Kirkland directs her narrative. Here, and throughout *A New Home,* she adopts an instructive tone, passing on her own hard-won rural wisdom to the "spoiled child of civilization" (185).

Though amusing on the surface, Kirkland's sketches contain at their core lessons in the development of public virtue, the democratizing power of knowledge, and the dangers of superficiality. Like other nineteenth-century women sketchwriters, Kirkland could publish her views about civic matters without fearing that she might be stepping outside her culturally defined gender role. Women in the United States had been chronicling and critiquing local and national events for generations. As Nina Baym has shown, Americans could look to a long tradition of female history-writing that, since the days of the early Republic, had validated women's "rights to know and opine on the world outside the home, as well as to circulate their knowledge and opinions among the public."[18]

Kirkland's civic-minded persona regularly echoes the voice and values of the republican mother; an eighteenth-century ideal that informs the history-writing tradition, this figure not only prepares her children to become model citizens but also has a "public destiny" as a teacher "of the entire nation, even of the world." [19]

Another adapter of the village sketch form, Alice Cary, also saw herself enacting the roles of teacher and historian, but her account of farming life in Ohio does not soften its hard lessons with the sort of humor that lightens the difficult truths recounted in A New Home.[20] Cary aims to "instruct readers who have regarded the farming class as essentially different and inferior" on how to appreciate the merits of an often-misrepresented population, yet she refuses to gloss over the deprivations of rural poverty.[21] In her Clovernook sketches, we again encounter a persona presenting accounts of everyday rural life from an insider's perspective. Even more than Kirkland, Cary focuses on the physical details of her environment, closely describing both interior and exterior scenes with the same specificity seen in Rural Hours. In the minor artifacts of domestic comfort and the small beauties of nature, Cary finds the only recompense for the often overwhelming hardships of existence. For although she, too, sees community life as interdependent, she emphasizes the sufferings that arise when neighbors and families let each other down, offering only brief glimpses of beneficial cooperation. Although the village of Clovernook sits in the ideal intermediate realm between city and woods, its potential for becoming a pastoral middle ground remains, like the talents of its less-privileged inhabitants, undeveloped.

As Mitford and Kirkland had before her, Cary emphasized her goal of presenting rural life simply and realistically. Although willing to embellish when composing the poetry that initially brought her national acclaim, Cary aims for "the simplest fidelity" in her prose (Clovernook, viii). She intended the sketches contained in Clovernook; or, Recollections of Our Neighborhood in the West (1851) to depict "natural and probable," "honest relations" (vii, vi).

Recognizing that most literary depictions of country people were highly improbable, Cary, like Kirkland, saw the need to correct accounts based on imagination rather than experience. As she tells us in her preface, "the masters of literature who at any time have attempted the exhibition of rural life, have, with few exceptions, known scarcely anything of it from participation, and however brilliant may have been their pictures, therefore, they have seldom been true" (Clovernook, vi). Having been raised in the rustic circumstances she describes, Cary can claim an authority the "masters of literature" lack, an authority—like that claimed by other sketchwriters—based on a detailed knowledge of people and place. In contrast to the privileged educated persona of *A New Home,* however, Cary's narrator speaks from the disadvantaged perspective of the poor rustic. Like Mitford and Kirkland, Cary writes for a middle-class audience, but instead of suggesting a shared worldview, she places herself outside their class position and attempts to make them understand the painful yearnings of those shut out from the advantages of bourgeois society. Whereas in *A New Home* readers laugh with the ill-prepared sophisticate who arrives in the country wearing thin-soled slippers, in *Clovernook* the audience suffers with the shoeless rustic girl embarrassed by the bare feet that mark her as inferior to a passing gentleman (*A New Home,* 6; *Clovernook,* 276).

The painful feeling of deprivation that the narrator and many *Clovernook* characters experience, however, is prompted more by a desire for status and education than a wish for material goods. The poor people Cary depicts yearn for the less tangible advantages that money brings, the chance to develop intellectual talents and participate in cultivated society. Over and over, we see characters whose desires for such advantages are thwarted, characters who know they possess great native abilities that will never be recognized (*Clovernook,* 60, 102, 191, 205). Judith Fetterley has called Cary's narrative persona the "entitled rustic," a speaker who despite humble beginnings feels she has a right to all the opportunities society has to offer and resents being denied the advantages to which she feels entitled.[22]

Cary, however, introduces the reader to many entitled rustics other than the narrator. The *Clovernook* sketches, unlike those of *Our Village* and *A New Home,* focus less on the speaker's actions and attitudes and more on the detailed scenes and situations she describes. In the first *Clovernook* volume, Cary's narrator, despite offering opinions in the first person and revealing that she lives in and knows the community well, rarely draws the reader's attention to herself as a participant in the events she depicts. Instead, employing what Fetterley calls a "poetics of detail,"[23] Cary paints a word picture of the "small things that make up the sum of human happiness or misery" (*Clovernook,* 150).[24]

Other American women writers, as Sandra Zagarell explains, also developed this sort of "hermeneutics of the everyday" in their community sketches.[25] Cary's interpretation of quotidian experience, however, is marked by a heightened sense of suffering. Her world is "full of bruised and crushed hearts and desolate spirits," and so she reminds us "we have need to be kind to each other" (*Clovernook*, 298–99). Yet too often those who should be kind are neglectful or repressive. Cary's sketches offer many examples of the oversize wounds inflicted by seemingly minor acts: cruel words, broken promises, selfish deeds (*Clovernook*, 193, 201, 290). But in an interdependent community, it requires only a little thoughtless behavior to disrupt the flow of life (*Clovernook*, 62).

Fortunately, there are thoughtful individuals in *Clovernook* to help counteract the misdeeds of the thoughtless, like the character of Aunt Jane, who understands the "blessings that are in the world—and with her own hand brings them near" (255). A "true comforter," Aunt Jane knows not to attempt to cheer a bereaved person with useless words, but instead she "sends a bowl of sweet milk, sometimes a loaf of bread or cake, sometimes the last newspaper. . . . These little things are not without meaning—they have a humanizing tendency . . . and stimulate us to do in return good deeds" (*Clovernook*, 255–56). The narrator offers some light to her often bleak worldview by acknowledging that "in the by-ways of life, there are a great many such good women as Aunt Jane" (*Clovernook*, 256). Such practical, hard-working people who know how to make the best of difficult situations are capable of finding contentment. The right attitude makes all the difference in rural life, as Cary illustrates in her sketch that contrasts the cheerful Mrs. Hall with the complaining Mrs. Troost (*Clovernook*, 69–70).[26] Destiny may not guarantee anyone happiness, but Cary makes clear that those who refuse to make any efforts on their own behalf because they mistakenly believe they have no control over their fates guarantee themselves unhappiness (*Clovernook*, 228, 243–44, 269).

In *Clovernook* the virtues of good people and the beauties of the landscape are all that mitigate the unrelenting facts of poverty and hard labor. Cary depicts a certain sympathy between natural elements and human emotions; changes in weather and animal behavior often reflect (rather than prompt) shifts in characters' feelings (*Clovernook*, 50, 228, 286). The majority of sketches begin and conclude with references to the seasons or to a death, emphasizing the cyclical quality of life. Although many of these moments are somber in tone, they are balanced by a few idyllic passages wherein someone finds contentment in the "middle ground" of a pasture or hillside and the sympathetic company of an understanding companion. The city, depicted negatively, offers no escape from the relentless labor required to maintain rural fields and homes (*Clovernook*, 231).

Characters do find brief respite, however, in natural settings. One such scene introduces two sisters who, in those few moments free from work, can be found "in a field of sweet clover sitting in the shade of a beautiful maple, just on the slope of a hill, washed at the base by a runnel of silvery water." "This favorite haunt" is a perfect intermediate spot, "on the one side, toward the willow valley; beyond which, dark and thick, stretched a long line of woods; and on the other side [the] white stones of the grave-yard . . . and [a] cottage" (*Clovernook*, 272). Here Cary suggests that despite the hardships it inflicts, this rural environment also possesses the ideal qualities of the middle landscape.

As she made clear in her preface, Cary's subject in *Clovernook* is the "pastoral life of our country," a life she distinguishes from the existence "in the far west where pioneers are still busy with felling the opposing trees, [and] it is not yet time for the reed's music" (v). Similarly, she notes that "the interior of my native state, which was wilderness when first my father went to it," has now become a place exhibiting as much "to interest us in humanity as there can be in those old empires where the press of tyrannous laws and the deadening influence of hereditary acquaintance necessarily destroy the best life of society" (*Clovernook*, v–vi). Clover-nook is blessed with a middle-ground location, neither as corrupt as the Old World nor as harsh as the new frontier. Cary expresses approval of the changes the first settlers made to the landscape, as well as faith in the gradual development through hard work of both people and communities (*Clovernook*, 81–82, 244). Progress may be slow and setbacks many, but even the struggling village of Clovernook is moving toward achieving its pastoral potential.

Susan Fenimore Cooper expresses this same faith in community devel-opment in her account of rural life in New York state. *Rural Hours,* like the volumes discussed above, chronicles the daily events of a single com-munity. This community, however, consists of an entire ecocultural net-work, including animals and vegetation. In Cooper's nature diary, one encounters ethnographic detail comparable to Cary's and civic-minded in-struction much like Kirkland's. Like these sketchwriters, Cooper aims for accuracy rather than imaginativeness, emphasizes life cycles rather than linear plot, and advocates communal rather than capitalistic values. What sets her "ecocultural sketch" apart from earlier works of village sketch literature, however, is its heightened sense of the interdependence be-tween human and nonhuman entities.[27] Cooper emphasizes the intellec-tual, emotional, and moral value in animals and vegetation, as well as their practical and aesthetic attributes. She focuses the reader's attention not on her own personality but on the multilevel meanings of all the things that surround her. Hers genuinely is a narrative of community, foregrounding the multiple aspects of place, rather than a narrative of a person, foregrounding one individual's thoughts.[28]

Although written "in journal form," the "trifling observations on rustic matters" that make up *Rural Hours* share many of the formal characteristics and thematic concerns of other nineteenth-century women's community sketches (3). The reader finds Cooper's narrative voice and structure—a community insider giving detailed accounts of circular journeys in and around her local environment—quite familiar. Each of her journal entries—offering brief accounts of community events, scenic landmarks, seasonal changes—could stand alone as a periodical sketch. Cooper shares the sketchwriter's concern with accuracy, prefacing her diary with the same protestations of realism we have heard from Kirkland and Cary. Her hope is that *Rural Hours* is "free from great inaccuracies"; at least, she reassures readers, "the following pages were written in perfect good faith, all the trifling incidents alluded to having occurred as they are recorded" (3). She advocates "truthful description" of both "inanimate nature" and "any fellow-man" (*Rural Hours,* 329). Like Kirkland's plain-speaking persona, she argues for simple language that fits its subject, lamenting, for example, the trend of giving plants "long, clumsy, Latin appellations, very little fitted for every-day uses," rather than the "pretty, natural names" provided in "olden times" when there "was some simplicity left in the world" (*Rural Hours,* 83–84).[29] Although respectful of science and academe, she does not hesitate to reject scholarly rhetoric in favor of everyday language. On this point, as on many others, Cooper—like the traditional woman sketchwriter—speaks with an authority derived from personal experience.[30]

With the confidence that comes from detailed knowledge of her local environment, Cooper freely engages in dialogue with the observers who came before her. She shows no hesitation in correcting the mistaken notions of other naturalists, especially those ideas, like the ludicrous theories about hibernating swallows, put forth by people "both learned and unlearned" who ignore factual evidence and "show a sort of antipathy to simple truths" (*Rural Hours,* 167). *Rural Hours* is, in one sense, a collection of such simple truths. Cooper encourages readers to adopt her value system, not by winning them over with witty commentary or impressing them with scholarly authority but, rather, by assembling a wealth of detail that validates the accuracy of her worldview. She illustrates interior and exterior scenes with equal sensitivity, breaking down, as Vera Norwood points out, the conceptual boundaries between "indoors" and "outdoors."[31]

Cooper finds equal variety and interest in listing the utensils hanging in a farm kitchen and recounting the many types of grasses in a meadow (*Rural Hours*, 98, 76). When looking out from the woods at the local lake, she finds the "archway of green branches" as "fine a frame" as "the elaborate mouldings of a great Gothic window" (*Rural Hours*, 21). Readers might reconsider their definition of greatness, of what has value and significance, as they see more of this community that encompasses both woods and village and includes animals as well as people. Here, the arrival of the first robins is a "great event," the death of a fawn is a great sorrow, the change of the seasons has great meaning (*Rural Hours*, 8, 151, 212–13).

In her reevaluation of the meaning of events others might deem insignificant, Cooper reminds the reader of the multilevel value of all things. For example, when discussing the benefits of realism, she argues that learning "to look at nature by the light of the sun, and not by the glimmerings of the poet's lamp" is "a great step . . . not only in art, but in moral and intellectual progress" (*Rural Hours*, 208). Accuracy in describing nature is not merely a stylistic choice but also has a moral dimension. Here and throughout *Rural Hours*, Cooper models the way antebellum thinkers often link ideas late-twentieth-century scholars have consigned to rigidly separated academic disciplines. As Brigitte Georgi-Findlay notes, in the nineteenth century, "science, art, and religion came to be regarded as parallel, mutually reinforcing modes of knowledge"; so in the writings of this era, as we see in Cooper's diary, "the discourse of natural history is continuously invoked in order to support religious and aesthetic beliefs." [32]

Cooper's ability to incorporate many modes of knowledge into her interpretation of a natural scene is nowhere more apparent than in her comments on the preservation of trees. In a fuller development of the communal value system Kirkland and Cary advocate, Cooper suggests an alternative to viewing resources with a profit-seeking, capitalist eye. She explains the "relative value of forests," showing readers that "independently of their market price in dollars and cents, the trees have other values: they are connected in many ways with the civilization of a country; they have their importance in an intellectual and in a moral sense" (*Rural Hours*, 133). Cooper frequently points out the historical, practical, and spiritual ways the "forest contributes to the wants of our race" (*Rural Hours*, 129). And like Kirkland, who critiques the way that "the very notion of advancement, of civilization, or prosperity, seems inseparably connected with the total extirpation of the forest" in Michigan (*Forest Life*, 43), Cooper suggests a redefinition of progress and profit.

Although she is hardly surprised that those "whose chief object in life is to make money" try to turn "timber into bank-notes with all possible speed," Cooper finds it "remarkable that anyone at all aware of the value of wood, should act so wastefully" (*Rural Hours*, 132, 134). Real social progress will be made only when people appreciate the living forest's value to the community more than the dead wood's value on the market. If the nation pushes forward with the capitalist's notion of progress, "another half century may find the country bleak and bare" (*Rural Hours*, 128). Yet Cooper, sharing Kirkland's and Cary's hope for eventual reformation, believes this bleak future can be avoided: "time is a very essential element" in the development of "true civilization," and "in the course of years we shall, it is to be hoped, learn farther lessons of this kind"; "when we have made this farther progress, then we shall take better care of our trees" (*Rural Hours*, 133, 134).

The village at the center of *Rural Hours* seems closer to "true civiliza-tion" than the nation as a whole; it is a community blessed with the ideal location and noble citizens of the middle landscape. Unlike the foolish folk who "left their fields untilled, while they followed the speculating hordes westward" in search of wealth and "unspoiled" wilderness, Cooper sees no need to look beyond the populated cultivated spaces of her local re-gion to find a potential paradise (*Rural Hours*, 245). Why search out new places when there is a "virtue in constancy" that gives "strength and pu-rity to every affection in life" and offers "a reward above all that fickle change can bestow" (*Rural Hours*, 29)?[33] And Cooper's neighbors have every reason to remain loyal, for in her narrative we once again encounter an ideal intermediate locale. Free from urban corruption, "it has a cheer-ful, flourishing aspect, yet rural and unambitious, not aping the bustle and ferment of cities," but it is still more developed than the "new lands on the prairies" (*Rural Hours*, 69, 78). Looking over the area's hillsides, Cooper sees a balance between the wild and the civilized: "there is an abundance of wood on their swelling ridges to give the charm of forest scenery, enough of tillage to add the varied interest of cultivation" (*Rural Hours*, 69).

This happy neighborhood owes as much to the "active, intelligent char-acter of the people" as to the "natural features of the country itself" (*Ru-ral Hours*, 89). Perhaps partly because she has less experience with hard physical labor than someone like Cary, Cooper idealizes the work that takes place in and around the farmhouse, echoing Jefferson in her depic-tion of a population that achieves moral superiority through its work (*Ru-ral Hours*, 99). In Cooper's view, a rural activity such as gardening is a "civilizing and improving occupation in itself"; it "makes people more industrious, and more amiable" (*Rural Hours*, 81). Such people enhance, rather than detract from, the natural environment. As Cooper notes in her nature sketch "A Dissolving View" (1852), she believes that "the hand of man generally improves a landscape." Yet it is crucial to remember one's place in the larger scheme of life: when man "endeavors to rise above his true part of laborer and husbandman, when he assumes the character of creator," then "he is apt to fail."[34]

The success of a person or a community depends upon such an acknowledgment of humanity's position as cultivator and guardian, rather than creator and owner, of the environment. Although closer to success than the inhabitants of Montacute or Clovernook, the population Cooper depicts in *Rural Hours* is not without flaws. Cooper acknowledges negative qualities: bad manners, infringement on others' rights, theft, poverty, cruel treatment of Indians, and so on (*Rural Hours*, 79–80, 112, 158). Yet Cooper has faith in society's potential for improvement. Like Kirkland, she speaks with the confidence of a republican mother, offering her country a plan that will help in its reformation.[35]

The model community of *Rural Hours* is an interdependent network. Throughout her narrative, Cooper brings natural and nonhuman entities inside the communal boundaries by giving them qualities usually reserved for humans. She invests plants and animals, especially birds and trees, with as much individuality as people. In *Rural Hours*, birds have distinctive families (23, 34, 47), violets seem like sisters (47), and neighboring trees have variations like those "observed in human beings among members of one family" (38). All these life forms are part of the ongoing historical and ecocultural continuum. But as Cooper's repeated references to the loss of native plants and species indicate, in such an interdependent environmental network, small changes can have broad-reaching impact. Just as "it often lies within the power of a single group of trees to alter the whole aspect of acres of surrounding lands," so, too, the presence or absence of one link in the environmental chain can have a great effect (*Rural Hours*, 6). The text of *Rural Hours* certainly indicates that Cooper shares environmental historian William Cronon's awareness that "human acts occur within a network of relationships, processes, and systems that are as ecological as they are cultural." In Cronon's view, describing our world today requires a "vocabulary in which plants, animals, soils, climates, and other nonhuman entities become the codeterminants of a history not just of people but of the earth itself," just the sort of vocabulary Cooper strove to develop more than a century ago.[36]

Today's readers have much to gain by considering Cooper not only as an important precursor of current environmental thought but also as an inheritor of the nineteenth-century women's sketchwriting tradition. Cooper, like her contemporaries Kirkland and Cary, employs a nonlinear narrative structure, depicts a single community with great detail, emphasizes a communal value system, engages in dialogue with earlier commentators, and idealizes a rural locale that has the attributes of the pastoral middle landscape. Yet Cooper puts these techniques and themes to unique use, broadening the definition of community to include the entire ecocultural network, presenting a powerful model of place-consciousness, and reaffirming a value system in which rural and domestic experiences really do matter. Placing *Rural Hours* in the context of other antebellum women's community sketches allows us not only to better understand antebellum women's literary history but also to appreciate Cooper's vital and original contribution to American nature writing.

NOTES

1. Thomas F. O'Donnell, foreword to *Rural Hours,* by Susan Fenimore Cooper (Syracuse, N.Y.: Syracuse University Press, 1968), viii.

2. Lawrence Buell, *The Environmental Imagination: Thoreau, Nature Writing, and the Formation of American Culture* (Cambridge, Mass.: Harvard University Press, 1995), 26. On village sketch literature as a women's tradition, see Elizabeth Ammons, introduction to *How Celia Changed Her Mind and Selected Stories* by Rose Terry Cooke (New Brunswick, N.J.: Rutgers University Press, 1986); Josephine Donovan, *New England Local Color Literature: A Women's Tradition* (New York: Frederick Ungar, 1983), 23–37; and Sandra A. Zagarell, "'America' as Community in Three Antebellum Village Sketches," in *The (Other) American Traditions,* ed. Joyce W. Warren (New Brunswick, N.J.: Rutgers University Press, 1993). On the development of the village sketch in New England, see Lawrence Buell, *New England Literary Culture: From Revolution through Renaissance* (New York: Cambridge University Press, 1986), chap. 13; and Perry Westbrook, *The New England Town in Fact and Fiction* (Rutherford, N.J.: Fairleigh Dickinson University Press, 1982).

3. Richard Wegner offers a serviceable definition of the sketch: "The distinguishing structural feature of the literary sketch is the displacement of plot by other fictional elements (notably the ones Aristotle terms character and spectacle). . . . The sketch purports to represent a 'picture' of imagined reality, as opposed to a 'story' of successive events" ("Hawthorne's 'Ethan Brand' and the Structure of the Literary Sketch," *Journal of Narrative Technique* 17 [Winter

1987]: 58). For a more detailed discussion of the sketch's formal properties, see also Wegner's "The Sketchbook of Nathaniel Hawthorne: Theory and Practice of Literary Sketching in the Nineteenth Century" (Ph.D. diss., University of Pennsylvania, 1987).

Like the periodicals in which they became standard fare, sketches had both high and low literary antecedents that linked them with the intellectual tradition of eighteenth-century literature as well as the democratic tradition of the almanac. On these influences, see Mary Von Tassel Murtha, "The Visible Circle: Nathaniel Hawthorne and the Literary Sketch in America" (Ph.D. diss., University of Maryland, 1991), 136–38. Anne Douglas also mentions the "Lockean empiricism" that formed "the intellectual underpinning of the sketch" (*The Feminization of American Culture* [New York: Alfred A. Knopf, 1977], 238).

4. Vera Norwood, *Made from This Earth: American Women and Nature* (Chapel Hill: University of North Carolina Press, 1993), 26.

5. Writers of the previous generation such as Lydia Sigourney (*Sketch of Connecticut,* 1824), Anne Newport Royall (*Sketches of History, Life and Manners in the United States,* 1826), Eliza Leslie (*Pencil Sketches,* 1833), and Caroline Howard Gilman (*Recollections of a Housekeeper,* 1834) had published texts exhibiting the inclusive social vision, ethnographic detail, domestic metaphors, and cyclical structure that would be employed in the following decades with increasing authority and inventiveness by other American women, including Cary, Cooper, and Kirkland.

6. For example, Rosaly Torna Kurth observes that Cooper's writing is "sometimes flat and spiritless" ("Susan Fenimore Cooper: A Study of Her Life and Works" [Ph.D. diss., Fordham University, 1974], abstract in *Dissertation Abstracts International* 35 [1974]: 2278A). David Jones concludes that "[a]s literature, *Rural Hours* varies from 'brilliant' in one passage to 'languid and pale' in another. This inconsistency . . . prevents it from being one of the truly great journals of the nineteenth century, like *Walden,* published four years later. . . . *Rural Hours* is not, like *Walden,* a multi-level book" (introduction to *Rural Hours,* xxxvii). James Franklin Beard similarly notes that despite earning praise in the nineteenth century, "*Rural Hours* is not comparable to *Walden*" ("Susan Augusta Fenimore Cooper," in *Notable American Women, 1607–1950: A Biographical Dictionary,* ed. Edward T. James et al. [Cambridge, Mass.: Harvard University Press, 1971], 1:382).

7. Buell, *The Environmental Imagination,* 265.

8. Susan Fenimore Cooper, *Rural Hours,* ed. Rochelle Johnson and Daniel Patterson (Athens: University of Georgia Press, 1998), 208. Hereafter cited in text.

9. On the alternative ways women writers depict the frontier, see Annette Kolodny, *The Land before Her: Fantasy and Experience of the American Frontiers,*

1630–1860 (Chapel Hill: University of North Carolina Press, 1984) and Brigitte Georgi-Findlay, *The Frontiers of Women's Writing: Women's Narratives and the Rhetoric of Western Expansion* (Tucson: University of Arizona Press, 1996).

10. Marx, "Pastoralism in America," in *Ideology and Classic American Literature*, ed. Sacvan Bercovitch and Myra Jehlen (Cambridge: Cambridge University Press, 1986), 50. When using the term "pastoral," I follow Marx in referring not to the classical literary definition but to the "meaning of pastoralism that prevails in ordinary discourse nowadays": "the worthy life represented" both by "fictive shepherds" and by "anyone (whether an actual historical person or a fictitious character) with a similar, as it were, shepherdlike view of life" (ibid., 42). Hereafter cited in text.

11. On the popularity of *Our Village,* see Shelagh Hunter, *Victorian Idyllic Fiction* (London: Macmillan Press, 1984), 228, n. 23. On Mitford's prose style, see P. D. Edwards, *Idyllic Realism from Mary Russell Mitford to Hardy* (London: Macmillan Press, 1988), 7–12; Hunter, *Victorian Idyllic Fiction,* 71–73; and W. J. Keith, *The Rural Tradition: A Study of the Non-Fiction Prose Writers of the English Countryside* (Toronto: University of Toronto Press, 1974), 87–101.

12. On Mitford's advocacy of realism and critique of sentimentality in literature, see Edwards, *Idyllic Realism,* 6; Hunter, *Victorian Idyllic Fiction,* 70; John L. Idol Jr., "Mary Russell Mitford: Champion of American Literature," in *Studies in the American Renaissance,* ed. Joel Myerson (Charlottesville: University of Virginia Press, 1983), 316, 318, 327; and Meredith B. Raymond and Mary Rose Sullivan, introduction to *Women of Letters: Selected Letters of Elizabeth Barrett Browning and Mary Russell Mitford* (Boston: Twayne Publishers, 1987), vii.

13. Although the categories are not defined absolutely by gender, nineteenth-century readers would have recognized readily the distinction between "fancy sketches" in the largely male tradition of Irving's *Sketchbook* and "life sketches" in the predominantly female tradition of Mitford's *Our Village.* The "fancy sketch" emphasized imaginative thoughts, presenting the reveries of a removed, genteel, passive narrator, typically identified as male and aristocratic. In contrast, "life sketches" emphasized realistic observation, presenting the experiences of an involved, democratic, active narrator, usually identified as female and middle class. On the imaginative and aristocratic qualities of the Geoffrey Crayon persona, see Thomas H. Pauly, "The Literary Sketch in Nineteenth-Century America," *Texas Studies in Literature and Language* 17, no. 2 (Summer 1975): 492 and Jeffrey Rubin-Dorsky, "Washington Irving and the Genesis of the Fictional Sketch," *Early American Literature* 21, no. 3 (Winter 1986–87): 228. On the popular male magazinists, such as Nathaniel Parker Willis and Donald Mitchell, who employed the fancy sketch form and developed urbane and detached narrators, see Douglas, *The Feminization of American Culture,* 236–38. On the dis-

tinction between Irving's narrative style and that of female sketchwriters, see Sandra A. Zagarell, "Expanding 'America': Lydia Sigourney's *Sketch of Connecticut,* Catharine Sedgwick's *Hope Leslie,*" in *Redefining the Political Novel: American Women Writers, 1797–1901,* ed. Sharon M. Harris (Knoxville: University of Tennessee Press, 1995), 59. On Mitford's middle-class perspective, see Keith, *The Rural Tradition,* 86. For an example of a nineteenth-century reader's clear differentiation between the two types of sketch, compare Edgar Allan Poe's description of Nathaniel Parker Willis's work with his commentary on Caroline Kirkland's writing in "The Literati of New York City," pt. 1, *Godey's Magazine and Lady's Book* (May 1846): 197 and "The Literati of New York City," pt. 4, *Godey's Magazine and Lady's Book* (August 1846): 75.

14. Mitford, writing of herself in the third person in the preface to the first edition of *Our Village,* explains that "if she be accused of having given a brighter aspect to her villagers than is usually met with in books, she cannot help it, and would not if she could" (quoted in Hunter, *Victorian Idyllic Fiction,* 69).

15. Caroline Kirkland, *A New Home, Who'll Follow?* ed. Sandra A. Zagarell (New Brunswick, N.J.: Rutgers University Press, 1990), 2. Hereafter cited in text.

16. On the popular and critical reception of *A New Home,* see my introduction to "A Bibliography of Works by and about Caroline Kirkland," *Tulsa Studies in Women's Literature* 18, no. 2 (Fall 1999): 299–350.

17. Caroline Kirkland, *Forest Life,* 2 vols. (1842; Upper Saddle River, N.J.: Literature House, 1970, 2 vols. in 1), 4–5. Hereafter cited in text.

18. Nina Baym, *American Women Writers and the Work of History, 1790–1860* (New Brunswick, N.J.: Rutgers University Press, 1995), 1.

19. Nina Baym, "From Enlightenment to Victorian: Toward a Narrative of American Women Writing History," in *Feminism and American Literary History* (New Brunswick, N.J.: Rutgers University Press, 1992), 106. On republican womanhood, see the essays in section 1 of *Toward an Intellectual History of Women: Essays by Linda Kerber* (Chapel Hill: University of North Carolina Press, 1997).

20. Along with Kirkland, Cary was one of the first American women to earn her living solely by writing. On Cary's popular and critical reputation, see Mary Clemmer Ames, *A Memorial of Alice and Phoebe Cary, with Some of Their Later Poems* (New York: Hurd and Houghton, 1873) and Judith Fetterley, introduction to *Clovernook Sketches and Other Stories* by Alice Cary (New Brunswick, N.J.: Rutgers University Press, 1987).

21. Alice Cary, *Clovernook; or, Recollections of Our Neighborhood in the West* (1851; Clinton Hall, N.Y.: Redfield, 1852), vii. Hereafter cited in text. I will be discussing only the first series of *Clovernook* tales in this essay; Cary also published a *Clovernook, Second Series* in 1853. Selections from both volumes are reprinted in the 1987 edition of Cary's sketches, cited in note 20.

22. Judith Fetterley, "Entitled to More than 'Peculiar Praise': The Extravagance of Alice Cary's *Clovernook*," *Legacy* 10 (1993): 104. Cary's narrator forcefully conveys the frustrations of the entitled rustic in the following passage: "of all situations, I conceive of none so really comfortless as that of a superior intellect, weighed down with petty oppressions which, in the first place, hinder its development, and, when through years of unaided and half-thwarted endeavor, it comes in some sort of light, hedge it round with circumstances that prevent its recognition" (*Clovernook*, 328).

23. Fetterley, "Entitled," 107.

24. To give one of many possible examples of Cary's use of detail: in one sketch, the narrator's close observations guide the reader's eye from the "curious ridges" and "tracks of the rabbits" in the outdoor snow, to a tree where a bird sits with "one shining red foot drawn up in the warm feathers, and one clasping the bough beneath," to a cottage interior where "crooked limbs of oak and maple, and smooth sticks of white ash" are "heaped up" near the "blue hearthstones," and "the gilt lettering shines from the shelf of books" and "the blue cups and nicely polished platters glow" (*Clovernook*, 254). Such concrete images convey as much about the character of this place as any narrative generalization.

25. Zagarell, "Expanding 'America,'" 59.

26. Kirkland emphasizes this same point, contrasting settlers with positive and negative outlooks; see, for example, *A New Home*, 75–78.

27. Buell, *The Environmental Imagination*, 26.

28. If we follow Cooper in considering the natural environment a part of the community, then clearly *Rural Hours* fits into the genre Zagarell calls "narratives of community," works that "take as their subject the life of a community . . . and portray the minute and quite ordinary processes through which the community maintains itself as an entity"; wherein "the self exists . . . as a part of the interdependent network of the community rather than as an individualistic unit" (Sandra A. Zagarell, "Narrative of Community: The Identification of a Genre," *Signs* 13 [1988]: 499).

29. This passage also illustrates Cooper's multilevel sense of value. She considers simple language important because the honest description of flowers achieves multiple goals. Those who would think only in scientific terms have too narrow a perspective and forget the domestic and historical significance of plant life. "It is really a crying shame to misname" flowers because they need names not only that serve scientific purposes but also that "mothers and nurses can teach children before they are 'in Botany'" and that allow American poets to "sing our native flowers as sweetly and simply as the daisy" (*Rural Hours*, 87).

30. Although Cooper does not often employ Kirkland's first-person "I," the persona of *Rural Hours* is equally, if not more, authoritative and confident than

the narrator of *A New Home*. Using the editorial "we," Cooper offers forceful opinions and critique as well as sensitive description. This editorial plural makes a persona seem less idiosyncratic and more representative. Hence, this was the voice chosen by scholars and magazinists who wrote essays and reviews meant to represent the opinions of their publications or institutions. Cooper, who, like many other sketchwriters, edited numerous works in addition to writing introductions, magazine articles, and children's stories, would have been very familiar with the quiet authority of this editorial voice.

31. Norwood, *Made from This Earth*, 42.

32. Georgi-Findlay, *The Frontiers of Women's Writing*, 43–44.

33. In focusing on her own local environment as a potentially ideal space, Cooper avoids the tendency of later environmentalists to place value only on unpopulated regions far from their own homes. As Krista Comer suggests, "the most troubling consequence of environmentalism's flight from history is that environmentalists fail to idealize the environments that most Americans, including themselves, actually inhabit" ("Sidestepping Environmental Justice: Natural Landscapes and the Wilderness Plot," *Frontiers* 18 [1997]: 78). Such revisionists, arguing that one should preserve one's own community and not consider people the enemy of the landscape, echo the views that Cooper, Cary, and Kirkland were expressing over one hundred years ago.

34. Susan Fenimore Cooper, "A Dissolving View," in *The Home Book of the Picturesque; or, American Scenery, Art, and Literature* (New York: Putnam, 1852; reprint, Gainesville, Fla.: Scholars' Facsimiles & Reprints, 1967), 82.

35. Cooper also exhibits her belief in the benefits of both village life and community reform in her 1869 *Putnam's Magazine* article "Village Improvement Societies," which asserts that "village life as it exists in America is indeed one of the happiest fruits of modern civilization," while also offering practical tips on how to further improve such communities ([September 1869]: 361).

36. William Cronon, "A Place for Stories: Nature, History, and Narrative," *Journal of American History* 78, no. 4 (March 1992): 1349. Cooper, in her rejection of linear narrative, might also reveal an awareness of the problems with reconciling form and content in environmental writing that Cronon identifies: "writing stories about environmental change, we divide the causal relationships of an ecosystem with a rhetorical razor that defines included and excluded, relevant and irrelevant, empowered and disempowered. In the act of separating story from nonstory, we wield the most powerful yet dangerous tool of the narrative form. . . . the very authority with which narrative presents its vision of reality is achieved by obscuring large portions of that reality" (1349).

Susan Fenimore Cooper, Catharine Beecher, and the Theology of Homemaking

> Drove several miles down the valley this morning in the teeth of a sharp wind, and flurries of snow, but after facing the cold bravely, one brings home a sort of virtuous glow which is not to be picked up by cowering over the fireside; it is with this as with more important matters, the effort brings its own reward.
>
> SUSAN FENIMORE COOPER, *Rural Hours*

In her first journal entry in *Rural Hours*, Susan Fenimore Cooper signals her adherence to one of the principal tenets of nineteenth-century American domesticity: fresh air is essential for the health of American women.[1] In *A Treatise on Domestic Economy* (1841), Catharine Beecher stresses that "walking and riding and gardening, in the open air" are necessary to "strengthen the constitution" of American women and counteract the dangerous effects of the "intellectual and moral excitement" to which they are exposed.[2]

Catharine Esther Beecher (1800–1878) was the chief architect of the dominant nineteenth-century American ideology of women's domesticity. In her best-selling *Treatise on Domestic Economy* and its sequel, *The American Woman's Home* (1869), she articulated a view of women as both morally superior and self-sacrificingly domestic. A woman's place was in the home, but Beecher strove to convince women of the exalted nature of that circumscribed place.

Domesticity, as constructed by and for nineteenth-century American women, is central to an understanding of Cooper's project in *Rural Hours*. The natural environment, for Cooper, was "an extension of her domestic sphere," as Vera Norwood has shown.[3] Cooper herself writes: "Home, we may rest assured, will always be, as a rule, the best place for a woman" (*Rural Hours*, 100). She does not construct an entirely new role for women independent of the dominant ideology, but, by extending domesticity beyond the familial home and into the natural environment, Cooper manages to escape the paradox, so pointed in Beecher's case, of being a domestic theorist who herself stands outside the domestic role she has created for other women.[4] Cooper's broader understanding of domesticity enables it to serve as a model not just for traditional homemakers but for all women and men who wish to create a home in harmony with the natural world.

The cardinal principle of Beecher's domestic ideology is an insistence on the benevolent self-sacrifice of American women, patterned on Christ's own self-sacrifice. She writes: "[woman's] great mission is self-denial, in training [the family's] members to self-sacrificing labors for the ignorant and weak. . . . She is to rear all under her care to lay up treasures, not on earth, but in heaven. All the pleasures of this life end here; but those who train immortal minds are to reap the fruit of their labor through eternal ages."[5] Cooper adhered to this principle of self-sacrifice—or, more broadly, to the notion that women were to act not for themselves but for others—but turned it toward the end of conservation. Women, and others involved in the conservation effort, become the caretakers of nature not only for themselves but for others, friends and strangers alike. Indeed, in discussing the conservation of trees, Cooper writes: "There is also something in the care of trees which rises above the common labors of husbandry and speaks of a generous mind. . . . In planting a young wood, in preserving a fine grove, a noble tree, we look beyond ourselves to the band of household friends, to our neighbors—ay, to the passing wayfarer and stranger who will share with us the pleasures they give" (*Rural Hours*, 134–35).

As in Beecher's version of domesticity, a woman's generous action has beneficial consequences that radiate beyond herself in ever-widening circles. But Beecher's principle of self-sacrifice, of "looking beyond oneself," is applied by Cooper not to storing up treasures in heaven but to preserving the treasures and pleasures of this earth. By shifting her emphasis from the care of the soul to the care of creation, Cooper begins to formulate an environmental theology.

Thus, while they adhere to the same understanding of women's domestic role, Beecher and Cooper differ in their theological understanding of the wider application of domesticity. Beecher's domesticity is evangelical, grounded in the imperatives of the New Testament to make converts of all nations. Cooper, however, understands domesticity as stewardship and more often finds her views supported by the Old than the New Testament.

She does not actively attempt to domesticate the world, as Beecher does, but rather attempts to find a place for herself in the inherently domestic order of nature. While Beecher relies on the New Testament with its evangelical and millenarian emphasis, Cooper turns repeatedly to the Old Testament, with its Mosaic laws and emphasis on the rhythms of rural life. By drawing out this comparison between Beecher and Cooper, I will demonstrate how Cooper moved toward transforming the nineteenth-century cult of domesticity, articulated by Beecher, into an ethic of care for the environment that in many respects anticipates the twentieth-century ecofeminist theology of Rosemary Radford Ruether.

The Nature of Domesticity

On the surface, Catharine Beecher and Susan Fenimore Cooper had similar conceptions of the landscape of home. In drawing up her plans for a Christian house, Beecher is careful to specify that her principles of housekeeping are of universal application, but they are chiefly applicable "to the wants and habits of those living either in the country or in such suburban vicinities as give space of ground for healthful outdoor occupation in the family service" (*American Woman's Home,* 24). Beecher envisions her Christian home as occupying the "borderlands," which geographer John Stilgoe defines as "a zone *between* rural space and urban residential rings."[6] This zone, which is essentially the residential countryside, is also identified by Stilgoe as the landscape favored by Cooper—the landscape of *Rural Hours.* This was a landscape whose value was chiefly moral, not agricultural.

The moral significance of a landscape is revealed by the presence of humans and their interactions with the land. In her discussion of gleaning, for example, Cooper comments on the absence of gleaners in America, saying, "[O]ur people, generally, are not patient and contented with a little; gleaning would not suit their habit. Many of them, probably, would rather beg than glean" (*Rural Hours,* 158). She continues in approval of European gleaners: "[H]umble as the occupation may be, it is yet thoroughly honest, and, indeed, creditable, so far as it shows a willingness to undertake the lowliest task for a livelihood, rather than stand by wholly idle" (*Rural Hours,* 159). This commendation of humble labor and rebuke against idleness again connects Cooper to the fundamentals of Beecher's domestic ideology. Beecher writes: "[E]very American woman, who values the institutions of her Country, and wishes to lend her influence in extending and perpetuating such blessings, may feel she is doing this, whenever, by her example and influence, she destroys the aristocratic association, that would render domestic labor degrading" (*Treatise*, 40). Domestic labor, however humble it may seem, is a proper pursuit for a patriotic American lady.

Catharine Beecher, however, has little directly to say about nature. Nature exists for her only as an adornment of the home; she deals with it only under the headings of "home decoration" and "domestic amusements." Under the latter heading, she encourages gardening as an activity that brings women into the open air and promotes good health. Nothing for Beecher is as beneficial as abundant fresh air. In addition to encouraging habits of "neatness and order," gardening also cultivates "benevolent and social feelings" by encouraging women to share seeds and cuttings from their gardens with neighbors and with the less fortunate members of the community. If seeds were liberally shared in this way, she says, "our country would soon literally 'blossom as the rose'" (*Treatise*, 296). For Beecher, gardening is another fertile sphere for domestic evangelism, another means by which the moral influence of woman can be disseminated far and wide from its domestic center.

Another domestic amusement sanctioned by Beecher is "the collecting of shells, plants, and specimens in geology and mineralogy, for the formation of cabinets" (*Treatise*, 297). Nature is, in a sense, domesticated as furniture. This notion of nature as furniture for the home becomes clear in Beecher's chapter on home decoration, where she introduces the idea of keeping a Ward case. A Ward case, she explains, is a small indoor greenhouse into which can be transplanted various ferns and wildflowers, such as the trailing arbutus, partridge berry, and anemone. She tells her readers confidently, "[W]e have succeeded, and you will succeed, in making a very charming and picturesque collection." She continues: "You can make in your Ward case lovely little grottoes with any bits of shells, and minerals, and rocks you may have; you can lay down, here and there, fragments of broken looking-glass for the floor of your grottoes, and the effect of them will be magical. A square of looking-glass introduced into the back side of your case will produce charming effects" (*Treatise*, 101). The American woman's domesticity is reflected back prismatically by the squares and fragments of looking-glass set into her creation. Nature is imbedded within—and reflects—domesticity.

Like Beecher gathering wildflowers for her Ward case, Cooper is frequently found gathering wildflowers for her home. In the same sentence she can remark on the rarity of lady's slippers and boast of gathering eighteen of them in a bouquet for her home (*Rural Hours*, 168). Like Beecher,

Cooper extols the virtues of gardening as moral instruction, noting that it teaches liberality, diligence, and order.

There is, however, a significant difference in Cooper's treatment of gardening as a moral pursuit. When Catharine Beecher commends gardening as a training in benevolence, she appeals to the example of Christ: "Our Savior directs us in making feasts, to call, not the rich who can recompense again, but the poor who can make no returns" (*Treatise,* 295). By sharing their seeds and rootstock with their poorer neighbors, women are following the example of Christ. For Cooper, on the other hand, this lesson in liberality need not be mediated through Christ. She writes:

> The bountiful returns which are bestowed, year after year, upon our feeble labors, shame us into liberality. Among all the misers who have lived on earth, probably few have been gardeners. Some cross-grained churl may set out, perhaps, with a determination to be niggardly with the fruits and flowers of his portion; but gradually his feelings soften, his views change, and before he has housed the fruits of many summers, he sees that these good things are but the free gifts of Providence to himself, and learns that it is a pleasure, as well as a duty, to give. (*Rural Hours,* 81)

While Beecher can only appeal to the example of Christ for moral instruction, Cooper's morality appears to grow directly out of the soil. The earth itself teaches liberality and instructs us in God's will.

This emphasis on the immediacy of the experience of nature reflects the influence of Cooper's Quaker background. Quakers also encouraged gardening as a useful moral pursuit; Cooper's own introduction to gardening was through her Quaker grandmother.[7] The Quakers emphasized empirical observation over speculative reasoning, believing that God was revealed through the works of his Creation rather than through abstract dogmas. The Quaker emphasis, furthermore, is not on Christ as the intermediary between God and humans but on a direct experience of God in Creation. Even when Cooper does devote an extended entry in *Rural Hours* to the teaching of Christ, as she does when discussing sparrows in her entry for December 9, her emphasis quickly shifts to the "revelation of the directness of the providence of God, the oversight and care bestowed by the Almighty on the meanest of His creatures" (*Rural Hours,* 260). Throughout *Rural Hours,* it is God's Providence that Cooper emphasizes, not the specific doctrines of Scripture.

Catharine Beecher envisions the family, home, and neighborhood as vehicles for spreading the doctrines of Christianity. In a chapter on the "Christian neighborhood," she writes of the influence spreading from a central village church: "The cheering example would soon spread, and ere long colonies from these prosperous and Christian communities would go forth to shine as 'lights of the world' in all the now darkened nations. Thus the 'Christian family' and 'Christian neighborhood' would become the grand ministry, as they were designed to be, in training our whole race for heaven" (*American Woman's Home*, 458–59). The family, home, and neighborhood form concentric circles, embracing an ever wider Christian community. At the center of these circles is the woman whose self-sacrificing labors conform to the example of Christ.

Cooper, too, has an expansive conception of home, but for her, home is an ecological entity rather than a vehicle for evangelism. Her most telling description of home comes not in *Rural Hours* but in her novel, *Elinor Wyllys*. In this description, it becomes clear that her conception of home is of a wider community that includes not only one's family but also one's neighbors, both human and nonhuman. She writes:

> To her [Elinor], Wyllys-Roof was home; and that is a word of a broader and more varied meaning in the country than in a town. The cares, the sympathies of a country home, embrace a wide circle, and bring with them pleasures of their own. People know enough of all their neighbours, to take part in any interesting event that may befall them; we are sorry to hear that A., the shoe-maker, is going to move away; we are glad to find that B., the butcher, has made money enough to build a new house. One has some acquaintance with everybody, from the clergyman to the loafer; few are the faces that one does not know. Even the four-footed animals of the neighbourhood are not strangers: this is the Doctor's Newfoundland dog; that is some old lady's tortoise-shell cat. One knows the horses, as well as the little urchins who ride them to water; the cows, and those who milk them. And then, country-folks are nature's free-holders; they enjoy a full portion of the earth, the air, the sky, with the thousand charms an ever-merciful Creator has lavished on them. Every inanimate object—this hill, that wood, the brook, the bridge, C.'s farm-house, and D.'s barn—to the very highway, as far as eye can reach, all form pleasing parts of a country home.[8]

Cooper goes on to contrast this with the city, where home seems to extend no farther than the domestic hearth. She concludes by saying, "No doubt, that with hearts warm and true, we may have a *fireside* in town; but *home* with its thousand pleasant accessories, *home,* in its fullest meaning, belongs especially to the country."[9] In this broad conception of home, Cooper displays a rudimentary understanding of home as biotic community, as *ecosystem* (*eco-*, from the Greek *oikos,* "home"). Home is a system of relationships of knowledge and affection extending beyond the domestic fireside even into the natural environment.

Instead of domesticating and miniaturizing nature within the Christian household, as Beecher does in her Ward case, Cooper sees nature itself as a larger household. Instead of constructing a domestic ideology in which nature served as moral furniture, Cooper finds domesticity and morality revealed directly in nature itself.[10] The divide between nature and civilization dissolves when both are seen as manifestations of domesticity, divine and human. Civilization, in other words, is not separate from nature but is simply a human expression of the domesticity inherent in nature.

Apocalyptic Homemaking and Sabbatical Homemaking

A central element of the environmental critique of Christianity, most prominently expressed by Lynn White in his essay "The Historical Roots of Our Ecologic Crisis," is that Christianity has been focused on the expectation of the world to come rather than on the care of the world in which we live now.[11] Millenarian expectations of a spiritualized promised land justified the neglect and domination of the earth. In the nineteenth century, two strains of millenarianism arose out of the Puritan tradition, one catastrophic and one progressive.[12] The catastrophic strain looked forward to the destruction of this earth and the establishment of God's Kingdom in Heaven. The progressive strain, represented by the Social Gospel tradition, worked toward "a virtual millennium . . . of peace and prosperity on earth" achieved through the spread of Christian democracy.[13] Catharine Beecher clearly belonged to this second strain and helped to develop it through her domestic ideology, which emphasized the role of women in providing the moral foundation for the spread of democracy. In her *Treatise on Domestic Economy*, Beecher writes of women's role in bringing about "the regeneration of the Earth" through their domestic labors:

The woman who is rearing a family of children; the woman who labors in the schoolroom; the woman who, in her retired chamber, earns, with her needle, the mite to contribute for the intellectual and moral elevation of her country; even the humble domestic, whose example and influence may be moulding and forming young minds, while her faithful services sustain a prosperous domestic state;—each and all may be cheered by the consciousness, that they are agents in accomplishing the greatest work that was ever committed to human responsibility. It is the building of a glorious temple, whose base shall be coextensive with the bounds of the earth, whose summit shall pierce the skies, whose splendor shall beam on all lands, and those who hew the lowliest stone, as much as those who carve the highest capital, will be equally honored when its top-stone shall be laid, with new rejoicings of the morning stars, and shoutings of the sons of God. (*Treatise*, 14)

Female domesticity is directed toward laying the foundation of this "glorious temple," in which God will be universally glorified through the institutions of Christianity and American democracy. Beecher's construction of human history is linear and progressive, focused on making this world a staging ground for the Kingdom of God in heaven. "It has been shown," she writes, "that the best end for a woman to seek is the training of God's children for their eternal home" (*American Woman's Home*, 23).

Catharine Beecher was clearly influenced in her strain of "progressive millenarianism" by the Calvinist traditions of the late eighteenth and early nineteenth centuries, perhaps best represented by her own father, the Reverend Lyman Beecher. The elder Beecher saw most of human history as a failed experiment. "The history of the world is the history of human nature in ruins," he writes. The hope for human civilization, according to the elder Beecher, is "a moral renovation, which will change the character and condition of men" and bring about a universal transformation, one that is "coextensive with the ruin." [14] It is the special calling of the United States, as a Christian democracy, to bring about this renovation of the earth. "Let this nation go on, then," he writes, "and multiply its millions and its resources, and bring the whole under the influence of our civil and religious institutions, and, with the energies of its concentrated benevolence, send out evangelical instruction,—and who can calculate what our blessed instrumentality shall have accomplished, when He who sitteth upon the throne shall have made all things new?" [15] Arising out of this nineteenth-century evangelical tradition, Catharine Beecher's construction of domesticity is pointed toward a Christian millennium in which God's kingdom will be established on earth through the far-reaching moral influence of American women.

Cooper, standing among a grove of old-growth pines, has a far more troubling vision of the millennium that raises the need for environmental conservation. She writes:

This little town itself must fall into decay and ruin; its streets must become choked with bushes and brambles; the farms of the valley must be buried anew within the shades of a wilderness; the wild deer and the wolf, and the bear, must return from beyond the great lakes; the bones of the savage men buried under our feet must arise and move again in the chase, ere trees like those, with the spirit of the forest in every line, can stand on the same ground in wild dignity of form like those old pines now looking down on our homes. (*Rural Hours*, 120)

Cooper's millennial fantasy is tempered by an understanding of the consequences of the irreversible destruction of America's natural heritage. While Lyman Beecher can speak of "multiplying" America's resources to regenerate the world, Cooper confronts the reality of threatened and diminishing resources. She is continually aware of the consequences of the expansionism, fueled by an evangelical zeal, that has driven the deer, the wolf, and the bear, as well as the bison and the American Indian, "beyond the great lakes." The recurring rumors of a "panther" later in *Rural Hours*, however, seem to confirm the possibility of Cooper's vision of wilderness restored: wild nature continues to exist, ready to rebound, beyond the margins of civilization. In Cooper's view, absolute wilderness, as represented by the panther, is as much of a threat as the extremes of urbanization or desertification. The solution lies in careful stewardship of the rural "borderlands" in which humans live in harmony with the rest of nature.

Cooper's vision of the civilized landscape reclaimed by wilderness is akin to the vision depicted by her father's friend, Thomas Cole, in his series of five paintings collectively entitled *The Course of Empire*. Like Cooper, Cole pays specific attention to architecture as an indication of humans' presence in and adaptation to nature. Cole's series of paintings depicts a landscape as it passes through stages: *The Savage State, The Arcadian State, The Consummation of Empire, Destruction*, and *Desolation*. In the foreground of the first canvas, a hunter pursues a deer with bow and arrow; in the final canvas, another deer grazes unmolested among the ruins. Each stage in *The Course of Empire* is marked by progressive changes in architectural details. In *The Savage State*, a circle of primitive tipilike huts stands in the background; in *The Arcadian State*, the circle of huts is replaced by a Stonehenge-like stone circle. *The Consummation of Empire* is triumphantly Greco-Roman, complete with Doric temples, marble porticoes, arches, and aqueducts. The savage hunt has been transformed into a group of figures on the pediment of a temple: Nature has been transformed into Art. Finally, in *Desolation*, the monumental structures have crumbled; on the capital of a single column in the foreground, a heron has made her nest. Cole, describing this canvas, wrote: "Violence and time have crumbled the works of man, and art is again resolving into elemental nature."[16] Cole's words suggest that if art can "resolve" into "elemental nature," then nature itself provides the elements from which art arises. This, at least, was the opinion of Cooper.

In her preface to *The Rhyme and Reason of Country Life,* Cooper subscribes in particular to the notion that architecture has its origins in the trees of the forest. Of Gothic architecture, she writes: "[S]carce a fine effect of the branching woods was not successfully repeated with great richness of detail in Gothic stone."[17] Architecture is organic; architectural ruins are simply a part of the cycles of nature.[18] Furthermore, even the furniture and domestic utensils with which our homes are furnished are derived from nature. She writes: "We seldom remember, indeed, how large a portion of our ideas of grace and beauty are derived from the plants, how constantly we turn to them for models. It is worth while to look about the first room you enter, to note how very many proofs of this you will find there. Scarcely an article of furniture, from the most simple and homely to the most elegant and elaborate, but carries about it some imitation of this kind" (*Rural Hours,* 316). She goes on, by way of example, to derive the origins of pottery from the forms of gourds found in the wild. Human domesticity arises organically out of the elements of domesticity in nature. When Cooper enters a home, she sees nature; when she goes out into nature, she sees a home.

This view of human architecture as arising organically from nature leads Cooper to connect cultural preservation with the conservation of natural resources. In her 1852 essay, "A Dissolving View," Cooper complains of the impermanence of American architecture; she writes: "[T]here is nothing old among us. If we were endowed with ruins we should not preserve them; they would be pulled down to make way for some new novelty."[19] In arguing for an organic architecture and for cultural preservation, Cooper envisions a rural society based upon a sustainable relationship to the fertile American land, blending old and new, native and European. In a sense, Cole's final canvas, *Desolation,* comes closest to Cooper's ideal landscape, in which human ruins are preserved and nature is regenerated. The stage is again set for human cultivation of the land, hopefully on a better model—a model that Cooper begins to envision in "A Dissolving View."[20]

Throughout *Rural Hours,* the recurring, cyclical patterns of nature are set against the linear decline of the postsettlement natural environment—

the loss of species and habitat, the harvesting of the ancient forest, and the invasion of exotic weeds. A pessimistic, even apocalyptic human view of history is set against nature's potential for quiet regeneration. This opposition is suggested in the contrast between the peaceful, diligent housekeeping of the migratory birds and the almost apocalyptic upheaval of the villagers' spring cleaning. Cooper's pessimism derives from the spectacle of humans living out of harmony with nature; her optimism derives from a knowledge of nature's resilience. A journal such as *Rural Hours* provides a transparent form for displaying a sensitivity to nature's cycles, its seasonal resilience from winter to spring.

The progressive millenarianism of the Beechers seeks to convert the world to the doctrines of Christianity and the principles of American democracy. The expected triumph of Christianity is, above all, the triumph of American Protestantism. For Cooper, on the other hand, the triumph of Christianity is the triumph of nature. Christianity seeks not the conversion of the earth into a Christian home but rather the stewardship of the home God has already provided in nature:

> No system connects man by more close and endearing ties, with the earth and all it holds, than Christianity, which leaves nothing to chance, nothing to that most gloomy and most impossible of chimeras, fate, but refers all to Providence, to the omniscient wisdom of a God who is love; but at the same time she warns him that he is himself but the steward and priest of the Almighty Father, responsible for the use of every gift; she plainly proclaims the fact, that even here on earth, within his own domains, his position is subordinate.[21]

This view still leaves room for a kind of evangelism, but Cooper's ecological evangelism seeks to cultivate the "love of nature" and spread the civilizing influence of the rural landscape. What again emerges is an argument not for millennial solutions but for sustainability: "The everlasting hills— the ancient woods—these are his [i.e., the countryman's] monuments— these tell him of the past, and not a seed drops from his hand but prophesies of the future."[22]

In rejecting the idea of permanent millennial fixes in favor of a vision of sustainability rooted in the Jewish sabbatical tradition, Cooper anticipates the ecofeminist theology of Rosemary Radford Ruether. A mature Christianity, according to Ruether, entails the establishment of a "right relationship" with the earth, in which human beings act as stewards of nature, and nature in turn sustains the lives and spirits of human beings. This sustainable relationship to the land is not fostered through paternalistic evangelism but through a maternal ethic of care.

An Ethic of Care

Catharine Beecher's domestic ideology involves an apparent contradiction. While it insists on the political subordination of women, it clearly assigns to women a superior moral position. In its Christian emphasis on "laying up treasures in heaven," it discounts the importance of political or economic power on earth. It is easy to apply a feminist critique to this ideology, arguing that a Christian belief in the rewards of heaven is used to justify domination on earth. This same argument can be extended to the domination of the environment. In its emphasis on the world of the spirit and the kingdom of heaven, Christianity can be seen as neglecting the stewardship of the earth. This combined critique of the domination of women and the environment is the essence of contemporary ecofeminism.

Coupled with political and economic disenfranchisement, Beecher's emphasis on "self-sacrificing labors" can be condemned as a slave mentality. But what happens when women are politically and economically empowered? Many ecofeminists would argue that women's relational construction of self provides the basis for a culturally and ecologically transformative ethic of care. If the self is seen as essentially a "self-in-relationship," there can be no self-sacrifice, only self-interest.[23] In her articulation of an "ecological spirituality," Rosemary Radford Ruether writes:

> Many spiritual traditions have emphasized the need to "let go of the ego," but in ways that diminished the value of the person, undercutting particularly those, like women, who scarcely have been allowed individuated personhood at all. We need to "let go of the ego" in a different sense. We are called to affirm the integrity of our personal center of being, in mutuality with the personal centers of all other beings across species and, at the same time, accept the transience of these personal selves.[24]

For Cooper, writing anonymously and laboring quietly in Cooperstown as her famous father's secretary, the liberation of ecofeminism was a long way off. But the seeds of an ecofeminist theology are there, particularly in Cooper's understanding of God's immanence in nature and of the interrelatedness of all things as they refer back to that immanent God. These seeds of an ecofeminist theology are particularly evident in Cooper's treatment of the biblical story of Ruth, an outsider to whom the humble rural occupation of gleaning offers a point of entry into a new community. From a relationship to the land grows a relationship to human society; the biblical story brings into play the linked ecofeminist concern for the earth and for women's societal position.

At the heart of the story is the relationship between Naomi and Ruth, mother-in-law and daughter-in-law. Naomi is only a surrogate mother to Ruth, but this model of surrogate motherhood may have appealed to the unmarried Cooper. Within a domestic ideology that idealized motherhood, Cooper was herself able to become a "surrogate mother" by extending a kind of maternal care to those around her—to her ailing father, to those aided by her philanthropy, to the natural world for which she was an advocate. Cooper demonstrated that marriage was not the only model of a covenantal relationship.

A modern feminist interpretation of the biblical Book of Ruth emphasizes the role of women in making the story of Ruth a story of *chesed*, of benevolence and loving-kindness. "As the most vulnerable members of a covenantal community," Judith Kates writes, "these women reveal the very heart of the biblical vision of human society and of God. They arouse the community to live up to its own ideals. The text presents them as acting out of *chesed* themselves and activating the *chesed* of those among whom they live."[25] In the same way, the ideology of the nineteenth century held that it was the role of American women to "arouse the community to live up to its own ideals." To Cooper, Ruth is very much a kindred spirit, occupying a similar moral position in society.[26]

The story of Ruth is closely associated in Judaism with the harvest festival called Shavuot. As Judith Kates observes, Shavuot is a celebration of renewed covenant between the Jewish community and God. The importance of this covenantal relationship was not lost on Cooper. As she draws to the end of autumn, Cooper returns one last time to the wheat fields for a discussion of the Jewish harvest festivals. The wheat field, at harvest time, is an illustration of the miraculous bounty that God bestows on humans through the products of the earth. The overarching relationship is between humans and God and is best expressed in God's gift of food from the earth and human gratefulness rendered back. She ends her discussion of Thanksgiving with this observation concerning the Jewish offering of first fruits prescribed in Deuteronomy: "A beautiful ceremony, indeed. Thus we see how full of this acknowledgment of the mercies of God in feeding his people, was the Jewish ritual. The Christian, in the same spirit of constant dependence upon Almighty Providence for the life of body and soul, has also been taught by Divine authority, whether rich or poor, humbly to pray for the boon of his daily bread" (*Rural Hours*, 250). Instead of looking for the fulfillment of God's promises beyond this earth, Cooper locates that fulfillment in nature, in the woods and wheat fields and gardens around her home.

Cooper's appreciation of the inherent domesticity of nature and of the multiple interrelationships within the natural world demonstrates a view of nature that is both "covenantal" and "sacramental." Rosemary Radford Ruether describes the covenantal view of nature as follows: "A covenantal vision of the relation of humans to other life forms acknowledges the special place of humans in this relationship as caretakers, caretakers who did not create and do not absolutely own the rest of life, but who are ultimately accountable for its welfare to the true source of life, God. This covenantal vision recognizes that humans and other life forms are part of one family, sisters and brothers in one community of interdependence."[27] This covenantal view of nature is supported by the sacramental view that sees nature as "an outward and visible sign" (in the words of the old Anglican catechism) of God's invisible presence. God binds the earth together in divine domesticity, which finds expression in the varied domesticity of God's creatures. In Cooper's vision, humans and other forms of life are part of the same household, interrelated and partaking of the domesticity instilled in them by God. Humans, by keeping their environmental house in order, fulfill their own part of this divine covenant. As Mary Catherine Bateson writes: "We must transform our attitude toward all productive work and toward the planet into expressions of homemaking, where we create and sustain the possibility of life."[28]

In her book on pioneering women naturalists, Marcia Bonta tells of being drawn to her subject while browsing through the open stacks of a large university library. One of the books she discovered was *Rural Hours*. The book aroused her curiosity, she says, and led her to revise her "whole vision of women's relationship to nature."[29] The result was a book that devotes chapters to such important scientists and natural historians as ornithologist Florence Merriam Bailey, environmental education pioneer Anna Botsford Comstock, and ecologist Rachel Carson. Cooper, however, is given short shrift: "As it turns out, Cooper was one of the least important of the women naturalists I eventually discovered. She devoted larger portions of her life to charitable works and to caring for her father and his literary reputation than she did to nature."[30] In her philanthropy, Cooper clearly was fulfilling her prescribed role in society as an unmarried daughter. Catharine Beecher makes charitable works the particular province of unmarried women (*American Woman's Home*, 20).

But Cooper's writing demonstrates that her charity and caring were extended also to the natural world, that she approached all of her relationships, including her relationship with nature, through this same ethic of care. In linking the human relationship with the earth to relationships within human society, Cooper anticipates the interconnected concern for social and environmental justice that characterizes contemporary ecofeminism. "In a multiplicity of forms," Mary Catharine Bateson writes, "caretaking is part of the composition of almost every life."[31] She concludes: "We need attention and empathy in every context where we encounter other living beings, and we need them to foster and protect all that we care for."[32] Cooper is important precisely because she demonstrated the importance of quiet observation and care.

NOTES

I would like to thank Professor Rachel Seidman, of the Carleton College History Department and Women's Studies Program, for taking the time to comment in detail on an earlier draft of this essay.

1. Susan Fenimore Cooper, *Rural Hours,* ed. Rochelle Johnson and Daniel Patterson (Athens: University of Georgia Press, 1998), 4. Hereafter cited in text.

2. Catharine Beecher, *A Treatise on Domestic Economy* (1841; New York: Source Book Press, 1970), 21–22. Hereafter cited in text. The standard biography of Catharine Beecher remains that of Kathryn Kish Sklar, *Catharine Beecher: A Study in American Domesticity* (New Haven, Conn.: Yale University Press, 1973).

3. Vera Norwood, *Made from This Earth: American Women and Nature* (Chapel Hill: University of North Carolina Press, 1993), 31.

4. The examination of this paradox forms the basis of Nicole Tonkovich's study of Catharine Beecher; see Tonkovich, *Domesticity with a Difference: The Nonfiction of Catharine Beecher, Sarah J. Hale, Fanny Fern, and Margaret Fuller* (Jackson: University of Mississippi Press, 1997).

5. Catharine Beecher and Harriet Beecher Stowe, *The American Woman's Home* (1869; Hartford: Stowe-Day Foundation, 1975), 19. Hereafter cited in text.

6. John Stilgoe, *Borderland: Origins of the American Suburb, 1820–1939* (New Haven, Conn.: Yale University Press, 1988), 9.

7. Susan Fenimore Cooper, "Small Family Memories," in *Correspondence of James Fenimore Cooper,* ed. James Fenimore Cooper, 2 vols. (New Haven, Conn.: Yale University Press, 1922), 1:12–13.

8. Susan Fenimore Cooper [Amabel Penfeather, pseud.], *Elinor Wyllys; or, The Young Folk of Longbridge. A Tale,* 2 vols. (Philadelphia: Carey and Hart, 1846), 1:43–44.

9. Ibid., 1:44.

10. As Lawrence Buell observes: "The shade tree and the sofa are not enemies but alternative forms of cultivation." Both have their place in the encompassing household of nature, which embraces human domesticity. See *The Environmental*

Imagination: Thoreau, Nature Writing, and the Formation of American Culture (Cambridge, Mass.: Harvard University Press, 1995), 407.

11. Lynn White Jr., "The Historical Roots of Our Ecologic Crisis," *Science,* March 10, 1967, 1203–7.

12. The history of these two strains of millenarianism is discussed by Rosemary Radford Ruether in *Gaia and God: An Ecofeminist Theology of Earth Healing* (New York: HarperCollins, 1992), 61–84.

13. Ibid., 77. The theme of the apocalypse and "ecocatastrophe" in American environmental writing is discussed in Buell, *The Environmental Imagination,* 296–308.

14. Lyman Beecher, *Works,* vol. 1 (Boston: J. P. Jewett, 1852), 316.

15. Ibid.

16. Ellwood C. Parry III, *The Art of Thomas Cole: Ambition and Imagination* (Newark: University of Delaware Press, 1988), 184. Parry includes reproductions of Cole's paintings from *The Course of Empire: The Savage State* (156, fig. 121), *The Arcadian State* (159, fig. 126), *The Consummation of Empire* (168, fig. 136), *Destruction* (181, fig. 148), and *Desolation* (184, fig. 153).

17. *The Rhyme and Reason of Country Life; or, Selections from Fields Old and New,* ed. Susan Fenimore Cooper (New York: Putnam, 1854), 23.

18. The notion of architecture as "organic" can be traced back at least to the eighteenth century and Sir James Hall's *Essay on the Origins, History and Principles of Gothic Architecture* (1785). For more on Hall, see Simon Schama, *Landscape and Memory* (New York: Vintage Books, 1996), 232–37.

19. Susan Fenimore Cooper, "A Dissolving View," in *The Home Book of the Picturesque; or, American Scenery, Art, and Literature* (New York: Putnam, 1852; reprint, Gainesville, Fla.: Scholars' Facsimiles & Reprints, 1967), 88–89.

20. This fantasy of refashioning the American landscape to resemble the English countryside is reminiscent of a similar episode in James Fenimore Cooper's novel *The Wept of Wish-ton-Wish* (1829). In the novel, an Indian raid causes the destruction by fire of a rough Puritan settlement in Connecticut; after this miniature apocalypse, Cooper fastforwards the action of his novel to a time several years later when the land has come to resemble an English rural landscape, with the ruins of the burned-out blockhouse still preserved.

21. Cooper, *Rhyme and Reason,* 28.

22. Ibid., 32–33.

23. For a fuller discussion of an ecofeminist construction of the self, see Val Plumwood, *Feminism and the Mastery of Nature* (London: Routledge, 1993), esp. chap. 7.

24. Ruether, *Gaia and God,* 251.

25. Judith A. Kates, "Women at the Center: Ruth and *Shavuot,*" in *Reading*

Ruth: Contemporary Women Reclaim a Sacred Story, ed. Judith A. Kates and Gail Twesky Reimer (New York: Ballantine Books, 1994), 198.

26. The biblical story of Ruth, as it figures especially in Susan Fenimore Cooper's *Elinor Wyllys* and in James Fenimore Cooper's *The Wept of Wish-ton-Wish,* is discussed by Lucy B. Maddox, "Susan Fenimore Cooper and the Plain Daughters of America," *American Quarterly* 40, no. 1 (1988): 131–46.

27. Ruether, *Gaia and God,* 227.

28. Mary Catherine Bateson, *Composing a Life* (New York: Plume Books, 1990), 136.

29. Marcia Myers Bonta, *Women in the Field: America's Pioneering Women Naturalists* (College Station: Texas A&M University Press, 1991), xv.

30. Ibid.

31. Bateson, *Composing a Life,* 140.

32. Ibid., 161.

LISA STEFANIAK

Botanical Gleanings: Susan Fenimore Cooper, Catharine Parr Traill, and the Representation of Flora

> And my dear Grandfather soon commenced my botanical education—being the eldest of the little troop, I often drove with him, in the gig, about his farms and into his woods, and it was my duty to jump out and open all the gates. In these drives he taught me to distinguish the different trees by their growth, and bark, and foliage—this was a beech, that an oak, here was an ash, yonder a tulip-tree. He would point out a tree and ask me to name it, going through a regular lesson in a very pleasant way. Such was the beginning of my *Rural Hours* ideas.
>
> SUSAN FENIMORE COOPER, "Small Family Memories"

Susan Fenimore Cooper's interest in botany is of foundational importance to *Rural Hours,* and the early cultivation of a botanical way of seeing that emphasized taxonomic classification as a function of the careful observation of increasingly refined natural details had a profound influence on her development as a writer and a naturalist. But Cooper's recollection of her early botanical education also suggests that the rich massing of accumulated natural details that gives *Rural Hours* much of its beauty and power has its origin in the gendered practice of nineteenth-century botanical study. Cooper's botanical ways of seeing and representing the natural are intimately linked with familial and domestic landscapes and thus connected with the leisure and pleasure those middle-class landscapes afforded. I want to focus here on the meaning and function of botany in *Rural Hours* and specifically on the ways in which Cooper's representations of her local flora emphasize the continuities between botany and gender as mid-nineteenth-century middle-class discourses. Placing Cooper next to her Canadian contemporary, Catharine Parr Traill (like Cooper, the first female nature writer in her national tradition), is useful to this project because the contrast helps illuminate Cooper's use of botany as a middle-class woman in a settled landscape. When seen in comparison, Cooper's and Traill's representations of flora reveal a shared and, in fact, transnational ideology of gender and domesticity but not of class. Each author approaches her local environment with a comparable awareness of botany as a gendered practice, but whereas Cooper's response to her local flora is almost fully aestheticized, Traill's is always tempered by an economy of utility.

In order to clarify the terms of this difference and before turning explicitly to botany, I will begin with the agricultural practice of gleaning and with the sustained interest each author took in gleaning as a type of women's labor appropriate to both the domestic sphere and the public space of domesticated nature. Employed as a frequent metaphor for their own literary pursuits, gleaning emblematizes their self-constructions as female natural history writers and points toward the primary influence of class and gender in their experience and representation of their local environments. By looking first at gleaning and then at the historical origins of botany as a gendered and genteel pursuit, I hope to show that the interconnections between gender, domesticity, and the "feminization" of botanical study are inseparable from Cooper's and Traill's representational practices as nineteenth-century women naturalists.

In the preface to *Rural Hours,* Cooper tells us that her book is "the simple record of those little events which make up the course of the seasons in rural life" and that this simple record was made only for her own "amusement." [1] Her conventional modesty is echoed and reinforced in her description of the "naturalness" of the enterprise: "In wandering about the fields, during a long, unbroken residence in the country, one naturally gleans many trifling observations on rustic matters, which are afterward remembered with pleasure by the fireside, and gladly shared, perhaps, with one's friends" (*Rural Hours,* 3). Cooper emphasizes that her book is a domestic enterprise, written not merely for herself but for others of her intimate circle, and she attempts to displace her authorial autonomy through the metaphor of gleaning. She seems, in fact, to have taken a particular interest in the agricultural practice of gleaning—the collection, bit by bit, of grain left behind by reapers. In one of the longest single entries in *Rural Hours,* she writes that the sight of cows in the fields after the harvest reminds her of the gleaners she had seen in European fields but that are absent in America: "In this part of the world, although we have once seen a woman ploughing, once found a party of girls making hay

The Respresentation of Flora   233

with the men of the family, and occasionally observed women hoeing potatoes or corn, we have never yet seen a sight very common in the fields of the Old World: we have never yet met a single gleaner" (158). By suggesting that *Rural Hours* is composed of "trifling observations" that have been merely, or "naturally," gleaned, Cooper invokes the practice of gleaning as a metaphor for the position of her work, and for herself as author, at the margins of literary and, by extension, national culture. As a simple and modest gleaner, she aligns herself with an economy of writing presumably subordinate to and dependent upon the figurative sowers and reapers whose primary labor produces the textual abundance that constitutes the harvest of America's literary enterprise. Her domain in *Rural Hours* is instead the superfluous and marginal, the residue of literary and scientific primary labor modestly and humbly gathered for private and domestic, as opposed to public and commercial, consumption.

Cooper's references to gleaning in *Rural Hours* function as a device to elide her own cultural labor as author, but they also recall us to the agricultural practice of gleaning as a gendered practice and, more specifically, a feminine form of agricultural labor.[2] Strangely enough, Cooper seems to approve of this type of women's labor even though it is clearly strenuous, backbreaking work; she approves of it, however, because it exists within an economy of charity, because it is a traditional practice, and because it represents a kind of domestic practice of the field. It is a gathering up of fragments that takes advantage of a kind of womanly strength, specifically, the meticulous attention to detail conventionally associated with the feminine and the domestic. Like the agricultural gleaner, Cooper recovers value from "trifling observations"—mere grains, or simple details accumulated through many small acts of seeing. But at the same time, gleaning the natural detail, as a type of ecological recovery enacted through writing, is rendered problematic by Cooper's position as a middle-class woman removed from the primary activities of agriculture. Cooper's strategies for gleaning the natural detail were not rooted in the work of the land but in the nineteenth-century genteel culture of botanical study, which worked to redefine women's relationship to plants in particular and nature in general.

Catharine Parr Traill (1802–99) also found gleaning an apt metaphor for her practices as naturalist and writer. The titles alone of her *Studies of Plant Life in Canada; or, Gleanings from Forest, Lake and Plain* (1850) and *Forest Gleanings,* the planned sequel to her successful emigration guide, *The Backwoods of Canada* (1836), suggest the pervasiveness of the metaphor in her work and thought. Traill, the sister of the more widely known Susanna Moodie, immigrated to Upper Canada from England in

1832, and her writing spans both the colonial and early national periods of Canadian literature. Her first book written in Upper Canada, *The Backwoods of Canada: Being Letters from the Wife of an Emigrant Officer, Illustrative of the Domestic Economy of British North America,* was published in 1836; during the 1850s she wrote a children's novel, *The Canadian Crusoes* (1852), and a work entitled *The Female Emigrant's Guide* (1854). Later, from the 1860s to the 1890s, she turned exclusively to botanical studies and natural history. Her last group of books includes *Canadian Wildflowers* (1868), *Studies of Plant Life in Canada* (1885), and *Pearls and Pebbles; or, Notes of an Old Naturalist,* published in 1894 when Traill was ninety-two years old. Almost all of Traill's writing originated as journal entries, drawn from her frequently difficult life as a settler on the shores of Lake Katchawanook, north of present-day Peterborough, Ontario. She also spent some years on the shores of Rice Lake, south of Peterborough, but after the death of her husband in 1860 returned to the Katchawanook area, where she remained until her death at age ninety-seven.[3]

I want to compare Cooper's and Traill's use of the botanical in order to pursue the possibility that they shared a transnational ideology of gender, domesticity, and class. But in doing so I must also acknowledge one particularly important difference that sets these authors apart. Traill was a pioneer woman who struggled throughout her life to maintain her middle-class status in the face of acute and chronic financial hardship. She was forced to perform some of the agricultural labor that Cooper is only able to witness as a distant observer in her more settled community in and around Cooperstown. Traill's attempt, while raising her seven surviving children, to maintain a subsistence level of agriculture for her family while also assuming the primary domestic labor of the pioneer woman rather seriously taxed her deeply held belief in her own sense of class superiority as expatriate gentry. Writing as a middle-class colonial woman from her isolated home in the backwoods of Canada gave Traill a way of reconnecting with the imperial center; her interest in botany in particular allowed her to participate in genteel culture and thus recuperate and assert her middle-class status. Traill was, like Cooper, a middle-class observer, yet she performed some of the agricultural work required of a female settler and thus was one of those "problematic" women whom Cooper disapprovingly observes laboring in the fields.

Like Cooper, Traill declares herself a "gleaner" of nature in a way that signals a gendered way of reading and writing the natural world, and the word demarcates a clear set of values and practices, both material and representational, that she shared with Cooper. For example, in the preface to her last published work of nature writing, *Pearls and Pebbles; or, Notes of an Old Naturalist,* a compilation of selected journal writings, Traill recollects her early childhood experience gathering "many pebbles hardly worth bringing home" on the beach in Southwold and concludes with a final paragraph on the significance of the "pearls" and "pebbles" she has gathered as a naturalist: "So, my readers, if you glean but one bright glad thought from the pages of my little volume, or add but one pearl to your store of knowledge from the experience of the now aged naturalist, she will not think the time wasted that has been spent in gathering the pebbles from note-book and journals written during the long years of her life in the backwoods of Canada."[4] Traill extends the practice of gleaning to the reader and, with the modesty of Cooper, suggests that whatever pearls exist in her natural history writings must be actively gleaned from among the pebbles—the seemingly insignificant or commonplace observations of nature that comprise the bulk of her entries. It is my contention here, however, that for Cooper and Traill gleaning symbolized a type of representational practice, a way of writing and reading the natural world. It functioned as, or was comprised of, a series of gendered perceptual habits and representational strategies that have their roots in both authors' participation in the genteel study of botany.

The promotion of botanical education for women and children arose out of the confluence of eighteenth-century science culture and the material history of European imperialist exploration. During the early 1700s, increasing numbers of previously unknown plants were flooding into Europe from the New World; Linnaeus, in an attempt to bring order to the expanding vegetable kingdom, introduced and promoted a sexual system of classification through which to marshal the individual specimens into newly created classes and orders. Simply stated, by examining the reproductive organs of a plant (the flower) and counting the number of male parts, or stamens, one could arrive at the class; these classes were then divided into orders by counting the number of female parts, or pistils. In *Cultivating Women, Cultivating Science: Flora's Daughters and Botany in England,* Ann B. Shteir suggests that the entire system "express[ed] a contemporary obsession with sex and gender difference": "[The sexual system] embodies clear and naturalized sexual differences and distinct gender boundaries; it asserts the biological incommensurability of the categories 'male' and 'female.' [Linnaeus's] highly naturalized and gendered theory about male/female difference in plant reproduction can therefore be read as illustrating a larger moment of reaction to cultural fears about blurred distinctions in sex and gender, and to gender ambiguity and shifting sex roles."[5] Popular translations of the Linnaean system published for female audiences were for the most part cleansed of their more controversial and erotic components and in this form assisted in promoting taxonomic botanical study as a fashionable middle-class pursuit. Thus botany soon entered the polite science culture of the eighteenth century as an appropriately genteel and feminine accomplishment. The sexual system, however, recommended itself to women and children of the middle class not because of its emphasis on sexual reproduction but because of its simplicity; in fact, it was so simple that the scientific study of plants was made possible, in Wilfred Blunt's phrase, for "any young lady who could count up to twelve."[6]

Botany became a remarkably popular pursuit in the late eighteenth century and developed into an influential form of polite scientific culture in England, colonies such as Canada, and former colonies such as the United States. In this sense both Cooper and Traill participated in an imperialist process of knowledge production to the extent that they provided an inventory or catalog of their local places that appealed to the Old World as the known world. But by the nineteenth century botanical study as a properly feminine pursuit had become strongly linked to prevailing discourses of domesticity and as such inevitably reflected conservative gender ideologies. Traill herself reaffirms this connection in her essay "Love of Flowers":

> If there be one study I would recommend to the attention of the female portion of my readers, it is the natural history of the vegetable world. . . . Whether our attention be directed to the simple star-eyed daisy . . . or to the magnificent dahlia in all its gorgeous hues—to the green moss, that vivifies the rude bark . . . or to the majestic pine that towers above his brethren of the woods . . . all is admirable—all is beautiful—and well fitted to awaken thoughts of holy contemplation in the mind—to lift it in grateful feeling towards that Almighty Being, who has graciously strewed the sinner's path with flowers. . . .
>
> The entomologist must inflict pain, or at all events, deprive happy creatures of a life of enjoyment, before he can perfect his studies . . . but the love of flowers may be pursued without incurring such risks, and the most feeling heart may delight itself in the occupation, without fear and without reproach.[7]

Traill's "natural history of the vegetable world" is aligned with the dominant discourse of "true womanhood" in its promotion of piety through natural theology, gentility, and feminine delicacy. It also encouraged nineteenth-century women to identify with their scientific objects: as one writer in *Godey's Lady's Book* suggests, the "pure-minded and delicate woman, who shrinks even from the breath of contamination" is like a flower in her "fragility, beauty, and perishable nature."[8] Such a woman would indeed feel the sting of reproach if she stepped beyond the bounds of genteel femininity, and these bounds were nowhere more firmly fixed than within the metaphorical and literal limits of the domestic.

Amateur botany for women, then, could not have attained its widespread appeal in the nineteenth century if it had not been aligned with conservative gender ideologies, and for the most part it reinforced rather than challenged the separation of public mainstream science from the private, amateur world of women's domestic botany. As Lora Romero reminds us, however, the "politics of culture reside in local formulations—and in the social and historical locations of those formulations—rather than in some ineluctable political tendency inhering within them," and thus we do need to "entertain the possibility . . . that some discourses could be oppositional without being outright liberating. Or conservative without being outright enslaving."[9] In her history of amateur botany in America, Elizabeth Keeney suggests that female botanizing, the study of plants in the field, did actually constitute a challenge to the more strict codes of feminine conduct:

> Indeed, the vigorous side of botany cause[d] a fair bit of controversy. . . . Even those like Wilson Flagg who championed female involvement in botany had reservations: "Even in this field [botany] they meet with obstacles not encountered by the other sex. A Young Lady cannot safely roam at will in any place at any distance . . . [W]hile a young man may traverse the whole country in his researches, his sister must confine her walks to the vicinity of her own home and to the open fields and waysides, and in those limited excursions she sometimes needs protection."[10]

Yet domestic botany was confined to the home and its immediate vicinity, although this changed as the century progressed. For the better part of the period, however, botany was as much a parlor activity as an outdoor pursuit, and women were often encouraged to have men physically collect the specimens that they would then press and identify at home. As Keeney suggests, the discourse of self-improvement that helped to promote botanical study as a feminine and appropriately pious pursuit was thoroughly coded within the rhetorics of natural theology, true womanhood, and domesticity. To this extent, it was a relatively restrictive, conservative, and middle-class practice.[11] But within the conservative dimensions of botanical study as practice, women were able to extend the bounds of what was considered appropriately feminine behavior, both in terms of an expanded participation in scientific culture and through increasing access to field work beyond the home.

Cooper and Traill certainly aligned themselves with the conservative strictures of domestic botany as a gendered discourse, reinforcing rather than negotiating the limits of culturally sanctioned femininity, but they also developed strategies for reading and writing the nonhuman environment that valorized their intimate connection to the home place. Their domestic, bioregional, and botanical way of seeing stressed attention to detail through a shared material culture and a shared material practice and emphasized a way of reading and writing the nonhuman environment that mirrored the cyclically repetitive, detailed, elaborate, and familiar order of domestic routine. Both women brought botanical study to the home and transformed the discourse within their respective social and bioregional contexts.

Both women were also no doubt aware that botanical study had not always been considered a genteel and benign leisure activity appropriate for middle-class women; in fact, the radical potential of female interest in (and simple exposure to) botanical discourse would have been recalled whenever the Linnaean system of sexual classification was promoted or denounced. The very simplicity that recommended the system for women and children also provoked questions of the moral consequences of women's involvement in an observational practice that gave them access to a fully sexualized "flora." Not only were they expected to diligently count floral sex organs, but they were also, like Linnaeus himself, in danger of seeing human analogues for the parts themselves and for the polymorphic and thoroughly un-Christian vegetable couplings essential to floral reproduction. Linnaeus was most explicit in discussing the analogy between animal and vegetable reproduction: "The calyx . . . is the marriage bed, the corolla the curtains, the filaments the spermatic vessels, the antherae the testicles, the dust the male sperm, the stigma the extremity of the female organ, the style the vagina, the germen the ovary, the pericarpium the ovary impregnated, the seeds the ovula or eggs." [12] The entire system, as Londa Schiebinger points out, was predicated on the arbitrary selection of male agency as the supreme determinant: "there is no empirical justification for this outcome; Linnaeus simply brought traditional notions of gender hierarchy whole cloth into science." [13] The irony of the system, however, is that it simultaneously sensationalizes and effaces its primary point of appeal, and this curious double vision was played out in Linnaeus's attempt to both circumscribe and circumvent the polymorphous nature of plant sexuality. Thus, in his allegorization of plant sexuality, Linnaeus took pains to normalize the relationships of male to female parts in terms of a relatively narrow canon of permutations. For example, even twenty stamens "sharing" the same pistil is still a (polyandrous) "marriage" if all parts share the same "bed."

Alan Bewell has suggested that the traditional association of women with flowers, in combination with the Linnaean system, encouraged the development of a botanical discourse that, "with its explicit focus on the sexuality of flowers, implicitly offered women a language for understanding and talking about their own sexuality, something that was supposed to remain hidden, a knowledge of which they, like the flowers, were supposed to remain innocent."[14] In the late eighteenth century, in fact, not simply sexual matters but questions related to gender and social inequality were discussed using botanical metaphors, as in Mary Wollstonecraft's "deconstruction" of the traditional associations of floral femininity (passivity, beauty, innocence, purity) in her critique of the "horticultural discourse on luxuriants" in *Vindication of the Rights of Woman* (1792).[15] In Bewell's view, the radical potential of botanical discourse was relatively short-lived, yet both Traill and Cooper, in their reactions against the Linnaean system, seem to be aware of the potential impropriety of delving too deeply into the realm of flora. What is at issue, then, in their use of the botanical is not only the modesty of their self-constructions as gleaners but also the way in which their negotiations of the vexed history of women's participation in botanical discourse frame their ways of seeing. Their adopted botanical vision demanded that they focus on a world of minute details, yet this appropriately "feminine" way of seeing, the actual practice of observing flora, offered a potential threat to the modesty and gentility it ostensibly guaranteed.

Traill and Cooper encode their resulting anxieties in different ways. Traill, as the more devoted and experienced amateur botanist, generally describes plants in a more scientifically rigorous way. In *Studies of Plant Life in Canada,* she seems compelled to coldly enumerate the pistils and stamens, even though she takes pains to assert that her book, written in a "familiar style," is not a book for the learned. "The aim of the writer," she says, "is simply to show the real pleasure that may be obtained from a habit of observing what is offered to the eye of the traveller,—whether by the wayside path, among the trees of the forest, in the fields, or on the shores of lake or river."[16] Nevertheless, each botanical observation provides a detailed description of the plant that includes a discussion of its reproductive organs. Traill's description of the Indian turnip (*Arisoema triphyllum*), for example, like most of her entries, provides a general description of the plant's habitat, a brief history of its common name, and a discussion of the plant's utility as either medicine or food. She adds a detailed description of the plant itself:

> The sheath that envelopes and protects the spadix, or central column which supports the clustered flowers and fruit, is an incurved membranaceous hood, of a pale green colour, beautifully striped with dark purple or brownish-purple. The flowers are inconspicuous, hidden at the base of the scape by the sheath. They are of two kinds, the sterile and fertile, the former, placed above the latter, consisting of whorls of four or more stamens, and two to four-celled anthers, the fertile or fruit-bearing flowers, of one-celled ovaries. The fruit, when ripe, is bright scarlet, clustered round the lower part of the round, fleshy, scape. As the berries ripen, the hood, or sheath, withers and shrivels away to admit the ripening rays of heat and light to the fruit.[17]

No one familiar with the morphological features of Jack-in-the-pulpit, with its suggestive combination of spathe and spadix, can fail to recognize Traill's dilemma here. Any close observation of the plant reveals a confusion of categories, since the patently phallic spadix actually contains the minute flowers. In other words, this particular plant represents a challenge to the purity, modesty, and innocence conventionally associated with floral femininity. Traill's description, only mildly sensual, nevertheless provokes a rather strange concluding paragraph in which she attempts to distance herself from the sexual (and political) meaning of her observational details:

> How well do I recall to mind the old English Arum, known by its familiar names among the Suffolk peasantry as "Cuckoo-pint," "Jack in the Pulpit" and "Lords and Ladies." The first name no doubt was suggested from the appearance of the plant about the time of the coming of that herald of spring the Cuckoo; the hooded spathe shrouding the spadix like a monkish cowl the second; while the distinction in the colour between the deep purplish-red and creamy white of the central column or spadix, supplied the more euphonious term of "Lords and Ladies," which to our childish fancies represented the masculine and feminine element in the plant; of course we dreamed not of the Linnaean system; the one was the Lord because it was dark, the other the Lady because it was fair and delicate. This was plain reasoning of the cause; children never reason, they only see effects. I am afraid that in many things I am yet a child.[18]

Unsurprisingly, Traill prefers the "more euphonious" or euphemistic name of "Lords and Ladies," a name she associates with the pre-Linnaean innocence of childhood; for her the name asserts the primacy of cultural sexual difference over biological sexual difference. And of course the name itself—"Lords and Ladies"—not only asserts the traditional associations of women and purity (the "fair and delicate" sex) but also recalls class distinctions, not least of which her own. As a "lady" botanist, Traill carefully reasserts her innocence by claiming that, like the flowers she observes, she is innocent of sexual knowledge; her status as a "lady" at this point depends upon her willful ignorance of the factual reality of the flowers she observes and records.

Unlike Traill, Cooper, with her acutely careful eye, must have observed the sexual organs of the plants that have such a central place in *Rural Hours*, but she does not record these particular details. Are we to conclude that she found no beauty worth noting amid the petals of the many wildflowers she gathered for the home? Given her repeated descriptions of the "modesty" and "grace" of the native flowers, it seems quite possible that she deliberately avoided this type of detailed observation. In fact, Cooper's flowers are so rigorously and consistently feminized within a cultural frame of reference that to call attention to their reproductive structures would potentially have upset both their purity and her own. At times, her insistence on "floral modesty" demonstrates the extent to which her botanical vision is subsumed within a feminine way of seeing that demands attention to the floral detail; yet certain details—the details that would, in fact, "deconstruct" the association between the pure woman as observer and the "pure" flower as object of the feminine gaze and "natural" analogue of the gentle female gazer—are revealing in their absence.

In contrast to Traill, Cooper's most careful descriptions are of those flowers that can be represented as feminine. For instance, the "skunk-cabbage" (like Traill's Indian turnip, an aroid) is simply "handsome"; the "unobtrusive" squirrel-cups "have a timid, modest look, hanging leafless from their downy stalks, as if half afraid, half ashamed of being alone in the wide woods"; violets "growing in little sisterhoods," gracefully and naturally prearranged for their admirer, are "a simple nosegay in themselves" and are thus observed "in the prettiest situations possible" (*Rural Hours*, 9, 29, 24, 47). Modesty, the prime virtue of Cooper's "native" flowers, differentiates them from "foreign" or European weeds and from the unnatural "hothouse flower." To this extent, her desire to valorize a particularly American "language" of flowers as a "native" language of common names leads her to reject the immodesty of Linnaeus's Latinate system of binomial nomenclature because it recalls the body and sexuality; even more importantly, however, the "dead language" is not only "uncouth" but "pompous" and "rough," as opposed to the "[p]retty, natural names" of "olden times" (*Rural Hours,* 84). Cooper, wanting to save the innocence of Flora from the cold reality of science, raises a patriotic objection to the scientific colonization of the "living blossoms of the hour" (*Rural Hours,* 83). She opposes the dry language of the "*hortus siccus*" to that of the "gay and fragrant May-pole" and appeals to a language that will promote a "natural, unaffected pleasure in flowers" (*Rural Hours,* 84). This language, apparently divorced from utility, will be a naming practice as modest as the flowers themselves, not dead but poetic, a purely aesthetic language purged of the post-Linnaean association of the floral world with sexuality, labor, utility, and commerce.

Like Traill, Cooper prefers the "more euphonious" names, although it is unclear to what extent these names should be "common," given that she distrusts the traditional naming practices of the rural poor (Cooper's "country people") and women.[19] For Cooper, the more poetic or "natural" name restores the flower to a world of leisure and pleasure or to the decidedly feminine realm of the beautiful as aesthetic object. Traditional, woman-centered ways of knowing flowers based on the labor of the field and of the stillroom are absent in *Rural Hours,* as are the female laboring body, the realm of production and utility, and the reproductive labor of the functioning flower. The gleaners, the women and children gathering berries, even Cooper herself only appear to disappear in *Rural Hours:* the other women's bodies enter the narrative only as models of appropriately feminine forms of domestic labor outside the home. Cooper's own body is wholly absent (as are the bodies and identities of her walking companions) except for the parasol that silently and continually reaffirms her status as a woman of leisure.[20] The modest flower, removed from the world of utility, labor, the body, and sexuality (like the genteel lady), is reified as an aesthetic object, and its sexual function is denied or repressed. Thus exalted, the flower's primary signification is purified and reduced to sheer ornamentation within the realm of the beautiful. As only the most "culturally" feminine (and ephemeral) part of any flowering plant, it seemingly ceases to exist for itself or in relation to its own body, mirroring the middle-class economy of female leisure in its existence as an object of and for display.

As perhaps the most concise example of this mirroring, the rose, the most perfect "emblem of womanly loveliness," acquires the symbolic or ideological valence of the natural virtues of femininity (*Rural Hours,* 75).

When Cooper notes that "the roses are opening at length" she anticipates the coming display, "when the village gardens will be thronged with thousands of these noble flowers": "How lavishly are the flowers scattered over the face of the earth! One of the most perfect and delightful works of the Creation, there is yet no other beauty so very common. Abounding in different climates, upon varying soils—not a few here to cheer the sad, a few there to reward the good—but countless in their throngs, infinite in their variety, the gift of measureless beneficence—wherever man may live, there grow the flowers" (*Rural Hours*, 70). These floral angels of the village gardens, these domesticated, cultivated roses, like Cooper's "healthy-hearted daughter of home," exist within an economy of divinely ordained charity: it is their very nature to exist for others as objects of pleasure, comfort, and beauty, and, like the domestic angel of the Victorian home, their "purpose and power" is to "cheer the sad" and "reward the good" (*Rural Hours*, 37). But, wary of the potentially unstable meaning of the rose's emblematic femininity (the roses/women are both "countless" and "infinite in their variety"), Cooper proclaims the wild, native rose as the true emblem of "womanly loveliness": "they have a grace all their own; there is, indeed, a peculiar modesty about the wild rose which that of the gardens does not always possess" (*Rural Hours*, 75). Cooper opposes the wild rose to the grafted tree rose, whose "very nature" is "pervert[ed]," robbed of her "drapery of foliage," her "veil of verdure." No longer "thoroughly rose-like" (and thus unwomanly), the "healthy-hearted daughter of home, the light of the house" (the wild, native rose) is contrasted with the grafted rose, "the meretricious dancer, tricked out upon the stage to dazzle and bewilder, and be stared at by the mob," her (its) "magnificent" body (flower) "exposed and explicitly manipulated as an object of desire" (*Rural Hours*, 75). The grafted rose simultaneously unveils an excess of meaning, an unnatural nature, the constructed "nature" of both woman and flower.

What is at issue here is not the opposition between the sexually commodified tree rose and the natural modesty of the wild rose but the fact of their ideological union symbolized by the graft itself. The "light of the house" and the "meretricious dancer" are not opposed but ideologically fused, grafted together by a cultural construction in which Cooper's attempts to fuse the feminine and the female, the rose and the woman, reveal a cultural dichotomy and not a natural balance. Instead, the veiling and unveiling, desexualization and sexualization of women and flowers results in a paradoxical transformation of the cultural meaning of floral femininity: the "wild" rose becomes the domesticated woman, and the domesticated rose becomes the "wild" woman whose publicly exposed sexuality sets her outside the moral bounds of mid-nineteenth-century patriarchal culture. In this way, Cooper's attempt to emblematize the American middle-class woman is an attempt to "naturalize" the domestic woman by domesticating the meaning of floral femininity within a national context. If the grafted rose is stripped of its modesty by the gardener, the American wild rose is stripped of its "wildness" by Cooper's fundamentally moral and aesthetic reading of the language of flowers, transplanted from the Old World and modified within a national context. The virtue of the wild rose is figuratively rooted in its literal roots as a native product of American soil, and so, to complete the connection, the middle-class American woman as "native" rose is no longer historically connected to conquest and settlement but is, rather, a wholly new, New World product of both nature and nation. At the same time, the representational graft that connects the American woman and the American rose, in its attempt to both nationalize and naturalize the mid-nineteenth-century domestic woman, reveals both rose and woman to be so intimately intertwined that it is impossible to determine whether either is finally a product of nature or culture. Like the virtuous woman who is virtuous because she is modest and modest because she is feminine, "whose roots are fed with her life's blood" (*Rural Hours,* 75), the economy of representation that is floral femininity becomes almost completely disassociated from the realm of the natural, unable to refer back to the very ground of its birth and generation.

Cooper's botanical vision of woman as flower mirrors a transformation in the aesthetic discourse of the beautiful in which beauty, by the middle of the eighteenth century, had become increasingly defined as both feminine and useless.[21] In fact, part of what Cooper's botanical representations suppress are other, competing historical discourses in which women and flowers (and plants in general) existed in a shared material culture, a culture that connected the utility of flowers and plants with the laboring, as opposed to ornamental, female body. Before the ascendancy of taxonomic botany, plant knowledge and plant lore were integral aspects of many women's lives because of their role in the gendered, domestic work of nurturing and healing.[22] These prior ways of knowing plants were eventually synthesized with or, rather, subsumed within or discarded by the discipline of scientific botany. Although Cooper and Traill, as middle-class women, wrote within the bounds of an increasingly feminized botanical discourse in the mid–nineteenth century, the record of their botanical gleanings reflects and reinforces this shift away from utility and toward aesthetics. Cooper, two generations removed from the experience of settlement, provides no evidence of her actual participation in the processes of the land. For her, the realm of flora functions as an extension of what Norwood calls "the domestic round" only to the extent that the domestic is itself purged of its associations with the laboring female body.[23] In *Rural Hours*, Cooper represents herself as a woman of leisure, strolling, admiring, recording, and recalling but never laboring in the landscape. Her social status is actually confirmed by what she does not do: she does not glean, or garden, or collect wild strawberries. But she does gather wildflowers to decorate the home, and this activity marks her relationship to the land as gendered and aestheticized, based on leisure and not labor.

Traill's botanical details, in comparison, do not exclude utility. Although self-conscious about calling attention to the labor that was necessary in "the backwoods of Canada," Traill strove to combine the proprieties of genteel domesticity with the demands of pioneer life by rejecting the type of taxonomic botanical practice that stressed collection and classification as a source of middle-class, properly feminine leisure. Yet Traill did collect and classify, practicing a type of domestic botany intimately linked to its source in British imperialist culture. Her botanical gleanings speak not only to the necessity of importing and domesticating ideologies of gender but also to the practice of domesticating the native flora of her backwoods home. In Cooper's American context, the botanical detail exists at the "border between the domestic and the foreign," or within what Amy Kaplan has recently called "manifest domesticity," domesticity "not as a static condition but as the process of domestication."[24] An ongoing, falsely dichotomous spiral of wild and cultivated, wilderness and civilization, nature and culture, foreign and domestic, national and local underlies the thought and material practice of these women as gleaners of the floral detail.

Like Traill and Cooper, I have focused on only a few details, emphasizing the discursive systems and material practices that they inherited and shared as New World women and only briefly acknowledging the ways in which they deployed and negotiated their relationships with the botanical—both the Realm of Flora and the specific local floras of their bioregional homes—within the complex cultural and political realm of the domestic. Attending to the details of their representations of flora forces us to acknowledge the extent to which the ideological codes that worked to define the boundaries of the domestic also worked to construct and limit their cultural field of vision. But these details also remind us that the natural and the cultural, like the domestic and its opposites—the public sphere, the wilderness—are not separate but inevitably, symbiotically intertwined.

NOTES

1. Susan Fenimore Cooper, *Rural Hours,* ed. Rochelle Johnson and Daniel Patterson (Athens: University of Georgia Press, 1998), 3. Hereafter cited in text.

2. For a discussion of gleaning as a gendered practice, see Peter King, "Customary Rights and Women's Earning: The Importance of Gleaning to the Rural Labouring Poor, 1750–1850," *Economic History Review* 44, no. 3 (1991): 461–76.

3. For a general introduction to the life and writing of Catharine Parr Traill, see Carl Ballstadt, "Catharine Parr Traill (1802–1899)," in *Canadian Writers and Their Works,* ed. Robert Lecker, Jack David, and Ellen Quigley, Fiction Series, vol. 1 (Toronto: ECW Press, 1983), 150–91.

4. Catharine Parr Traill, *Pearls and Pebbles; or, Notes of an Old Naturalist* (Toronto: William Briggs, 1894), xxxvi.

5. Ann B. Shteir, *Cultivating Women, Cultivating Science: Flora's Daughters and Botany in England, 1760–1860* (Baltimore, Md.: Johns Hopkins University Press, 1996), 17.

6. Quoted in Jennifer Bennett, *Lilies of the Hearth: The Historical Relationship between Women and Plants* (Camden East, Ontario: Camden House, 1991), 105.

7. Catharine Parr Traill, "Love of Flowers," *Literary Garland,* n.s. 1 (1843): 41–42.

8. Quoted in Elizabeth Keeney, *The Botanizers: Amateur Scientists in Nineteenth-Century America* (Chapel Hill: University of North Carolina Press, 1992), 72.

9. Lora Romero, *Home Fronts: Domesticity and Its Critics in the Antebellum United States* (Durham: Duke University Press, 1997), 4, 6.

10. Keeney, *Botanizers,* 74–75.

11. Ibid., 69–82.

12. Quoted in Alan Bewell, "'On the Banks of the South Sea': Botany and Sexual Controversy in the Late Eighteenth Century," in *Visions of Empire: Voyages, Botany, and Representations of Nature,* ed. David Phillip Miller and Peter Hanns Reill (New York: Cambridge University Press, 1996), 174–75.

13. Londa Schiebinger, *Nature's Body: Gender in the Making of Modern Science* (Boston: Beacon Press, 1993), 17.

14. Bewell, "Banks," 175.

15. Alan Bewell, "'Jacobin Plants': Botany as Social Theory in the 1790s," *Wordsworth Circle* 20, no. 3 (1989): 137.

16. Catharine Parr Traill, *Studies of Plant Life in Canada; or, Gleanings from Forest, Lake and Plain* (Ottawa: A. S. Woodburn, 1885), i.

17. Ibid., 21.

18. Ibid., 22.

19. Cooper asserts that the "[f]armers and their wives, who have lived a long life in the fields, can tell you nothing on these matters" (*Rural Hours*, 83), whereas Traill includes the common names (and uses) of local plants gathered from "old settlers' wives, and choppers and Indians" throughout *Studies of Plant Life* (3).

20. Even though Cooper asserts that "it has always looked well to see man, or woman either, working in a garden" (*Rural Hours,* 28), there is no indication in the text that she herself gardens, whereas Traill discusses her efforts as a gardener, particularly in relation to the domestication and cultivation of native plants, throughout *Studies of Plant Life.*

21. For a discussion of the relationship between botany and aesthetic discourse in the late eighteenth and early nineteenth centuries, see Peter Gerard O'Sullivan, "The Botanical Sublime: Natural Science, Aesthetics and the Cultural Politics of Beauty, 1750–1830" (Ph.D. diss., University of Pennsylvania, 1994).

22. For a wide-ranging discussion of the relationships and associations between women and plants, see Bennett, *Lilies of the Hearth.*

23. Vera Norwood, "Pleasures of the Country Life: Susan Fenimore Cooper and the Seasonal Tradition," in *Made from This Earth: American Women and Nature* (Chapel Hill: University of North Carolina Press, 1993), 25–53.

24. Amy Kaplan, "Manifest Domesticity," *American Literature* 70, no. 3 (1998): 582.

In Response to the Women at Seneca Falls: Susan Fenimore Cooper and the Rightful Place of Woman in America

The July 14, 1848, number of the *Seneca County Courier* contained the following short announcement:

SENECA FALLS CONVENTION

WOMAN'S RIGHTS CONVENTION.—A convention to discuss the social, civil, and religious condition and rights of woman, will be held in the Wesleyan Chapel, at Seneca Falls, N.Y., on Wednesday and Thursday, the 19th and 20th of July, current; commencing at 10 o'clock A.M. During the first day the meeting will be exclusively for women, who are earnestly invited to attend. The public generally are invited to be present on the second day, when Lucretia Mott, of Philadelphia, and other ladies and gentlemen, will address the convention.[1]

Buoyed by the support for the sentiments expressed at the meeting in Seneca Falls, the leaders—Elizabeth Cady Stanton, Lucretia Mott, and Mary and Elizabeth McClintock—held a second one in Rochester on August 2. Like a pair of thunderclaps in the still heat of that drought-ridden summer, these conventions stirred a storm of comment in newspapers far and wide.

That same summer, Susan Fenimore Cooper, daughter of novelist James Fenimore Cooper and an aspiring writer in her own right, was visiting her aunts in Geneva, New York, a stone's throw from Seneca Falls.[2] By the summer of 1848, she was writing journal entries that would be collected and published in 1850 as *Rural Hours,* in which she discussed many issues confronting Americans. Her occasional commentary on the rightful place of woman in American society in this text is especially interesting because it is among the earliest discussions of the subject, pro or con, in the post–Seneca Falls era.[3]

For most late-twentieth-century students of mid-nineteenth-century American history and literature, the conditions under which women then lived seem unbearably constricted. In 1848 American women had virtually no legal standing and no political power, at least through the electoral process. A Philadelphia newspaper, the *Public Ledger and Daily Transcript,* summed up a common attitude of the time in its response to the woman's rights conventions of 1848, saying, "A woman is nobody. A wife is everything. A pretty girl is equal to ten thousand men, and a mother is, next to God, all powerful" (*History of Woman Suffrage,* 804). Readers of Susan Fenimore Cooper are often disappointed that she, a single woman published and acknowledged for her intellectual ability, did not support efforts to allow her financial autonomy and a role in electing governors who would support her right to equal treatment under the law. Instead, she wielded her pen to oppose the effort led by Stanton, Mott, Anthony, and others to provide women with equal rights under the law and the right to vote. Her opposition to the rights-of-woman arguments expounded in these early conventions was subtle. However, as it became apparent that gentle suasion would not quell the rising sentiment for female suffrage, Miss Cooper's arguments against it grew pointed and specific in the post–Civil War period.[4]

While her position seems an inherently contradictory position to readers in our own time, it did not seem so to many women writing in the middle decades of the nineteenth century. Other influential women writers, notably, the Beecher sisters and Sarah Josepha Hale, editor of *Godey's Lady's Book,* advocated roles for women that kept them in the home, fortifying it and, by extension, fortifying, even barricading, the nation as the collective home from foreign and potentially malevolent influences. It has also been argued that these women writers, by defining the home and women's role in it, made it possible for women to move outside the home, most notably into print.[5] Thus, Susan Fenimore Cooper's *Rural Hours* could be viewed as defining America's domestic natural history as part of America's identity, setting it aside from foreign species. Using American natural history as a springboard, Miss Cooper went on to discuss many issues facing America at the time. Among these, she expressed sentiments mirroring those laid out in what late-twentieth-century writers have dubbed the "cult of domesticity."

Domesticity was but one response to the considerable turbulence of the second quarter of the nineteenth century throughout Europe and North America. Writing in the *New York Herald,* the paper's proprietor, James Gordon Bennett, alluded to the numerous political upheavals in Europe in 1848, a year eventually called the "Year of Revolutions":

This is the age of revolutions. To whatever part of the world the attention is directed, the political and social fabric is crumbling to pieces; and changes which far exceed the wildest dreams of the enthusiastic Utopians of the last generation, are now pursued with ardor and perseverance. . . . By the intelligence, however, which we have lately received, the work of revolution is no longer confined to the Old World, nor to the masculine gender. The flag of independence has been hoisted, for the second time on this side of the Atlantic; and a solemn league and covenant has just been entered into by a Convention of women at Seneca Falls, to "throw off the despotism under which they are groaning, and provide new guards for their future security." Little did we expect this new element to be thrown into the cauldron of agitation which is now bubbling around us with such fury. (Quoted in *History of Woman Suffrage*, 805)

In his comments on the Seneca Falls meeting, Bennett acknowledged the correspondingly charged atmosphere of the United States at the same period. Having led the way in political revolution in 1776, America was following up with economic, industrial, social, and religious revolutions of varying scope and scale. Westward migration, industrialization, urbanization, immigration, increased social mobility, and economic turbulence caused by an indecisive banking system and trade imbalances all engendered social upheaval, and well before the midcentury, progressive ideas posited by reformers of many stripes were receiving considerable attention.

Central New York State, where Susan Fenimore Cooper spent virtually all of her adult life, was called "the burned-over state" during the 1830s and 1840s for the numerous religious revivals and camp meetings held in the region. These appealed deeply to people displaced by so many new and conflicting forces. While evangelical preachers ranted about hellfire and damnation, other potentially disturbing ideas about social reorganization arose. Utopian groups, especially the Fourierists at New Phalanx, New Jersey, and the Perfectionists at Oneida, New York, threatened the hierarchical, patriarchal order posited by mainstream American theologians of the period. Like the Shakers earlier, these peculiarly American groups offered different roles within an altered power structure, especially for women. Communal child rearing, work outside of traditional domestic management, and inclusion in the community power structure offered potential fulfillment for women displaced within American society.[6]

The mainly female audience of two hundred who attended the two-day convention held in the sweltering July heat of a central New York State summer in 1848 demonstrated the agitation felt by at least a certain cadre of women. The Declaration of Sentiments read at the meeting and signed by sixty-eight attendees used the revolutionary Declaration of Independence written seventy-two Julys before as its model. The Declaration of Sentiments described the injustices to woman practiced by man through the American legal system. While relatively local papers failed to comment on the events of the meeting at Seneca Falls, the *Rochester Democrat* noted with derision, possibly tinged with concern lest those standing for the rights of woman might receive a fair hearing:

> This has been a remarkable Convention [held in Rochester on August 2, 1848]. It was composed of those holding to some of the various *isms* of the day, and some, we should think, who embraced them all. . . . The great effort seemed to be to bring out some new, impracticable, absurd, and ridiculous proposition, and the greater its absurdity the better. In short, it was a regular *emeute* of a congregation of females gathered from various quarters, who seem to be really in earnest in their aim at revolution, and who evince entire confidence that "the day of their deliverance is at hand." Verily, this a progressive era! (Quoted in *History of Woman Suffrage,* 804)

"Insurrection among the Women," the title of an article in the *Worcester (Massachusetts) Telegraph,* also reveals the concern with which the women's conferences were viewed (see *History of Woman Suffrage,* 803).

In mid-nineteenth-century America, the predominant editorial, literary, religious, and political voices generally worked to avoid open insurrection among any of the young nation's disaffected and, for the most part, disenfranchised populations, including Native Americans, African Americans, new immigrants, the growing industrial poor, and, after 1848, women. Thus in 1848 and 1849, when Susan Fenimore Cooper was composing the journal entries that she would publish as *Rural Hours* in 1850, the rights-of-woman issue was new and the discourse varied, but the rhetoric and activity of reform ideas of all kinds as an alternative to upheaval were well established in America. Miss Cooper, herself, was the promising scion of two American families—the Coopers and the Delanceys—who had played important roles in developing a new republic at once linked with its European forebears and traditions and separate from them. Her grandfather William Cooper had established Cooperstown, New York, where his granddaughter lived and set *Rural Hours.* In *A Guide in the Wilderness,* William outlined his plan for the successful settlement of the American wilderness, breaking with tradition by establishing freehold tenure rather than tenancy. Miss Cooper's father, James Fenimore Cooper, was arguably America's best-known writer in the mid-1800s. Emotionally rooted in the landscape surrounding Otsego Lake, James became a student of the Romantic movement as a young man. He melded Romanticism with his sense of the American past to create some of the nation's most enduring stories. These helped define and elaborate America's past for the young and uncertain republic.

Susan Fenimore Cooper wrote with a consciousness of her role within that family and within American intellectual society. She continued her father's exploration of the relative merits of aspects of the emerging American culture and the meaning of being American. Though Miss Cooper prefaced *Rural Hours* as "the simple record of those little events which make up the course of the seasons in rural life," a careful reading suggests that she intended to cut much wider and deeper than that disclaimer suggests.[7] In *Rural Hours* we find commentary on a broad range of issues relating not only to American nature but also to facets of American culture. She was well aware of the social and economic turbulence of the time and almost certainly recognized the potential appeal that many reform ideas—among them the rights of woman and female suffrage—had for people displaced by a variety of economic and social forces.

Among the displaced were Native American people, whom she discusses in considerable detail in her entry for July 17. She notes: "There are already many parts of this country where an Indian is never seen. There are thousands and hundreds of thousands of the white population who have never laid eyes upon a red man. But this ground lies within the former bounds of the Six Nations, and a remnant of the great tribes of the Iroquois still linger about their old haunts, and occasionally cross our path" (*Rural Hours*, 108). As prominent citizens of the village of Cooperstown and the occupants of one of the village's largest houses, the Coopers received many visitors. She recalled one visit by three Iroquois men, among them the Reverend Mr. Kunkerpott. Of them she wrote: "when no longer warriors and hunters, [they] lose their native character; the fire of their savage energy is extinguished, and the dull and blackened embers alone remain. Unaccustomed by habit, prejudice, hereditary instinct, to labor, they cannot work, and very generally sink into worthless, drinking idlers" (*Rural Hours*, 111). While her judgmental tone reveals a distaste for the men's current demeanor, she acknowledges their displacement through the disappearance of their traditional tribal culture. She is, however, quite taken with three Oneida women who visit. They are "meek in countenance, with delicate forms and low voices" (*Rural Hours*, 108).

Miss Cooper perceives them as positioned between untamed nature and her own civilized culture and suggests that they retain the essential, perhaps natural, gentleness of the female sex despite being heathens and savage (*Rural Hours,* 109). She proposes that woman has a natural reticence and gentleness embodied in these Oneida women, who are barely exposed to the temptations available to the girls of her own village or of the larger towns. The native women are vessels containing true female virtue, preserving their own domestic ways in the face of loss of tribal lands and the ensuing disappearance of the Iroquois way of life. As white middle-class women were cast in the role of protector of domestic virtue and exemplary lights of the home, so too are these Oneida women protecting their own domestic virtue from outside forces. Miss Cooper praises their continued wearing of clothes related to their traditional costume, saying, "[T]hey seem to be the only females in the country who do not make a profound study of the monthly fashion-plates" (*Rural Hours,* 112).

The native gentleness and lack of concern for material goods among the Oneida women differed from that of girls living in towns, or even in the rural village of Cooperstown, whom Miss Cooper describes in a passage dated July 3:

> Those [girls] who live in our large towns, where they buy even their bread and butter, their milk and radishes, have no idea of the large amount of domestic goods, in wool and cotton, made by the women of the rural population of the interior, even in these days of huge factories. Without touching upon the subject of political economy, although its moral aspect must ever be a highly important one, it is certainly pleasant to see the women busy in this way, beneath the family roof, and one is much disposed to believe that the home system is healthier and safer for the individual, in every way. Home, we may rest assured, will always be, as a rule, the best place for a woman; her labors, pleasures, and interests, should all centre there, whatever be her sphere of life. (*Rural Hours,* 99–100)

Increasing industrialization, especially in textile manufacturing, had made serious inroads on what observers like Miss Cooper perceived to be the predominant way of life of the early Republic. Mills opened up wage labor to girls and young women, as well as boys and young men, and by the late 1840s numerous farm-bred girls worked in textile mills in New York and New England.[8] Many girls were dislocated from the traditional pattern of living at home until they married and developed interests and concerns unrelated to the rural pattern of life esteemed by Susan Fenimore Cooper.

Though an innovative thinker on issues relating to the conservation of American nature, Miss Cooper deplored the potential changes in traditional American family and community structure that might further result from some reformers' ideas. She noted in an 1874 manuscript opposing female suffrage that women had "much higher and noble work to do than dabbling in politics."[9] Woman, as wife and mother, was the "light of the home" who exerted a gentle, civilizing influence on brutish man. She was the spiritual flame around which children and husband gathered like moths in a lamp's glow. Miss Cooper compared "the gentle, healthy-hearted daughter of the home, the light of the house," to the naturally beautiful wild rose, in contrast to the clipped and hybridized garden roses, which reminded her of "the meretricious dancer tricked out upon the stage to dazzle and bewilder, and be stared at by the mob" (*Rural Hours,* 75). But the light of the home could be easily sullied by the world outside the door of her family home; she could so easily lose her spiritual strength and endanger the souls of husband and children entrusted to her.[10]

The argument was familiar; journalists expressed these sentiments in vigorously antagonistic terms following the women's conventions of 1848. In Albany the *Mechanic's Advocate* stated that meeting the demands made at Seneca Falls "would set the world by the ears, make 'confusion worse confounded,' demoralize and degrade from their high sphere and noble destiny, women of all respectable and useful classes, and prove a monstrous injury to all mankind" (quoted in *History of Woman Suffrage,* 803). The *Lowell (Massachusetts) Courier* served up the same rhetoric with mockery:

> The women folks have just held a Convention up in New York State, and passed a sort of "bill of rights," affirming it their right to vote, to become teachers, legislators, lawyers, divines, and do all and sundries, the "lords" may, of right now do. They should have resolved at the same time, that it was obligatory also upon the "lords" aforesaid, to wash dishes, scour up, be put to the tub, handle the broom, darn stockings, patch breeches, scold the servants, dress in the latest fashion, wear trinkets, look beautiful, and be as fascinating as those blessed morsels of humanity whom God gave to preserve that rough animal man, in something like a reasonable civilization. (Quoted in *History of Woman Suffrage,* 804)

The message was clear. Woman was incapable of filling her God-given role if she cluttered her mind with politics. Susan Fenimore Cooper noted on December 16 that "[t]he position of an American housewife is rarely, indeed, a sinecure" (*Rural Hours,* 268). Rather, she had the care of the souls of her household to see to, and so her domestic sphere, set aside from the male political one, was divinely ordained, purposed to protect home and heart from incursion.

Susan Fenimore Cooper drew many examples from nature, the stuff of America's individuality, to support her views of woman's domestic role in America. Nature, the product of the Creation, the dwelling place of the deity, and the mainspring of the American imagination, was divinely ordained and so the perfect source of lessons in correct behavior. Like a clergyman crafting a homily, she drew lessons from nature illustrating family life and maternal devotion to support her views on American behavior, including the domestic role of woman in the young nation. An avid birdwatcher, she observed the family behaviors of songbirds. Of the nuthatch, she remarks, he "is a remarkably good husband, taking a vast deal of pains to feed and amuse his wife, and listening to all her remarks and observations in the most meritorious manner" (*Rural Hours*, 20). Husbands were to respect and care for their wives, who played important roles in organizing the home and raising the children. Orioles, she notes, "are just as well behaved as robins—harmless, innocent birds, bearing an excellent character. We all know how industrious and skilful they are in building; both work together at weaving the intricate nest, though the wife is the most diligent" (*Rural Hours*, 21). Husband and wife were to build a home together, though the woman's task was to work most diligently in furnishing and developing the family's domestic life, while the man worked beyond the home to support its continued smooth running. Nesting birds also provided inspiration for maternal devotion and selflessness:

> By nature the winged creatures are full of life and activity, apparently needing little repose, flitting the livelong day through the fields and gardens, seldom pausing except to feed, to dress their feathers, or to sing;—abroad, many of them, before dawn, and still passing to and fro across the darkening sky of the latest twilight;—capable also, when necessary, of a prolonged flight which stretches across seas and continents. And yet there is not one of these little winged mothers but what will patiently sit, for hour after hour, day after day, upon her unhatched brood, warming them with her breast—carefully turning them—that all may share the heat equally, and so fearful lest they should be chilled, that she will rather suffer hunger herself than leave them long exposed. (*Rural Hours*, 23)

Woman's most important job was that of mother. Her individual needs and desires must necessarily be subjugated for the good of her children and the home they required. Perhaps the upholsterer bee's homemaking impressed her most. This Old World insect, according to her description, painstakingly builds a subterranean nest for a single egg, lines it with a brilliant red upholstery of poppy petals, and supplies it with food. Then "the careful mother replacing the earth as neatly as possible" seals up the nest to await the birth of the new generation (*Rural Hours*, 123). For a single offspring, this insect expends virtually all of its life energy. Through self-sacrifice, woman achieved power. In the words of the *Public Ledger and Daily Transcript*, "a mother is, next to God, all powerful" (quoted in *History of Woman Suffrage*, 804). A woman's quintessential identity was in creating, maintaining, and defending the home and her offspring against invasion of all sorts.

Miss Cooper also suggests that women who "trifl[e] with their own characters" by giving in to their own desires and going beyond their God-given role would necessarily lose the respect of their community and their own self-esteem. She parallels the behavior of the "cow-pen black-bird," or brown-headed cowbird, with such women in yet another lesson from nature:

> It is well known that the cow-pen black-bird lays her eggs in the nest of other birds; and it is remarked that she generally chooses the nest of those much smaller than herself, like the summer yellow-bird, the blue-bird, song-sparrow, among our nicest and best behaved birds. One might almost fancy, that like some unhappy women who have trifled with their own characters, the cow-bird is anxious that her daughters should be better behaved than herself, for she is careful to choose them the best foster-mothers; happily, such a course has often succeeded with human mothers, but with the bird it seems to fail. There is no such thing as reformation among them. (*Rural Hours*, 255)

Miss Cooper notes that, unlike woman, who has free will and may make choices, the bird is guided only by biological destiny. Woman may, by her choices, improve or diminish herself. Woman must choose her proper Christian role, illustrated by nature and by the Bible. In so doing, she accepts domestic roles, for which she is best suited, in exchange for man's protecting her from harm.

This exchange was based partly on the perceived necessity to protect woman because she was thought naturally inferior in both physical and mental strength. If she was to exert power within the home, thus acting in the best interests of the American nation, she must not be overpowered by malevolent forces. Writing of her travels in America in 1837, Harriet Martineau felt this was carried too far. She observed that middle-class American women got little physical or mental exercise, noting, "The ladies plead that they have much exercise within doors, about their household occupations."[11] Martineau opposed this claim, saying that if American women would only get out and walk, they might not feel so physically weary or be so mentally dull. Even though Susan Fenimore Cooper was a vigorous and intrepid walker, as a review of her routes in the Cooperstown area reveals, she nevertheless described women generally as weak and incapable of taking care of themselves. On July 11 she comments:

> We American women certainly owe a debt of gratitude to our countrymen for their kindness and consideration for us generally. Gallantry may not always take a graceful form in this part of the world, and mere flattery may be worth as little here as elsewhere, but there is a glow of generous feeling toward woman in the hearts of most American men, which is highly honorable to them as a nation and as individuals. In no country is the protection given to woman's helplessness more full and free—in no country is the assistance she receives from the stronger arm so general—and nowhere does her weakness meet with more forbearance and consideration. (*Rural Hours*, 106)

This follows a discussion about women doing field chores in which Miss Cooper notes how unusual it was to see women in the fields in her region but that female gleaners were commonplace in Europe. Furthermore, in Germany she had even seen a woman and a cow yoked together pulling a plough while the husband drove the team. These scenes, which might illustrate woman's potential hardiness, shocked Miss Cooper's sensibilities. For at least one leader at Seneca Falls, however, similar scenes led to different conclusions. Elizabeth Cady Stanton remarked:

> Let us now consider man's claim to physical superiority. Methinks I hear some say, surely, you will not contend for equality here. Yes, we must not give an inch, lest you take an ell. We cannot say what the woman might be physically, if the girl were allowed the freedom of the boy in romping, climbing, swimming, playing whoop and ball. . . . The Croatian and Wallachian women perform all the agricultural operations in addition to their domestic labors, and it is no uncommon sight in our cities, to see the German immigrant with his hands in his pockets, walking complacently by the side of his wife, whilst she bears the weight of some huge package or piece of furniture upon her head. Physically, as well as intellectually, it is us that produces growth and development.[12]

Like Martineau, Stanton thought that American women might not be physically weak if they only got exercise.

Susan Fenimore Cooper's arguments for the roles she advocated for women, even those derived from nature, are amplifications of ones commonly held by Christian theologians of the period. As a devout Episcopalian, Miss Cooper was inclined to rely on the interpretations of scripture presented to her by her clergymen, rather than acting as her own interpreter. Lucretia Mott, a Quaker and a believer in the Quaker doctrine of the priesthood of the self, declared that women "had all got our notions too much from the clergy, instead of from the Bible" (quoted in *History of Woman Suffrage*, 76). Thus when Episcopalian Susan Fenimore Cooper presented the Old Testament story of Ruth and Boaz, it was in terms typical of Christian theologians of the time. She wrote, "One never thinks of gleaning without remembering Ruth. How wholly beautiful is the narrative of sacred history in which we meet her! . . . her history is all pure simplicity, nature and truth, in every line" (*Rural Hours*, 160). Ruth, a young widow, returns to Bethlehem, her husband's native city, with her widowed mother-in-law. We see Ruth "*cleaving* to the poor, and aged, and solitary widow. . . . from that instant we love Ruth" (*Rural Hours*, 161). Ruth works to maintain the domestic circle even after her husband's death. When she discovers that Boaz, the wealthy man who owns the fields where she is gleaning, is related to her husband, she follows Jewish law and lies at Boaz's feet when he is sleeping to remind him of his duty to protect her as a woman of his family by marriage. Boaz accepts the responsibility. Thus Ruth, by appealing for protection following the law rather than "following young men," preserves her dignity and earns protection within the domestic sphere of her husband's family. Indeed, Susan Fenimore Cooper notes of her peers generally, "[I]t must be woman's own fault if she be not thoroughly respected also. The position accorded to her is favorable; it remains to her to fill it in a manner worthy of her own sex, gratefully, kindly, simply; with truth and modesty of heart and life; with unwavering fidelity of feeling and principle; with patience, cheerfulness, and sweetness of temper—no unfit return to those who smooth the daily path for her" (*Rural Hours*, 106). Woman's selflessness is a fair exchange for the effort man takes to protect and care for her.

By the time she published *Rural Hours* in 1850, Susan Fenimore Cooper had clearly formed strong views about the correct behavior of the American woman and her place in America. In *Rural Hours* she focused her argument on women's behavior and the forces—especially the increasing tendency of girls to leave home—she perceived as altering traditional values. While she never discusses female suffrage in *Rural Hours,* it seems certain that she was responding to many other issues discussed at the Seneca Falls conventions and subsequent meetings. Her discussion of some issues and not others mirrors the character of the women's conventions from the late 1840s through the 1850s and into the 1860s. The meetings of this period provided a forum for discussion, and so women with wide-ranging views and concerns came. Not all supported female suffrage; at Seneca Falls only a third of those attending signed the Declaration of Sentiments.[13] The *Mechanics Advocate* of Albany, New York, described their activities, activities common to all reform efforts of the early nineteenth century: "The women who attend these meetings, no doubt at the expense of their more appropriate duties, act as committees, write resolutions and addresses, hold much correspondence, make speeches, etc., etc." (quoted in *History of Woman Suffrage*, 802). A second paper noted that "they design, in spite of all misrepresentations and ridicule, to employ agents, circulate tracts, petition the State and National Legislatures, and endeavor to enlist the pulpit and the press in their behalf" (quoted in *History of Woman Suffrage*, 803).

The women who led these conventions had developed these skills in other reform efforts, most notably abolition, and, in fact, abolition and the rights-of-woman issue remained closely linked for nearly two decades. During that period, the leaders of the women's conventions maintained a more-or-less united front and kept the issues of the rights of woman, including suffrage, more or less in the public eye, and a range of opinions was voiced from within this loosely organized group of reformers. Events in 1867, however, divided the group, and later writings on the subject of the rights of woman must be viewed in relation to the schism caused by the Kansas referenda on black and female suffrage of that year. Suffrage for neither group was permitted in national elections, but states could choose to allow them to vote at the state and local levels. The young Republican party, the party of Lincoln and of the emancipation of African-American slaves, sought to expand its supporters and feared linking black suffrage to female suffrage, a far more volatile issue that might alienate potential supporters. In hopes of improving their support, the Republican legislature divided female and black suffrage into two separate referenda. Neither passed, but the split resulting among women willing to support black suffrage before female suffrage and those insisting that the issues remain linked to achieve universal suffrage divided the leaders of the rights-of-woman movement for good.

Under the leadership of Elizabeth Cady Stanton and Susan B. Anthony, female suffrage became the leading and most highly visible argument. Susan Fenimore Cooper noted in her 1870 "Letter to the Christian Women of America," published in *Harper's Monthly*, that this new group "claim[ed] for woman absolute social and political equality with man. And they seek to secure these points by conferring on the whole sex the right of elective franchise, female suffrage being the first step in the unwieldy revolutions they aim at bringing about. These views are no longer confined to a small sect. They challenge our attention at every turn. We meet them in society; we read them in the public prints; we hear of them in grave legislative assemblies." [14] The discourse had changed in both emphasis and volume, becoming more focused on female suffrage and better publicized. In 1867 John Stuart Mill, the English philosopher, published his essay "The Social and Political Dependence of Women," calling for female suffrage following a series of petitions for female suffrage in Parliament. [15] In her "Letter," Miss Cooper cites Mill's essay and rebuts his ideas by expounding the predominant clerical view on woman's rightful place in society and opposing female suffrage.

In her "Letter," Susan Fenimore Cooper argues that woman, as a sex, will always be subordinate because of her inferiority to man in physical strength and intellect. Further, she recommends Christianity as the belief system that best provides for woman's well-being, saying:

> No system of philosophy has ever yet worked out in behalf of woman the practical results which Christianity has conferred on her. Christianity has raised woman from slavery and made her the thoughtful companion of man; it finds her the mere toy, or the victim of his passions, and it places her by his side, his truest friend, his most faithful counselor, his helpmeet in every worthy and honorable task. It protects her far more effectually than any other system. It cultivates, strengthens, elevates, purifies all her highest endowments, and holds out to her aspirations the most sublime for that future state of existence, where precious rewards are promised to every faithful discharge of duty, even the most humble. But, while conferring on her these priceless blessings, it also enjoins the submission of the wife to the husband, and allots a subordinate position to the whole sex while here on earth. No woman calling herself a Christian, acknowledging her duties as such, can, therefore consistently deny the obligation of a limited subordination laid upon her by her Lord and His Church. [16]

The subordination inherent in domesticity becomes power because woman's work is as important as man's, because it is a Christian duty. Miss Cooper goes on to detail the "gendered spheres" argument, concluding it by saying, "Women have thus far been excluded from the suffrage . . . from the conviction that to grant them this particular privilege would, in different ways, and especially by withdrawing them from higher and more urgent duties, and allotting to them other duties for which they are not so well fitted, become injurious to the nation, and, we add, ultimately injurious to themselves, also, as part of the nation." [17] Thus, gendered spheres and the domestic role of woman continued to be an issue of national importance, possibly national survival, in the post–Civil War era. American women must exert their powers to protect and enhance the home and insure America's future.

In both the "Letter" and a manuscript dated 1874, Susan Fenimore Cooper worried that most women would misuse their votes if they were granted the elective franchise. She wrote in 1874 that most women were both above political interest and incapable of using their vote wisely and would thus compromise the stability of the nation:

> Let us hope that the wild theories which demand Female Suffrage may never be carried into effect in this our good State of New York. Our women have already much higher and more noble work to do than dabbling in politics. To force the vote upon them would be to *degrade* them. If unhappily Female Suffrage should ever become a legal measure the downfall of Free Institutions would follow inevitably—the amount of political corruption would then become utterly unendurable. It would be *the beginning of the end*. Bribery would increase a thousandfold. Not that women are so mercenary. They are less mercenary than men. But they care little for political questions as a rule—their minds are filled with other matters—they would give their votes thoughtlessly, or the ignorant and unprincipled would sell them as a matter of course. The demagogues would be more powerful than ever. Mostly[?] female voters would trifle away their votes, and what good would it do that the remaining ten in every hundred would vote more wisely, and conscientiously than most men do? [18]

The 1874 manuscript reiterates the noble calling of domesticity for middle-class American women and insists on a difference in interests and abilities between man and woman. In her 1870 "Letter," Miss Cooper expanded on this idea, writing, "Men are born politicians; just as they are born masons, and carpenters, and soldiers, and sailors. Not so women. Their thoughts and feelings are given to other matters. The current of their chosen avocations runs in another channel than that of politics—a channel generally out of sight of politics. . . . The interest most women feel in politics is secondary, factitious, engrafted on them by the men nearest them. Women are not abortive men; they are a distinct creation." [19] As distinct creations, women have distinct, divinely ordained tasks. Suffrage is not among them.

As the discourse of the rights of woman shifted from a loose discussion among a variety of concerned citizens in the 1840s and 1850s to a set of more specifically argued agendas held by different groups in the late 1860s, the most vocal and visible being those calling for female suffrage, so too did Susan Fenimore Cooper's writing on the issues. Thus she moved from her more general discussion on the rightful place of woman in American society posited in several entries in *Rural Hours* in 1850 to an argument focused mainly on opposing female suffrage using the clerically based doctrine of the difference between the sexes by the 1870s. Her entries in *Rural Hours* are especially interesting because, unlike contemporary journalistic commentary, they are a woman's gentle, reasoned discussion of opposing and widely held views. Couched within the larger issue of American domesticity presented in the rural journal and so gently introduced, the subject of the rightful place of woman might be missed by a casual reader. In 1850 the issue was so new and considered by many so laughable that its potential threat must have seemed easy to quell, and the text can be read as a kind admonishment to women to reinforce their important domestic role in American society for the good of the young nation. But the call for legal and political rights for woman was not so easily put down; rather, it grew and was refined, and its supporters had to be addressed directly in reasoned terms. Miss Cooper's "Letter" of 1870 and her manuscript of 1874 can be seen as refinements and elaborations of the themes she first discussed in *Rural Hours,* to which she returned in light of the shift in the discussion of the call for the rights of woman, especially female suffrage. Miss Cooper never changed her mind on the subject of votes for women. When she died in 1894, women in some Western states could vote in state and local elections, but national suffrage was still many years away.

NOTES

1. Elizabeth Cady Stanton, Susan B. Anthony, and Mathilda Joslyn Gage, *History of Woman Suffrage, Volume I, 1848–1861* (New York: Arno and the New York Times, 1969), 67. Hereafter cited in text. Though a potentially biased source, this history of the fight for female suffrage collects many useful and rather ephemeral sources, including numerous newspaper clippings.

2. James Fenimore Cooper to Mrs. Charles Jarvis Woolson (Hannah Cooper Pomeroy), June 1, 1848, in James Franklin Beard, ed., *The Letters and Journals of James Fenimore Cooper*, 6 vols. (Cambridge, Mass.: Harvard University Press, 1960–68), 5:368–69.

3. During the nineteenth century, literature of the suffrage movement referred to the rights of "woman" rather than "women," apparently in contrast to "man" rather than "men." This essay uses the nineteenth-century term in most instances.

4. While it is unusual to refer late in the twentieth century to a maiden lady as "Miss," Susan Fenimore Cooper would, I believe, have been surprised at the very least to be referred to as "Cooper." She would have thought of herself as "Miss Cooper," and so she is referred to in this essay in this way.

5. For a discussion of these arguments, see Amy Kaplan, "Manifest Domesticity," *American Literature* 70 (September 1998): 581–606.

6. See Dolores Hayden, *Seven American Utopias: The Architecture of Communitarian Socialism, 1790–1975* (Cambridge, Mass.: MIT Press, 1976) for encapsulated discussions of these groups as well as others and their relationship to their buildings and planned landscapes.

7. Susan Fenimore Cooper, *Rural Hours,* ed. Rochelle Johnson and Daniel Patterson (Athens: University of Georgia Press, 1998), 3. Hereafter cited in text.

8. See Rosalynn Baxandall, Linda Gordon, with Susan Reverby, *America's Working Women: A Documentary History, 1600 to the Present* (New York: W. W. Norton, 1976) for a discussion of the changes in work patterns for woman in the early nineteenth century.

9. Susan Fenimore Cooper, Manuscript, April 7, 1874, Chicago Historical Society, Archives and Manuscripts, Chicago, Illinois.

10. See Harvey Green, *The Light of the Home: An Intimate View of the Lives of Women in Victorian America* (New York: Pantheon Books, 1983) for a discussion of the light of the home and the cult of domesticity.

11. Harriet Martineau, *Society in America* (New York: Saunders and Otley, 1837), 262.

12. Elizabeth Cady Stanton, "Address Delivered at Seneca Falls, July 19, 1848," in Ellen Carroll DuBois, *Elizabeth Cady Stanton and Susan B. Anthony: Correspondence, Writings, and Speeches* (New York: Schocken Books, 1981), 31.

13. For discussion especially of this early period of the movement, see Ellen Carroll DuBois, *Feminism and Suffrage: The Emergence of an Independent Women's Movement in America, 1848–1869* (Ithaca, N.Y.: Cornell University Press, 1978). For more general discussions, see Miriam Gurko, *The Ladies of Seneca Falls: The Birth of the Woman's Rights Movement* (New York: Macmillan, 1974); and Christine Bolt, *The Women's Movements in the United States and Britain from the 1790s to the 1920s* (Amherst: University of Massachusetts Press, 1993).

14. Susan Fenimore Cooper, "Female Suffrage. A Letter to the Christian Women of America," *Harper's New Monthly Magazine* (August 1870): 440.

15. John Stuart Mill, the English political philosopher, published his long es-

say, "The Social and Political Dependence of Women," in 1867. It went through numerous printings and was read on both sides of the Atlantic.

16. Cooper, "Letter," 439.
17. Ibid., 442.
18. Cooper, Manuscript.
19. Cooper, "Letter," 445–46.

Susan Fenimore Cooper's Published Works in Chronological Order

Elinor Wyllys. A Tale. Anon. ed. J. Fenimore Cooper. 3 vols. London: Richard Bentley, 1845.

[Amabel Penfeather, pseud.] *Elinor Wyllys; or, The Young Folk of Longbridge. A Tale.* Ed. J. Fenimore Cooper. 2 vols. Philadelphia: Carey and Hart, 1846.

Rural Hours. "By a Lady." New York: George P. Putnam, 1850. The subsequent publication history of *Rural Hours* includes a two-volume edition (London: Bentley, 1850); Putnam's illustrated edition (1851); Putnam's 3rd and 4th editions (1851); an illustrated edition (Philadelphia: Willis P. Hazard, 1854); a second edition by Bentley, bearing the title *Journal of a Naturalist in the United States* (1855); an edition from Putnam "with a new chapter," which is entitled "Later Hours" (1868); the last edition of the full text (Putnam, 1876); the abridged edition—some 40 percent shorter than the 1850 text—from Houghton Mifflin (1887); a reissue of the abridged edition, edited by David Jones (Syracuse University Press, 1968); a paperback reissue of the Jones edition (Syracuse University Press, 1995); an edition of the full 1850 text, edited by Rochelle Johnson and Daniel Patterson (University of Georgia Press, 1998).

"The Lumley Autograph." "By the Author of 'Rural Hours,' Etc." *Graham's Magazine* 38 (January 1851): 31–36, (February 1851): 97–101.

"A Dissolving View." In *The Home Book of the Picturesque; or, American Scenery, Art, and Literature.* New York: Putnam, 1852. Reprint, Gainesville, Fla.: Scholars' Facsimiles & Reprints, 1967. 79–94.

[John Leonard Knapp.] *Country Rambles in England; or, Journal of a Naturalist with Notes and Additions, by the Author of "Rural Hours," Etc., Etc.* Ed. Susan Fenimore Cooper. Buffalo: Phinney & Co., 1853.

Rural Rambles; or, Some Chapters on Flowers, Birds, and Insects. "By a Lady." Philadelphia: Willis P. Hazard, 1854. The identity of this volume's author is yet to be uncovered. Jacob Blanck states that the editorship of this volume is "generally credited to Susan Fenimore Cooper, but *BAL* has been unable to locate any positive evidence that she was, in fact, the editor of this compilation" ("Susan Augusta Fenimore Cooper," in *Bibliography of American Literature,* 9 vols. [New Haven, Conn.: Yale University Press, 1955–91], 2:312).

The Rhyme and Reason of Country Life; or, Selections from Fields Old and New. Ed. Susan Fenimore Cooper. New York: Putnam, 1854.

Mount Vernon: A Letter to the Children of America. New York: D. Appleton and Co., 1859.

"Sally Lewis and Her Lovers." *Harper's New Monthly Magazine* 18 (April 1859): 644–53.

Pages and Pictures, from the Writings of James Fenimore Cooper, with Notes by Susan Fenimore Cooper. New York: W. A. Townsend, 1861.

Church-Yard Humming-Bird (Cooperstown, New York), July 20, 1865: [1–2, 3, 4]. Lead article and six contributed items.

The Cooper Gallery; or, Pages and Pictures from the Writings of James Fenimore Cooper, with Notes. By Susan Fenimore Cooper. New York: James Miller, 1865. Reprint of *Pages and Pictures* (1861).

"Fragments from a Diary of James Fenimore Cooper." *Putnam's Magazine* 1 (February 1868): 167–72.

"Hospital Notice." *Freeman's Journal* (Cooperstown, New York), May 29, 1868: [3].

"Passages from a Diary by James Fenimore Cooper." *Putnam's Magazine* 1 (June 1868): 730–37.

"Bits." *Putnam's Magazine* 2 (August 1868): 145–48.

"The Battle of Plattsburgh Bay: An Unpublished Manuscript of J. Fenimore Cooper." *Putnam's Magazine* 3 (January 1869): 49–59.

"The Eclipse: From an Unpublished ms. of James Fenimore Cooper." *Putnam's Magazine* 4 (September 1869): 352–59.

"Village Improvement Societies." *Putnam's Magazine* 4 (September 1869): 359–66.

Appletons' Illustrated Almanac for 1870. Ed. Susan Fenimore Cooper. New York: D. Appleton and Co., 1869.

"The Magic Palace." *Putnam's Magazine* 5 (February 1870): 160–62.

"The Chanting Cherubs." *Putnam's Magazine* 5 (February 1870): 241–42.

"Insect-Life in Winter." *Putnam's Magazine* 5 (April 1870): 424–27.

"Madame Lafayette and Her Mother." *Putnam's Magazine* 6 (August 1870): 202–13.

"Female Suffrage: A Letter to the Christian Women of America." *Harper's New Monthly Magazine* 41 (August 1870): 438–46, (September 1870): 594–600.

"Two of My Lady-Loves." *Harper's New Monthly Magazine* 45 (June 1872): 129–33.

Introductions to the fifteen volumes of the "Household Edition" of the *Works of James Fenimore Cooper.* New York and Cambridge, Mass.: Houghton Mifflin and Co. [Hurd and Houghton], 1876, 1881–84.

"Rear-Admiral William Branford Shubrick." *Harper's New Monthly Magazine* 53 (August 1876): 400–407. Reprint, *Rear-Admiral William Branford Shubrick. A Sketch.* New York: N.p., n.d.

"Mrs. Philip Schuyler: A Sketch." In *Worthy Women of Our First Century.* Ed.

Mrs. O. J. Wister and Miss Agnes Irwin. Philadelphia: J. B. Lippincott and Co., 1877. 71–111.

"Otsego Leaves I: Birds Then and Now." *Appletons' Journal* 4 (June 1878): 528–31.

"Otsego Leaves II: The Bird Mediæval." *Appletons' Journal* 5 (August 1878): 164–67.

"Otsego Leaves III: The Bird Primeval." *Appletons' Journal* 5 (September 1878): 273–77.

"Otsego Leaves IV: A Road-side Post-office." *Appletons' Journal* 5 (December 1878): 542–46.

"The Wonderful Cookie: A True Story." In *Wide Awake Pleasure Book*. Boston: D. Lothrop and Co., 1879. 348–53. Reprint, *Wonder Stories of History*. Boston: D. Lothrop and Co., 1886.

"The Hudson River and Its Early Names." *Magazine of American History* 4 (June 1880): 401–18.

"The Adventures of Cocquelicot. (A True History)." *St. Nicholas: An Illustrated Magazine for Young Folks* 8, no. 12 (October 1881): 942–46.

"Small Family Memories." In *Correspondence of James Fenimore Cooper*. Ed. James Fenimore Cooper. 2 vols. New Haven, Conn.: Yale University Press, 1922. 1:7–72. Cooper dates this document "January 25, 1883."

"Thoughts on Parish Life." *Churchman: The Faith Once Delivered to the Saints*, June 30, 1883: 722–23; July 7, 1883: 20–21; July 14, 1883: 50–51; July 21, 1883: 79–80; July 28, 1883: 106–7; August 4, 1883: 131–32; August 11, 1883: 162–63; August 18, 1883: 187–88; August 25, 1883: 218–19; September 1, 1883: 247; September 8, 1883: 273–74; September 15, 1883: 298–99; September 22, 1883: 328–29; September 29, 1883: 355; October 6, 1883: 383–84; October 13, 1883: 415; October 20, 1883: 440.

"Missions to the Oneidas." *Living Church*, February 20, 1886: 709–10; February 27, 1886: 720–21; March 6, 1886: 736–37; March 13, 1886: 753; March 20, 1886: 768–69; March 27, 1886: 784; April 10, 1886: 28; April 24, 1886: 60–61; May 1, 1886: 75–76; May 15, 1886: 107–08; May 22, 1886: 123–24; May 29, 1886: 139; June 5, 1886: 155.

"Orphan House of the Holy Saviour." In *A Centennial Offering. Being a Brief History of Cooperstown, with a Biographical Sketch of James Fenimore Cooper*. Ed. S. M. Shaw. Cooperstown, N.Y.: Freeman's Journal Office, 1886. 182–84.

"The Thanksgiving Hospital." In *A Centennial Offering. Being a Brief History of Cooperstown, with a Biographical Sketch of James Fenimore Cooper*. Ed. S. M. Shaw. Cooperstown, N.Y.: Freeman's Journal Office, 1886. 180–82.

Appletons' Cyclopaedia of American Biography. Ed. James Grant Wilson and John Fiske. 6 vols. New York: D. Appleton and Co., 1886–89. Cooper is listed among the "chief contributors."

"A Glance Backward." *Atlantic Monthly* 59 (February 1887): 199–206.

"A Second Glance Backward." *Atlantic Monthly* 60 (October 1887): 474–86.

"The Orphanage Fund Pledged." *Freeman's Journal* (Cooperstown, New York), May 4, 1888: [3].

"Financial Condition of New York in 1833." *Magazine of American History* 22 (October 1889): 328–30.

"The Life of Hattie Brant." *Churchman: An Illustrated Weekly Newspaper-Magazine,* December 14, 1889: 748–50.

"The Childhood of Bishop Heber. I." *Churchman: An Illustrated Weekly Newspaper-Magazine,* July 19, 1890: 81–83.

"College Life of Bishop Heber. II." *Churchman: An Illustrated Weekly Newspaper-Magazine,* August 16, 1890: 205–6.

"College Life of Bishop Heber. III." *Churchman: An Illustrated Weekly Newspaper-Magazine,* August 23, 1890: 232–33.

"Boyhood of Bishop Heber." *Churchman: An Illustrated Weekly Newspaper-Magazine,* September 13, 1890: 319–22.

William West Skiles: A Sketch of Missionary Life at Valle Crucis in Western North Carolina, 1842–1862. New York: James Pott and Co., 1890.

"The Talent of Reading Wisely." *Ladies' Home Journal* 9 (February 1892): 18.

"A Lament for the Birds." *Harper's New Monthly Magazine* 87 (August 1893): 472–74.

"An Outing on Lake Otsego." *Freeman's Journal* (Cooperstown, New York), April 12, 1894: 2.

"The Cherry-Colored Purse. (A True Story)." *St. Nicholas: An Illustrated Magazine for Young Folks* 22, no. 3 (January 1895): 245–48.

Susan Fenimore Cooper's
Letters and Manuscripts

We list here chronologically the known letters and manuscripts in Cooper's hand together with several letters to her. This list is intended as an aid to further research into Cooper's life and work, not as a complete record of all surviving papers, most of which, doubtless, have yet to be located and collected. We include with each entry some indication of the contents of the letter or manuscript. Unfortunately, several of her letters are preserved without evidence that identifies the person addressed. Unless otherwise stated, Cooper writes from Cooperstown, New York.

Abbreviations

Beinecke   Beinecke Rare Book and Manuscript Library, Yale University, New Haven, Connecticut
JFC   James Fenimore Cooper
NYSHA   New York State Historical Association Library, Cooperstown
SFC   Susan Fenimore Cooper
VA   Alderman Library, University of Virginia, Charlottesville

1. Letter to Mrs. Hansom, October 26, 1846, The Historical Society of Pennsylvania, Philadelphia. Asks a minister's wife to recommend a new chamber woman for their household.
2. Letter to James Fenimore Cooper, Geneva, New York, June 21, 1848, Beinecke. Regrets that she will not see her father on his way to Detroit; enjoys driving about with "Peter who makes a very good whip" and who seems content despite the "great misfortune under which he labours"; impressed with the "conclave of surplices" at an ordination ceremony performed by the "Bishop," "quite grand compared to our own little parish church"; includes a description of a new college chapel that Dr. Hale showed them; Aunt Martha has planned an excursion to Crooked Lake; wishes JFC to purchase either at Niagara or Detroit "some Indian curiosities," which they "four" can send to European friends, "which will have more interest for them than anything else from this part of the world"; SFC thinks JFC will "like Mr. Hobart," who "has just given up three hundred dollars of his salary . . . on account of the church debts"; feasts on Aunt Martha's strawberries three times a day; about the coming "great election": "As I am never a very good partizan I have

taken the liberty of ranking myself on the *Rough-and-Ready* side for the present; being a woman I conceive myself . . . privileged to take any political subject wrong and foremost, and accordingly *Men, not Measures* is my device"; "Your affectionate child / Susan F. Cooper."

3. Letter to Andrew Jackson Downing, October 2, 1849, NYSHA. Thanks Downing for providing information about the willow and for his offer of a willow cutting, which she cannot accept because the weeping willow does not thrive in her region.

4. Letter to James Fenimore Cooper, March 3, 1850, Beinecke. Thanks JFC for his praise of *Rural Hours;* "To satisfy yourself, and my dear Mother, has always been a chief object of my authorship, and hitherto I have met with little enough of encouragement from other quarters"; the "remainder" of the "Rural Hours" manuscript "was sent off by express on Monday" to Putnam; asks JFC to "call at Stanford and Swords ? for the M.S. of *Devotions for the Sick;* I have no other copy of it, and perhaps it may some day find a publisher"; "Perhaps our Sunday School Publisher may take it one of these days"; on the recent birth of "Cally's little boy" SFC finds she is "quite a baby-fancier. It actually makes me smile sometimes to find myself already caring so much for this little rogue—such things come by nature as Dogberry says of reading and writing"; "as ever, dutifully and affectionately your daughter / S. F. C."

5. Letter to G. P. Putnam, June 24, 1850, Beinecke. SFC has received all the sheets for *Rural Hours,* "and the printing process is over at last"; JFC has forwarded the sheets to England; SFC notes "one or two slight errors in the Dedication, and a change in the Title Page"; "As regards the Title Page, I wish the words *A Lady* changed to a smaller type."

6. Letter to Mrs. Laight, July 20, 1850, Special Collections, The Ohio State University Libraries, Columbus. Announces that a bound copy of *Rural Hours* will arrive "In a day or two"; JFC had already had Laight read it in proofs.

7. Letter to Mr. Jay, September 2, 1850, VA. Asks Jay to find a public library in New York that would lend books to the "country folk" in Cooperstown; her "patch work labours" are often delayed by not having needed books.

8. Letter to Miss Jay, July 28, 1851, VA. Eight-page account of JFC's illness, confirmation in the church, spiritual condition, and that he has stopped even dictating to Charlotte. Rather full portrait of family circle.

9. Letter apparently to Richard Bentley, August 6, 1851, Beinecke. Disappointed by sales of *Rural Hours* in England; "The good success I have had in America has led me to prepare another work for the press, which will shortly be printed. It is called *The Shield, a Narrative;* and relates to the habits, and life of the red man, before his intercourse with the whites, or rather to his condition at the period of the discovery. Many historical essays, giving information on the antiquities and customs of the race, when first seen by the Europeans, have appeared here lately, and it is to embody these in a charac-

teristic tale that the narrative has been written. It seems to me likely that in this case the tables may be turned, and *The Shield* from the nature of the subject may proove more intersting in the old world than a record of our simple rural life. Should such proove . . . to be the fact it will also help the sale of Rural Hours. I have taken much pains to give the book accuracy in all its details. In your June letter you proposed to take the work on the same terms as Rural Hours, and I now wish to know if such are still your views. The first Chapter will probably be printed within a month."

10. Letter to George Putnam, August 27, 1851, G. P. Putnam Papers, Manuscripts and Archives Section, New York Public Library. Cooper explains why she has not yet sent the first chapters of "The Shield" and asks Putnam to keep searching for JFC's introduction to "The Towns of Manhattan," which he is certain was included in a recent package to Putnam.

11. Letter to Master Samuel Francis, August 29, 1851, Department of Special Collections, Memorial Library, University of Wisconsin–Madison. Grateful response to a family friend's son's request for a sample of SFC's handwriting; Master Francis's father was apparently a physician who "left his business, friends, and home, to travel two hundred miles to an out of the way place" to visit JFC, "his old friend," "at a distance from the best medical advice and too ill to be moved himself."

12. Letter to R. W. Griswold, October 2, 1851, Boston Public Library. Thanks Griswold for his intent to honor JFC's memory in some way.

13. Letter to George Putnam, October 11, 1851, G. P. Putnam Papers, Manuscripts and Archives Section, New York Public Library. A lengthy (eight-page) discussion of editorial matters relating to the manuscript of JFC's "The Towns of Manhattan," which Putnam is preparing for publication. SFC also explains that as soon as she is able to check certain natural history facts cited in "The Shield," she will send the first chapters to Putnam.

14. Letter to Miss Jay, October 26, 1851, VA. SFC's mother thanks Miss Jay for her letter of condolence; a description of JFC's last pleasures, demeanor, and smile.

15. Letter to R. W. Griswold, November 24, 1851, Boston Public Library. Response, by way of refusal, to his proposal to publish an edition of unpublished JFC manuscripts, even though they need money, and he promises some.

16. Letter from G. P. Putnam, New York, December 2, 1851, Beinecke. "Your favor of Nov. 28. With proofs of Towns of Manhattan & 'The Shield' was duly rec^d." Putnam explains that her desire to "re-model" the "whole work"— meaning "Towns of Manhattan"—is not feasible; she should have told them sooner, before they had "commenced printing"; "The expense of the sheets already printed would probably be about $150 or $175." "I shall proceed with Mdm Pfeiffer's work & The Shield as rapidly as possible—presuming you can furnish the copy as rapidly as it is wanted."

17. Letter to Frederick Phinney, March 27, 1852, Beinecke. Humbly agrees to

write an introduction and notes for an edition of John Leonard Knapp's *Country Rambles in England* (1829), which Phinney will publish.

18. Letter to Sir, June 25, 1852, VA. Declines writing about homes of American writers and an article about JFC.

19. Letter to Sir, July 2, 1852, VA. Complies with request for daguerreotype, possibly of JFC, although she thinks he would have a better image for his book if he had a sketch made.

20. Letter to Richard Bentley, Geneva, New York, October 20, 1852, Rare Book and Special Collections Library, University Library, University of Illinois at Urbana–Champaign. Complains a bit about sales of *Rural Hours;* willing to let him publish "The Shield" on the same terms; hopes for better success; she would not mention money if she didn't need it.

21. Letter to H. S. Mandall, Esq., Secretary of State, Albany, June 18, 1853, The Historical Society of Pennsylvania, Philadelphia. Thanks him for a copy of the new "Documentary History" and several books from the State Library that are helping her with a volume she is now preparing; notes the difficulty of getting books in Cooperstown; her brother appears to have asked this official to help his sister.

22. Letter to John D. Hart, Esq., June 12, 1854, The Historical Society of Pennsylvania, Philadelphia. SFC just returned from a winter in Washington, D.C.; Hart is welcome to extracts from *Rural Hours;* notes that since *Rural Hours* she has edited Knapp; *Rhyme and Reason* is now in press; apparent response to Hart's query about what she has published since *Rural Hours.*

23. Letter to Rear Adm. William Branford Shubrick, November 10, 1854, VA. *Rhyme and Reason* to be published this week and a copy to be delivered to Shubrick; playful affection shown for "my dear Commodore"; references to war between England and Russia.

24. Letter to Mrs. Banyer, January 26, 1855, VA. Thanks for a package of books; description of a winter evening spent reading and their book-easel.

25. Letter to Redfield and Company, Publishers, October 24, 1855, Duyckinck Family Papers, Manuscripts and Archives Section, New York Public Library. Proposes that Redfield publish her diary of "a summer passed in a country house in Switzerland, and that of an autumn passed on the shores of the bay of Naples." She refers to it as "a sort of European Rural Hours," which would "probably contain about three hundred pages of common duodecimo page." This seems not to have been published.

26. Letter to Sir, January 26, 1857, VA. Declines request for JFC's autograph and states her general rule to decline all such requests.

27. Letter to Eliza, February 3, 1857, VA. Thanks for a volume of "Memorial Sermons."

28. Letter to "My dear sister," Geneva, New York, July 12, 1858, Mount Vernon Ladies' Association Library, Mount Vernon, Virginia. SFC is pleased to be locally involved in the restoration of Mount Vernon: "Most of us have

more patriotism than we are aware of, and it is pleasant to have the feeling aroused under a form more generous and dignified, than a fourth of July Oration, (of the common sort), a Buncombe speech in Congress, or a fire-man's procession—the usual channels into which one's everyday love of country flows."

29. Letter to Mary Morris Hamilton, Geneva, New York, July 27, 1858, Mount Vernon Ladies' Association Library, Mount Vernon, Virginia. SFC formally accepts her local role in the restoration of Mount Vernon.

30. Letter to "Gentlemen," November 1, 1858, VA. Reference to revising historical articles and submitting a "little tale" to be published anonymously.

31. Letter to W. H. Averell, November 18, 1858, NYSHA. Thanks Averell for assistance with the Charity House Fund.

32. Letter to unknown youth, January 26, 1859, VA. Polite, encouraging letter to "a mere youth" who wrote to SFC.

33. Letter to Mr. Jay, June 16, 1859, VA. Thanks Mr. Jay for the photograph of Judge Jay; remarks at how fast life seems to go sometimes.

34. Letter to Rear Adm. William Branford Shubrick, April 26, 1860, VA. Asks permission to dedicate *Pages and Pictures* to her Commodore.

35. Letter to Rear Adm. William Branford Shubrick, December 7, 1860, VA. Announces publication of *Pages and Pictures;* he should receive a copy soon. Charlotte and SFC watch the dark clouds of the Civil War gathering from their "quiet womanly home"; if JFC were alive, his "clear tones" and "powerful pen" would be heard; no one seems to be effective today in this way.

36. Letter to "Sarah," March 11, 1864, VA. Sends certification Sarah requested to attach to the page of JFC manuscript she has; envies Sarah for being close to their friends in Washington, D.C.

37. Letter to "Madam," April 2, 1864, private collection of Allan Axelrad. Grants a request for a sample of JFC's manuscripts; includes a page from the "Water Witch" manuscript; "We had just decided that we could not afford to give up any more of his hand-writing, having already sent about two hundred pages to the different Fairs throughout the country."

38. Letter to "Seward" [?], August 23, 1865, Department of Rare Books and Special Collections, University of Rochester Library, Rochester, New York. Solicits his name and influence as an honorary member of the Thanksgiving-Hospital Society.

39. Letter to anonymous, October 21, 1865, NYSHA. A request for assistance with the county hospital.

40. Letter to Sir, June 2, 1869, VA. Denies request for JFC autograph—this and all others.

41. Letter to Sir, September 8, 1869, VA. Laments trouble she is having helping a girl whose grandfather is her legal guardian; SFC can't do any more because of the legalities.

42. Letter to W. W. Cooper, March 30, 1872, VA. Thanks for transcript of Wil-

liam Cooper's "pamphlet," which she had never seen before; this helps with a volume she's now preparing.

43. Letter to W. W. Cooper, October 7, 1872, VA. Response to his query about obtaining a copy of SFC's edition of Knapp; grateful for an apparent compliment for her *Rural Hours*.

44. Letter to Sir, February 22, 1873, Historical Society of Pennsylvania, Philadelphia. Thanks him for the copy of grandfather's letter, as of "*great service*" to her; she has almost finished her transcription of the "Guide to the Wilderness"; she'll send his copy of the volumes she's using the "Guide" for and will be disappointed if he does not approve of the use she has made of it; he will be acknowledged in the publication; reference to "that dreadful fire at Boston" and to the loss of her home twenty years ago when she was away.

45. Letter to W. W. Cooper, October 21, 1873, VA. Letters (two) to both W. W. Cooper and his wife (?); SFC has been too busy for "pleasure writing"; her last Cooper aunt, Mrs. Isaac Cooper, died at age ninety.

46. Two-page manuscript against female suffrage, April 7, 1874, Archives and Manuscripts, Chicago Historical Society. SFC suggests that the institutions that sustain democracy itself would collapse if women were allowed to vote.

47. Letter to W. W. Cooper, August 8, 1874, VA. Response to his request for Cooper family history information; she doesn't know much.

48. Letter to Mary Shubrick Clymer, January 14, 1875, VA. Seeks information about the Paraguayan Expedition and President Buchanan's message about it from 1853; she can't write much because it is physically difficult for her.

49. Letter to W. W. Cooper, October 16, 1875, VA. She is very busy lately with a sick aunt (De Lancey) and orphanage teacher and matron, whose absences she fills; also correcting proofs of her introductions to the new edition of JFC's novels.

50. Letter to Mary F. Barrows Cooper, February 23, 1878, NYSHA. Explains SFC's recent cold and asks to borrow books.

51. Letter to W. W. Cooper, October 2, 1878, VA. Informs him of the illness and approaching death of a family friend.

52. Letter to "Madam," March 18, 1880, NYSHA. SFC sends her "Adventures of Cocquelicot" for publication in *St. Nicholas* magazine.

53. Letter to John B. Peaslee, Esq., Superintendent of Public Schools, Cincinnati, Ohio, April 12, 1883, Special Collections, Baker Library, Dartmouth College, Hanover, New Hampshire. Thanks him for his interesting letter and encloses a copy of *Rural Hours;* "The subject of Forestry is one in which I have been very deeply interested for many years. In a volume on Country Life published long since under the title of '*Rural Hours,*' I already deplored the extravagant and senseless destruction of trees in our country, not only wild forests, but lesser woods, and groves, and single trees of unusual beauty. There has been really a recklessness of this subject which may be called barbarous, and utterly unworthy of the civilization on which we pride ourselves.

But most happily our people appear to be awaking to the vast importance of this question, in different parts of the country"; thanks him "for including my Father's name in your Authors' Grove"; return address on envelope: "From Miss Susan Fenimore Cooper, daughter of J. Fenimore Cooper." A copy of Putnam's 1876 edition of *Rural Hours* signed by John B. Peaslee is held by the Cincinnati University Library.

54. Letter to Mrs. Mapes Dodge, February 4, 1884, NYSHA. SFC submits a sketch to *St. Nicholas* magazine.

55. Letter to Gentlemen of the Ben W. Austin Lee Literary and Historical Society, October 15, 1884, Anthony Collection, Manuscripts and Archives Section, New York Public Library. A brief note of gratitude for membership in the society.

56. Letter to "Madam," October 22, 1885, VA. Declines assisting with an exhibition, the *Three Americas,* in New Orleans; she has no "sectional" feelings against the South; a blanket woven by native Alaskan women is superior to "Crazy Quilts"; hopes the "Women's department" recognizes that the best exhibits of their work are well-trained children; actually women have more to do than men.

57. Letter to unknown, November 4, 1885, Charles Roberts Autograph Collection, Haverford College Library, Haverford, Pennsylvania. Writes to say she doesn't know the person the unknown writer asked about.

58. Letter to "young friend," February 17, 1886, VA. Sending "scrap of my Father's" hand that he requested; she likes JFC's novels also, "though I am not a boy!"

59. Letter to unknown, November 29, 1886, private collection of Allan Axelrad. Grants a request for a piece of JFC's manuscripts; SFC encloses a fragment of a page from the "Water Witch" manuscript.

60. Letter to Thomas Bailey Aldrich, October 31, 1887, Houghton Library, Harvard University, Cambridge, Massachusetts. She offers the *Atlantic Monthly* pages she wrote in the summer of 1827, when her family resided in the village of St. Ouen, near Paris: "I took them out of a Box sometime since with a number of volumes of my youthful Diary, intending to burn them all. But on looking them over I became interested in many of the details—the Diary goes back so far, sixty years, there have been so many changes since those days, and there are so many little touches connected with my father, that I read them with an interest I had not expected." The youthful pages apparently were not published.

61. Letter to Mr. Sheldon, December 27, 1887, NYSHA. A note of thanks for a Christmas package sent to the orphanage.

62. Letter to Mr. Sheldon, December 27, 1889, NYSHA. A note of thanks for candy sent to the orphanage.

63. Letter to Miss Emo E. Stickney, February 13, 1892, *Otsego Farmer*, July 29, 1938. This is the only piece of Cooper's private correspondence known to

have been published. She asks Miss Stickney to serve as the assistant superintendent of the orphanage. At the time of this letter, Cooper was two months from her eightieth birthday. Because copies of the *Otsego Farmer* are rare, we reproduce the text of the letter in full:

February 13, 1892.

My dear Emo:

I am thankful to say that I am recovering my usual strength, but the attack has been rather a severe one.

As I lay awake at night last month, the thought occurred to me with some force, that it would be wise perhaps, and most for the advantage of the Orphanage, that I should ask for some relief in my cares. After thinking very seriously on the subject for some weeks and with earnest, humble prayer for guidance, I wrote to the Bishop. I told him that I thought it would be for the best that an assistant superintendent should be appointed to aid me with my work, and asked that this assistant should be Miss Stickney. An advisory committee of three resident trustees could at the same time be appointed to help us in emergencies with special assistance.

Such is the outline of the plan. The Bishop is entirely satisfied and even much pleased with the suggestion. He enters into the plan heartily. He wishes it carried into effect this spring.

The details will of course have to be settled after full consideration. I would ask for a measure of relief at certain points and you also would require special relief and assistance at other points.

I earnestly hope, my dear Emo, that you will consent to act as my aide de camp under these circumstances. Think over this subject, pray over it, and let me hope for a favorable answer to

Your affectionate old friend,
Susan F. Cooper.

64. Letter to "the Boys and Girls at the Orphan House of the Holy Saviour," January 1, 1893, NYSHA. SFC sends in her "New Years Letter" admonitions to the orphans; signed "your affectionate Orphanage Mother, Susan F. Cooper."

65. Letter to Mrs. Foot, January 26, 1893, VA. SFC's namesake niece was mentioned in a Washington, D.C., paper, not SFC, who hasn't been there since "befo' de war"; 1880 was her last trip to Albany and last trip away from Cooperstown.

66. Letter to Mr. Husbands, November 15, 1893, NYSHA. SFC assures Husbands that "the cutting from the Rochester paper was taken . . . from *Lament for the Birds.*"

67. Letter to Mlle H. Boissard, n.d., VA. In French, apparently in her hand of the late 1840s or early 1850s.

ALLAN AXELRAD is professor of American studies at California State University, Fullerton. He is the author of *History and Utopia: A Study of the World View of James Fenimore Cooper* (1978). His essays on James Fenimore Cooper have appeared in such journals as *American Literature* and *American Quarterly*.

MICHAEL P. BRANCH is associate professor of literature and environment at the University of Nevada, Reno, where he teaches courses in nature writing and American literature and helps direct the Graduate Program in Literature and Environment. He is a cofounder and past president of the Association for the Study of Literature and Environment (ASLE) and is current book review editor of the journal *ISLE: Interdisciplinary Studies in Literature and Environment*. He is coeditor of *The Height of Our Mountains: Nature Writing from Virginia's Blue Ridge Mountains and Shenandoah Valley* (Johns Hopkins University Press, 1998) and *Reading the Earth: New Directions in the Study of Literature and Environment* (University of Idaho Press, 1998).

LAWRENCE BUELL, John P. Marquand Professor of English at Harvard University, is author of *The Environmental Imagination: Thoreau, Nature Writing, and the Formation of American Culture* and the forthcoming *Writing in an Endangered World*.

MICHAEL DAVEY received his Ph.D. from Ohio State University and is currently adjunct assistant professor of English at John Carroll University. He has written on Melville and James Fenimore Cooper and is currently at work on a book-length study of the cultural work and historical hermeneutics of the Leatherstocking Tales.

JENNIFER DAWES is a Ph.D. candidate in the Literature and Environment Program at the University of Nevada, Reno. Her primary interests include nineteenth-century American women writers, western women's narratives, and sentimental fiction. She is an adjunct faculty member in the English Department of Idaho State University.

DUNCAN FAHERTY is a doctoral candidate in the Department of English at the City University of New York Graduate School and University Center. His dissertation focuses, in part, on the development and history of landscape design in the antebellum United States.

WAYNE FRANKLIN, Davis Distinguished Professor of American Literature and chair of the English Department at Northeastern University, has written *The New World of James Fenimore Cooper* (1982) and several other books. Currently at work on the first modern biography of James Fenimore Cooper, he also edits the interdisciplinary American Land and Life series for the University of Iowa Press.

TINA GIANQUITTO is a graduate student in Columbia University's Department of English. Her dissertation work on nineteenth-century American women nature writers enables her to satisfy two passions: a love of dusty library stacks and a fascination with the outdoor world. She currently teaches courses in literature and in political philosophy at Columbia University and in American literature and the environment at SUNY–New Paltz.

ROBERT HARDY lives in Northfield, Minnesota. His poems, essays, and short stories have appeared in numerous publications. Most recently, his poetry was featured in *33 Minnesota Poets,* ed. Emilio and Monica DeGrazia (Minneapolis: Nodin Press, 2000). His new translation of Euripides' *Iphigeneia at Aulis* was performed by the Carleton Players at Carleton College in May 2000. He holds a Ph.D. in Classics from Brown University and has published scholarly articles on Vergil, James Fenimore Cooper, and Edith Wharton. He has also been a Classics professor, a stay-at-home father, and a substitute elementary school teacher.

ROCHELLE JOHNSON has published articles on Susan Fenimore Cooper in *ISLE: Interdisciplinary Studies in Literature and Environment, Thoreau's Sense of Place* (University of Iowa Press, 2000), and *Reading under the Sign of Nature* (University of Utah Press, 2000). With Daniel Patterson, she edited Cooper's *Rural Hours* (University of Georgia Press, 1998). She is assistant professor of English at Albertson College of Idaho, where she teaches courses in American literature, environmental studies, and gender studies.

ERIKA M. KREGER completed a dissertation about nineteenth-century American women writers and the periodical sketch form at the University of California, Davis. Her recent publications include "'Depravity Dressed up in Fascinating Garb': Sentimental Motifs and the Seduced Hero(ine) in *The Scarlet Letter,*" *Nineteenth-Century Literature* (December 1999) and "A Bibliography of Works by and about Caroline Kirkland," *Tulsa Studies in Women's Literature* 18, no. 2 (Fall 1999). She is currently coediting, with James McClure and Peg Lamphier, *The Letters of Salmon P. Chase and His Daughters* (forthcoming, Kent State University Press).

LUCY MADDOX is professor of English at Georgetown University and editor of *American Quarterly.* Among her publications are two previous essays on Susan Fenimore Cooper.

RICHARD M. MAGEE completed his bachelor's degree at the University of California at Berkeley and is a Ph.D. candidate at Fordham University. He is currently writing his dissertation on Susan Fenimore Cooper while teaching at the State University of New York Maritime College in the Bronx. He is the author of the articles "Beach Reading: Defoe and Dana in the Intertidal Zone," in *Reading the Sea: New Essays on Sea Literature* (Fort Schuyler Press, 1999) and "Sentimental Ecology: Susan Fenimore Cooper's *Rural Hours*," in *"Such News of the Land": American Women Nature Writers* (University Press of New England, 2000).

LISA WEST NORWOOD is completing her doctoral work in American literature at Stanford University. Her dissertation, "Storied Grafts: Land Use, Monuments, and Sense of Place in Antebellum America," includes chapters on Charles Brockden Brown, Lydia Maria Child, Cornelius Matthews, Susan Fenimore Cooper, and Herman Melville.

DANIEL PATTERSON is a specialist in Colonial American literature and in the history of writing about nature. He is coeditor, with Rochelle Johnson, of Susan Fenimore Cooper's *Rural Hours* (University of Georgia Press, 1998). His articles have appeared in *Early American Literature* and *Legacy: A Journal of American Women Writers*. He lives in Caldwell, Idaho.

JESSIE RAVAGE earned her M.A. at the Cooperstown Graduate Program of History Museum Studies and works as a historical research and exhibits consultant in Cooperstown, New York. She researched, wrote, and designed an exhibit about Susan Fenimore Cooper's *Rural Hours* in 1995 that has appeared in the Smithy-Pioneer Gallery, at Hartwick College, and at Castleton State College. From 1997 to 2000 she wrote a biweekly column for a Cooperstown newspaper, commenting on excerpts from *Rural Hours* and placing them in an historical context.

LISA STEFANIAK is a doctoral candidate at McMaster University. Her dissertation, "At Home on the Land: Domestic Ecologies of Place and Self in the Bioregional Writings of Catharine Parr Traill and Susan Fenimore Cooper," is an ecocritical and transnational reassessment of Cooper's and Traill's gendered representations of nature as domestic space. She is completing a new edition of Traill's *Canadian Crusoes: A Tale of the Rice Lake Plains* (forthcoming, Broadview Press).

INDEX